EDUCATION FOR DEMOCRACY
IN WEST GERMANY

EDUCATION FOR DEMOCRACY
IN WEST GERMANY

Achievements — Shortcomings — Prospects

Edited by Walter Stahl

With an Introduction by Norbert Muhlen

Published for Atlantik-Bruecke by
FREDERICK A. PRAEGER, *Publisher*
New York

BOOKS THAT MATTER

Published in the United States of America in 1961
by Frederick A. Praeger, Inc., Publisher
64 University Place, New York 3, N.Y.

Library of Congress Catalog Card Number: 61—14811

Printed in Germany - Hafen-Druckerei Hamburg

Preface

This book endeavors to give a comprehensive and objective picture of the efforts being made in the German Federal Republic to educate the German people for democracy.

Since it has often been said that political education cannot as yet be called successful in West Germany, we also want to contribute to a better understanding of the many and serious difficulties which German educators are facing and are striving to overcome.

To a large extent foreign criticism of West German political education and, for that matter, of German democracy as such, is based on the misrepresentation of facts which originate from the efficient and dangerous Communist propaganda campaign directed against the German Federal Republic. The reader of this book, we hope, will be better equipped to distinguish between constructive and destructive criticism of Germany.

While the falseness of the Communist allegations is refuted by the contents of this book, it is by no means an apology for post or prewar Germany. On the contrary, all the shortcomings of contemporary German democracy are frankly stated and admitted. But they are placed in the right perspective. For, as Senator Thomas J. Dodd in his speech on "Anti-Semitism, the Swastika Epidemic and Communism" (March 15, 1960), has said: "It is not enough to be able to distinguish right from wrong. There are many gradations of evil, and the civilized society distinguishes between them in its structure of laws. Similarly, it is not enough to be able to distinguish the beneficent from the harmful, the safe from the dangerous.

"Without a sense of proportion we should find ourselves equating petty larceny with rape, measles with leprosy, a toy chameleon with a crocodile.

"In the balanced mind, in the same society, everything is scaled, everything has its measure or its value."

Thus, through this book we would like not only to inform our American friends of the achievements and the shortcomings of democracy in Germany but also to enable them to see the different aspects of the entire German picture in proper proportion.

In recent years a multitude of books and papers on Germany have been published. All of them have been written for a wide group of readers. In those, the basic facts of German life after 1945 have been outlined and explained.

This book has been compiled for the scholar, the student, and the interested layman who would like to dig deeper into the problems of postwar Germany. Originally, a more comprehensive book on the present status of democracy in West Germany was planned. However, the subject of this book proved to be sufficiently extensive and important to justify a monograph. All other subjects related to the question of how strongly democracy has taken roots in the German Federal Republic will be treated in a second volume, which will appear in the autumn of 1961.

The articles contained in this book represent the opinion of the respective authors. With the exception of the first article ("The Present Status of Democracy in Germany") and the bibliography (Part VI), the articles and reports were not specifically written for this book but have been selected from a large number of periodicals, books, manuscripts and newspapers. The fact that they were, with a few exceptions (see Appendix), not written for foreign consumption will, we believe, enhance their objective value for the American reader.

This book is published by *Atlantik-Bruecke* (Atlantic Bridge), Hamburg which is a non-partisan group of private citizens who desire to further better understanding between the United States and Germany. We sincerely hope that this book will serve not only as an interesting source of information, but will also contribute to some small degree toward this goal.

The source of each selection is indicated in a note at the foot of the page. The source notes constitute a complete list of acknowledgements. Special thanks are due to those who have contributed unpublished material. We are particularly grateful to Marcia L. Kahn, European Representative of the American Council on Germany, Inc., who helped on many aspects of the manuscript.

<table>
<tr><td>Arnold Bergstraesser</td><td>Walter Stahl</td></tr>
<tr><td>Chairman</td><td>Executive Director</td></tr>
</table>

Note to the Reader

The American and the German school-systems are so different that there are no equivalent terms for the various forms of schools except elementary school. Even more complicated is the rendering into English of terms such as *Politische Erziehung* or *Sozialkunde,* not only because of the different structures and traditions of the American and the German democracy but even more so because in Germany political scientists and pedagogues are still trying to agree on commonly acceptable definitions.

We should therefore like to draw the reader's attention to the report on "Training Instructors for the Teaching of Social Studies" (II B 3). As this report originally was written for UNESCO comparisons between Germany and the Anglo-Saxon countries are made and many important definitions are given, most useful to the reader of this book.

The Editor.

CONTENTS

PART V.   GERMANY AND THE GERMANS

PART VI.   RESEARCH

APPENDIX

Introduction

"Have the Germans really changed?" Is it possible that yesterday's Third Reich has become today's *Wunderkind* of the Western World, as some appearances seem to indicate? And if it is true that this change has taken place — will it last? Or, must we expect another reversal?

Questions of this kind are frequently — and understandably — raised in this country. In fact, a huge question mark seems to have succeeded the Swastika as the symbol of Germany. The free world is ready to rejoice at the transformation of its new ally, but it cannot quite suppress the deep and dread memories of only yesterday. What is more, it cannot quite suppress the misgivings that come with these memories, and this uneasiness is shared also by a great many Germans themselves.

In this extraordinary volume, German authors present a collective progress report on the political education of their people. The editor has painstakingly assembled what German experts — with a small number of competent foreign observers admixed — have to say about the challenges, shortcomings, methods, and achievements in their special fields of educational endeavor. Their observations range from grade schools to television audiences, and from the academy to the army barracks. Their composite report with all its little-known facts of great general interest supplies essential material for an answer to the question-marked German problem of today — and of tomorrow.

Originally, most of the papers and articles in this volume were written for German readers, a fact which might well increase their value to American readers eager to know what Germans "really" think and say. Even the translation — often leaning toward the literal rather than the idiomatic, and sometimes more faithful to the German original than to American usage — retains the special flavor of the subject, that is, of Germans struggling hard to educate their fellow-citizens in that civic spirit which hails from the Anglo-Saxon world. The editor has wisely and fairly included contributions of varying view-points culled from official and other memoranda as well as from the daily press, learned journals and private reports, in order to present a composite picture closely reflecting the many-sided reality. After publication of this volume, one must hope that it will be less easy — and less easily forgiven — when some American students hold forth on "lasting German characteristics" and harp on outdated stereotypes while they ignore the important, stimulating latest developments.

The majority of writers in this volume seem to agree with H. G. Wells who remarked (as a pessimist or an optimist?) that history is a race between education and catastrophe. Since they have witnessed the Nazi tyranny, and are still witnessing

1

the Communist terror, they are acutely aware of the meaning of catastrophe — and passionately eager to overcome its ever-present threat. From their compendious essays we gain the distinct impression that education is advancing in this German race against its antagonist, despite all the perplexities and hurdles in its way.

Only dreamers assume that "republicanism," as the Founding Fathers called it, could be taught as if it followed the three R's merely as a fourth; few, if any of the contributors to this volume seem to be dreamers. Whether in Germany or elsewhere, the political educator's job is never done — the nature of man and of the society in which he lives impede any hope for perfection. ("Knowledge of human nature is the beginning and end of political education," Henry Adams noted.) But even within this universal limitation, to educate Germans in the democratic ways and spirit has been — and still is — a particularly difficult undertaking.

Although the Germans did not enter their school of freedom, tolerance and civic intercourse as complete novices, their first term at that school — circa 1945 to 1949 — was as inauspicious as could be. In those chaotic years their nation-wide classroom was haunted by hunger, destruction, division, moral ruin, the decaying heritage and memories of their recent past; those were not conditions under which a people might be interested in, or understand, let alone strive for a new dignity of the person in a new community. Although for the opposite reason conditions seemed hardly more propitious in the decade of the 1950's. Throughout this period — marked by recovery toward national independence and individual well-being, — when many Germans were busily, happily, almost exclusively absorbed in their private prosperity, the majority had little patience for education in the civic art of give-and-take, nor much desire for a noble common purpose. After the motto had been "everybody for himself" if he wanted to survive, the survivors would rather maintain this attitude, and enjoy the pleasures of survival. Nevertheless, even then a growing number of individual Germans sensed — and expressed — their desire to bring about a new German society in which collective decency and individual responsibility, in brief, the *bonum commune*, prevailed.

The third term of Germany's democratic education set in with the 1960's — almost on the day, in fact, on which the decade began. Swastikas painted by hoodlums, morons, and other Nazis on Christmas Eve of 1959 triggered a shock of recognition among the German majority. In the months that followed they felt that the time had come for them to build barriers against the approach of a new catastrophe, and the main barrier was to be political education. Since that time, Germany has witnessed an impressive effort to build this barrier.

The educators belonged mostly to what has been called Germany's moral elite; by occupation they were in the main statesmen and politicians, priests and clergymen, students and scholars, army officers and trade union officials, in addition to professional teachers; in short, members of the same occupational groups from which had also come the men and women of the German anti-Nazi resistance in the 1930's and early 1940's. But in the late 1950's and 1960's they were powerfully strengthened by the most vigorous and alert segments of the younger generation.

A second, no less significant difference from previous decades was based on the fact that they embodied not only the most active political tendency, but almost the only discernible active political tendency. True, there remains a rather deep gap between the moral elite — which numerically is by necessity a small minority — and the majority with their "terrible mass of ignorance, indifference, apathy and insensitivity," as an official recently denounced it. But in their egocentric, *unpolitisch,* unhappy lethargy, they merely ignore rather than oppose the educators, and they passively tolerate the offensive of the democrats while before they had forced them into the defensive. Today, Germany's moral elite has ceased to be at cross-purposes with Germany's political leadership; now both tend to strive for the same goals — the latter, by action; the former, by educating the citizenry, first and foremost the young.

In Germany's experimental class-room formal political education, as well as the less formal, though systematic education by mass media, face a second difficulty which can also be observed elsewhere, while it appears in Germany in a particularly acute shape. Whether Germans are told about the facts of political life in school proper, or, say, in editorials, or radio scripts, or lectures, their educators must tread an extremely narrow, winding path between two self-defeating, though seductive aberrations. On the one hand, they must avoid the pitfalls of indoctrination which would proclaim democracy and its values as almost absolute if not pseudo-religious idols, and which would deny the freedom of thought, expression, choice. On the other hand, however, they must also avoid the opposite mistake of a positivistic, relativistic approach which denies the duty to take sides between freedom and tyrannies, between obligation and sin, between good and evil. While on occasion both approaches have been used in the name of democracy both are equally anti-democratic in themselves. Since Hitler's fall, Germans are particularly sensitive toward, and suspicious of, indoctrination in blind acceptance of political ways and values. In turn, a purely pragmatic education in democracy is particularly unlikely to withstand the assault of other political doctrines in the case of present-day Germany where the spiritual and historical roots from which democracy grows, are still weak.

But in addition to these general difficulties which, though, appear more difficult in Germany than, say, in this country, German political educators also had to face a heavy load of special national difficulties in their valiant attempt. First they had to solve the riddle of who would teach the teachers. Many among them had played an active role in past political events, and therefore felt reluctant to discuss these past events — but in German political education this subject cannot be avoided. The same dilemma frequently beset parents and other adults. The curriculum of political education posed another moot question. Is it advisable, some well-meaning educators asked, to acquaint our young too closely with too many facets and details — more precisely, crimes and horrors — of recent national history? The reactions of the adolescents might take unexpected directions, perhaps not at all those at which their educators were aiming. The discussion of some of these problems will provide the reader of this volume with a better understanding of the great problems which German political education had, and still has, to face.

In light of all these difficulties, the progress made up to now is the more gratifying. True, the groundwork had been laid by history itself when Germany, not at all by her own will, graduated from that school of hard knocks which Goethe praised — "He who has not been tormented has not been educated" (*Wer nicht geschunden wird, wird nicht erzogen.*) But after this experience, a more formal and purposeful effort of education undertaken by Germans themselves has begun to "form the common mind," and it still goes on with unmistakable vigor. Over the past few years, this writer on travels throughout Germany witnessed the serious attempt of Germans to awaken the young generation to new, healthy political life; I also watched the happy response of the young themselves. When I listened to the instruction periods of army recruits and to the political quiz contests of high-school youngsters, or when I observed the youthful audiences of the sensationally successful anti-Nazi plays and motion pictures, I was as deeply impressed as when, conversely, I noticed the contemptful silence answering the tired tirades of totalitarians.

If Germany succeeds in the great attempt of democratic self-education — and the contributions to this volume strongly suggest that she will — this success shall transcend her much-admired economic recovery. Surely both the economic and the political efforts complement rather than contradict each other. Yet to reconstruct "the common mind" excels the reconstrucion of real estate and production power. For it leads to a new society which permits its citizens to be free men, and which wholeheartedly joins the community of free nations. The present volume indicates that Germany is on her way to this goal which is also an American goal.

New York City, January 1, 1961.   Norbert Muhlen

Part I.   Basic Trends

The Present Status of Democracy in West Germany

By Walter Stahl

It is the unanimous opinion of unbiased foreign experts and observers of the Federal Republic that the democratic development of the country has made gratifying progress. Democracy in Germany seems to be more consolidated in 1960 than even the very optimistic could have expected in 1945.[1] German and foreign experts are just as unanimous however, that one of the weakest points in the structure of German democracy is that of the political education and training of the youth of the country — and of the adults as well.

This fact is not surprising when one bears in mind that a genuine and deep-rooted democratization of the German people must necessarily be a difficult and lengthy process. It should not be compared, for instance, with the reconstruction of the economy in a highly industrialized country which had been destroyed by the war. Here the requisite elements of reconstruction — skilled workers, experienced management, know-how, etc. — already existed. Democratization of the Germans necessitates the changing or replacement of deeply-rooted and, in part, centuries-old processes of thought and forms of behavior. In other words, the whole cultural atmosphere of the country must be changed.[2]

An important prerequisite in this respect is a change at the top, for the bulk of the population is inclined to conform in its action and thought — for reasons of social prestige — with that of the more elevated social classes. This makes itself manifest even to the extent of superficialities such as the prevailing fashion of the moustache at the time of Emperor Wilhelm II. It is therefore very encouraging for democratic development that, in the Federal Republic, for the first time in German history, every position of authority in the state and in society is occupied by democratic elements. That wasn't even achieved in the Weimar Republic. Today only democratic parties are represented in the Federal Parliament and in the legislative bodies of the *Länder*. The powerful labor unions, the industrial associations, the churches, the large youth associations, the press and radio, all have their feet firmly planted on the soil of democracy and are doing their best to make their respective contributions towards its consolidation. It is true, however, that something of the democratic manner is still left to be desired, particularly in German politics. The *Deutscher Ausschuß für das Erziehungs- und Bildungswesen* (German Committee on Training and Education) rightly drew attention to this in a statement on the anti-Semitic smearings (December 1959/January 1960). The personal element, for example, is hardly ever kept out of political debates. The telegram of congratulation by a defeated American presidential candidate to his successful opponent always arouses astonish-

[1] See Appendix.
[2] See Lewin, *"Cultural Reconstruction"*, Part V.

2

5

ment in many circles in Germany; in others, it arouses admiration or even envy. This kind of attitude, unfortunately, does not yet appear to be the order of the day in this country. It is to be hoped, however, that in this respect a change will also gradually occur. The coalescence of the world is having an increasingly favorable effect on the influence of the West, particularly of America, on Germany. This can be seen in incidents of everyday life, even in the language. The American election in the fall of 1960 was followed with tremendous interest in the Federal Republic in the press, on radio and T. V. by all classes and age groups of the population, almost as if it were their own. Kennedy's visit to his defeated opponent — which was reported on with pictures in every newspaper — made a great impression here, particularly on the younger generation.

One must also take into consideration the fact that the world, and Germany with it, has changed decisively in the past twenty years. Of the 55 million inhabitants in the Federal Republic over 22 million had either no experience whatever, or no conscious experience, of National Socialism. Their impression of Germany, Europe and the world is formed by completely different developments, facts and aims as was that of the youth of 1914 or of 1933. The coalescence of Europe, the Federal Republic's membership in the Atlantic Community, the East-West conflict, the appearance of the Asiatic and African nations in the limelight of international affairs, automation, nuclear energy, jet aircraft, space research and, in Germany itself, "Prosperity for Everyone", and the levelling of class distinctions; but also the partition of Germany and Europe, the insular situation of Berlin, the industrial and consumer society, the steadily increasing secularization and commercialization of all spheres of life determine the world-picture of the youth of today. In this confusing and alarming social and technical-industrial revolution which is spreading at increasing speed across the globe, they see their little country entirely dependent in its freedom, its security and its prosperity, upon its integration in the Western World. There is in this world-picture no longer any room for nationalism or dreams of omnipotence.

The Germans, old and young, have learned that democracy works. The prestige of Parliament has, in contrast to the Weimar Republic, increased steadily since its establishment. They know that they are now economically better off than at any time under Hitler or Wilhelm II. These facts can hardly be overestimated in their effect on the further consolidation of German democracy.

The question, "Will democracy survive this time?", I should, therefore, like to answer with a decisive "Yes!" Certainly it is true that the confirmed and active democrats in the Federal Republic are confronted by a still overwhelming majority of anti- and semi-democrats or democratic fellow-travelers. The political indifference of the masses is justifiably deplored and cannot be taken seriously enough. It is also true that nationalistic or Nazi (including anti-Semitic) feelings and ideas still linger on in many German hearts and minds in spite of the gruesome Hitlerite object lessons. These feelings and the resultant ideas can, however, be psychologically explained. Nearly all of those who harbor them, need them in order to compensate their feelings of guilt, shame or inferiority.[3] These people need them to justify themselves to themselves, their children and their fellow-men. One can only disperse them by clarifying to their own conviction to those who held them, the real reason for their feelings.[4] It is an absolute necessity for the moral recuperation of our people that this be done. For "a people which thrusts out of its historical

[3] See Adorno, "What does Digesting the Past Mean?", Part II, 8, 3.
[4] See Adorno, op. cit.

consciousness that, which charges it with guilt, thus evades not only its responsibility for that for which it is to blame, and for those towards whom it is to blame, but in so doing does worst of all towards itself".[5]

A further explanation for this phenomenon may probably be found in the fact that Hitler's fascination for the masses of his supporters had two main reasons. He gave them a feeling of protection and security and satisfied the human desire for a feeling of importance. His followers felt their importance as leaders in a small or big way in the innumerable organizations created by the Nazis or even as mere members of the party or of a social class such as the peasants or the workers whose importance for the common good (very similarly to the Communist system) was continually being emphasized by Nazi propaganda. Moreover, Hitler enabled every German who felt inferior or frustrated to project his desires for power and security onto him, the *Fuehrer*, or the German people as a whole and then to identify himself with the leader or the national collective. The individual was thus able to compensate his inferiority complex.

Those of the older Germans who today still harbor nationalist or Nazi ideas may well do so because they unconsciously miss that euphoric experience of feeling important. The German Federal Republic does not lend itself to this kind of identification though quite a few people (of the same type) nowadays again speak of the German *Tüchtigkeit* (efficiency) which produced the "economic miracle".

Yet the psychological explanation alone is not sufficient. Add to this that people still infected by Nazism often show a lack of knowledge and judgment. One must have both in order to *understand* that the Nazi system because of its nature had to be criminal.[6]

Many of these people would indeed be better off, as far as knowledge and judgment are concerned, if they would not, on account of the psychological difficulties referred to, resist accepting the instruction and enlightenment offered via mass media in ample measure since the end of the war. But here, too, a remarkable change has been taking place for about two years now. Since 1958 concentration camp trials have been taking place uninterruptedly in German courts throughout the country. Hardly a day has since passed when the press has not reported — often in considerable detail — on these proceedings. Under the impression of the horrifying confessions and evidence given by the accused, many adults have obviously changed their attitude.[7] The intelligent and interested section of the younger generation is taking every opportunity of becoming acquainted through films, exhibitions, books, etc., with the facts of the Nazi period.[8]

These are encouraging developments. If they strengthen in the German people the feeling that all politics must be limited by the postulates of morality an important work of education has thus also been achieved. This alone is, of course, not enough, for one may indeed teach democracy with great pedagogic effect but not exclusively by means of the negative example of the Hitlerite rule of blood and terror. Much more must be done and that commences, as the American example shows, already in the kindergarten and in the companionship of family life.[9]

In assessing to what extent democracy has been consolidated in Germany, two questions must, in my opinion, be considered quite separately. One is often con-

[5] Heinrich Weinstock: *"Der Nationalzozialismus im Schulunterricht"*, Gesellschaft — Staat — Erziehung, No 8, 1959, p. 339.
[6] See *"Study of National Socialism by 17-18-years-old High School Students"*, Part II, B, 2.
[7] See Appendix, *"Germans Eye Prosecution of Nazis"*.
[8] See Chapter *"Mass Media"*.
[9] See Part V, *"Cultural Reconstruction / The Special Case of Germany"*.

fused with the other or else no difference at all is made between them. This is probably the main reason for the stability of German democracy being the subject of so many differing evaluations. The first question is: "Can a 30th January 1933 occur again in Western Germany?". The second is: "Have the Germans really become democrats?". The first question must be answered definitely in the negative, the second with the answer: "Not yet in the majority".

There is no doubt that a liberal, parliamentary and constitutional democracy has been created in Western Germany as a form of state and society. It is borne and supported by a strong constitution and by the democratic governing class which holds all the positions of power in state and society. The enemies of democracy in the Bonn state are, in contrast to Weimar, powerless and devoid of influence. For this reason and on account of the radical change in the entire world situation referred to above, a repetition of the 30th January 1933 appears to be completely out of the question.[10])

On the other hand, however, the majority of the Germans cannot yet be regarded as democratic in the same way as the Americans, Swiss or British are democratic. Apart from the fact that each country can only constitute a democratic form of society according to its mentality and national character, it takes considerable time to achieve its realization. In the 15 years which have passed since the war, certain beginnings, at the most, have been made in this respect. To develop these and put them to effect is the principal task of the educationalists. But not only of the educationalists, for if they were left only to their own devices they would be faced with a hopeless task. Everyone must co-operate. The politicians in the first instance, the parents, every qualified German in his own field, large or small.

The differences between Bonn and Weimar, such as, for example, the continued development since 1949 towards a two-party state, are usually well-known to pessimistic critics of the young German democracy. They still draw attention, however, in their genuine or affected concern, to the nationalistic or Nazi residues of feelings or ideas among the German people. They fear that at the first severe test which democracy in Germany would have to undergo, the anti-democratic potential still in existence would sweep aside all constitutional and other barriers. I do not share these fears.

Firstly, because these nationalistic sentiments exist mainly among the old and older generations. Their numbers are therefore being reduced by natural causes from year to year. Secondly, because the great majority, even of the older people, cannot do otherwise than recognize the difference in the world situation since 1940. They must feel that their emotional nationalistic or Nazi sentiments which they may give vent to in their beer parlor, among their workmates or in their family circle, are only the expression of completely unrealistic wishful thinking, for the same people obviously act quite differently when they have to make rational decisions which immediately affect their fate and that of their families. What other explanation is there for the fact that the right-wing radical parties obtain fewer votes from year to year? At the last federal election, the democratic parties, who all supported the unification of Europe and the integration of Germany into the Atlantic Community, with a total poll of 88.2 % of the electorate, received a total of 98.7 % of all votes cast. The right-wing radical parties received only 1.06 % and could not secure a single seat in the Federal Parliament.[11])

---

[10]) In connection with this question see Fritz René Allemann: *Bonn ist nicht Weimar.*
[11]) Of the remaining 0.24 % the neutralist Bund der Deutschen obtained 0.2 %.

One need not necessarily interpret this election result with respect to the portion of the population under discussion as being an endorsement of Bonn and its foreign policy. It does show at least, however, that the vast majority of the Germans feel happy in the Federal Republic and are not interested in any radical alteration of the present situation. Naturally, as is the case in every country in the world, the economic factor also played an important part in this election. But the same applies in the reverse manner also to Hitler's success. All the historians and experts are unanimous that without the economic crisis of the nineteen-thirties and its mass misery, the NSDAP would never have come to power. The responsibility for their misery was then attributed by the masses to the democratic parties. The masses, however, had no democratic alternative. They turned to the right or left-wing radical opposition, for the difference between then and now was that there was no *democratic* opposition. However, economic crises on the scale of 1930 will, in all probability, never occur again. We have since learned how to meet them.

My contention that even the majority of those in the Federal Republic who are still nationalistically or Nazi infected, at least accept the German reality of 1960 is also borne out by the results of the following polls of public opinion.

The Best Type of State

About three-quarters of the adult population of the Federal Republic is in favor of democracy as the type of government best suited to the Germans. The proportion of those questioned has thus again risen in comparison with the analogous poll of 1958. The number of those in favor of a monarchy or of an authoritarian regime is in this year also very small.

This question, put by the EMNID Institute of Public Opinion Research[12]) to a representative section of the adult population of the Federal Republic in May 1960,

"Which type of government do you think is best for us Germans?"

elicited the following answers:

Type of Government preferred	1953 %	1954 %	1955 %	1956 %	1957 %	1958 %	1960 %
Democracy*	57	66	70	67	69	66	74
Monarchy	11	10	10	8	5	5	5
Authoritarian Régime	8	7	4	4	2	3	2
Indifferent or Other Nominations	1	2	3	1	3	5	1
No Opinion	23	15	13	20	21	21	18
	100	100	100	100	100	100	100

A considerable proportion still, as in the previous poll, give no opinion. When examining the results within the sociological groups, it will be noticed that a quarter of all those in the 16—21 years age group were of no opinion and also

---

[12]) These and the following poll results are taken from EMNID INFORMATIONEN, No. 19 (May), No. 28 (July), No. 35 (September), and No. 40 (October), 1960, published by EMNID Institute, Bielefeld.
* Or Republic, or "present policy".

that the proportion of those of no opinion in the 21—30 years age group is still above the average for the total population.

Those, however, who actually lived through the period of the German Empire were in favor of a monarchy to a degree above the average. In the 50—65 years age group, 8 % prefer that type of government, and of those over 65, no less than 16 %.

	Democracy	Monarchy	Authoritarian Régime	Indifferent or other Nomination	No Opinion	
	%	%	%	%	%	%
Total	74	5	2	1	18	100
Age Groups						
16 up to 21	68	3	1	2	26	100
21 up to 30	72	2	3	2	21	100
30 up to 50	78	3	3	1	15	100
50 up to 65	73	8	3	0	16	100
65 upwards	65	16	1	1	17	100

Within the occupational groups, the state officials and employees show up as the best democrats, 86 % of them being in favor of "democracy", "republic" or something on similar lines. The pensioners — as has already been shown by the results classified under age groups — hold pro-monarchist convictions to a relatively greater extent than the other occupational groups. The proportion of those of no opinion among the occupational groups is higher than average among the farmers and lower among the officials. In the other occupational groups the proportion of those of no opinion is roughly approximate to the average of the general population.

	Democracy	Monarchy	Authoritarian Régime	Indifferent or other Nomination	No Opinion	
Occupational Groups	%	%	%	%	%	%
Workers	72	4	3	1	21	100
Employees	78	3	2	0	17	100
Officials and Employees of the State	86	4	1	1	8	100
Professional and Self-employed People	78	4	4	1	13	100
Farmers	64	7	2	1	26	100
Old Age Pensioners	69	12	2	1	16	100

When analyzing the results according to the degree of education of those questioned, the fact becomes evident that the proportion of those of no opinion sinks very considerably with increasing education. This increase in readiness or ability to make a statement among those of higher educational standards, goes almost exclusively to the credit of the nomination of "democracy".

	Democracy %	Monarchy %	Authoritarian Régime %	Indifferent or other Nomination %	No Opinion %	%
Educational Standard						
8 or 9 Years of Schooling (Volksschüler)	71	5	2	1	21	100
10 Years (Mittlere Reife)	80	6	4	0	10	100
13 Years and More (Abitur and possibly academic studies)	87	8	1	1	3	100

Democracy Means Freedom

The outstanding characteristic of democracy is, in the opinion of about half the adult population of the Federal Republic, freedom. This was shown by the results of a representative poll carried out in March 1960 by the EMNID Institute of Public Opinion Research. In analysing the results of this poll, not only those statements by the people questioned relating to personal freedom of movement or to economic freedom, but all replies which referred to freedom of speech, freedom of press and freedom in the deeper sense of the word, were listed under the heading of "freedom".

The actual replies given to the question,

"What in your opinion is the most important characteristic of democracy?"

show particularly clearly the opinion held regarding the term "freedom", — "that one can open one's mouth", "everyone is entitled to his own opinion", "to be able to speak openly", "a life in freedom", "freedom of the people, the Jews too".

	1953 %	1955 %	1956 %	1957 %	1958 %	1960 %
Freedom	40	36	47	42	48	49
People's Government	12	22	21	23	20	26
Justice	4	3	3	5	3	4
Economic and Social Progress	2	2	1	2	2	1
Several other Characteristics	5	5	1	6	3	2
Negative Characteristics	10	7	4	6	4	3
No Opinion	27	25	23	26	23	23
	100	100	100	100*	100*	100*

*Some interrogated gave more than one answer.

"Yes" to the Defense of Europe

The obligation of Germany to participate in the framework of European defense was endorsed, according to the results of a representative poll carried out by the EMNID Institute of Public Opinion Research in June 1960, by 71% of the adult population of the Federal Republic. 15% opposed this liability and 14% were of no opinion. Of the entire population, the question,

"In your opinion, has Germany responsibilities in the framework of European defense?"

has been answered since 1951 as follows:

	1951 %	1952 %	1953 %	1954 %	1956 %	1957 %	1958 %	1959 %	1960 %
Yes	47	44	59	65	64	58	68	73	71
No	24	27	23	25	26	31	25	18	15
No Opinion	29	29	18	10	10	11	7	9	14
	100	100	100	100	100	100	100	100	100

For or Against "A Man Like Hitler"?

The adult population of the Federal Republic is dissociating itself more and more obviously from the political personality of the Hitler type. A representative poll in the Federal Republic in August 1960 (last poll August 1958) showed that 85% of those questioned were against "a man like Hitler" and only 5% in favor. 10% withheld their opinion. The question asked was phrased as follows:

"If the opportunity arose now, as in 1933, to vote in an election for or against a man like Hitler, how would you vote?"

As can be seen from the following illustration of trends so far, the numbers in favor of "a man like Hitler" are the lowest proportion since the polls were commenced in 1953. Part of the 10% of those of no opinion may, however, be added to the category of those questioned who are in favor of a man like Hitler and the proportion of those "for" could thus be increased by a slight percentage which could not be determined beforehand. The table gives the following picture:

	1953 %	1954 %	1955 %	1956 %	1957 %	1958 %	1960 %
For	12	15	14	12	15	10	5
Against	67	81	76	82	74	81	85
No Opinion	21	4	10	6	11	9	10
	100	100	100	100	100	100	100

The following is a breakdown of the latest poll results according to age groups, with the comparative figures for 1958 in brackets:

Age Groups	For %		Against %		No Opinion %		%
16—25 years	3	(7)	81	(80)	16	(13)	100
25—30 years	5	(12)	87	(78)	8	(10)	100
30—50 years	6	(11)	86	(82)	8	(7)	100
50—65 years	5	(10)	86	(83)	9	(7)	100
over 65 years	4	(10)	87	(83)	9	(7)	100

These results are gratifying even if one accepts them with every reservation appropriate to questions of such a very emotional nature.[13])

One may therefore well say, summarizing the foregoing, that at present and in the foreseeable future, the young[14]) West German democracy does not appear to be endangered, but instead, — given no catastrophes in world politics — can be expected to consolidate calmly and steadily. When one considers the other countries in the world, it can hardly even be disputed that the Federal Republic now ranks among the comparatively few countries whose internal and foreign political decisions are guided much more by common sense than by extremism or nationalistic fervor.

However, we must not let ourselves be lulled by this encouraging and reassuring picture given by the Federal Republic as a whole, into relaxing our efforts in the political education and training of the youth and adult population of the country. On the contrary, these efforts must be pursued with the greatest possible energy and tenacity, for it is not nearly enough that, due to existing conditions and the political and economic successes of the democratic governing classes, a situation has been established which renders impossible a repetition of the 30th January 1933. There is more at stake in the world today, — the survival of the democratic way of . life itself. It is threatened everywhere, not only in Germany and, in point of fact, from the inside, by the development of an industrial mass society which is curtailing to an increasing degree the margin of freedom of the individual, and from the outside, by the totalitarian and militant ideology of the East. The Germans, therefore, are given a challenge to play their part in this fateful struggle in which the entire free world finds itself engaged.

Are they in a position to do this? Three prerequisites must be fulfilled towards this end,

1) an adequate knowledge of the world's political and economic affairs,

2) a firm standpoint, based on the moral values of Western civilization, and

3) personal readiness to defend the democratic way of life, everywhere and at any time.

These prerequisites are fulfilled at present only among a minority of the German people. The majority is politically ignorant, uninterested and indifferent.

If it is a fact that the German people have always been lacking in interest and consequently, of having little knowledge of politics, this is possibly true today in an even greater measure. The masses have become tired. Their mental energies are exhausted due to the demands made upon them by Hitler, the war and the exigencies of the years immediately afterwards. As a reaction to all this they seek refuge in the security of a world of illusions in which there is nothing but parochial harmony and a minimum of problems. Or else they live in a world of dreams as conjured up for them by films and the illustrated magazines. Reality makes them uneasy and anxious. Politics are an important part of this "dreadful"

---

[13]) See Jaide "Attitude of Young Persons of Today to Values" (Part II).
[14]) One should keep in mind that the "young" German democracy has a tradition of a hundred years. Since 1848 when the German democrats asserted themselves for the first time the German democratic forces have steadily become stronger though sometimes stopped in their advance (e.g. under Bismarck) or brutally suppressed (under Hitler). Even Bismarck could not govern against the Parliament. In 1912 the Social Democratic Party became the strongest party in the Reichstag. Weimar was the first (partial) victory of democracy. But for the fearful odds under which the Weimar Republic hat to labor it might have become a complete victory. Therefore it is correct to speak of the "young" German democracy only in the sense that today for the first time *all* positions of power in the state and in the society are held by democrats. In this connection see Alfred Rapp, *Bonn auf der Waage*, Union Verlag, Stuttgart, 1959.

reality and are therefore repressed. It is no coincidence that these illustrated magazines which ignore reality and its demands and, instead, dish out to their readers a dream world of the extraordinary, or the equally unreal illusion of perfect security, have circulations running into millions. As similar phenomena can be observed in other Western countries (although perhaps not to the same degree or exclusivity as in Germany), one wonders whether this development has become a general tendency in the West, a sort of "holiday from history".

The Polish Catholic, parliamentary representative, and writer, Stefan Kiesielewski, an admirer of French culture, wrote, after a tour of Denmark, France and the Federal Republic in the autumn of 1960:[15])

> "The West European countries today represent tremendous material energy; they comprise a mobile, ant-like industrious and brilliantly organized market of consumption and production. The first thing that strikes the bewildered tourist is the extent and organisation of the network of public and commercial services. He is then fascinated by the production. He needn't even visit a factory. It is quite enough when he sees what the production puts onto the market.

> "I would give the entire Polish literature if Poland could quickly achieve this standard of organisation and consumption which exists in some countries of the West today."

'However, the Catholic and emphatically non-Marxist does not like it in the present-day West:

> "The people there are over-tired, absorbed by the nature of modern work, exhausted by the tempo of life, by continually having to deal with machines and cars, and by the incessant hustle and bustle; they wear themselves out in worrying about material progress, are careful, notwithstanding their activity, and do everything to conserve their energies."

'Kisielewski is horrified that the interest in political events, in the fate of mankind, has waned to such an extent in the West. He states that people there are only concerned with material matters and no longer with ideas, that the great philosophers, artists and writers, in respect of whom Poland is so envious of the West, eke out an existence in their own countries on the edge of society and have no influence worth mentioning on that society. Kisielewski, who is much more at home in Western than in Eastern thought, discovered to his consternation that he could no longer find a common language in his discussions with people in the present-day Western world.

'It is true that West European integration has produced important results and national peculiarities in Western Europe have thus receded into the background to a considerable extent so that one could speak of a new universalism; behind this universalism, however, is concealed also a petty, egocentric, Philistine provincialism. 'Kisielewski, the Catholic and old friend of France, makes no bones about the fact that he was very glad to return to his very poor and Communist Poland.'

Indifference and "Philistine provincialism" in Germany is not limited by any means to the older generations, of whom, in view of that which they have been through since 1914 or since 1930, one could perhaps understand their desire for peace and a feeling of security. Even the youth, and the educated youth at that, is for the most part, of a similar attitude. It is mainly interested in three things: personal

---

[15]) From *Die Welt*, November 29th, 1960

security, economic progress and a feeling of security in a harmonious family life. During a discussion evening with his students, held by the Rector of Hamburg University in November 1960, one of them said, and thereby stated the opinion of the majority, "Our need for security is the reaction to two world wars, to a dreadful present and to the need of the older generation for security". In a public opinion poll instituted by the Bavarian Broadcasting Service among 18—30-year olds, (250 young men and girls of all occupational grades and social classes were questioned,) one of the questions asked was, "Is there anything for which you are prepared to devote your entire personal energy, perhaps even risk your life?"[16])

The question was deliberately formulated as a challenge and the replies are correspondingly full of passion and frankness, — as was desired. One opinion, a deep-rooted one, shows up like a colored thread in a drab pattern in hundreds of statements, the opinion that "one need no longer render unto Caesar that which is Caesar's". This scepticism is directed at authority and people in general, these impersonal powers which could again at some time in the name of an idea — any idea — demand risk and sacrifice. This is refused.

"'I am prepared to devote my entire personal energy", writes, for example, an 18-year old high school pupil, "to attain a goal — a profession — I have set for myself. I would not be prepared to risk my life so quickly. To risk one's life for the fatherland, truth and similar things, is for the idealists. The saying "You can be assured of the fatherland's gratitude" is a joke. This was drummed into my father too, and when he came back home after the war he had gone to the dogs, physically and mentally..."

Another student, six years older, studying business management, stated: "I would not be prepared to die for the fatherland, for the traditional scholastic values such as honor, human dignity and freedom — in particular, I would not be prepared to die for our much vaunted Western freedom, which for many is only an ideological justification for unscrupulous high life..."

When Schelsky, the sociologist, in his book, *Die skeptische Generation,* speaks of political readiness of belief and ideological activity having been destroyed at the root among the young generation of today, by far most of the letters confirm this total absence of political thinking in the consciousness of young people. But this strict rejection is not the last word. It is nearly always accompanied by the acknowledgment, quoted as a matter of course, that they are prepared to risk and sacrifice everything for their neighbor, the beloved people. "... but this I know," writes a 19-year old laboratory assistant, "I would never give up my life for a political idea... In any case, I would give my all for one individual person, but never anything for a generality, as these are usually lost forces..." And a 17-year old ship's steward confessed, "The only thing for which I would risk my person, yes, even my life, would be my mother. For a state or even a church, I would, honestly, — and you want us to be honest — not do so: ... we never really know what is actually going on up at the top."[17])

---

[16]) From *Die Zeit,* August 22nd, 1958, *Wie junge Leute sich das Glück vorstellen,* by Barbara Bondy.

[17]) A very interesting and very thorough study by Professor Walter Jaide (published in the supplement of the weekly paper "Das Parlament" of November 30, 1960) could not be included in this book. It presents another, a much more favorable, view on the attitude of the 15 — 18 year old boys and girls. A poll had been taken between October 1958 and April 1960 of about 550 young people living in Lower Saxony, Bremen and Hamburg who were born between 1941 and 1944. Instead of formal interviews or questionaires, the method applied here was that of carefully prepared exploratory talks not only on political subjects but on all questions of vital significance to young people. In order to obtain the most representative results possible, a widely dispersed sample of boys and girls had been selected including representative numbers of the gifted and the less gifted, shy as well as

It may be that the youth of other countries also reacts to the complex of questions on ideals, heroism and spirit of sacrifice with dissociation and scepticism. That this is the case in Western Europe can be presumed from the results of a similar poll taken in France.

Be things as they may in other countries, what a large proportion of the younger generation — and of the adult population — in the Federal Republic have not yet grasped is the fact that their civic ideals and desires can only be fulfilled within the framework of a democratic way of life which the state guarantees and they must consequently support this state and be prepared at all time to defend the democratic way of life. Instead of this we find that youth, like the adults, has an increasing tendency to demand more and more from the state without a correspondingly growing readiness to identify itself with it. However, this deplorable absence of state-consciousness in the Federal Republic is motivated not only by this general tendency which can also be observed in other European countries. As a result of the partitioning of Germany, the Federal Republic is regarded to a large extent as a temporary measure. This renders the creation of state-consciousness exceedingly difficult.

What the youth of Germany lacks is a great objective, an objective which lifts them out of the daily routine. Man needs an imperative. He must feel challenged to co-operate in the great tasks of his people and his era — small as his personal contribution may be. There is in all conscience, no shortage of great objectives in a world in which the survival of freedom is at stake and in which more than half the human race is under-nourished or sick. These objectives must be set forth in a concrete manner.

In order to be able to set them forth, one must first of all make them understandable to the young generation. The will to devote themselves to these tasks must be aroused in them. Political education and training must endeavor to achieve both these ends. They must, therefore, in the first instance, constitute training in morality towards one's fellow-men, whether they be our own countrymen or the distressed peoples of Asia and Africa, because "a nation which only works and earns money, but has no actual objective, goes to rot. A generation on which no other demands are made than to keep the wheels of the economy busily moving, will, being devoid of spirit and soul, undoubtedly perish."[18])

---

talkative ones, those from villages, small towns and cities, students of primary, vocational and middle schools.
Professor Jaide summarizes the result of the poll as follows: "The often quoted tendency to avoid problematic issues, the embarrassment, the indifference or indolence seem no more rampant in this new generation. It cannot be characterized by them since the other voices are predominant. It is my opinion indeed (for which I cannot give any further reasons in this connection) that with the seventeen year olds a new generation with specific characteristics is coming into being, the essential traits of which are different from the ones which are typical of the "sceptical generation" as Schelsky called it. "Hitler killed innocent women and children, he also murdered the guiltless Jews. We cannot point to those facts often enough and we must do everything in our power to avoid a recurrence of such madness!" This statement is typical of the attitude towards racism of the vast majority of those interviewed. Only very few young people showed indifference to the Jewish question and only 4 out of 550 showed an anti-Semitic attitude."
"These young people", it says in the study, "have formed their attitudes and conceptions through newspapers, radio, youth forums, classroom discussions, "Nacht und Nebel", "Anne Frank" etc.; they regret that they do not receive more thorough instruction on the subject and that instead the adults (parents, teachers) hush up the facts or cover them up with excuses."
This confirms my opinion that since about 1958 (possibly under the influence of the KZ trials before German courts which began around that time) not only a change of opinion can be observed with many adults, but that also young people, moved by the cruelties which had been committed by Germans, have begun to inform themselves on their own about the German past. (see also part III, THE MASS MEDIA)
Professor Jaide's study will be reprinted in full in volume 2 of this series which will be published in summer 1961.

[18]) Dr. Marion Gräfin Dönhoff in her article on the assistance for under-developed countries: "Nur Geld?", in DIE ZEIT, November 12, 1960.

Abraham Lincoln was firmly convinced that democracy would infuse new life into a suffering and oppressed world. "This conviction is the classic expression of the idea that the mission of the United States of America is to foster the ideal of the free and independent individual and to demonstrate it unwaveringly to the peoples of the world ... This concept of America's destination presented the average democrat, whose narrow view of the world hardly extended beyond the main street of his small town, with a romantic vision in which he perceived his own modest efforts at righteousness as being very significant for the whole world."[19]

It would certainly not be possible, even with the greatest effort, to make political and economic relationships of an ever increasingly complicated world comprehensible for the average man. Such understanding requires considerable intellectual capability. If the large majority of Germans would not only be aware of the fact that they are living in a free country, but would also recognize the value of this freedom and accept the consequences which it implies, then much would already be achieved. This should be the first aim for the political education of the broader masses of the population.

The question why the multifarious and energetic efforts in the sphere of the re-education of the German people since 1945 are not met by a commensurate success can be explained to some degree by the explanations given above. In addition to these difficulties mentioned, one should take into account that democracy can only be taught by democratic means. Red China has doubtlessly proven with its system of "brain-washing" that an entire population can be re-educated more quickly and successfully with other methods. Therefore the youth in Eastern Germany knows more about National Socialism and its crimes than its counterpart in Western Germany. And perhaps for this reason anti-Semitism has been more thoroughly overcome there. Neither the people in Red China, however, nor those in Ulbricht's state have been educated to be democrats. By the state of political education in Western Germany one realizes that democracy is not at all an easy way of life.[20]

In spacious America democracy naturally developed under a plentitude of fortunate circumstances. One cannot really imagine how any other form of government could have developed there.[21] The historical development of Germany with its small, narrow, and over-populated land area, surrounded by strong and aggressive neighbors has run a different political course. Present-day German teachers are daily confronted by their pupils, students as well as by their own colleagues with indigenous traditions, deeply-rooted ways of thinking and living. Aside from their general problems there is a series of other, more specific ones. Dr. Felix Messerschmid, Director of the Academy of Political Education in Tutzing, has summed them up in the following way.

The task of opening the minds of the youth of the German Federal Republic to the social and political entity of their nation and the world in which they

---

[19] Ralph Henry Gabriel, *Die Entwicklung des demokratischen Gedankens in den Vereinigten Staaten von Amerika.* Berlin: Duncker and Humbolt, 1951.

[20] That does not of course mean that democratic leadership in Germany cannot and should not energetically realize their educational aims. The Board of Education in Hamburg supervises the teaching of contemporary history in all of their schools through surprise visits made by school-inspectors. Inadequate teachers are removed and replaced by qualified successors. President Heinrich Lübke, who was recently interviewed over television by Dr. Klaus Mehnert, commented that, "I have visited eighteen school-classes this past year and have seen how much the pupils have learned from the teaching of social sciences that will later serve as a basis for their political understanding. I should, however, like to say that my visits in the *Ländern* have convinced me that the teaching of social sciences in the schools has taken on more importance than ever before. *Bulletin des Presse- und Informationsamtes der Bundesregierung,* 2. Dezember 1960.

[21] See Gabriel, op. cit., particularly Chapter 1.

will one day have to find their place and prove their mettle is not conceivable without a minimum of understanding of recent German history and the present-day German situation. Such an undertaking would comprise three aims: information (basic familiarity with the subject-matter), knowledge (practical understanding of the structure of a democratic society under certain circumstances), and education (an attitude corresponding to such knowledge and experience). In a nation that has been geographically, politically, and ideologically divided after a catastrophy without equal (National Socialism, World War II, total destruction of its political order), it would be a difficult task which would be confronted with set-backs that could only be overcome by the greatest perserverence and tenacity over a long period of time. In addition to this, moreover, important academic presuppositions could not be further developed in Germany, as in other countries, because of the isolation of Germany during the Nazi era. Capable scholars often went into the "inner" emigration for two decades and consequently were condemned to silence or the "outer" emigration and could therefore not be heard and lost contact with developments in Germany. For this reason the academic principles in the Federal Republic must be furthered at the same rate as the educational ones.

The solution of this task is confronted with difficulties, which originate from the lack of specialized training and also from the resistence (in one quarter) of the teachers themselves. This is due to the fact that the bitter experiences of 1939 to 1945 and the misdirected methods of de-Nazification after 1945 have consequently resulted in an insurmountable disinclination on the part of the teachers to commit the same error twice and a preference to restrict themselves to less dangerous fields than those assigned to them. The idealistic standard of education at German institutions of higher learning offers justifications for an escape into non-political spheres.

The willingness of students to discuss political problems is generally present. However, their mistrust of their father's generation in this sphere, a generation that had not been able to prevent National Socialism, is a considerable obstacle. It is not to be surmounted by dry and objective instruction. Thus is it understandable that a survey of the Frankfurt Institute of Social Research shows that social studies "arouse little interest and a connection between social studies and deeper political consciuousness cannot be ascertained."[22]

The influence of the parents often obstructs the teaching of social science. K. Barthel differentiates parents into three groups: those who support the efforts of the school; those who oppose them; and those who keep silent out of insecurity and shame, but also out of grounds of opportunism or indifference. These attitudes of the parents are reflected by the students and often present the teachers with an additional difficult task.

Dr. Messerschmid continues:

Nevertheless this frank description of conditions should in no way justify a resignation to this judgment.

There are many schools in which these difficulties are well-handled and where the factual as well as the psychological obstacles are surmounted and a

---

[22] Juergen Habermas in *Gesellschaft — Staat — Erziehung*, No. 8, 1958. See Part II, Chapter Five.

believable presentation of social and political circumstances is made possible through educational methods.

The students themselves further such instruction in many schools through voluntary study-groups, student-meetings, and field-trips. In a number of schools a student organization called the Political Study Group of High Schools has been founded which is independent of but sponsored by the teachers.

Inspite of inherent difficulties there has been positive success and encouraging advances in the Federal Republic. Whoever has read this book would neither deny that German democratic leadership has an insight into the problems of political education nor underestimate that they are earnestly endeavoring to promote a profound understanding of the German past and to make the democratic system safe for the future. People abroad do not know much about these problems and the efforts that are made to solve them, but rather more about actual or alleged failure of democratic education in Western Germany. That is probably due to the fact that all over the world the sensational "makes" news and appears in the headlines of the front pages of the newspapers, while, on the other hand, the real facts are printed on the back pages, if at all. One need only think of the publicity that was given to the swastika-smearings in Cologne (Christmas, 1959).[23])

The world-press contributed, even if unintentionally, to the resulting chain-reaction. Such reports were welcomed by those who are interested, for one reason or another, to keep a picture of the Federal Republic alive for the peoples of the world which hardly differs from that which Nazi-Germany offered. Every expert on German affairs knows that these destestable misdeeds were absolutely atypical of the political and social climate in the Federal Republic.[24]) One was therefore very favorably impressed in Germany by the objective reporting of the serious American press, which consistently evaluated the events in an appropriate manner. Here, for the first time, the confidence which the young German democracy has won in the United States of America under the leadership of Chancellor Adenauer was reflected in the American press at a critical moment.

The Germans, however, know very well and understand fully — in view of their recent past — that they have many enemies in the United States, as well as every-where else in the world, and that the mistrust toward Germany can also be very easily awakened in many, who would like to trust Germany. One is, therefore, the more thankful in Germany that our former enemies, and foremost the Americans, were so immediately willing to accept Germany once again into the family of nations and to believe that the German people would not be a hopeless case with regard to the democratization of their country. I am convinced that the American faith in the basic goodness of mankind has greatly contributed to the co-operation of the Germans in accepting democracy. The democratic leadership of Germany needs this encouragement and appreciation of their efforts. A disregard of what is actually being achieved in the Federal Republic as well as a persistent and unjustified criticism, of isolated and atypical occurrences would only impede the endeavors of German democratic leadership.

Therefore, in conclusion, something should be said about the origins of the malicious agitation against Germany which is unfortunately believed to some extent abroad.

---

[3]) These events will be dealt with in a section of a second volume of this series under the title "Anti-Semitism". All the other antidemocratic occurences and developments in the Federal Republic will be discussed extensively.
[24]) See Gruson, Appendix.

The smear-campaigns launched in other countries against Germany originate to a large degree in the Communist sphere and, at that, primarily in the Eastern zone of Germany. There is no need to give a detailed explanation of why the Kremlin and its puppet regime in Pankow would be greatly interested in employing all the means at its disposal to discredit the Federal Republic in the eyes of its allies. In their inflammatory articles and radio broadcasts meant for their population as well as for the nations abroad, the Federal Republic is described as being a militaristic, revengeful state that is ruled by former Nazi-generals, Junkers and capitalists, which continually agitates and prepares for an atomic war against the freedom-loving "German Democratic Republic". As an example of this a "Memorandum of the Government of the Democratic Republic" which was submitted as recommendation to UNESCO can be found in the appendix. It is characteristic of communistic propaganda that facts are distorted and that half-truths are intermingled with lies. Sensational news of this sort is being spread abroad by the enemies of the Federal Republic in countries that are friendly to her.

Another source of criticism is to be found in the Federal Republic herself. I refer here to purely destructive criticism, for there is no lack of constructive self-criticism in the Federal Republic. This destructive criticism is expressed by a number of left-wing intellectuals and publicists. Such was also the case in the Weimar Republic. At that time left-wing intellectuals unintentionally helped to bury the young republic. Fortunately this sort of criticism does not influence the average German of today.

That is, at least, a positive side of the political indifference of the larger segment of the German population. However, this sort of criticism finds an audience outside of Germany and because it originates in the Federal Republic it probably is therefore more readily believed than the communistic propaganda. For this reason the danger of this sort of criticism must be pointed out. Although there is much truth contained in this criticism, there is, due to its onesidedness, a completely distorted picture of the political, economic, and social conditions in the Federal Republic.

The enemies of Germany are able to give an appearance of authenticity to their smear-campaign by their quoting of West German publicists. Only recently the communistic newspaper *Neues Deutschland* devoted an entire page to the reprinting of excerpts from Erich Kuby's book *Alles im Eimer* (All Gone To Pieces). In a caption Kuby was introduced to the unsuspecting readers as a "bourgeois writer from Western Germany". In reality he and his associates reside in the Federal Republic because of obvious reasons, but their spiritual home is more in the Communistic part of Germany.

There are many sharp observers in Western Germany who know how to evaluate properly the dangers which threaten democracy from this quarter as being more critical than those from so-called Neo-Naziism.[25] The journalist, Johannes Gaitanides, a very perceptive analyst, has however pointed out with very sound arguments that the German intelligentsia cannot prove dangerous for German democracy.[26] Inspite of this it will be necessary to prepare the Germans, with their disasterous tendancy toward perfectionism, and especially the younger generation, against these "Hidden Persuaders" by means of political education.

---

[25] "In this respect they are right. Naziism is dead in Germany whether it is "old" or "new"." Cf. Hans Helmut Knütter, *Ideologien im Nachkriegsdeutschland. Eine Studie über die Nachwirkung des Nationalsozialismus.* Bonn: Ludwig Röhrscheid, 1961.

[26] Cf. Appendix, Johannes Gaitanides, "A word about the impotence of our literature."

1944 — After an Air Raid

1945 — Refugees

Just Released from Prison-of-War-Camps in Soviet Russia

Camp Friedland Near the Iron Curtain (1955)

Nevertheless there is an element of truth in the criticism made by the intelligentsia in Western Germany which must be taken seriously. This criticism comes from the fear that the Germans do not recognize the major problems of our age or are unable to solve them. Of course, this does not apply to the Germans alone but to the modern world as a whole. I suppose that the West German intelligentsia makes the "corrupt and economic wonder", the Federal Republic, the object of its strong attacks only for the sake of argumentation and out of resentment.

We live in an era of Revolution, such as the world has not known since the beginning of time. From my point of view, our major problem lies in the fact that Man must now show a moral maturity that measures up to the advances of the technical, industrial, and social revolution that began one hundred and fifty years ago and which seems to be reaching a new peak today. Instruments of power are given to nations and greater possibilities to shape his own life to the individual! These can be used by the community or the individual either for self-destruction or for the beneficial fulfillment of their responsibilities. In this connection I should like to quote a few note-worthy remarks by Eduard Spranger.

Every civilization can be compared with a system in which one tries to find a set of values. The participants in this endeavor, who are replaced from generation to generation, must have the conviction that this synthesis of values is worthy of preservation. It would be disasterous should they no longer understand the meaning of their cultural ideals; it would be dangerous could they no longer maintain the process physically; but it would be fatal if the moral powers were no longer adequate.

Decay does not begin with general immorality. It is already to be found in an individualistic way of life which usually is evident in the *fin de siècle*. The individual may still very well lead an orderly life, but he no longer feels himself to be a responsible member of a community. Even at a time when the *Decline of the West* was not yet a topic of discussion, we were taught at the humanistic high schools to appreciate the example of community-spirit in Antiquity. Not only was the spirit of Athens praised, but also that of Sparta and Rome. That was often no more than a modest appeal for "patriotism". Today we shy away from such appeals after having become guilty of an uncontrolled outburst of nationalism. It should, however, not be forgotten that a people, a fatherland, and a state, as Fichte said, are only forms in which the higher destiny of Man takes shape. One must be willing to sacrifice oneself for the State and the Ideal. A democratically organized society requires them even more than a monarchy, which operates a well-trained bureaucracy with traditional ideas of honor.

We know very well what the individual conscience requires. We are conscious of the responsibility which we have to bear in our respective professions. But that is not sufficient. We must know what the duties and responsibilities of civilization are. This extension of consideration results directly from the idea that free individuals must sustain their civilization and with that their state. Once we have begun this experiment, we must follow it through to its ultimate conclusion.

That is, however, not a matter for technical science and in this quarter the most brilliant engineering mind could not help us. In this matter it is not a question of providing us with means but with personal values. All methods are relative; each is related to the ideals which it has set up as being worthwhile. The goals that we set for ourselve decide whether technology will be benevolent or malevolent. Finally it is a question of what sort of aims we should choose. And only after this decision has been made can we approach the Absolute. By the Absolute, we mean the source of the final and ultimate purpose of mankind. Religiously speaking, this means God.

Because the superstructure of culture has been erected over and above free individuals, there must be an ultimate governor in every mature individual which reflects the Absolute. (Reflection, recommitment, we should keep in mind, translate the Latin word *religio*.) A civilization which is not founded on a real religious basis is actually nothing more than "an experiment". One may experiment with different methods, but not with the ultimate destiny of mankind.

Our present civilization is a society with unlimited means at its disposal. Old fairy tales and myths abound with examples of how catastrophic it can be for Man when his "possibilities" and "means" exceed beyond his ethical standard. In such periods of excess a completely different sort of "drive" is required which cannot be harmonized with the chain of events and has its own goals and under certain circumstances impedes the mechanical course of development. Basic moral qualities are of this mettle.

Such qualities must at least develop proportionately with the stocks of natural energy, if the latter are to continue to effect the same success later as they did earlier. That is simply not the case. One the contrary, Man is inclined to waste his reservoirs of energy and means the more carelessly, the more accessible they are to him. *What he can do, he will do.* His ability to evaluate his desires properly becomes less apt. That is not only true with respect to economy — one need only think of the trivial case of water — but above all to the ethical self-criticism of what may be desired and — on a higher plane — what ought to be desired."[27]

I believe that this spirit should be the leading idea of the education of modern man and especially of the German people as well. In this frame of reference the great task of the German nation today is to come to grips with the past in order not to lose their souls and to become responsible citizens through education, in order to be immune to the demogogy from the left or right, and to become world-citizens so that they can participate judiciously and vigorously in the fight against hunger, ignorance, and fear and thereby also to take part in the world-wide contest between freedom and totalitarianism. These problems must be solved by the German people if they are to take their rightful place once again among the civilized nations of the world, after having fallen into the nightmarish abyss of barbarism.

---

[27] Eduard Spranger, "*Leben wir in einer Kulturkrise?*", *Wo stehen wir heute?* Gütersloh: Bertelmann, 1960, pp. 20—21. Cf. Karl Friedrich Kindler, "Not und Aufgabe der politischen Erziehung", *Gesellschaft, Staat, Erziehung.* Heft 2, 1960, pp. 85—86. "In his treatise *De regime principum at regem Cypry* (circa 1266) Thomas Aquinas raised the question some seven hundred years ago — as had Cicero in his *Somnium Scipionis* — how a ruler, if he were good and just, would be rewarded by God for the charge and burden of ruling and for the great responsibility of his office. Thomas believed that the ruler would be rewarded for his capability in ruling for the good of the state — beyond wealth, glory, and fame — and would thereby be near God in a special way. A ray of this hope should fall to the lot of every citizen in a democracy who participates in the community in a self sacrificing fashion in the fulfillment of his part in the sovereignty of the state and the wise and just order of the community. If, in addition to all other endeavors, we succeed in making a person understand the religious aspect of politics and the fulfillment of civic tasks as being on essential act in the realization of the religious basis of the state, then we can hope that he will fulfill his daily civic responsibilities not only with an eye to their purpose and effectiveness, but to their ultimate nature."

Part II. Youth
A. Basic Attitudes

"Attitude of Young People of Today to Values"[1]

By Walter Jaide

I.

The theme of this lecture is also the subject of an investigation now being made, with the German Bureau for the Study of Youth Questions as its sponsor, and so I would like today to give you some points from this investigation.

As one can hardly preface an interim report like this with an outline of the philosophy of values or of motivation psychology (which would really be the right thing to do), I shall confine myself to giving you an idea of what has been covered in the investigation.

It is a pilot survey, and thus a wide scope has been allowed and an endeavor made to cover everything in which the individual boy or girl believes and which they try to follow, in other words everything which, at the level of a more or less conscious and considered motivation, helps to determine their attitude and behavior.

With an eye on considerations of system and on empirical diagnoses we can best group and examine the relevant factors of motivation under three headings: standards — examples to be followed — ideals (if I may begin by giving them these simple names).

With young people we find standards in the form of single standards of values, tenets, commandments, principles (fairness and justice, for instance) or, one degree lower (if you like), rules for living, proverbs, standards of behavior and adaptation ("not to be different"); or we find instead merely the licence of an attitude which is not guided by any standards — "as occasion demands".

In contrast to this, the examples which some follow present comprehensive, integrated programs for the shaping of one's life — whether they be embodied in fellow humans (one's father, for example), or traditional figures of social, regional or national origin, (such, for example, as the honest artisan), or whether they are required in response to calls of religion and exemplified among the followers of Christ. Those who do not respond to such comprehensive guidance, those who are unable to identify themselves with such a total idealization of the control of existence, will seek a more anonymous guarantor of their conduct by conforming with the habits and aims which they see far and wide around them (at different levels) or just in their closer surroundings. So much for the heuristic assumption. Many young people, moreover, worship film stars, athletes, singers or players whom they hear on records; the evaluation of such people as ideals must, however, be on a different plane.

From examples to be followed, as from standards of value, we may advance to higher ideals; for instance, a young person may extend his personal tenet of truthfulness to the concept of truth and the pursuit of truth, to which he may

---

[1]) Lecture given at the twenty-second Congress of the German Psychology Society, Heidelberg, 27. 9. to 1. 10. 1959.

3*

dedicate his life as a research worker or a lawyer; another may be so inspired by the model provided by Albert Schweitzer that he devotes himself to serving his fellow men. A central value such as this may provide an appreciation of life which may serve as a norm and criterion for one's commissions and omissions.

Other young people may forego such celestial ideals in favor of a successful career, social preferment and an easy life, and in doing so they may not be clear in their own minds how far higher values are included or necessary. Others again will probably refuse to adopt any specific point of view and will tarry in the antechambers of circumstantial, wary reservations.

It is against the background of these problems, then, that the young people covered by the survey have been questioned; they were asked whether, and at what level, they were acquainted with values like these, whether they accepted them and acted accordingly, of what these values consisted, why and how they came to adopt them.

II.

The question of what technique to use in these surveys poses many problems. If value is attached to findings which will present a cross-section and be statistically representative, every kind of questionnaire, both written and oral, can be employed. In this way we get responses which are, it is true, of great interest for our subject, revealing certain general tendencies — but probably only to the extent that the questions are limited to points of fact and to wishes — limited, that is to say, to the use made of money and time, church attendance, club membership, important points from the subject's life history and general background, his wishes for a career and for his future.

The limits on the utility and reliability of such formal, factual methods are reached when one inquires about past events and about the reasons why, say, a young man no longer belongs to a certain group, about the combination of factors connected with the group, the family and the individual which led to his leaving the group, and into the values which played a part in motivating the decision. Moreover the symptomatic value of the young person's answer to the questions, whether put in the form of a questionnaire or a formal interview, is difficult to ascertain; it is unclear whether it is just a borrowed opinion or an adopted conviction, or a genuinely effectual attitude — a motive that for the subject is dominant — and why and how he adopted it.

From the questions on wishes, too, it is difficult to find out what subjective standing attaches to a wish in the mind of the young person concerned — whether it is a Utopian idea, something regarded as a matter of course, an objective he has been forced to accept or a target that can be reached with a certain amount of effort.

Incidentally, there are, even among the factual questions, some which are unexpectedly complicated (the father's profession for instance) and those in which the question has been inadequately formulated or put in a form which is not sufficiently neutral (e.g. Have you someone whom you emulate? a friend?). It is only by trial and error that it is possible to see how questions like these are interpreted and how they "get across".

This is even more true as soon as we try to move from questions of fact and wishes to reasons, attitudes, combinations of motives and their etiology. We might, for instance, ask (as has been done): "Do you look upon your job as a 'burden' or as the 'fulfillment' of your life's ambitions?" "Are you 'interested' in politics?" "Is there an 'idea' which could fill you with enthusiasm?" But then we should have to reckon with the fact that not only would such expressions be variously interpreted and evoke different shades of feeling, but they would even be felt to have an out-dated, pretentious flavor, much to the detriment of the replies that would be made. Psychometric methods, in spite of skilful combinations, variation and grading of the question and answer item are, in my opinion, unequal to the task. Over and above this the statistical results will be ruined by the silent third of those who hold no opinion whatsoever, have no previous experience or views — and by the large number of answers given out of embarrassment or vulgarity, of which there are always examples, with difficult questions like these.

In the case of our investigation a procedure aimed at producing a monograph lay behind the system of questionnaires intended to give to earlier qualitative findings subsequent quantitative confirmation or confirmation of group distribution and to show the boundaries of the findings. Only in this way is the procedure offered a field in which it is fruitful. Personal contact between the young person and the investigator, therefore, was the basis of our method, and its chief means was exploration — repeated, methodical exploration, extending widely over the relevant subjects such as school, job, home, leisure, church, religious teaching and confirmation classes, plans and aims for the future in general, politics.

This round of exploration incorporated:

a list of 32 catchwords in 4 groups (Ten Commandments — seventeenth of June — five-day week — Soraya) and the young people were asked to select several of these for discussion with the investigator;

in the same way: a list consisting of eight fictive characters ("would you like to be a person who...");

Twenty pictorial reproductions of the Cross — proclamation of a kaiser — country idylls — assembly shop;

and (instead of the tiresome moral anecdotes) the story of a forced landing on water by St. Exupéry, which has been found to be excellently adapted for the discussion of the problem of guilt.

All this was done with the object of creating a more informal and less strained atmosphere in the all too direct contact between the young person and the investigator during the investigation (as is of course also done by the essays or diary sketches on the subject), so that the young person is offered as wide a range as possible for projection and that, for certain phases of the investigation at least, roughly comparable conditions are established and numerically definable answers obtained.

This, however, in no way means that we escape the general problems and limits of the exploratory method, which I may assume here are familiar to you. To these we must, because of our subject, add two further difficulties:

The first I may illustrate by a comparison with investigations of wishes for careers; however ill-defined and clumsy the replies on a choice of career, they at least refer to one and the same world of careers, which actually exists today. When we turn to values, however, there is in the minds of most boys and girls nothing which exists objectively, absolutely (and to which they could, of course, adopt an attitude of doubt or opposition). Rather, their choice of an attitude is made amid a number of partly contradictory religions, philosophies, doctrines, ways of life and social habits which in any case are interpreted, undermined and twisted by everyone as he thinks fit. In other words, the young people's thoughts and conclusions display such syncretic variety that the investigator would need to possess an extensive philosophical and theological background to be able to proceed far enough in the identification, classification and evaluation of the statements — both in the interviews and also during the subsequent analysis.

When, for example, the question of guilt is raised, the boy or girl of today is able to find a dozen different solutions and conclusions with which the investigator must be fully familiar if he is to ask questions and listen to the answers in his capacity as an expert. (This is something which remains a stumbling-block in investigations on this subject — much more troublesome than the problem of obtaining results which can be put in sufficiently objective form and give a sufficiently true picture.)

The second difficulty is usually brought up by the question: is present-day youth different in fact, more unstable, more thirsty for stimuli, and so on, than were ... or does it only express itself in quite a different way? For purposes of this survey this means that the statements obtained from the young person need to be checked in the light of observation of his actual behavior in daily life as well as in special test situations. What part he really does play in the family, at school, at work, in his club; how he would react when without warning he is faced by the relevant problem, etc. — all these things must be added to his statements in order to verify and interpret them. In our case this was made possible by a small group of specially trained teachers. Even allowing for scepticism about the accuracy and objectivity of the schoolmaster's (concealed) observation of his pupils, we must agree that such a combination of exploratory and biographical items, if carried out over a lengthy period of time (about a year), is the most likely to realize the object of our survey — as far as method and purpose are compatible at all and we do not have constantly to find a compromise between the methodological requirements and the practical possibilities open to us.

Naturally, the quantitative results of an intimate monographic procedure such as this cannot be great. It cannot yield more (and not less, just as in other disciplines), than a study of consciences (in our case with 200 young people), but its qualitative evaluation can provide an instructive picture of the attitude taken to values and its background. We were obliged to choose the subjects for our survey from a particular age-group (15—17 years, born between 1941 and 1944), within a limited area (Lower Saxony, Bremen, Hamburg), and to take approximately equal numbers from both sexes, from all kinds of schools, including trade schools, and the various types and sizes of dwellings — in other words, not on a random basis.

III.

Since the material obtained in this way does not allow for either cross-sectional findings nor, so far, for findings by groups, it is best broken down and analyzed by a system of interpretation which seeks to identify types. The way in which the subjects dealt with the questions put will serve as a characteristic which decides the types. In relation to their general stage of development the boys and girls varied in the degree and type of forcefulness, self-assurance, critical ability, finesse and insistence with which they come to grips with the traditional values. Accordingly our monographs may be divided into three types (each with two variants). Using a great deal of simplification, I should like to call these:

the naive

the aloof

and the seekers.

The girls of the naive group have hardly started to tackle problems or decide for themselves as yet. They cling firmly to fixed opinions and canons of behavior which have not, so far, been subjected to doubt, been exposed to the need to make a choice or been shaken by critical experiences. They have taken them over from their ordered, socially normal surroundings, from the people with whom they have the most immediate contact, whose authority they recognize unquestioningly and whom they wish to be like.

They have almost no "problems", inner tensions or conflicts but they possess a reliable moral sense, are industrious at school, tactful and respectfully receptive, and they have something akin to an ideology which they can recite. The tenor of their remarks is simple and straightforward, reminiscent of confirmation classes or books written for young girls.

With the boys there is an even more emphatically conservative attitude, bound up with an almost reactionary interest in history and politics ("should like to have lived earlier"). Domesticity, grace at table, thriftiness, rambling, severe school discipline or, in some cases, artisan training, patriotism, Bismarck, sterner justice — these form the inventory of their interests as taken over direct from their families, schools, churches or youth-groups. Here we can still find social characters taken as examples to be followed (the independent artisan, the farmer) if the type is exemplified for the boy by his father or an uncle. A good deal of stress is laid on good behavior (in the sense of strictness and self-denial).

These cases consists of thoroughly active, helpful, popular boys (class spokesmen, youth-group workers) who do their school work or apprenticeship assiduously but not pushingly, or who are particularly bright and sure in the calling they choose. What they lack — so far — is the impetus which carries them to the adventure of finding their own intellectual vantage-point, of seeking guidance in many quarters and of deciding between several possibilities ("everything has its proper place").

These young people show no drastic symptoms of anxiety, frustration, insecurity, lack of ties, exposure to danger, or scepticism. Their attitude to school, work, family, money, leisure and religion is unsophisticated and is characterized by timeless reasonableness and naturalness. So even this sort of thing exists!

The sub-variety of this type is on the contrary marked by a lack of maturity and mental activity. In place of a respectful acceptance of values, the representatives of this group show uncritical entanglement in the rules of behavior. Instead of attachment to those nearest to them they display infantile servility instead of heteronomous guidance, and dull unawareness. In examining their cases allowance must be made for the difficulties caused by a strict upbringing at home, domineering educators, retarded physical development, lack of intelligence, pamperism, etc. It is almost impossible to carry on a conversation with them. They are childishly astonished at the nature and scope of the questions, they answer in evasive turns of phrase, such as "I don't know; yes, actually; I think so too" or in stereotype formulae and proverbs ("One has to pay for one's misdeeds", "A good deed a day") and they accompany their inadequate replies with mime and gestures which indicate that too much is being expected and asked of them.

With these young people one is left anxious about what will happen to them, with their still unformed opinions, when later in life church and school send them out to make their way in the world.

One answer may, perhaps, be found when we sketch the uninterested sub-variety in our second or aloof group.

For them, grappling with ideas starts mainly by way of emancipation from accepted values — in a carefully indirect way behind the facade of harmless amusements, of adaptation without friction, of perfectly respectable opinions — anything so as not to attract attention and to have to stand up for one's convictions ("well, that's what people believe", "everyone does it").

Higher tenets are not attacked, but are gradually allowed to lose their force and become ineffective ("who acts on them nowadays anyhow?") so that according to circumstances the subject may act in whatever way is convenient or advantageous and can fall back with a minimum of friction on life itself, as they do not want to miss anything and least of all to be pinned down by his fellow men, by examples to be followed or by principles.

The ties with parents and teachers are very much loosened, there is an attempt to escape from the sometimes stuffy respectability of home, they are out and about a great deal, always have something to do, and they draw from cheap novels and films and the like the ideas for their appearance and their behavior. Even for these young people, however, the stars of the screen, football field and the old princely houses do not play the part of examples who should be copied, for it is just these boys and girls who prefer to remain "themselves" or to "take life as it comes". The stars serve as persons who are admired and loved, and are to be partly imitated, they serve too for the projection of illusory, compensating, braggart wishes ("one day like Lizy"). In all this the young people remain almost as reserved in their attitude towards the prominent members of their dream-world as nearly everyone does towards the great of this world.

Girls and boys form cliques, display teenage behavior and in doing so they show certain puberal features which are characteristic of their generation; these cannot be regarded as mere protracted infantile unwillingness to face problems, or as a hasty conformity with grown-ups, but as an explicit disassociation, an artificial primitiveness, an intentional refusal to deal with everything which grown-ups responsible for them find problematic and of binding force. ("I never racked my brains about God and that sort of thing — we've never spoken about democracy and that sort of rubbish".)

There is a clear distinction between the uninterested and the actual sceptics (Schelsky). With the latter, liberation from inherited values and the unfolding of their own independence leads to a conscious grappling with problems. They experience, recognize and doubt the different possible solutions (as far as they are available to them) and arrive, somewhat hastily and not without complacency, at a new, well-defined attitude — that of the sceptic; in other words they criticize as a sham the idea that standards of values, examples to be followed and even ideals have ever been taken seriously or can ever be usefully applied in actual practice, and they wonder whether these things do not foster hypocrisy and abuse and, in their impracticability and unworldliness, do not merely burden and mislead mankind ("why shouldn't one be a coward if it saves oneself and others a lot?" "Ideals are a dirty business, they only lead to unhappiness.") They admit that one needs a certain support and an inward sense of decency, but people have always had a sense of decency anyway. All norms for living which go beyond utility and enjoyment they thus strip of their transcendental value and their tradition, because these seem to them to be at best bearable and practicable when looked upon as secularized, routine motives immanent in behavior. This emphasis on immanence, though so strongly supported only by the sceptics, also plays a part with other young people, and probably provides one of the features to be noted in the overall characterization of these age-groups — though this does not mean that the sceptic can just be taken as their prototype.

These young people are only too willing to discuss freely and at lenght (the girls even more aggressively than the boys) but they are extremely touchy about any traditional formula which does not fit into their view of life. They constantly put things into quotation marks and consistently use a jargon of understatement (it is possible to recognize something but not to "admire" it or "be enthusiastic" about it — a book may be read with "interest", but never with "profit".

The result of a process of guidance and emancipation on these lines, lasting several years, is, it is true (up to now), not much more than the desire for a private life as lived by the middle classes, troubled neither by the subject's own wishes nor by any general social responsibility ("I want to be left in peace at last and to live, just live and do as I like — to be the plain Honest John of my day", said one who might have been speaking for many others.) We should in fact be grateful to them that they continue to live at all, for many of them possess an underlying strain of fatalism and pessimism. Many of them see in birth control and "never getting married" an essential aim in life, while others take refuge in Utopias (such as a world state). (One of them keeps a balance sheet of the advantages and disadvantages of life, so as to be able to put an end to things himself on the basis of the balance).

If the aim of these young people was to belittle concepts of values, the third type, the seekers, succeed in coming to grips in a constructive manner with problems ranging over a wide field of ideas on several planes, and this leads them towards new and personal ties. With them it is possible to speak, in the fullest sense, of a struggle and a search which they do not treat lightly. Some of them remain for a long time in the phase of doubt and disapproval (girls, by the way, no less often than boys); many revel in lofty dreams; many of them soon reach a firm faith and sense of values. From all of them we may expect further consolidation from an honest, healthy way of life.

They look upon the world not as a piece of machinery which creaks along more or less well while they stand on the sidelines, but as a range of problems, difficulties, errors and tasks which interest and appeal to them. They have quite discriminating views on guilt and suffering, on the meaning of life, on the tension between command and obedience, and they are receptive of lofty ideals and human greatness. In their choice of career, unselfish motives play a part. For the most part they have active relationships and responsibilities within the family, at children's services, youth-groups, and are hesitant in their contacts with the opposite sex. With all this goes a certain reserve *vis-à-vis* the indifferent *massa perditionis* or Philistines among their relatives or in their class at school.

They too are more inclined — as are most of the young people — to quote as examples that they follow, people they know personally from their own circle (family, friends, or even the place where they work) rather than collective examples taken from public life, from among well-known figures in politics, science and art.

An exception to this rule is Albert Schweitzer, who for schoolchildren has become an idol standing for escape from personal egoism. Clearly, our modern society has not yet brought forth any fascinating, graphic ideals which establish a standard. No young person aims at being a "consumer of leisure" or a "lowincome shareholder" or a fighter for Western freedom. One comfort in all this is that they do not deceive themselves in such matters.

Corresponding with the reservations towards heroes and symbolic figures — also shared by these young people — and the falling back on ideals in their more immediate surroundings, we find a tendency to be less ready to discover and accept a perfect example and more inclination to accept part-characteristics ("I do not know anyone so perfect, but I can put together the good qualities of a number of people"). Many invent ideal figures and project all kinds of desirable virtues into them, as can be seen in the way they put together an almost standard catalogue of worthy ideas when questions are put to them on their friends, their teacher, their father and so on. This in no way means — and these young people would not claim that it did — that they can no longer find examples worth following. Rather, it points to a healthy confidence in themselves and a more liberal readiness to accept their elders — beginning with their own parents — in a way which is neither forced nor conventional. In all this can be seen the reserve of mass reactions and of being uprooted.

We are left with the subgroup among the seekers who are reluctant to name and acknowledge an example they can follow. They decry very subtly the danger of mere imitation, of self-delusion or of showing off, of losing courage or of self-disparagement, and they make much of the difficulties of a valid transfer to the actual circumstances of their own life; finally they cling to the incomparable individuality of their own personality, using almost the formula of Meissner. ("I want to shape my own life, according to my own ideas" — this from a 15 year old village girl.)

Consequently they exaggerate the drawing of conclusions from their own doings and experience, from which they try to extract for themselves a whole view of life, although they are also ready to accept suggestions from those who are more mature. As a rule they put their point of view and their convictions modestly and thoughtfully.

The sub-variety of this type, the convinced ones, behave very differently. They are esoteric people who have been roused, converted, liberated, and they put forward their absolute opinions with extreme clarity in a rigidly theological, philosophical or political phraseology. They have no doubt whatsoever that their ideals can be put into practice. With all respect to such a determined attitude, it is impossible to overlook the fact that we are dealing here, in most cases, with unbalanced young people, worried about approval of themselves; their close association with small groups is the reverse side of their insecurity.

The professions of faith, which they put forward like a formula, are supported by virtues, principles and abnegations which they can reel off ("Correct, honest, tolerant, firmly religious, real manliness, true soldier's spirit, genuine Prussian spirit" as one of them puts it). In this way many a vital question is subjected to a somewhat drastic solution or dismissed with dialectics.

IV.

I hope you will understand if I have had, from time to time, to use, without further ado, evaluation terms which have already done heavy service and which have no clear-cut, single signification, in the attempt to reduce several hundred pages of minutes to a few pages for a lecture — a thing which would not have been possible if I had used merely descriptive terms. By giving a picture of the three types I have merely tried to show the great variety of style, force and direction encountered when we investigate the efforts of these boys and girls to cope with problems; I wanted, too, to draw just two conclusions from the work: first, that there seems to be no justification for hastily stating in tones of resignation that there is no more "youth", no peculiarly youthful dynamic in the progress through the ages of man.

Next, it seems incorrect to me that in describing these age groups we should go on using the usual negative generalizations, which only apply to particular groups or types. There have probably always been the naive types, the "Couldn't care less", the heretics, the honest seekers and the orthodox. It is likely to be very difficult to work out whether the relative strengths in these types shift so very much from one generation to another (whether, for instance, the number of those really without ties has in fact increased appreciably). We have no truly comparable investigations at our disposal and are apt to see past generations through rose-colored glasses and to use them rather carelessly as a norm by which to judge our present findings.

With my subjects — up to the age of 17 — the timeless characteristics and conservative stamp are of almost more significance than the features which might be considered ephemeral and typical of the generation. I rather think that we are apt to oversimplify the moulding power of contemporary conditions when we reduce their manifold aspects to an abstract formula ("industrial society") and then expect that in the light of this formula the times will immediately exert a one-way influence on "youth". Probably, however, we all shape our lives — as do our young people — rather despite such a formula than in immediate conformity with it. For this reason the degree of soundness and stability which these age-groups take through life with them should not be overlooked. For the same reason we should not assert that they are in general more seriously "endangered" than other, earlier generations.

Naturally, it is possible to analyze this danger more closely, according to types and forms, but we must not paint it in such general and extensive terms. For if there is one thing that these age-groups find uncongenial and irritating, it is the dramatic picture of dangers, shortcomings and duties painted by the somewhat more sentimental generation of those who are describing them. On the other hand most of these young people elect to follow a sensible, undramatic, but sincerely and reliably managed middle way of life, influenced by their dislike of self-expression, their inclination to avoid change and to seek the middle way. This does not, however, mean that they are entirely opposed, in a negative or sceptical sense, to every up-lifting and fixing of existence. They will be able to play their parts pretty well, and they will perhaps be, in this way, sounder than the florid prototypes of earlier generations. They have developed their own habits of levelling down their ideas and of using understatement, and these have led to many an error in judgement of their true outlook and their actual conduct. It is only when one has seen through the understatement and taken care not to fall into the error of doubtful comparisons and generalizations that one begins to understand what this world and its values really mean to these young people.

Attitude of Young Persons to Politics [1]

By Dieter Geldschlaeger

What is the basic attitude to politics of the young people towards whom efforts at political education are directed? What are their basic political views, and to what extent are they prepared to accept political instruction, to form political decisions and to take part in politics?

Inquiries among German youth have been carried out over a period of about ten years. Some of the results of these inquiries seem to have produced disturbing revelations. Thus the question, not very aptly put, of "Are you intersted in politics?", was answered at various times in the negative by 60 % to 70 %. The number of those uninterested was always higher among girls than among the boys, in one case the figure was as high as 87 % of girls questioned.

Another question which was frequently put concerned one-party or multi-party government. Here too the results were disturbing. In 1952, 56 % of the young people questioned stated that they were in favor of a single party; in 1951 during another poll 40 % were in favor of a one-party government. It may the that a slight change in the statistics of inquiry has meanwhile taken place, but no fundamental difference in these figures is to be expected. Does this mean that the situation is not a very hopeful one? "But it is in dealing with such individual questions that this mean that scientific action first begins" (Schelsky).

In the chapter entitled, "Youth's attitude to politics and public life", of his book on juvenile sociology, The Sceptical Generation, 1957, Helmut Schelsky[2]) attributes the political attitude of the majority of young people in Germany to two essential attitudes. One is the pre-political reaction against political duties, the other is the consumer attitude extended to the sphere of politics.

The pre-political reaction against political duties expresses itself for example in a resignation towards all political happenings, an ignorance of even the most elementary political facts, and in the judging of political relationships by general human standards. The reasons for such a reaction are obvious. They are connected with the abstruseness, the unmethodical character of political procedure in a democracy which operates under present-day conditions, the rationalist structure of which leaves little room for the play of feelings. Its frankness rejects any compulsory commitments, and its restriction to substantive decisions takes the place of the role played by the person in smaller and more intimate spheres. All these characteristics make it clear that close restrictions are placed upon political understanding in a democracy of this type, indeed it may be said that the restrictions are all the closer, the the less extensive the education. Schelsky points out that the inclination to a one-party government is far stronger among primary school

---

[1]) Excerpts from Bericht ueber die Probleme und die Versuche der politischen Bildung unter jungen Menschen in der Bundesrepublik Deutschland. (Report on the Issues involved and the Attempts made at Political Education among the Youth of the German Federal Republic, prepared during the summer and fall of 1960 — a Manuscript.)
[2]) Helmut Schelsky, Die Skeptische Generation, Diederichs Verlag, Cologne, 1958 (second ed.)

pupils than among high school pupils and students. The reasons for the lack of interest in "politics" — just this very word seems to exert rather a repulsive than an attractive influence on young people — is expressed by young people themselves in such phrases as "we are still too young for that" and "that's a matter for the specialists", or, among girls, "that's men's business". But if, instead of asking "Are you interested in politics?" some specialized question is asked, a surprising interest is displayed among young people. This interest is all the greater, the more the matter in question affects the persons polled. A certain precocious caution with regard to politics may sometimes be evoked in young people, in that they take over the opinion of older adults ("a burnt child dreads the fire"), without having assimilated the corresponding experience. In conclusion, Helmut Schelsky decides that the great majority of young people are in favor of democracy, and that — apart from a small minority — no conscious anti-democratic feelings are to be found anywhere, and that the attitude of German youth in general may be termed "unpolitically democratic".

As regards German university students, Gole Mann observed in 1960 that they are "critical, unprejudiced, polite, open-minded, ready to work, with no trace of nationalism, with no trace of hate or self-conceit or hazy romantic ideas. They are fundamentally different from the academic youth of 30 years ago, and if things were to go wrong, it would not be their fault this time".

Hand in hand with this not absolutely unsympathetic attitude, which is often quite innocent, with this pre-political reaction against political duties, goes, as has been said, a consumer attitude towards political affairs, towards the state of the administrative authorities, which may be attributed to a prevailing conception of basic values which Schelsky, in agreement with other sociologists, defines by the terms "peace and quiet, security and complete individual freedom". It is taken more or less for granted by German youth that these values exist, a claim is made to them, even in the bosom of the family children are taught that they are entitled to them, and here already the desire to expect a great deal from the state is encouraged. This desire is not necessarily balanced by a readiness to give up too much to the state. Contrary to all assertions regarding militarist leanings on the part of German youth, a distinct reluctance to serve in the federal army continues to be distinguishable, which is in no small part due to this lack of readiness to make a personal sacrifice for the state. Schelsky also points out that nothing is less likely to be found among young Germans than a respect for authority with regard to official institutions and representatives. Schelsky describes the "dilemma typical of our age" which is revealed here: "while making the maximum claims upon state welfare provision, there is a conviction that all claims on the part of the state to influence private life in any way should be rejected, as is bureaucracy. The interrelations have become so vast and complicated that a personal knowledge or conception of their urgency is impossible".

Schelsky himself says that these remarks apply to the majority of young people in Germany, but that a recognition of the necessity of political activity and political education also exists. Thus a 20-year old infants' nurse writes: "the present generation should be given more opportunities for a general political education on a democratic basis..." And another young man writes: "In this generation there is a large class of young people who are anything but uninterested in politics. A class which discusses problems of the day keenly, and which has opinions and ideas of its own. A class which would very well be able to take over political tasks one day, which inwardly realizes its responsibilities, and which indeed has in part a guilty conscience that it has not yet passed from the stage of being interested in politics to taking an active part in politics. For the greater part they are put off by the hubbub which surrounds party politics, and by the way in which all those taking part, now and again deviate from the common course upon which they all should be set to perform a few party political gymnastics. Other people, who are by no means unintelligent, have no idea where to begin, or what possibilities even exist. There are many other reasons. That does not mean to say, however, that this class of undecided persons is a class of disinterested or indeed unusable persons". Walter Gross-Hartlage and Karl Rauch, who in 1959 published a volume of sayings by 20-year old Germans[1]), reach the conclusion from similar remarks: "that the teaching of civics and the foundations of political education to the growing generation must be intensified and expanded". One special aspect of the political attitude of young persons is contained in their attitude to the existing youth organizations. Investigations have shown fairly clearly that between 30% and 40% of juveniles up to the age of 25 have joined youth organizations.

It has been proved that this figure remains relatively constant over a number of years. It has also been shown that considerably more young men work in youth groups than do young women, and that this difference is specially marked in rural areas in contrast to large towns. There is also general agreement that at about the age of 20 an abrupt break in the contacts to the youth organizations tends to take place. These observations are summed up in the expressions "aversion to organizations" and "weariness of organizations" among young Germans. Theodor Wilhelm has spoken critically on this: "the reason for many complaints about 'poverty of social contacts' or 'lack of community spirit' among young people may be attributed to the community experiences of the adults themselves, which are not suitable as a precise gauge for measuring the social susceptibility of the young".

It has been shown, namely, that new attempts in the field of juvenile welfare, such as unconventional club-like unions, possibilities of meeting one another in the "Homes with the Open Door", have been able to attract a large number of young people who were adverse to the youth organizations. A young man who belongs to such an unconventional circle writes: "this is a free and easy group, which is in no way organized or has any sort of tendencies. I am against organizations, whether of political parties or the churches. The former are prejudiced, the latter often, at any rate in the youth groups, terribly childish."

Helmut Schelsky draws two conclusions from his analysis of the attitude of young people to political events. Information on political happenings, instruction regarding political inter-relations, familiarity with the course of politics are good, but they are only possible within limits. It is a misleading idea to assume that all political events can be related to a familiar scheme of things, to personal connections and to human emotions. It is, therefore, necessary, in addition to the instruction, that a critical dissociation from politics should be maintained — as protection, so to speak. In the course of their report Walter Grosse-Hartlage and Karl Rauch come to the conclusion: "The share of the twenty-year olds in public life is not excessive, but is doubtlessly larger than that of the thirty to fifty year olds. All the comments of the young people on this subject are also at the same time a question put to the adults, as a group and as individuals."

---

[1]) *Zwanzigjaehrige haben das Wort*, Paul List Verlag, Munich, 1959.

...An attempt has been made to determine more precisely from whence the political opinions of young people originate, and what part school and home play in this connection. The result was as follows: It was found in the course of an enquiry among pupils of Frankfurt secondary schools about the sources from which their knowledge of the National Socialist era derived, that source No. 1 was the books they had read, while home and school occupied the 2nd and 3rd place respectively among younger schoolboys, the positions being reversed in the case of older boys. The detailed break-down of these results is exceedingly informative: "No schoolboy who considers Hitler's policy to have been good names his school as the source of information, but mostly indicates his home and often books as source No. 1. ... The correction of knowledge already acquired ... presents the most difficult problem. The answers given by the schoolboys allow of the conclusion that — despite the bombed-out cities — the book-cupboards apparently still contain masses of history books written from the perspective of the National Socialist time ..." When 256 elementary school pupils in a north German city (children between the ages of 10 and 15, almost exclusively members of working-class families) were questioned, only 24 had obtained information on Semitism from their parents, while the remainder had informed themselves through book-club magazines, radio and television programs and their school.

**Modern Class Room. Inscription on Wall in Background reads:
A Divided World — A Divided Germany**   Photo: Windtstosser-Nuettgens — Bavaria

A Class Room in a Primary School

Photo: Peter Cornelius — Bavaria

A Chemistry Class

Photo: Peter Cornelius — Bavaria

Friends

Photo: Oskar Poss — Bavaria

B. Political Education in the School

The West German School System [1]

By Ernst Matthewes

The States of the Federal Republic of Germany have jurisdiction over the German schools. There is neither a Federal Ministry of Cultural Affairs nor Federal legislation regarding school matters. Nevertheless, the school systems throughout Germany are uniform in their principles, organization and curricula. The certificates, examinations, and privileges are mutually recognized in all States. During the years immediately following the end of the war, difficulties developed because of differences in the priorities accorded to the foreign languages to be taught. A few states had English as the first foreign language, others had French ranking first, and the classical secondary schools (Gymnasien), began their foreign language programs with Latin. However, these differences were resolved several years ago. With the exception of the Gymnasien which still prefer Latin, all schools throughout the Federal Republic now teach English as the first foreign language.

The similarity of the various German school systems devolves in part from their common tradition. Also the systems are coordinated by the Cultural Affairs Ministers of the various States who have established a Permanent Conference with its own secretariat. Although operating without legislative mandate, this group, in conjunction with an advisory committee of school experts, all operating under the aegis of the Ministers, has been instrumental in assuring a standard approach over a wide range of common problems.

The jurisdiction of the states over school matters inhibits a centralism which, as in every intellectual field, would be particularly harmful to schooling. Vigorous schools can only operate where, despite all the required regulations, sufficient leeway is left for teachers' associations, parents' committees, and schools to get in direct contact with the supervisory offices. Granted that a Federal Ministry of Cultural Affairs could promote greater unification, it would necessarily give administrative bureaucracy priority over creative impulses. Further, it would place school policy more centrally in the political arena than is the situation at present. Since State Cultural Affairs Ministers belong to different political parties dependent on the political composition of their State parliaments, their discussions and joint decisions are free from partisan political controversy.

By tradition, the German school system comprises three branches, the elementary schools (Volksschulen), the "intermediate schools" (Mittelschulen), and the secondary schools, all of the latter now being called Gymnasien. The first years at the elementary school (Volksschule) are known as basic schooling (Grundschule) which must jointly be attended by all children. As a rule basic schooling takes four years; however, in Berlin it takes six years, and in Hamburg and Bremen both four- and six-year programs are found. After basic schooling, the children shift over to one of the three types of schools. The decision on subsequent schooling depends on the choice of the parents and the talents of the children as measured by special tests or placement tests.

For a few years the duration of basic schooling was a much disputed issue, especially in the city-states of Hamburg, Bremen, and Berlin. These three city-states had introduced school laws providing for six years of basic schooling. Furthermore, they

[1] From Meet Germany, 1960, published by Atlantik-Bruecke.

had given some kind of equality of status to the three school types. An attempt was also made to combine the three differing types in one school system without interfering with their particular programs.

Despite remarkable pedagogical successes, such school reform failed to win public support. The public was afraid that the more gifted children would suffer if the general education of all children should continue too long. The consensus was that after four years of basic schooling, children should be sent to the appropriate type of school. Such schools should be kept strictly separate from each other.

In most states elementary school (Volksschule) lasts eight years, in a few states nine years. The idea of raising the elementary schooling to nine years is winning more and more support. In most states intermediate schooling (Mittelschule) begins after grade IV at the basic school, — in the city-states after grade VI at the basic school — and leads the pupils to a final examination in grade X. The term "Mittlere Reife" (medium maturity) has been generally adopted for this final intermediate-school diploma which entitles the holders to enter medium-level careers and to continue their education at full-time vocational schools.

The secondary schools (Gymnasien), to be entered after grade IV and/or grade VI at the basic school and taking nine or seven years, respectively, lead to the "Abitur", the final secondary-school diploma, which gives the holders the right to enroll in colleges and universities.

It is difficult to say a great deal about the pedagogic aspect of the German school system as it reflects the various tendencies of pedagogic trends during the last decades. However, it must be said that the results of the pedagogic reform have taken root over the breadth of pedagogic life. Old-fashioned teaching, where the teacher dominates and the pupils simply accept what is offered to them, is seldom found anymore. In all phases of the curriculum the active cooperation of the pupils is invited; the pupils are trained to acquire learning through their own efforts, through thinking on their own, indeed, under their own responsibility. However, in contrast to the reform movement between the two world wars, there is now lacking in modern society a dynamic, passionate belief in the inherent power of educational and cultural forces. Many reasons can be found to explain this restraint. Certainly, one of the major reasons is that, after the catastrophes of the past, visions of an ideal future no longer appear credible. More consideration is given to hard facts and the forces in being which are apt to shape life today and tomorrow.

In this respect German schools are confronted with two problems which have effectively, and partly also successfully, been tackled, namely selecting from the huge volume of material to be taught and bringing education to bear on the problems of modern life.

People are becoming more and more aware that the volume of the traditional school curriculum is too large for the pupils to cope with intellectually. Pupils are expected to learn so much that they have little opportunity to think on their own. It is agreed that this problem can only be solved by selective learning; by concentrating on a few subjects in which the pupils will comprehend the interrelations and principles involved. Indeed, this concept is generally recognized but it is difficult to select the subjects which can be taken as typical. It is also difficult to obtain general agreement among the pedagogues concerning the selection of subjects to be made.

Numerous proposals and suggestions have been offered concerning the number of subjects to be covered, but it is not expected that decisive changes in the curricula will be made in the foreseeable future.

This is not so much due to the slowness of the school administrations, perhaps not even due to the attachment of the teachers to the conventional and traditional subjects but rather it is quite likely that the public finds it hard to drop from its own frame of preference the memories of the old school days. The solution is also made more difficult by the demands which trade groups, scientific institutions, and other groups make upon the school system.

Considerable progress can be noted in increasing the emphasis on bringing education closer to actual life. Efforts are made at school to bring the pupils closer to the actual facts of present-day life, to social, economic, and political interrelations. In all schools, at the elementary schools as well as at the secondary schools and naturally most notably at vocational schools, educational thought is turning more from abstract theoretical knowledge to the concrete facts of life. It would be wrong to believe that this development has already been completed but considerable improvement can be noticed everywhere.

The demand for learning "in touch" with present-day life is most noted in the demand for political education. The term "political education" has several meanings and the distinction between them is not always clearly marked. There is first the knowledge of the instructions of public life, i.e. civic education in the very meaning of the term, but — and especially this was stressed recently in a delightfully forceful manner — the schools must not be satisfied with passing on knowledge regarding civic institutions. They must increase the emphasis on recent and current history, thus arousing within young people the will for political decisions and political responsibility. Last year, this issue was frequently under vigorous public discussion.

It must not be forgotten that, during the first years after 1945, there was a certain reluctance among many teachers to include recent history in the curriculum. This reluctance was understandable because many parents and teachers had supported Nazism in one way or the other. The readiness to teach modern history is thus not only a pedagogic but also a human problem. However, it is gratifying that, among the new generation of young teachers, issues of current history win more and more acceptance as a part of school life. One may speak of sound progress. Leading school administrations and teachers themselves make great efforts to train the teachers to teach the most recent past. It is correctly pointed out, however, that not too much compulsion must be exercized. Political education can only be fertile and lasting when, among the students as well as among the teachers and parents, any suspicion of political guidance from higher up is avoided. The Germans, in view of the experiences during the Nazi regime, have become very sensitive to any form of "training" in political thinking. Although the method of political education has met with certain pedagogic and human problems, the clearly evident fact can be noted that an overwhelming majority of the German school youth think along democratic lines and are internationally minded. The European idea in particular has found wide support at schools. Anti-Semitic and totalitarian tendencies can hardly be found among present-day youth. Combatting such tendencies is not a serious problem for the schools.

More difficult is the task of arousing young people's interest in politics. This is the real pedagogic problem. It is noteworthy that members of the student councils have for years energetically demanded that political education be given more intensive treatment; an indication that the youthful elite are aware of their political responsibility. It must be said, however, that most students are indifferent to political thought. It is very difficult to make a definitive judgment at this juncture. Experience has shown that wherever schools have made serious efforts at political education not only has it presented no problems, but rather strong interest among the students has developed quickly.

Political education is assisted by the continuing development of student participation in school self-government. Here, too, experience varies. Such development, if actively promoted by the school administration, requires understanding and assistance on the part of the teachers.

Educators as well as businessmen are now discussing the issue of an extension of the years of school attendance. At present, compulsory school attendance varies depending on the state from the 6th to the 14th or the 15th school year, a period of eight or nine years. The extension of the time at school has become necessary in view of the basic change in the position of the young boys and girls at work. More years at school are intended to prolong their time of childhood as well as to give the school a chance to ready the pupils for practical work without anticipating training for specific trades. Pedagogic circles are now amidst a lively discussion of whether this task can better be met by elementary schools or by vocational schools.

In Germany all young people are compelled to attend vocational schools up to their 18th year of life or up to the time when they complete their apprenticeship, whichever comes earlier. On the job the young people receive their practical training for their trade. One or two days per week, they attend the part-time vocational school *(Berufsschule)* which supplements training on the job, by providing some theoretical background. In small towns and rural areas vocational schools cater to the apprentices of various trades in joint courses while vocational schools in big cities are specialized by a specific trade. Besides these part-time vocational schools, supplementing practical training on the job, there are also full-time vocational schools which take the place of training on the job. In contrast to *Berufsschulen* (part-time vocational schools) they are called *Berufsfachschulen* (professional schools.) Most of them take care of young people bound for homemaking and commercial employment. Completion of apprenticeship training is marked by an examination held by the state-approved associations of the trades concerned, i.e. by the Chamber of Commerce or by the Chamber of Handicraft. After passing the final examination the young people are entitled to attend technical schools *(Fachschulen)* in order to prepare for higher-ranking positions in the economy. Technical schools for building contractors and engineers are the best known types of such schools.

During the last years the German vocational school system has made much progress, both externally and internally. The vocational schools have successfully tried also to offer a general education as a part of practical training. The goal is not only to provide general education by giving special lessons in addition to the lessons concerning strictly vocational training, but also to make evident the general interrelations of economic, social and cultural life by confronting them with the specific trade. Although good results have already been obtained in this field, very much must still be done theoretically as well as practically.

Recently some additional contacts between vocational schools and schools of general education have been established by the introduction of the so-called "second way of education." The energy devoted to this concept of the second way of education can best be understood by the concern not to let any talent remain undeveloped and to give all gifted persons a chance to attain the highest possible standards regardless of what their educational background might have been. The "second way of education" is interpreted in two ways. On the one hand, it refers to institutions through which, outside the secondary schools, the privilege can be obtained to apply for enrollment in colleges and universities. Persons who for one reason or another had no chance to attend secondary schools, will be able to attain this right by taking part in special programs. Such programs include evening secondary schools for adults, examinations for gifted persons, special maturity examinations for graduates from technical schools for engineers, etc. On the other hand, the second way of education is also interpreted to mean something completely different, not just as a substitute for education at secondary schools. Prominent pedagogues are of the firm belief that, besides the traditional form of general education, work in specific trades can also lead to general knowledge and experience.

This discussion is still in its infancy. However, it is very likely that far-reaching changes in thought about education will be brought about. Particularly the efforts of the elementary school to win an identity of its own might win strong support and new impulses from this side. It is considered most urgent to give assistance to the elementary school, since about two-thirds of the youth attend elementary schools. This trend is a characteristic feature of the present pedagogic situation in Germany. The elementary school can reasonably be assisted only when it is possible to provide a unique program, and not to be satisfied with an imitation of more advanced education on a watered-down basis. The special program consists chiefly of establishing itself by confronting the student with concrete situations, through practical work in hobbycrafts, and though direct contact with social and cultural events.

Basically, there is far-reaching agreement among the pedagogues in Germany. However, the ways to implement what has been recognized as good in theory must still be found. Promising beginnings can be seen.

For about a year, active public discussion has centered around a memorandum compiled by the German Committee for Educational Matters (Deutscher Ausschuss für das Erziehungs- und Bildungswesen). The members of this committee, all public spirited citizens from private life, were appointed by the Ministry of the Interior and by the Permanent Conference of the State Cultural Affairs Ministers. After a number of drafts covering separate issues had been prepared, a skeleton plan for the standardization and reorganization of the public schools of general education was presented, the result of five years of committee work.

The plan envisages common four-year basic schooling, followed by a two-year course for slow learners (Förderstufe) for all pupils. This latter step would be an innovation in the German school system.

The present Volksschule (elementary school) would be based on the Förderstufe as a three-year Hauptschule (main school). The Mittelstufe (intermediate school), leading up to grade XI, would be given the name of Realschule, while all secondary schools would be known as Gymnasium. Only candidates for the classical schools, to be called Studienschule (school of studies), would make the changeover directly from the Grundschule (basic school) and not via the Förderstufe (promotive step).

Discussions regarding the skeleton plan are in full swing. They are increasingly concentrating on the introduction of the Förderstufe and the special position envisaged for the Studienschule. Regarding all the other points, general agreement has been reached. The present status of the skeleton plan is that of a recommendation of the State Cultural Affairs Ministers. The future will show to what extent the reform ideas contained in it will actually be carried out.

The fate of the skeleton plan, and the readiness of the school authorities to carry out the proposals of this plan, will furnish clear evidence of the readiness of the German school system to adjust itself to the changes in modern life.

Structure of the German Educational System

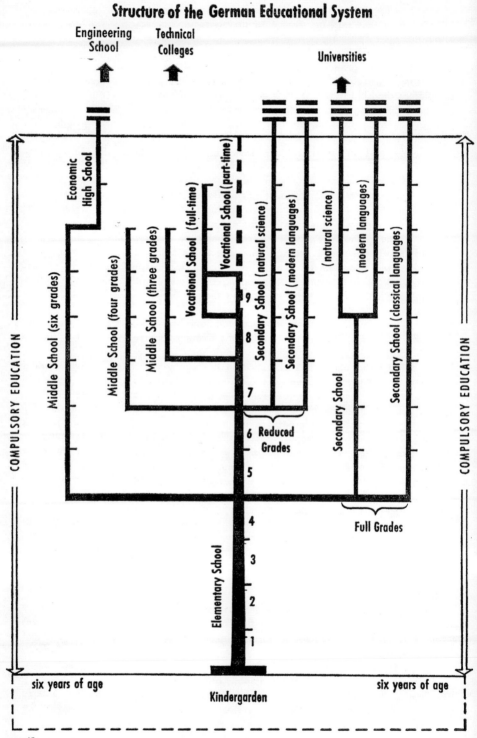

Political Science and the High School *

By Felix Messerschmidt

The efforts of the past ten years to determine the place of political education in the schools and to establish it there, meet with certain obstructions which are often not taken sufficiently seriously. If we wish to be more successful than were the first efforts made by a German Republic, we should do well to face up to these obstructions. I shall enumerate some of these, namely those of particular importance for our subject and for this report.

Let us begin with the fact that political science constitutes a new task, indeed an additional subject in schools in which the old subjects are already bursting their bounds. This overthrows the very precarious balance between the subjects. Political science, like philosophy, geography, music and art, is a disturbing factor, which does not square well with the rigid timetable of the high school. Political science is indeed in a more difficult position than the subjects named, since a powerful tradition in the high schools is opposed to it, and it has scarcely any allies. Even history, which as a subject is closest to it, disassociates itself — at least from political science as a subject. Indeed there is a tendency for the former to annex the latter. But it would be possible to strike an honest bargain between the two, since the two fields, both as regards material, as well, if looked at closely[1]), in regard to their aims, are interdependent upon one another, provided that the learning of history is not misconstrued as a study of what is long past, but permits the growth of political consciousness out of historical perspective, and provided that political science is not limited to a study of institutions and training for team behavior.

There is a tendency in some Federal states to guard against the possible disturbing effect which the introduction of a new subject might have, by specially emphasizing political education only as a principle in teaching. Political education is, of course, as a principle, indispensable. Every branch of culture, every subject has some political content, and throws a light upon the general political workings and the structure of our social and political order which should not be disregarded. It will be a lengthy task to work out these relationships and the form in which they should be presented, whereby an implicit danger should not be disregarded, in regard to which I would refer to the report "Political Science and Education"[2]) of the *Deutscher Ausschuß für Erziehungs- und Bildungswesen* (German Committee on Training and Education). The justified demand that political education should be

---

*) From *Moeglichkeiten und Grenzen der politischen Bildung in der Hoeheren Schule*, Schriftenreihe der Bundeszentrale fuer Heimatdienst, Vol. 52, 1960.

[1]) Felix Messerschmid, The Task of Political Education in School and in History Teaching. *Geschichte in Wissenschaft und Unterricht* ("History in Research and Teaching"), 1935, page 463 et. seq.

[2]) Recommendations and Reports of the *Deutscher Ausschuß für das Erziehungs- und Bildungswesen* (German Committee on Training and Education), 2nd series, Ernst-Klett Verlag, Stuttgart 1955, p. 41: "The demand for the teaching of civics as a principle rests upon the fact that every aspect of education has political references, which should be evoked. This demand of the Weimar constitution is rightly revived today, although there is a tendency here and there to evade actual political education. If the conception of justice and the limitation of specific political science is lost sight of, the demand for civic education as a 'principle' may lead to grave danger. The subordination of all subjects taught to a political principle has the misleading result of making capital for political propaganda out of independent teaching material. Programs of study in the totalitarian states demonstrate the abuses to which this demand may lead".

recognized as a principle is frequently, however, combined with the "evident tendency to avoid actual teaching of political science", or at least ignorance of what is required in political education, which cannot be carried out merely in principle. This desire to evade must be a source of deep concern to everyone who has become conscious of the danger to which liberal order is exposed in the world of today, and who as an educator feels responsible for this order. In duty to ourselves, our pedagogical mission, which at the same time is a political one, and to the groups and authorities who employ us, we must not permit any unclearness to creep in here, it is for this purpose that we have met. We have learned how slight a protection ivory towers can give those entrusted to our charge and to ourselves, and how speedily they are demolished if we do not take care. This appeal, unfortunately, springs from an experience which will never cease to exert its influence upon our lives.

Let us ask ourselves, therefore, where this desire for evasion comes from, but for the present omit from the mass of actuating motives those due to failures we have ourselves not yet overcome. Next there is a large class of persons who are strongly opposed to political education. Just as ethics are essentially understood as individual ethics, high school education is largely conceived as individual education, a process for each separate individual as such. Each should receive an all-round education, the leading idea in the schools — whether held secretly or openly — is still the homo universalis. Anyone who has ever attempted to take this educational aim seriously for himself and his pupils will have been forced to realize that it has become unachievable and impotent . . .

We shall need to accept the fact that the chief feature of the German conception of education is still an aesthetic and literary one. The conception of education derives from the great days of German learning, from Classicism and Romanticism. The changes which have taken place since then, and the secular tasks for training and education which they have brought with them, have not yet been fully assimilated into this way of thinking.

I have detailed provisionally some of the reasons for the antagonism between the high school and political science. In my opinion it has been more difficult since 1945 to establish political science in the high school than in any other type of school.

A real change will only take place when it is unreservedly recognized — and this is the basic thesis of this report — that in a free society and a free political order, political science and education ore an indispensable and essential constituent of education in its fullest sense.

The demand, therefore, is not primarily for an addition to the work, but for a change of thought, and there is not much hope of political science being a success in the high schools, if the tension between the traditional conception of education and this task is not relaxed, as long as political science is regarded and taught as an isolated affair. Education can only be the personal integration of everything innate to human existence in the religious, intellectual, social, economic and political fields. Political science would, accordingly, be a failure from the beginning, and would rapidly degenerate into a mere study of information and probably soon into indoctrination, were it not understood as an integrated — nay more, as an integrating part of the education of the complete man, however specialized this may be. This conception of education, however, is by no means general and undisputed; moreover safeguards are required against its being confused with totalitarian theory and practice.

It must first of all be understood that this sympathy for our former style of education needs qualification. Ever since the Middle Ages European education has been in the sphere of the cotemplative life, and, owing to its origin, signified religious rebirth. It is true that training in chivalry and gentlemanly education, which developed in the 17th and 18th centuries, were more closely related to politics and social life, but in thought and practice education, above all in Germany, has remained, to a certain degree, in contradistinction to active life. Highlights of European and German education owe their character to this unpolitical attitude, and we should do well not to allow the truth concerning this unpolitical development of our educational system to be lost to history, lest after totalitarian political absolutism, we should unintentionally fall into the error of democratic totalitarianism. This danger would arise if the question of the right place to be occupied by politics in the whole system of education were not to be considered at all, and all aspects of our system of existence were subjected to politics and interpreted in its light.

Such a development would deprive all non-political spheres of their intrinsic content and inevitably bring about their final decline. There are of course subjects and whole fields which are not focussed upon politics, and which must be "sought and loved for their own sake[3]". Our political order may be defined by saying that it upholds a system of existence in which politics serve as an instrument whose function it is to protect superordinate fields. Otherwise they destroy what they pretend to protect, and the alleged democratic politician prepares the way for totalitarianism. According to our conception of mankind and the social system, man does not exist for the sake of some ends or other; politics are not autonomous but must make life worth living for all mankind. This is the purport of the list of basic rights in our constitution. In the sphere of education it means that there are subjects which in no way may be subjected to politics. The political constellation which has developed since the second world war would become meaningless were the efforts of the free world to end in our existence becoming exclusively a matter of politics and were we to permit our opponents to force their laws upon us.

After this precautionary statement against the totalitarian idea of politics and political science, it can and must be said with the necessary frankness that the contemplative conception of education, the traditional German Idealistic Education, has, through the political and social changes and revolutions, the excessive developments in technology, the predominance of politics at home and abroad, declined in its effectiveness and credibility. It no longer suffices, indeed it is fatal, to think that education makes a man a citizen of an ideal kingdom elevated above the depths of the daily life of society, work and politics. After 1945 it was demonstrated very emphatically that this unpolitical conception of education had not given us a sense of responsibility for the shaping of public affairs or the ability to accept the challenge which the 20th century has made to us Germans. That such remarks should meet with so little understanding above all in the high schools, indeed that they have in part been bitterly rejected, only goes to show how little our thoughts on education have actually been concerned with the experience which we (the West Germans) have behind us. We have seen "the mark of the beast" with our own eyes, as no previous generation in German history. Since then peace can never return to our schools until we can say with absolute conviction that we have done what was in our power to prevent the beast from returning. This is the important point. It is useless to ask whether the school can be of greater or less

---

[3] "Recommendations and Reports of the German Committee on Training and Education", 2nd series.

avail. Our time is short, let us therefore postpone this question until we have done all we can. Granted that education must be an all-round affair in which all subjects share in proportion, it is certain that education in ethics and religion are of basic importance for political education. But we have learned that it does not suffice to be a righteous or indeed a pious man to follow the right course in politics. We have indeed seen that righteousness and piety, unpolitical righteousness and politically blind piety, can be abused by totalitarian rulers and turned into forces working in their own interests. Unpolitical ethics and religiousness are particularly liable to fall a victim to certain totalitarian slogans, since although they make man able to endure sacrifice, they do not make him able to decide whether the purposes for which the sacrifices are demanded are politically right and worthy. The same may be said of an esthetic education. Hoelderlin has said that it is the poets who create what is of lasting value. Anyone who wishes to quote this as an argument against political education, however, should read *Hyperion* right through and not pass over the most bitter parts. A strong influx from the outside world is what the high schools need to prove the value of esthetic, ethical and religious education.

Political problems in the world of today have become so comprehensive and urgent that they can no longer be mastered by political means alone. Both points of view, therefore, are interconnected. On the one hand it is not possible to regard the social and political fields as an isolated, statically fixed group of questions assigned to those professions directly concerned, nor is it possible to fulfill the purpose of education, to fashion the "imperfect man" of today into as fully developed a human being as possible, to enable the stunted beings of our time to grasp and acknowledge the abundance of actuality, without incorporating politics in general education as a sphere in which every man plays a part, and for which he is to a greater or lesser extent responsible. The state can only become human if its citizens regard it as belonging to them, and the individual can only attain human integrity if, realizing the importance of society and state and espousing these causes as far as lies in his power, he becomes integrated through these tasks and so manifests his own personality. Totalitarian thought might be described as a deficiency disease, since it only takes root where the multiplicity of human relationships and spontaneous social links have become increasingly weakened among the public at large and the supporting systems have broken down, that is, where society no longer (or, as in pre-revolutionary Russia, not yet) fulfills its proper function in priority to the state. The usurper is then not far away. The unpolitical man, however, is also a deficiency symptom, since he excludes from his thoughts and his life the wider conception of the calling of the body politic as a unity, and, leaving the more troublesome side to others, becomes fossilized. Today we must grasp and acknowledge the inevitability of this argument, and revise our whole ideas on education in view of the consequences of this interdependence. Whoever refuses to do so has already taken up sides against the system of political freedom. Democratic lip-service is worthless. (The totalitarian state is always able to exploit lip-service as acclamation of itself.)

Our educational system has not as yet proved capable of meeting these demands[4]), many of those responsible for this system and many of those who work

[4]) The unanimously adopted theses I—IV of the Study Group of the Annual Meeting of the Curatorium "Indivisible Germany" in November 1959 read: —
"I. In the present situation of Germany our educational system is, more than ever before, faced with the task of safeguarding and strengthening the spiritual unity of the nation. The efforts towards political reunification cannot succeed unless the spiritual unity of our people is preserved.
"II. German education is thus faced with a historical task of major importance. The significant point is to preserve the national consciousness, and, while critically examining our past, to prove

under it are awake to the resultant danger to our existence. The danger is all the greater because at home lack of watchfulness and of reliable preparedness on behalf of all classes of society, under all circumstances to stand up for the existing liberal order in spite of all its deficiencies, imperils the change of withstanding the unrelenting political, military and ideological pressure from abroad in times of crisis. Laborious and punctilious measures of defense do not help much. We must recognize that the most crucial task of youth and adult education is to counteract the tendency of the politically unsteady German to reject active responsibility outside his own personal circle, to bury himself in the crowd and to sacrifice freedom to this security. It may be that this tendency was also at other times characteristic of the mass of the people and has troubled popular educators. Pestalozzi[5]) writes: "In general mankind does not value freedom as long as he is happy, even if he is only moderately happy, he is too fond of a quiet life and a full stomach to be prepared to risk these things too easily. This, it is true, is not a speech in his favor, it means, in other words, that he is ready to be tied to his feeding trough, provided it contains fodder. — A man who is only half happy is ready to remain a slave, and it is part of his nature that only bitter experience of misery brings him to risk, in the cause of freedom, what you, Fatherland, are prepared to risk". But what was supportable, perhaps, in former and more stable times, because it was firmly rooted in an unshakeable patriotic consciousness and in an order safeguarded by the traditional acceptance of authority, can only lead to catastrophe under the present-day constellation. It ends in an individual or a group seizing power; and between oligarchy, mob-rule and dictatorship there are many hidden and open forms of loss of freedom.

We do not deny, therefore, that German education although unpolitical, has been of a high standard, and while demanding a new conception of education which responds to the dangers of our time, we shall not derogate former types of education. But the truth remains that an educational system today which does not incorporate a link with politics and which does not lead to an understanding of the basic elements of our political order, and to the readiness to acknowledge this order and to taking an active part in it, has failed in its purpose. This new conception of education must be regarded as typically modern, it is an outcome of the times and perhaps limited in its duration. Our task is, under pressure from the crying needs of the time, to develop a form of education which no less corresponds to truth than did the earlier and unpolitical educational system.

Experience, moreover, goes to show that political science will not be able to hold its own against the humanities in the high school unless its foundations are sufficiently deeply laid. We must, therefore, concern ourselves with the directives issued to the high schools. Publications on this subject in recent years, however

---

the existence of those cultural and moral values which are indispensable to the rebirth of our reunited nation.

"III. The profession of faith in a reunited nation is by no means opposed to the education of the young German as a citizen of the one world of the 20th century, rather is it the prerequisite for this. Since the Second World War German scholars and teachers, in close collaboration with their colleagues from many other countries of the world, have, with this in view, worked together for an obective molding of the teaching of history in particular and for training our youth in the spirit of international understanding. This work should be continued and expanded with determination, in order to help to overcome the tensions and antagonisms of our age through better knowledge of all nations.

"IV. The German school of today is, as an institution, not in a position to do justice to its task in the field of political instruction of our people and our youth. In the interests of German unity and the peaceful order at which we aim, German education must be expanded to be able to solve this task better in future".

[5]) Edition Seyffarth V., 327.

varying they are individually, have at least one thing in common, the realization that the politically educated person must be more than just educated in politics, he must possess a general education. Politics is an activity which organizes mankind in a purposeful way. Such purposeful organization, however, can only be carried out in a worthy fashion by some one who knows what is required for human existence and its needs. For this reason political education can be defined and fulfilled only in connection with education as a whole. This must cover, not only humanistic subjects, but also studies bearing on the institutions and customs of nations, that is, society, economy, law and government, finance and power, not only Lessing and Stifter, Mozart and van Gogh, but also Marx and Lenin, production, the market, employment and other things, for example, the division of Germany. And all this not as a side-line of high school education, but in a way which enables the complicated existence of modern civilization to be mastered, in order that this may not become a decadent culture doomed to destruction. If such mastership is to be attained, however, strenuous and unrelaxing efforts must be made to illuminate all the important factors bearing upon this existence. The beginnings of this must take place in the schools, by elementary instruction in the fundamentals, as is appropriate everywhere to schools. We shall have heavy work in selecting what is worthwhile and necessary from the mass of material at our disposal, and perhaps in drawing up an outline syllabus. Above all in working out a theory of teaching of political science and its place in the system of pedagogics. This is of urgent importance, if we are to proceed beyond the experimental stage of individual teachers, schools and *Laender*, and crystallize the available and constantly growing experience into a teachable system. Pedagogic concensus of opinion, taking the aspect of juvenile psychology into account, will tend towards the teaching of the structure upon which a free governmental and social system is built, and towards political anthropology. Questions of special methods of political science will need careful consideration, side by side with those of didactics. The science of politics itself will be able to give us indispensable aid in all these matters, but it cannot relieve us of the necessity of working out the relationship between matter and method, of solving the task of political education; in this sphere as well the relative autonomy of pedagogics must be acknowledged.

But let us restrict ourselves to the educational task of the high school. This received its traditional character from the idea of the general education of man. I should like to make some comments on this.

The fact is generally overlooked that the original conception of this idea, i.e. that of Wilhelm von Humboldt, went far beyond that later established in the humanistic *Gymnasia*. The Humboldt idea applied to the nation as a whole, the *Gymnasium* — in modern terms — was to be a sort of differentiated standard school. Today we must admit that this was unrealiable, at least in the society of the 18th and 19th centuries, partitioned off into classes, and reft by religious differences. But this original idea has acquired new force today. In an open society no longer built on class differences, education can no longer be a closed affair, either socially or otherwise. We must "insist that our basic ideas of education are carried out throughout the whole of society. The elite of the highly educated, upon whose existence and intellectual powers the fate of our cultural life depends, can therefore only be conceived as an open elite, admission to which is not closed to any productive class, but which runs sectionally through all classes and groups as an elite of the open-minded, objective thinkers" to quote the words of Buber, "an elite of the well-informed, clever, responsible and leading members of all productive classes and groups"[6]). This is a demand which is by no means based upon mere sociological views, as the testimony of Martin Buber goes to show. It demonstrates that today, as at the beginning of the 19th century, the educational task of the schools is also determined by the educational requirements which arise from conditions of the day, conditions which have developed out of past history and are not determined arbitrarily. The term educational requirements should, however, not be taken as only having a practical bearing; this matter-of-fact expression might be misunderstood and shock the ear of the classicist. The educational task of the high school is not unchangeable, unless it is to be agreed that it is a form of "heroic downfall". It must be discovered and formulated anew with the changes in historical development. Such a claim implies that this educational task is largely determined by the political trend of the age, to which Pestalozzi's words seem directly to apply: "without political education a sovereign people is a child playing with fire, who at any moment may bring his house into danger". Moreover politics themselves should be handled by a large class of politically educated persons, if they are to safeguard a liberal and worthy system of government, and should not be left in the hands of mere functionaries and commissars or an increasingly exclusive caste.

What is meant by the "educational requirements" referred to above? No teacher can fail to see that the process of education of the individual is dependent upon connections beyond the individual. What are these connections? Proceeding from the bottom upwards, the first to be named is the disposition and the inherited characteristics, as determined by origin and family. Further there are the connections with society, nation and state, with history and culture. These play a reciprocal role in wide spheres of the life of each individual. They enter into him and play their part in his make-up, and he again shapes them and so exerts his influence on other individuals.

As long as these connections are safeguarded, sturdy, orderly and permeated with tradition, they have an idealism of their own and exert a strong influence on education. How strong, has been seen in the negative sense, when they proved rotten, when after 1933 these connections were almost entirely reversed and their former molding and protective function had been destroyed. Our educational system shows its weakness, complexity and susceptibility when this supra-individual order collapses and the individual must fend for himself, no clear and universal will any longer exists, and he is surrounded by an atmosphere of general uncertainty or even helplessness. Only when this state of affairs is clearly recognized does the problem of training and education today stand out in its full relief. To be educated means that the individual has been shaped by a characteristic ideal which at one and the same time encompasses and penetrates thought, existence and action. The requirement that this picture should not exist merely theoretically as an "ideal of education", but should represent binding, acknowledged and actual standards, as expressed in the cultural, social, economic, legal and political order, which therefore play their part in forming and educating, this requirement is the determining factor for the success of public education.

A responsibility which can scarcely be met is laid upon institutions of education and training today, simply because public influence no longer functions, or indeed may be inimical or obstructive to education. What is needed in such a case is a uniform, integrated and graded primary education, which would constitute a

---

[6]) Walter Dirks, *"Politische Wissenschaft"*, Supplement to *"Parlament"*, 23rd December 1953.

foundation and a security for the new form of existence which has begun to be built up. The mere recourse to former educational theories will not bring us success here. Let us leave aside the question of the obligation imposed by the neo-humanistic ideal of education, which is generally evoked in this connection. It has long lost its general binding force. The struggle between it and what is termed *Realbildung* (priority of science and modern languages), which began in the second half of the 19th century and which reflects in the sphere of education the change in the disposition of our lives, is not actually realized because only the more obvious losses are seen, and not the crying need which it expresses; the consciousness of the radical changes which science has brought about is suppressed, technology as a new force in life is denied or overlooked. Now that the patriachal system has finally and completely broken down, the politically responsible citizen of the future will only be able to carry on this new order, which, if it remains a merely formal functional system is bound to come to grief, if a fundamental change in the pedagogic outlook takes place. This condition of the institutional structure of the democratic system is only very slowly being realized and acted upon. It therefore continues to be a shortcoming of our higher education, that the pupils have imbibed a very great amount of knowledge in certain fields, but that they have not been sufficiently informed concerning important spheres of our public policy and the demands they make upon the individual; life has not been understood and taught as an entity, guided from one central point, but falls for them into separate parts which are precariously connected with one another.

It has not been unforgettably impressed upon them that maturity demands that all the powers of body and mind and the whole of one's energy must be at the service of the organization which defends liberty, and that it is necessary to know what are the constitutional elements of this organization which under no circumstances may be encroached upon. It is this very knowledge which in the past was lacking to many well-intentioned educated persons. For them, as for the Greek citizens, education lay beyond the world of practical affairs, the workaday world, which they left to its own mere materialism. The attitude of intellectual withdrawal from everyday existence, from working day life in which the important factors are earning a living and providing food, clothes, dwelling and warmth, coal and oil, the conflict of power and interests, but in which at the same time the shape of our future existence as a people and a nation, law, peace and justice, the preparations for reunifaction play a part, this attitude which tends to assign all these things to the others, the common crowd of the world of materialism, and to set education apart in a world of its own, must be overcome. Whoever replies that this would mean sacrificing culture to technology, and education to mere training, fails to see that it is a question, not only of the salvation of technology, economics and politics, which are all part of our culture, but also of reintegrating education in the sum total of our lives, of preventing the danger of a segregated sphere of learning, which would be unable to yield any organizational resources for the desperate state of affairs in the world. The task which lies before the high schools is to incorporate the new world into education, a world which according to Ortega y Gasset has been created by three principles, liberal democracy, experimental science and industrialism, and to prevent the human spirit from becoming detached from it. Individuality must be made more manifest in the school, not only in the realm of character and religious training, but also in that of practical affairs. Political science will perhaps be able to make the largest contribution to this, since it falls to politics to a very great extent to determine the order governing this technical civilization, the order which upholds our existence and safeguards its liberty. After what has been said at the beginning concerning the falsification of political argument under totalitarian systems, the opinion that political science in the high school would be at the cost of classical, perhaps more integrating subjects, is certainly not worth discussing.

We have up to now been concerned with the incorporation of political science in the syllabus of the high school, and will now turn to some of the more important questions of the actual teaching of the subject.

In education the method must always correspond exactly with the aim. Functionaries can be trained by authoritarian methods; the free citizen only in an atmosphere of freedom. Success in political training and education, therefore, can only be achieved if the schools themselves are permeated with a spirit of a free community organization. The school, for example, in which young people are to gain their first experiences of political order on a small scale, should not be run on magisterial lines, and the teacher who is only even distantly related to the policeman on the corner, will fail to achieve his task. Everything depends upon young people being allowed to experience freedom with responsibility, both at school and in the youth organizations, they should learn that the amount of liberty which can be granted them, the amount of freedom which they may acquire, is in proportion to the amount of responsibility they are prepared to undertake, beginning with small responsibilities in accordance with their age, and leading up to assuming a leading role in school government. This experience is no less important than their contacts with the authorities themselves, those connected with the actual teaching or with the organization, as well as those who hold personal or religious authority. Both experiences are indispensable. Educational trends which do not allow for a good balance between a basically free organization and a helping, directing, restraining, if necessary, also a resistant and commanding authority, are not suitable for political training and education.

Political science, also, must not restrict the sphere of personal decision, such as is the aim of political indoctrination, and legitimate for the methods of party politics. What is important here is a fundamental political insight. Thus great restraint should be exercized in introducing current politics into school teaching. These events should be used in order to draw attention to the underlying fundamental political facts, but not in order to take up sides. There is no place in the school for something which will have been forgotten next year. Political science aims at general clarification, stimulates a political habit of thought, and so prepares the way for the basic political decisions of the individual, but does not fixate these singly beforehand.

The question discussed in schools under the title "political science as a principle or a subject" is not a genuine question.

In accordance with what has been said above it should be a matter of course that the schools (or the institutions connected with adult education) should be so organized as to form an example of a free system, in which joint responsibility is shared by the pupils, and in which activities connected with sport, the arts and music, etc., are conducted on communal lines. In addition, almost the whole of the teaching material, all subjects to a varying degree, have some political content, and it is a matter of integrity for the scientist and a duty of the teacher to draw upon this content as well. These political connections must therefore not be suppressed. Political education acts as a "principle" everywhere. Added to this are the various forms in which the pupil himself may play an active part in teaching (group studies, working groups etc.), which awaken and train a sense of responsibility for others, for the team spirit and for the proper approach to a subject.

The political education which can be given in this way as an underlying "principle" of teaching and school life is of the greatest importance. If it is limited to these forms alone, however, there is danger that the actual aims of political science will not be attained. In addition to drawing upon the political content to be found in all subjects, special teaching in the form of a separate subject, or special lessons expressly devoted to political considerations and to the teaching of elementary political knowledge necessary for understanding and becoming familiar with the basic political set-up, is required. This political education is intended as a preparation for taking an active part in political life. The basic knowledge which is to be taught as a separate subject may be subdivided into: a) elementary sociology, which deals with the basic forms of social behavior and awakes a consciousness of the social environment in the mind of the pupil, b) fundamental questions of the legal and economic systems, covering matter which experience has shown to be difficult or even impossible to introduce into the teaching of other subjects, and which unless treated as special subjects are either omitted altogether or at least not in accordance with their political and social significance, c) study of the most important institutions, political parties, non-parliamentary groups, the churches, trade unions, corporative institutions, d) current tendencies, insofar as these are indispensable to an understanding of current politics, i.e. are of basic political significance. These four fields reappear at all stages, even in the primary school, and at each higher stage are dealt with more comprehensively and in greater detail. In the senior year of secondary school, "e" is added, the study of political ideas as the crystallizing interpretation of basic political forces.

Difficult problems for the teaching of political science arise from the following: politics today are not just a context of material and service objectives, which needs to be understood. This is only part of it. The facts of politics today cause deep-seated perplexity. As is generally realized, the determining forces are so over-powering, the field in which politics plays a part is so comprehensive, the influences so complicated, that, as has been said already, political problems can no longer be mastered by political means alone. This applies even to domestic politics. Completely new methods are therefore needed, an original outlook undistorted by any ideologies, a freer judgement, a more fitting mode of attack. This means, however, that it does not suffice for political science today to be just one more of the many subjects, however highly one may rate the importance of the body of informative knowledge. It must, in addition, to put it shortly and generally, arouse a new attitude and new forces, and discover new standards. Moreover the teaching of political science must commence far earlier and more simply than formerly, it must train people to be capable of political action, and this begins in the primary school. The training of those powers required by a man in order to be capable of political action must therefore begin at the pre-political stage. This is due to the fact that "the path followed by a young man through the various stages of his development, must be considered as proceeding from the pre-political field into that of actual politics"[7]). The powers necessary for specific political activity either receive preparatory training at this pre-political stage — as for example is still done in an excellent manner among the Anglo-Saxon nations — or

[7]) "Recommendations and Reports of the German Committee on Training and Education", 2nd series.

Editing a School Magazine

Photo: Georg Fabian — Bavaria

School Kindergarten

Photo: Werner Luecke

they will be found to be lacking at the adult stage — as is largely the case in Germany. It is most difficult in a society such as ours to work out practical exercises suitable to the young. But a beginning has been made. These must be developed and made generally applicable. The subject might be discussed here of the necessity of developing school life as the form adapted to youth, and what is needed for this.

Many problems point to the fact that, if the actual tasks of political training and education are looked at rightly, these are also problems of the politics of today. Consider for example the question of political science and political parties — a knotty point for most of those concerned with political education and training. Political science must point out to the young that political parties cannot be dispensed with, otherwise it would fail in its purpose. That the political parties mediatize the citizens is a matter for regret. But without such mediatization no possibility of participating in political decisions any longer exists, and the result is the totalitarianism of one single party. If this is understood, it becomes clear that no political training can exist detached from the parties or in contradiction of the party system.

The solution is to be sought, not in conflict but in partnership. The right solution is to be found through partnership in the field of mutual distress and within the bounds of possibility. Such an attitude is made objectively possible through the fact that the non-totalitarian parties, despite all their differences, hold certain convictions and many historical links in common. If these common features are denied, democracy immediately becomes impossible. And with this the possibility of a joint political education collapses. It tends to be replaced by political training for a mere struggle for power, and this means a victory for the totalitarian point of view without a war and without a change of regime. Our fate would then be sealed and lost, and not only our political fate.

Another important problem is referred to in the closing sentence of the report quoted above. It says "political education in youth is a prerequisite of good politics. But political education of the people as a whole takes place mainly through politics themselves. The efforts towards political education will come to grief, therefore, if politicians do not realize the educational effects which for good or for bad are the outcome of their actions". This appeal cannot be overlooked. On the other hand "German perfectionism", which considers itself relieved of the obligation to concern itself with politics just because democracy contains so many failures, is disastrous. The English say, "we prefer democracy, because it is so inefficient". There is a widespread opinion that one should only speak like that when politics are stable, under secure circumstances. I consider this wrong. Democracy is in actual fact no less permanent than a dictatorship. The fact that it requires more patience is not an argument against it. On the contrary. This "so inefficient" means that the patience which it demands is a safeguard against cutting through knots. Such results in totalitarianism. We prefer democracy, because it is so inefficient. We Germans should note this.

The central problem of our government is the problem of power and its rightful administration. All studies, sociology, civics, social politics, are remarkably in agreement in bypassing this problem, they either suppress it or idealize it. A political training and education which evades it, instead of facing up to it and making a profitable task of it, is not worth anything. Political science must therefore include the ethics of the use of power, the cultivation of backbone and will-power. Just to say, you must be brave, you must be just etc., does not of course amount to education. But this is a problem with which the whole of education is faced and not political science alone.

It must however be said quite openly that the teacher who intends to educate politically, will not take refuge in mere sociology, or economics, or institutional organization, or political sentiments, or mere rules of conduct, but will attack the subject of politics where it reaches its full expression, as a problem of power, which can and must be sought out, whether in the social, economic or governmental field.

This is, however, where the real crux of political science lies. It can be overcome if we demonstrate that totalitarian regimes by no means represent excesses due to the exaggerated value given to the state, but that they resolutely destroy state and politics, and that the state, that is ordered and controlled power, is the only force which can give effective protection against this determined demolition and the destruction of liberty. A further realization is required, namely that the tolerance of democracy is not unlimited, it is only extended to those who observe the conditions of a free order. "Under no circumstances should democracy be understood as a regime which allows the enemies of democratic liberty to organize its downfall". As Justice Murphy expressed it, in a finding of the American Supreme Court "Basic rights and freedoms are not a suicide pact"[8]). Fear of taking part in political action, insofar as it is not simply civil cowardice, is due to ignorance of these facts.

One failure of the common form of political science is that it restricts itself to the level of argument. The forces underlying politics to which Hitler owed his success, are ignored: emotion, resentment, dreams, utopia, symbolism, *Weltanschauung*, myths etc. It would be wrong to dismiss the German inclination to dream as romantic sentimentality or muddled introspection. It can lead to powerful action, or make people capable of extraordinary sacrifices and altruism. The democratic formalism of the usual political education is blind. If I judge it correctly it does not appear real to the youth of today, and can be knocked over by the first political magician who comes along. I do not of course mean that we should imitate totalitarianism. This would be to betray the only political idea upon which we in this assembly are all agreed, and which is to be the mainstay of our political education, liberty. It is harder for us, since we have no political doctrine at our disposal which can employ the magic of a cunning propaganda in its service, and to which one need only sacrifice the liberty of one's own thoughts and judgement to be certain of political redemption. And the "idea" of democracy, namely not to declare any definite idea as officially binding, is not easy to understand. It requires differentiated thought. This makes our study of political science so very difficult.

In addition to this, and not only due to its history which was marked by two defeats, our German democracy is a dismal affair. We are inclined to be too critical and too sober. Has sufficient use been made of the opportunities to lend our system of government and administration more lustre, even, I may say, to arouse more sentiment concerning it? Are, for example, films like "Ernst Reuter", "Hermann Ehlers" and others, which are made for schools, utilized sufficiently and in the right way? It would be found that they can be very moving. Mere argument does not get close enough to young people, there are other ways of laying the foundations of political science than only in the field of pure reason. This is too little understood, and the closest attention needs to be given to this aspect of the

---

[8]) Eric Voegelin, *"Demokratie im Neuen Europa"*. In *Politische Bildung im demokratischen Staat,* address at the opening of the Academy for Political Science in Tutzing, 1959.

54

teaching of political science. We must do conscientiously what is done unscrupulously in totalitarian lands, where the abuses still point to the permanent neglect of this whole sphere in the democratic camp.

Finally in this connection there is the theoretically still unsolved problem, that a gap exists between democratc doctrine, between the standards and articles of the Constitution, and the actual conditions of political life. This cannot be denied. If these standards and articles are preached to young persons with any power of criticism, and they begin to look around and discover that this is only a special sort of ideology, namely a democratic ideology, then they are already practically lost for democracy, they see the contradictions and cannot solve them. It is not as though contradictions which cannot be solved, and which constitute one of the tasks of politics, should be passed over. They should be pointed out, and one should hope and trust that young people are capable of facing up to problems, if they are shown where they come from. Democracy means that the nation should regard its government as an organization of communal life to which it voluntarily agrees and of which it is the bearer. It should therefore, with all due seriousness, participate in the tasks and decisions of the state, and be answerable for its sovereignty in certain fields, and for the law and order which it has appointed and preserves. But the relation between the people and the state, between the form of government and the citizen, is not without its problems in Germany, and not alone in Germany. Democratic values are not always considered unassailable, as has already been pointed out, the will to freedom has distinctly weakened during the past few decades. Although for many centuries of European history this will has been the force behind significant movements, including those among the masses, today totalitarianism succeeds far more easily in moving the masses, and liberty is thrust into the defensive. There is a breach between democratic teaching, the claims it makes for itself, and actuality, which is not determined by an allegedly sovereign, responsible people, capable of judging and deciding, but to a far greater extent by functionaries, bureaucrats, financial magnates, managers etc. The task of political science can therefore not be solved through the traditional ideas of democracy. It has been pointed out by philosophers that democratic values of earlier times have received their historical stamp through a cult of the individual personality. They express the claim of the many, that each single one may be able to develop as an individual, capable of free and independent judgement and of responsibility for political decisions. The difficult position in which political training and education finds itself today may be explained by the fact that it often employs arguments and statements which no longer hold much power of conviction, and which are frequently received by young people with a shrug of the shoulders and looked upon as withered idealism and ideologies which are remote from reality. Political education is so difficult today because German polity has not yet become clearly defined, it cannot even define itself. This is partly due to the fact that the Federal Republic — and this should not be forgotten — is a provisional arrangement, and will remain so until reunification takes place, even though this provisional character is not such that it has no binding force. In regard to both the provisional as well as the binding character of our state, attention should always be drawn to the Preamble of the Basic Law. Political science must understand this problem. A merely formal or indeed negative definition of democracy will not suffice.

It seems to me that youth has a more sensitive and alert feeling than many adults for the fact that the old type of democracy has reached a critical stage. We can speak with the tongues of angels but will still achieve nothing, unless we accept this indisputable crisis of the democratic way of life as our starting point. The question is, how, in spite of this, or indeed because of it, what is worthy of being aimed at in the sphere of politics and of being defended as a possession can be made evident and practicable. How can the minimum of binding force and trust-worthiness be gained in a state of political parties and associations, which is needed to carry it through periods of severe economic and political crisis? One reason for the collapse of the Weimar Republic was the inability to solve this question. Youth, like the masses, is very ready to say that it is all a fraud and then to stand aside. If this problem is passed over, as often happens, then political education becomes ineffective, it does not "take". We are called upon to work out how this is to be done. A theory of the teaching of political science does not lie ready, fixed and detailed. But for the genuine educator this affords a pedagogic opportunity, and not a reason for retiring into the safe tower of the traditional school subjects, where he only needs to repeat what tradition has passed on to him in regard to content and method. Here he can seek the way step by step, together with those who are before him. This can be most fruitful pedagogically, although it demands a certain courage, but a cowardly teacher is no more use than a cowardly politician.

This brings us to the final problem, which perhaps constitutes the toughest core of our subject. Recently a teacher with great experience in the teaching of political science put forward the theory that "the teaching of political science today should not, as in the case of almost all other teaching, be set in the usual field of tension between young and old, in which the elder persons are the ones who hand on information which has remained unchallenged for generations and who hold the key to a stable realm of experience. Since the relationship of the older generation today to National Socialism was marked by error and failure, and it has therefore forfeited its superior position as an experienced teacher, and since in many cases the elders are indeed unable to detach themselves from the political ideas and ideals which were hammered into them, although these have been refuted by historical events, political education must paradoxically be effected by the younger generation, even in the face of the older generation, those who according to their age should be the teachers, must themselves be educated"[9]. How far this may be correct is obvious to all those who keep their eyes open and acknowledge honestly what are the prerequisites both of political and of pedagogical political activity.

But all the same we must guard against the pessimism which may result. Error and failure may produce mastery in teaching, provided the individual can digest this sad experience and work upon it objectively. The older generation has gone through a practical course in political training, which could make it far better able to teach political science than any generation before it. Will it summon up the necessary courage, the victory over itself, the bravery, the modesty before the generation of its sons and daughters, which will restore its credibility? Let us recall the magnificent scene in the last act of *Faust*, in which Faust, who, up to the end, has remained entangled in failure and error, is given the task of teaching the celestial youths. *"Doch dieser hat gelernt, er wird uns lehren"* (This man has learned indeed, he will be our teacher). It is up to each individual whether he is able to pass on this lesson.

---

[9] Konrad Barthel, *"Schule und Nationalsozialistische Vergangenheit"* in Gesellschaft — Staat — Erziehung, Vol. 6, 1959, p. 246, Vol. 7, p. 301.

National Socialism in the Eyes
of 15 and 16 Year-Old High School Pupils

By Rolf Schoerken

When, as so often happens, a teacher's work is compared to that of a gardener — planting, nurturing and cherishing — it should not be forgotten that before planting the ground has to be thoroughly cleared and tilled. To no sphere of secondary school teaching does this apply more emphatically than to that of political education. Nothing can be accomplished here until the litter of half-truths and prejudices cluttering up the pupils' minds (no less than those of many adults) is brought to light and swept away.

This account of an investigation in a field exceptionally bedevilled with political prejudice is intended to assist in clarifying the pre-conditions which make any kind of political education possible in the middle grades. Hitherto attention has been mainly focussed on political education in the upper grades. It is unfortunately only too easy to forget that pupils of 15 and 16 years of age are particularly susceptible to prejudice and cliché, because they are passing through a very plastic and unstable phase of their development. The political half truths picked up during this intermediate stage between childhood and adult life, when the critical faculties are incompletely developed, are extremely difficult to eradicate later on.

The first school history course, ending with a treatment of National Socialism, is completed during the ninth school year. What do pupils of this age and grade know about Hitler and National Socialism before these have been handled in class?

Ninety-five ninth grade boys were asked to write free and candid answers to the question: "What do you know about Hitler, and what you think of him?" The resulting essays revealed a large measure of common ground, suggesting that their contents may well be typical for 15 and 16-year-old high school pupils. The common features are observable both in the boys' knowledge and in their powers of judgement.

The source of this knowledge is only mentioned expressly in relatively few cases (about 20%), but in others the origin can be deduced indirectly. There is no doubt that illustrated magazines are the chief source, followed a good way behind by movies, radio broadcasts, books and youth group discussions. The essays unfortunately provide no reliable information on the most interesting source of all — parents and the home. Only a few boys mention that Hitler and National Solialism are discussed at home. It may be assumed, however, that many boys are reluctant to cite their parents as a source of information, particularly in a written piece of work. Many significant touches in their expressions of opinion nevertheless justify the conclusion that the influence of parents (or at least of trustworthy adults) is greater than the boys' statements indicate directly. It is reasonable to infer that on a scale representing frequency and strength of influence the home would come after the illustrated magazines and on a level with the movies. One revealing fact is that the most pronounced value judgements on Hitler are to be found in the small group which does quote the home as a source of information. One boy who mentions that his father often talks to him about the Nazi period calls Hitler "the biggest gangster who ever lived". Another writes: "I know all this from books and conversations with my father, with whom I often discuss such things. I think Hitler was the best statesman of all time." We can see how the boys tend to repeat their

[1]) From *Gesellschaft — Staat — Erziehung — Blaetter fuer politische Bildung und Erziehung* published by Felix Messerschmid, Friedrich Minssen and Otto Seitzer, Ernst Klett Verlag, Verlag Moritz Diesterweg No. 5, 1959.

parents' opinions (always the father, by the way!), very possibly in an exaggerated form.

Turning to the actual content of the essays, we perceive immediately that the factual knowledge of the boys is generally extensive but always partially erroneous. By picking out the correct items from the whole range of replies one could obtain a surprisingly accurate picture of the Hitler period. However, no single account is entirely free of error and many contain gross distortions.

In the average pupil's array of basic facts the most prominent elements are the following: Hitler's origins were humble; he came to power on account of his ambition, assisted by his gift of oratory; he solved the unemployment problem by autobahn building; he persecuted the Jews, overran Austria and Czechoslovakia, became a maniac and declared war on half the world; at first the German soldiers were successful on all fronts, but they were defeated in the end because of the enemy's superior strength and Hitler's incapacity as a military commander. The Jews were exterminated — a terrible crime which remains a shameful blot on our reputation today.

It is thus already evident that most of the boys possess a certain basic knowledge and are capable of arranging it fairly adequately. As regards details and chronological sequence, however, there is often the greatest confusion. Remarkably enough the boys frequently have a much more accurate picture of the pre-1933 rise to power than of the sequence of campaigns, victories, defeats and other major events of the war. It might well be supposed that boys of 16 would be particularly interested in military matters, but most of them know surprisingly little about World War II. The reason for this is hardly likely to be that ninth grade youngsters of today are more mature than their forebears and therefore take no interest in war, but simply that they cannot grasp its extreme complexity, so manifest in the last war. World War II covered such a multitude of events that a boy of 16 is not yet capable of surveying it in perspective. His background knowledge has been acquired at random and he has never approached the material systematically. Most of the pupils at least know of the campaigns in Poland, France and Russia; of Stalingrad, Rommel in Africa and U-boat warfare — although these crop up in every conceivable sequence — and of the finish in the "Führer's" air raid shelter. In the cracks and crevices between these fixed paving stones, as it were, there blossoms a most peculiar flora. Four names constantly recur, with an extreme over-estimation of their political and military importance: Rommel, Heydrich, Canaris and Nebe (the latter was Chief of the German Police publicized by articles in illustrated magazines). There is also much exact detail about the battleship *Graf Spee*. This "inside knowledge" is undoubtedly drawn from the newspapers and movies. Its danger lies not so much in its sensational flavor, which is dissipated quite soon, as in the fact that it imperceptibly produces a false sense of proportion. It is even fair to assert that the more detailed and accurate the pupils' knowledge of these specialized aspects is, the greater is the danger of their acquiring a false or at least a biased historical picture. If a boy knows a great deal about Heydrich he will be tempted to use this information as a fixed point in trying to understand the other phenomena of the period, which can of course only lead to distortion and absurdities. A good example of the perverted judgements that ensue, although at a different level, is to be found in the essay of a pupil who discourses at length about Hitler's success in tackling the problem of juvenile delinquency and praises this as his greatest achievement. It is not chance alone that has fixed these four names in the ninth graders' minds. In Rommel, for instance, they have a figure they feel they may, with a clear conscience, (after all the English themselves say so!) worship as a hero, crowned with a halo of courage and the knightly virtues. At the other extreme they have an arch-villain — usually Heydrich, sometimes Himmler. Apart from these there are the invisible "powers behind the throne" who control the bewildering tangle of happenings from the background, emerging seldom into the open but with all the threads in their hands. This "black-and-white" style of portrayal, which we find constantly in the illustrated magazines appeals to the mind of the ninth grade youngster confronted with history. Difficult material and psychological issues impossible for him to understand are reduced to the simplest terms and thus brought within his grasp. In the end history becomes fiction — made by a gang of stock figures, the hero, the villain, the powerful wire-pullers behind the scenes, it is not far removed from the comic strip.

In comparison with these dangers the cruder errors of fact appear relatively innocuous: "Hitler himself was descended from Jewish ancestors"; "Hitler joined the SPD (Socialist Party)"; "Hitler worked hand-in-hand with the Communists"; "He was a gangster before he entered politics"; "America offered him assistance against Russia"; "At the beginning of 1941 the Emperor and Empress were murdered by Communist agents in Austria. Adolf at once sent his army to march into Poland" (sic). On closer examination, however, we perceive that it is not a matter of sheer mistakes in detail. The boy who writes that America wanted to help Hitler against Russia is clearly not able to imagine that the United States fought against Germany, in company with and allied to Russia. He is simply transplanting the present-day situation into the past. Other pupils show an inclination to cover up their lack of knowledge by bold invention or combination of facts, being subsequently hardly capable of distinguishing between the true and the fictitious.

When a boy writes: "In my opinion Hitler knew nothing about the majority of SA and SS crimes committed in Himmler's and Heydrich's name", we recognize the first contours of the landscape of legend, and realize that we have reached a dangerous point. Legends stick more deeply and obstinately in the mind than mere errors, and are not to be eradicated by simple correction. Their irrational foundations have to be broken down. "Expunging the myth" from historical legends always means grappling with the obscure and inaccessible realm of prejudice; but in the given case we must explore further. Historians are aware that the stereotyped thought pattern: "Our leader is innocent; it is only the unscrupulous underlings who have besmirched their hands with blood" has existed in all eras — not that this makes it any the less harmful. It arises from a compulsion to believe in the purity and nobility of the leader and the cause, even in the face of obstacles and defeat; to maintain one's faith at all costs, even against one's better knowledge. This urge to believe is a basic component of all ideologies.

The pupils' essays are surprisingly rich in legendary elements. The most harmless variety includes, for instance, the tale of Hitler's "carpet chewing" (in his rages). The legend of Hitler's origins in the version he spread himself appears with conspicuous frequency: a child of humble parentage, he experienced early and at first hand the nation's dire need — hence his desire to save Germany. More dangerous are the tentative new versions of the "stab in the back" legend — of treachery in various forms: Hitler could not trust his generals; or Africa was lost by treachery, because "the English knew every time Rommel received fresh supplies". The old stab in the back seems to have become split up into a series of minor "pricks", since it is only partial setbacks and not the total defeat that are attributed to treason.

It would be misleading to convey the impression, however, that these ninth grade boys' minds are stuffed with Nazi prejudices. Hitler is praised in only about 10 % of the contributions, in 3 cases with an aggressive tone; 30 % condemn him vigorously, often just as violently; while 60 % first weigh up the pros and cons carefully before arriving at a derogatory judgment. Speaking generally, therefore, there can be no question of a Nazi "infiltration" of the youngsters, or even of their being receptive to National Socialist ideas. Only from 4 or 5 essays can one infer with fair certainty that parents or other adults have exerted a definite National Socialist influence on the boys. Even if we are at first appalled by the frankness — not to say brazenness — with which these boys trumpet forth the Nazi slogans as though nothing had happened in between, we should not forget that these are to a large extent the expression of an "oppositionist" urge and a temptation to exaggerate. There is certainly no reason to underestimate their potential harm, but on the other hand we should not ignore the fact that only a few isolated cases are exposed to this type of influence. The other boys' occasional praise of Hitler and National Socialism is almost always due to typical limitations in their powers of reasoning and judgment; of this more later on.

Most conspicuous of all are three common features which appear in practically all the essays, with such few exceptions that they may be accepted as part of the stock knowledge and thinking of any ninth grade pupil. First: Hitler built the autobahns; second, Hitler exterminated the Jews; third, Hitler developed megalomania[1]).

We are familiar with the fact that among adults it is typically the "incurables" who are fond of pronouncing the cliché about the autobahns, which might at first suggest that this is clear evidence of Nazi influence on the young. Against this there is the fact that the boys who have violently anti-Hitler views also mention the autobahns. No doubt we must bear in mind that in the automobile age, with so much interest focussed on transportation, especially among adolescents, any boy will some time ask how the autobahns came to be built, and the answers received are rarely likely to be politically colored. In recent years the persecution of the Jews has been repeatedly thrust into public consciousness through the newspapers, court cases, films, radio and books, and we may assume that there is no ninth grade schoolboy who is unfamiliar with the basic facts about the extermination of the Jews. The third point reflects one of the stock opinions held by many contemporaries who personally experienced how Hitler relentlessly pursued a hopeless fight to the bitter end, and who take the view (or in this way attempt to grasp the incomprehensibilities and excesses) that only a person who had lost his senses — i.e. a maniac — could have been capable of such action. This commonly uttered idea has simply been taken over by the boys.

Although not a single boy ignores the extermination of the Jews, this certainly does not mean that the 16-year-olds have thought through the whole question on their own. If we attempt to put ourselves in the adolescent's shoes we realize at once that with the best will in the world he cannot possibly grasp the Jewish problem yet. The history of anti-Semitism is extremely complex and an objective assessment demands very full and accurate knowledge of political, social and financial conditions in the 19th and 20th centuries.[2]) Quite apart from this, however, such a boy is not yet in a position to cope with the problem by himself. He knows that millions of Jews were murdered, recognizes this as a ghastly atrocity, and wants

---

[1]) The German term — "Groessenwahn" — is comparatively colloquial but usually stronger than an English rendering such as "swollen-headed". Tr. note.
[2]) For literature cf. Hannah Arendt, *Elemente und Urspruenge totaler Herrschaft*, Frankfurt a. M., 1955.

first of all to know the reason. It is an obvious step to the conclusion: such an atrocious effect must have had an equally atrocious cause. How should it occur to a boy of 16 that millions of human beings could have been killed for the sake of a prejudice, a vindictive grudge? As a "sufficient reason" he may then see only two alternatives — "wicked Nazis" or "wicked Jews"; one or the other of them must have been monstrously wicked, is the next stage in his reasoning. The Jews are the guilty ones in the eyes of 5 boys, the National Socialists in the opinion of practically all the rest — the overwhelming majority. A few pupils, however, evade the question of guilt and only set down the facts.

The following type of judgement is common: "In my view Hitler and his minions were the greatest gangsters that have ever lived"; "I consider Hitler was a mean and despicable guy who thought of nothing but his own power". In the few essays which are anti-Jewish in character we find the old anti-Semitic prejudices: "He (Hitler) had the Jews persecuted; they had seized practically entire control of the nation's finance. A wholesome public life was gradually restored." The next quotation almost takes one's breath away: "There is danger at hand. With ruthless disregard for the people Jews are forcing their way into high position. The people are being exploited and betrayed. Hitler puts an end to this state of affairs, first by expelling the Jews and then by annihilating them. The people are Aryan and must not be contaminated by foreign or Jewish blood. The Jews are led to the gas chambers. Much that happens is unjust, but much is just, too." In such instances adult influence cannot fail to be recognized. By himself a ninth grader would never come upon phrases such as "wholesome public life" ("Volksgesundung"), and "foreign blood". The final sentences are particularly revealing. The boy starts off in a sure and emphatic manner. Then he mentions the gas chambers and simply cannot avoid at least seeing the evil; but he only says: "Much that happens is unjust", and then rushes to the loophole "but much is just, too," which puts everything straight again, he feels. Here we are already confronted in miniature with the attitude that has almost become normal in the world ideology: the evasion of genuine understanding by taking refuge in the rigid obstinacy of a preconceived opinion.

Another boy who puts the blame on the Jews invents his own incriminating evidence. He asserts that the Jews had been planning to overthrow the government and were persecuted for this reason. However deluded this idea, it fits the psychological make-up of a 16-year-old boy far better than those previously quoted, and in his case one is not necessarily induced to presume some anti-Semitic influence.

The third point — that Hitler "developed megalomania", or simply "became a maniac", "went mad", "turned crazy" — is probably also associated in the ninth grade boy's mind with the persecution of the Jews. The boys look for a tangible, understandable reason for the "liquidation", can find none and are forced to comfort themselves with the idea that Hitler must have been a maniac or lost his reason, since such crimes would otherwise be quite inexplicable. In this way an average boy of 16, knowing next to nothing of "Weltanschauung", ideologies, party programs and totalitarian methods of government, has accomplished all the reasoning of which he is capable, and one must appreciate that within his limits he has even managed to be consistent. The statement: "Hitler turned crazy" dismisses the problem for most boys, and they do not feel the need of further reasons and motives to explain all the horrors.

By contrast, it is at this point that the more mature boys awaken to a consciousness of the real problem, and the initial steps towards independent reflection and reasoning begin to emerge. "Hitler's hatred of the Jews in my opinion is nothing more

61

than the 'revenge of the little man'. You might call it that. The intelligentsia was too much for him. Instead of getting at them by hard, solid work he tried to get at them like that. I think it is a great pity to have a prejudice against another people. I love all mankind, and really we ought to love Israel most of all, because they're not only a small, brave and very efficient people but also God's chosen people." "The German people must try hard to make up to the Jews for what they suffered."

"What Hitler did to his own people seems to me to be one of the worst sins in history. Hitler made the people crazy, so crazy that they followed him almost unthinkingly through all the hell of a world war." The mentally alert pupils move on almost as a matter of course from the historical and political plane to moral issues — and include themselves as well. Here, without any external inducement, they are themselves taking the first step towards a sense of political responsibility — unquestionably a most welcome sign.

The ninth grade schoolboy's powers of judgement in relation to historical subjects are certainly limited. This emerges most clearly in the comments on World War II. Although there is no sign of patriotic pathos or an upsurge of romantic emotion, war still appears to most of the boys as a more or less sporting affair. In war the bravest men win, and the German soldiers were naturally the bravest. If they lost in spite of this some scapegoat must be found to bear the blame. It is obviously extraordinarily difficult for the boys to admit Germany's military defeat. They seek a culprit to bear the guilt — Hitler's mania, betrayal of state secrets or the overwhelming material superiority of the enemy. A scapegoat seems to be essential.

The boys' attitude to war is strikingly similar to their attitude towards football matches: it goes without saying that you support the home team, and of course it's the better team. If it nevertheless loses the match one player must have let the others down, or the other side didn't play fair. The Allies' overwhelmingly superior resources are regarded by the boys as "unfair odds" and they reason: if both sides had had the same chance we should inevitably have won. Thus the question of war guilt, and indeed any moral judgment on war, escapes the boys' attention. Only one boy opposed the sporting conception of war, writing: "I'm inclined to think the treason was really a good thing. Otherwise the war in Germany would have lasted longer and caused even more destruction." Although even this boy cannot manage without the theory of betrayal (which?) he does at least recognize that war is primarily a matter of destruction and suffering and only in the second place concerned with courage.

This thinking in terms of sporting achievement is apparent at other points, too. Ideas derived from the world of sport such as fairness, success, victory and honor have a high place in the ninth grade boy's scale of values. Hitler is praised because he "achieved things" — autobahn building, full employment — and above all because he was a German. Many boys obviously go by the principle: if you criticize Hitler too severely, and only Hitler, you are being unfair to Germany. They do not yet see that the whole point of criticism is responsible and moral reflection, and are afraid of honor being violated — "honor" again being conceived in terms of football teams with partisan associations.

It is this approach which lands the boys in peculiar conflict. Not one of them can evade the fact that Hitler was responsible for the collapse of Germany and caused immeasurable suffering. It is extremely revealing to watch how the majority of the boys escape this dilemma. At this point the limits of their critical faculties become especially clear.

First, nearly all the boys realize that unprejudiced and objective judgement is a paramount necessity. They try their best to achieve it. This is done as follows: they draw up two columns, one for the "plus" points and one for the "minus" points, in their minds. Hitler's "good" achievements go into the first, the failures and crimes into the second. Then they draw a line and add up. The result in most cases runs: Hitler did a lot of good, but a great deal more bad. The bad predominates, so he must be condemned. Sixty percent of the boys proceeded along these lines.

The boys' desire for objectivity is undoubtedly a welcome sign, even though it is usually accompanied by a strong distrust of adults. "To lots of folks the phrase 'National Socialism' is like a red rag to a bull. But didn't many of those who now run it down so much perhaps vote for it in 1933?" "You hear it said that the Nazi period was the darkest epoch in Germany's history. The question is whether this is true. Those who are now against the Nazis quote as their strongest argument the poisoning (sic, but see note)[1] of the Jews, and those who support the Nazis on principle use the building of the autbohns as their argument." The boys' demand for objectivity is there, and they make the first move — albeit an incomplete one — in that direction themselves. From school teaching they have acquired some idea of objectivity, e.g. they know from early lessons in natural science that correct results can be obtained by quantitative weighing up. They now approach historical subjects in the same way. As an example: "To begin with, Hitler wanted Germany to lead the world in commerce and industry. In this he succeeded. But I think the way he treated the Jews and the insane was quite wrong. On the whole I condemn him." Here the 'plus', 'minus', drawing the line and adding up are quite plain.

Under the heading of 'false categories of thinking' belongs the use of the word 'mistake'. "Altogether about 4 to 5 million Jews were killed. I think that was a big mistake." "Till then there's probably nothing to blame Hitler for, but then he made mistakes. He ordered the Jews to be persecuted." Here the ninth grade boy applies the modes of thinking proper in natural science not only to history, but to moral issues as well, so that a crime suddenly becomes a mere mistake.

The real reason for these false judgements is probably that a boy of this age is not yet in a position to create his own complete picture of a historical phenomenon, an epoch or a person. To him people and history are made up of a number of isolated factors. He arrives at his overall picture by giving these factors a plus or a minus sign and then doing a sum. Hitler had his good and bad points. If you collect as many of his characteristics and political achievements as possible and balance them out you will, he thinks, get the right total picture. The individual factors are always seen quantitatively, never qualitatively, so that any item is virtually comparable with any other. The boy enters autobahn building on the plus side and the extermination of the Jews on the minus side without noticing that they belong to entirely different dimensions which cannot possibly be compared. He sees no fundamental distinction between considerations of morality and usefulness, humanity and political success. The danger of this false association of radically different categories is that the impulse towards objectivity and justice, which the boys undoubtedly possess, can imperceptibly switch over to the most extreme injustice without their even noticing it.

At this point it is clear enough that the ninth grade boys' deficient understanding of history and politics is not so much due to gaps or mistakes in knowledge as to

---

[1] Note: phonetically the German word for "poisoning" — Vergiftung — is not so unrelated to the terms "Vernichtung" (annihilation) or even "Vergasung" (gassing), as the English equivalents might suggest. Tr.

incompletely developed faculties of judgement. When this is borne in mind pro-Hitler views need not be immediately suspect as alarming political signs, but may reasonably be attributed to lack of clarity in thinking, partly due to their age. It is, of course, impossible to overlook the startling resemblances between some of the opinions offered by ninth grade boys and those of many adults today. The phrases about autobahns and treachery, the tendency to think solely in terms of success, to see everything in black and white are just as widespread among adults as among juveniles. Nevertheless in both cases one must be careful not to assume that the motivation behind such utterances comes from Nationalist Socialist "infection". Is it not more likely that many adults suffer from the same basic deficiencies in their capacity for judging political issues? Merely to grasp the substance and structure of a phenomenon such as National Socialism requires certain intellectual powers which not everybody can command, and an ethical judgement in the political field is an even rarer plant. Utility and success, appeals to so-called 'realistic' thinking, partisan feeling or self-interest often enough prove stronger than ethical arguments. Thus even if the ninth graders' essays have indicated that deliberate National Socialist influence is rare, the result is not of a kind to set the teacher's mind at rest. The danger is, in fact, only on another plane. Whoever is unwilling or unable to judge human action primarily by ethical standards is at least potentially exposed to any form of political seduction. His ears will not be open to National Socialism in particular, but to the words of any demagogue.

What are the implications of all this for political education in the school? First and foremost — it must be moral education. When the pupil has grasped that the familiar autobahn cliché does not belong to a category of ideas which can possibly do justice to a period of history, when he recognizes that the comparison between autobahn building and the annihilation of the Jews is extremely dangerous — then, and not till then has he absorbed the basic concepts of political education. Thus history teaching admittedly becomes much more than just teaching a 'subject', and the teacher must constantly be reaching far beyond its boundaries. Nor can he do without the help of other school subjects, especially German, which is indispensable for the development of moral and humane standards of judgement. Political education can never be a task for one subject only; it must encompass all subjects which provide stimuli for the development of ethical judgement.

How do 16 and 17 Year-Old High School Pupils Regard Questions of Recent History? [1]

By Kurt Fackiner

That we Germans have not mastered our past has become a catchword. As it is common knowledge we need speculate no longer about it. And apart from that we have enough immediate problems. We should now finally draw a line under it and not always rummage about in the past. This is an attitude often adopted today. One is angry at the donkeys that try to eat the grass which in turn is slow enough in growing.

---

[1] From *Gesellschaft — Staat — Erziehung*, No. 4, 1959.

Certainly this attitude can hardly be found in the newspapers, and then only on rare occasions among readers' letters. It is one of the most peculiar aspects of our post-war period that we have various layers of public opinion on our past. What newspapers, magazines and radio state is only the opinion of a small minority. Only a little of it penetrates into the broad mass of the populace. At best, the actual attitude is only thinly rationally superimposed. This opinion is supported in detail by an investigation report published in 1955 by the Frankfurt Sociological Institute[2]).

This condition is so important to our life that we must concern ourselves with it. "Unmastered", as an epithet of our past, threatens to become the distinguishing title behind which we take refuge.

When one comes to terms with these questions in teaching social science, one quickly realizes that one is dealing with quite unique "material". The object is, after all, namely, the conceptions and opinions of the pupils themselves. It appears to me that in a position such as this, teaching can only be fruitful if one is aware, firstly, why the pupils are so very intensely interested in these questions and, secondly, if one tries to clarify the nature of the results of this interest, and thus which attitude the pupils adopt towards these problems. The question as to the reasons of the great interest of the pupils in events in our recent history must be answered mainly by youth psychology. The memories of their own experiences — destroyed cities, flight — and discussions with their parents, certainly also assure a personal interest in the problems of this period. But it appears to me in the end to be something else, something more decisive. The young person sees, even although only unconsciously, his own history, his own personal development in the history of his own people. After the collapse of his childhood world of values, he seeks standards of lasting value which he hopes to find also in the history of his own people. Every newly won value is then applied in retrospect once more to history itself. If the events of history stand up to this critical examination his personal sense of value rises as the individual feels a sense of self-justification in association with these events. Should the past not stand up to this test, his own sense of value suffers and all the more so, the closer the period in question is to the present day. This can lead to the flight of the young person into an inner world of ideals which loses its connection with the outside world, and can also lead to the collapse of the world of values which he has gained or to a simple closing of his eyes in face of the facts. It is certainly a bitter fate to find so little of value in the recent political history of one's own people.

As the second condition of coming to terms fruitfully with problems of recent history, I already referred to the mental attitude of the pupils to these questions. Everyone who engages in conversation with pupils gains his own experience in this respect. It is bound up with the personality of the teacher in each case, with his contact with his pupils, his political attitude, in its widest sense, and, as a whole, with the particular discussion group. This experience can be very fruitful for teaching if it does not remain incidental and isolated, but assists in finding a structure of thought in which the pupils can come to grips with the facts of recent history.

That is why I have tried, by questioning 250 pupils of various high schools in Frankfurt, to obtain a basis for a systematic investigation of these questions. The questioning was confined to sixth, seventh and several eighth grades[3]). The sixth and seventh grades were chosen for the following reasons: in the sixth grade the history

---

[2]) *Gruppenexperiment*, Europaeische Verlagsanstalt, Frankfurt.
[3]) The sixth, seventh and eighth grade at secondary school correspond to the tenth, eleventh and twelfth school year.

course at the time of questioning (autumn) had only proceeded at the utmost as far as 1914, and the pupils had thus not yet become systematically acquainted with the following period. In addition, the discussion of the constitutional state and the right of resistance had not yet taken place in the majority of the sixth grades. The seventh grades — according to entries in their schoolbooks and to their educational program — had discussed recent history in class at the end of the sixth grade, i.e., six months prior to the time of questioning. It was thus possible to ascertain what the pupils bring with them in knowledge and attitude before teaching takes effect and, secondly, it was possible to see how the teaching here took effect. Eighth grade pupils were enlisted in order to make spot checks as to how this development continues with increasing judgment.

Five questions were put to the pupils in writing and were to be answered briefly within an hour. The results were handed in without the pupils' names. At the time of questioning I was not teaching in any of the classes questioned, but about half the classes were known to me. The questions were formulated as follows:

1. What influence, in your opinion, had the Treaty of Versailles (1919) on political developments in Germany?
2. How, in your opinion, was it possible that the political events in Germany in the year 1933 came about?
3. There is no doubt that we Germans have committed an injustice towards the Jews. What do you suggest doing in order that we can settle this problem?
4. You know that our people are not united in their judgment of the event of 20th July 1944[4]). What would be your standpoint on this question?
5. The political events of the years 1933 till 1945 are also assessed differently among us. How would you assess the policies of Hitler?

The replies to the first two questions are not substantially of interest in this connection but throw light on the way in which the pupil regards political events. The Treaty of Versailles was, for the great majority of the pupils, the cause of the seizure of power by Hitler, of the Third Reich and finally, of the Second World War. Human actions are regarded in a causal relationship. Freedom of action and responsibility of the individual are thus denied. Such a fundamental attitude of thought on the part of the pupils must from the outset distort any evaluating settlement with our recent history. Still more: standards of responsible political bevahior, constitutional state thinking which instruction in sociology might drive home, can only then be obligatory for the pupil when the exclusively causal connections of historical events are removed. There are sufficient proofs in the pupils' statements before me that causal and free linkage of historical action are placed side by side and the causal view is always chosen when responsibility is uncomfortable. This is psychologically understandable but none the less disturbing on this account.

In the following I shall report broadly on the replies of the pupils to the last three questions. I would rather not, with two exceptions, quote the pupils' replies as they would probably, in the isolation of their limited numbers, give a false picture.

One of the most scabrous chapters in the mental life of our people is the question of our relationship with the Jews. It will be difficult and take a long time to arrive at an unencumbered relationship. The pupils are reluctant to acknowledge blame in this respect, repressing and often not acknowledging the facts as such. Their statements of opinion are extreme and become even more so with increasing years.

---

4) The German Resistance' attempt on Hitler's life.

This is shown also by the fact that among the older pupils the proportion is greater of those who do not answer this question. It is worthy of note therefore that the pupils who have discussed this problem certainly in the history class and often also in the sociology class, react more negatively than the others. It appears to me that the school's teaching on this subject is repudiated. This deduction is supported by the increase in statements by seventh grade pupils, asserting that it is not yet possible at present to make any objective assessment of this question and nothing reliable can be said by anyone in this respect for the time being. Apart from that we should all only have one opinion on this question.

From the pupils' statements various groups of replies can be classified. To begin with, the statement that the Germans are to blame for the extermination of the Jews provokes about half the pupils to such an extent that they state their opinion on the matter before they answer the actual question. These statements appear to me to be more important than the replies to the questions themselves as they are more fundamental. None of the sixth grade pupils say that the Germans bear no blame for the fate of the Jews, which is disputed by 2% of the seventh grade. We must remember, however, that a reaction of silence is just as likely as a spontaneous statement of opinion. 25% of the sixth grade and 19% of the seventh grade pupils admit German blame.

The reply of one seventh grade pupil is revealing in regard to the attitude of the pupils to the question of German blame.

"The injustice to the Jews cannot be made good with money as is being done by the Federal Government. It is not only Jews but also several European nations which are affected. If reparations are to be made here, then they must be made for everyone. But we are not in a position to carry this out in order to do the thing really effectively. All reparations should therefore be stopped. That is just war. Perhaps other countries too, and not only Germany, are to blame."

In every turn of phrase, in its very choice of words, this statement is self-contradictory. The first sentence states an opinion which is to be respected in every way and which is now prevalent among us in the upper sphere of public opinion. The adversative appendage of the second sentence already betrays resistance against the full acknowledgment of this statement even although injustice is substantially admitted on an even greater scale. And now the "logical" conclusion is established. If we thus make reparations, then for everyone. Then again the adversative conjunction at the beginning of the sentence: "But we are not in a position to carry this out." Therefore stop the reparations. The injustice is regarded (if that were at all objectively possible) as even greater, so great, that reparation greatly exceeds our capabilities.

In order to render it remote, the blame is piled up to a great height. The conceptions, of reparation and blame thus interblend. And thus follows, finally, out of the limitation of our economic means of reparation, not only its repudiation but also that of blame altogether. The sentence: "That is just war", removes it into the realm of fate where limits are set to the powers of man in any case. As, however, other states were also involved, part of the blame is now unloaded onto them — admittedly, only "perhaps". The writer feels himself absolved from blame by the fatalistic "that is war".

This example also holds good for quite a number of similar statements. The attitude can be appreciated psychologically but goes no further. Certainly one is shocked when on the other hand one reads in the reply of a seventh grade pupil which he wrote, obviously under the influence of the documentary film "Night and Fog": "I am ashamed to be a German, ashamed that I come from a nation such as this." It will be very difficult to heal these mental wounds.

My third question to the pupils required suggestions for solving the problem set us by the National Socialist injustice to the Jews. It is evident in the replies that the older pupils are more sensitive in their reactions than the youger ones. Nearly 17 % of the seventh grade — as opposed to 10 % of the sixth grade — give no reply. The proportions are reversed with pupils who can make no suggestion of a solution. This is evidence that the sixth grade pupils have indeed less knowledge than their fellow-pupils who are one year older. The percentage of sixth grade pupils who would like to see the reparations question solved "politically realistically" is strikingly large. They understand by this that our reparation services towards Israel should conform to the opinion of the Arab nations on this problem as these nations are important for us as customers of our industrial export trade. The repudiation of reparations increases among the pupils from the sixth to the seventh grades in the same way also, however, as the endorsement of the German reparations policy, even although on a smaller scale. The number of sixth grade pupils who endorse the present reparation policy and of those who repudiate it balance at 17 %. Among the seventh grade pupils the majority repudiate the policy (23.6 % against 19.8 % endorsements). Numerically more sixth grade than seventh grade pupils support better reparations than are being made today. As against that, the grounds given by the seventh grade pupils for improved reparations were qualitatively more valuable. If one adds the number of replies of those who endorse the present reparations policy to those who desire a better solution, the classes are on equal terms (6th: 35.4 %, 7th: 34.9 %). The numbers here give a confusing and contradictory picture. The inner tension towards this question is greater with the seventh grade pupils than with the younger ones.

With the question regarding the assessment of the event of the 20th July 1944, the replies are on the whole similar in their significance to those to the preceding question. It is apparent that the ethical judgment of the older pupils is more strongly developed than in the younger ones; as against that however, they think more "politically realistic", i.e., they study events from the aspect of their utilitarian value. That the actions of the 20th July are of themselves to be assessed positively is the opinion of 11.3 % of the sixth grade as opposed to 18.8 % of the seventh grade. 32 % of the sixth grade, however, are of the opinion that if the attempt had been successful, the result of the war would have been more favorable for Germany; only 15 % of the seventh grade shared this opinion. The picture given by the total results is rather deranged, however, by the replies from one sixth grade class. In this class the question of the right of resistance was discussed very intensively in the religion lesson. The ethical opinions of this class — the discussion did not lead to a collective opinion — are amazingly mature. Regarded as a whole, the opinions of the pupils on the 20th July are decidedly more straightforward than those to the previous question. But here, too, exaggerated one-sided opinions increase with age.

What opportunities and tasks for sociological education arise out of this complex of problems need not be accentuated. With an event such as that of the 20th July 1944 a happy encounter of the pupil with our recent history, with his past, becomes possible. Such instances can help in accepting the entirety of the past, in acknowledging it factually and thus creating the possibility of a sound attitude towards the past and the future and thus towards the present. Certainly, the isolated consideration of the 20th July in the sociology class must not lead to perversion of the

Lecture Hall at a West German University

Photo: Willy Pragber — Bavaria

Girl Scouts

Photo: Bundesbildstelle Bonn

A Studentenheim (Students' Residence) in Frankfurt/M.

Photo: Eduard Renner — Bavaria

facts and to regarding the whole of recent history from the viewpoint of the German internal opposition. That would also be an obstacle to acceptance of the past and would not stimulate the forces which would help to prevent such developments in the future.

An assessment of Hitler's policies was the point of the last question put to the pupils. Here the replies of the seventh grade are decidedly more considered than those of their younger fellows; it is true that they also more often withold their opinions. It is interesting that here, too, in the search for something positive, the entity of Hitler's home and foreign policies is dissected and also a temporal separation is made into an early good and late bad policy. Thus 23.5% of the sixth grade (as opposed to 20% of the seventh) judge Hitler's policies as being good to begin with. The home policy is regarded by 30% of the sixth grade (as opposed to 13.2% of the seventh) as good and they separate it from his foreign policy. 10.6% of the sixth (as opposed to 5.7% of the seventh) assess Hitler's policies simply as good. As opposed to these, the statements of 11.3% of the sixth grade and 36.7% of the seventh describe his policies as bad. Here a positive influence of the school appears to take effect with increasing age.

One more reference to the values of "people and nation" in the pupils' replies, appears to me to be important in this connection. That no conscious reality is attached to these two words appears to me to be substantiated by the fact that of all the 250 pupils questioned, only two mentioned the partition of Germany — in connection with their assessment of Hitler's policies. That is a peculiar phenomenon, particularly when one bears in mind the attempts to repress the feeling of guilt regarding the injustice towards the Jews; the feeling of guilt which nevertheless depresses us considerably because these atrocities were perpetrated just by Germans in the name of the people. It is also peculiar in view of the attempt to support to a large extent Hitler's policies. The national feeling — so greatly overtaxed during the National Socialist era — appears to have suffered such a shock that even today it still appears to react only in a roundabout way via the sense of personal value out of the subconscious.

Here, too, is an important task for sociological teaching in which once more the question as to the "how" of the solution must be very searchingly asked.

I should like to relate one final observation. With a large number of the pupils not all the questions are assessed according to the same standards. Thus it often happens, for example, that one pupil opposes the injustice to the Jews and emphasises that all men are equal, and then, some few lines later, fully condones Hitler's internal policy. Others acknowledge the attempt on Hitler's life as actually being a good action but believe at the same time that they can support his policies. Even if one can regard these phenomena as being partly the unconscious endeavor of the sense of personal value to find as many examples of value as possible in one's own national past, it is clear that the ethical judgment of the pupil is still not binding to any great extent for him himself. Only thus are such self-contradictory assessments possible.

Here again the question remains as to the means of effecting an alteration. Sociology cannot act alone on such questions. It appears doubtful whether our school in its present form is at all capable of satisfactorily solving such problems. On the contrary, it appears to block even the most fruitful approaches out of fear of concentration on subjects, which is construed as specialization.

A Study of National Socialism
by 17 and 18 Year-Old High School Students [1]

By Gerhard Reyl

The catchwords about our "undigested past" were constantly recurring in social studies lessons with my twelfth grade class. The first impulse towards an unprejudiced study of the National Socialist ideology came during "question time" — a period in which the pupils can put questions on practically any topic and the teacher gives an answer on the spot, if he is able. If not, the reply is postponed until the next lesson. During one of these question periods the following criticism was voiced: "Our teachers don't tell us the truth about National Socialism. They either put us off with convenient platitudes or they're embarrassed and won't say a thing. What are we to believe?"

I countered with questions of my own: "Are you aware that at Hitler's order millions of Jews were murdered?"; "Are you aware that Hitler suppressed free speech?"; "Are you aware that Hitler rode roughshod over international law?", etc. The boys then drew attention to the positive achievements of National Socialism and described the Nazi crimes as excesses — perversions of something that had originally been quite sound. In the case of some pupils I was struggling right from the start against the intangible shadows of discussions at home. About 50 % of the boys supported my views from religious conviction. About 30 % were non-committal. About 20 % fell back on the positive elements — autobahn building, abolishment of unemployment, etc.

Thereupon I declared that I myself — nine years old in 1933 — had been a supporter of Hitler. I had given my allegiance to the National Socialist ideology without any critical study of its foundations. In fact before 1945 I had not even read Hitler's Mein Kampf right through. In this respect I undoubtedly shared the company of numerous ex-Nazis, above all of many "incurable" Nazis. Certainly it was not to be expected that Nazism would return after all the evils the German people had experienced; but uncritical, parrot-like repetition of the latest political slogans was still current today among Germans. Such an attitude led to idolatry of the State, and all State worship ended up in some form of inhumanity. My pupils themselves recognized that this danger could only be averted by making a thorough study of the now closed historical chapter of the dictatorship.

This realization was the starting point of a six months' study of National Socialism as revealed in the testimony of the Nazis themselves. I distributed to the class all the available copies of the following books: Adolf Hitler, Mein Kampf; Alfred Rosenberg, Der Mythus des 20. Jahrhunderts; Gottfried Feder, Das Programm der NSDAP; NS-Briefe (correspondence); Schulungsbriefe des Gaues Hessen-Nassau der NSDAP (training circulars issued to a local party division). Since Heinrich Himmler's book, Die SS als antibolschewistische Kampforganisation and Baldur von Schirach's book, Die Hitlerjugend were not obtainable we used two studies instead: Arno Kloenne's Die Hitlerjugend and Ermengard Neusuess-Hunkel's Die SS.

I should begin by saying that I very soon managed to induce the boys to voice their opinions freely and candidly. This was primarily due to the fact that I had openly admitted my own National Socialist past.

[1] From Gesellschaft — Staat — Erziehung, No. 5, 1960.

It soon became evident that a critical evaluation of the National Socialist material was a very difficult task for the boys. I then distributed 14 subjects throughout the class, asking them to prepare impartial accounts based on the above sources; the topics included Rosenberg's race teaching, the principles of Hitler's foreign policy, the history of the Hitler Youth, the history of the SS, the concentration camps, etc. After each piece of work had been presented to the class I attempted to start up a critical discussion. The pupils' response to this initial approach was not very promising. Their helplessness produced a host of questions which again landed me in monologs. By about the fifth essay session, however, they were beginning to grasp some of the fundamental errors of the National Socialist ideology themselves. Their first attacks were directed against the Nazi "State perfectionism" and the race theories. By the end of the series three points had emerged which the boys felt to be of cardinal importance:

1. Was the National Socialist race-teaching materialistic?

2. The logical consequences of the race theory (euthanasia, the Jewish question, the gipsy question, eugenic "improvement" ('Aufartung'), "breeding for the Nordic type" ('Aufnordung').

3. Was the criminal nature of National Socialism already inherent in its ideological basis?

For the final discussion of these questions we resolved to hold a joint meeting with the other two parallel twelfth grade classes in our school. For preparatory purposes copies of the essays and the results of our own discussions were distributed to all teachers and pupils who were to take part in the general meeting. The boys had eight weeks in which to study this material, and the final discussion itself took up six school periods. The pupils ran the discussion themselves, under their own leaders (the preparations had been made by a special committee of schoolboys), and the school Principal and teachers of religion, history, social studies and biology who were present only gave information in reply to questions directed expressly towards them. During the discussion the boys revealed a knowledge of National Socialist ideology thorough enough to have aroused the envy of any ex-pupil of a special Nazi training school. This probably accounts for the outstanding results achieved by the general meetings, which as far as space allows I should like to summarize below. The conclusions are taken from the written record of the joint discussions.

Point 1.
a) The aim of the National Socialist race teaching was to apply knowledge derived from animal breeding to human beings, and to breed a *Führervolk* ('master race') without any regard for the human soul and its autonomous nature. Man, however, is both the expression of a God-given spirit and a biological organism — a being between beast and angel. Since the National Socialists recognized only the biological aspect of man, their race teaching was materialistic.

b) In its overweening national pride the Nazi party contemplated breeding a "superior race", which was to represent the extreme opposite of the Jews.

c) Every dictatorship needs some scapegoat; the National Socialists' was the Jew. One regrettably negative view prevalent among the pupils, and widespread in Germany, was not entirely dislodged during the plenary sessions. Although the Nazis' treatment of the Jews had to be condemned for its inhumanity, the Jews themselves — especially the Eastern Jews who had migrated to Germany after World War I — were to blame for their fate because of their behavior. This point received thorough treatment during a critical evaluation of the discussions in religion and social studies.

Point 2.

a) Euthanasia was a consequence of the materialistic viewpoint expressed in *"Recht ist, was dem Volke nützt"* (Whatever benefits the nation, is right). Some pupils upheld the Christian view: "No man has the right to destroy the image of God, his body or his soul. People who are a danger to the community should be separated from it, but on no account should they be killed." There were still some boys who said: "The insane are a burden to the State. All ballast must be eliminated." They were defeated in the debate.

b) The gipsies were treated like the Jews. The motives for getting rid of them only differed in part from the motives of anti-Semitism.
   1. They were a different people, a foreign race.
   2. They could not be incorporated in the economic system as a source of labor.
   3. The attempt to make them settle failed.
   Nevertheless the gipsies must not be denied the right to follow their own way of life among the settled populations of Europe.

c) "Eugenic improvement" or "breeding for the Nordic type" was a futile and preposterous chimera (see Point 1.) and a dire injustice. Parts of the SS "standing orders" and "Germanization measures" in Poland were cited as examples of "Nordic" eugenic practice.

Point 3.

Mein Kampf and the *"Parteiprogramm"* served as a basis for discussing the question: "Was the criminal nature of National Socialism already inherent in its ideological basis?"

Conclusions

a) The race teaching was inherently criminal, since practical application of the theories inevitably led to the abuse of fundamental human rights.

b) The suppression of free throught and religion was also wrong. The totalitarian claim, already set forth in Hitler's *Mein Kampf*, resulted inevitably in this crime.

c) The practical consequences of the notions *Volk ohne Raum* (a people without space to live) and *"Gemeinnutz geht vor Eigennutz"* (benefit to the community has priority over the individual) could not be other than crimes. The uncertainty of justice under Hitler's rule and the expansionist policy which ended in war proved this.

The results of this study indicate that questions concerning recent history certainly appeal to the boys. They demand objectivity of presentation and a frank confession about his own past on the part of the teacher. At the beginning of the enquiry they were always asking me: "But how could you, as a thinking man, ever have believed all that?". The more they delved into the history of the Nazi party and the Nazi ideology, however, the better they understood the conditions which produced and accompanied this enormous and disastrous mistake of a whole generation. To me the most important outcome of the entire study was one boy's observation after the joint meetings: "We too are still capable of being infected by tyranny in some form or other. We can only arm ourselves against this danger by conscious democratic living." As a follow-up to the study the boys read Alan Bullock's book on Hitler in the translation published by the Droste-Verlag.

A Conference of 18 and 19 Year-Old High School Students Discussed Recent History [1]

By Andreas Hillgruber

The *Landeszentrale fuer Heimatdienst*[2]) in Hesse had invited 36 boys and girls from the top classes of high schools and three high school teachers to a short conference at the *Evangelische Akademie* in Arnoldshain i. T. The object of this gathering, which was planned for the 11th and 12th December 1959 under the leadership of Dr. Hannah Vogt, was to hear what high school pupils themselves had to say on the much debated topic of contemporary history, to learn their views on specific questions of interest to their teachers and to receive any criticism they had to offer. On this occasion, therefore, the students were to become the teachers. Everything depended on the pupils' speaking their minds frankly and honestly. The fact that this was achieved to an astonishing degree in the short time available may be ascribed not least of all to the open-minded and free atmosphere of the *Evangelische Akademie,* which also sent a member of its regular staff, who had been working for some time on problems of contemporary history with a youth group in Frankfurt, to attend the conference. The success was primarily due, however, to the group of 36 boys and girls, all of them exceptionally interested in contemporary history, who, within a few hours, were cooperating in team study and attacking the problems with deep seriousness and penetrating thought.

During the initial plenary session, aimed at discovering their conception of contemporary history and what place they thought it should occupy in the school program, they were comparatively reticent and some of their replies and interpretations appeared to follow the "desired" conventional pattern of "school" answers; but the feeling of still being in some way "at school" was rapidly lost during the group work that followed, which was devoted to the question: "What are the pros and cons of contemporary history study?" Any residual inhibitions were in fact completely broken down by the evening, when, after a documentary movie on the *"Machtergreifung"* (Seizure of Power), compiled by T. Ellwein and K. O. von Aretin, a free informal discussion developed. This started with problems raised by the film and then opened out in breadth and depth until in the course of the night (some small groups did not break up until 4 a.m.!) cardinal questions such as guilt and reponsibility for the past came to the fore. After this first day, so exceptionally revealing and full of impressions for the teachers present, who had by common agreement kept as far as possible in the background (the pupils appointed their own leaders and recorders for the study groups), the following day's developments only served to strengthen the feeling that these strongly roused and agitated youngsters, who were increasingly putting questions of their own to the adults, should really not be sent home without having received a reply to at least some of their most urgent queries. Since in the one day left even a moderately satisfactory solution of this problem was out of the question (the primary aim of the gathering, as already indicated, had been to provide information for the teachers) it was arranged that the whole group should meet again in Arnoldshain during the second half of March, 1960, to enable the teachers, as far as possible, to satisfy these questing spirits in a way which was not possible on the first occasion.

[1]) From *Gesellschaft — Staat — Erziehung,* No. 5, 1960.
[2]) Land Organization for Civics.

With this in mind the teachers presented themselves to the pupils in the afternoon for a "question period" lasting about 1½ hours, and were confronted with numerous questions of great variety. Only a fraction of them could be answered on the spot, of course, but the important thing was to give the youngsters the feeling that their questions were not being treated in a stereotyped fashion, but with full seriousness. This question time was both the climax and the final session. It was preceded in the morning by group work on various problems, such as "Is it too soon to attempt a judgment of the 'Third Reich'?", "What standards of judgment can be applied to the period?", "What were the 'ideals' of National Socialism?". During the mid-day break the pupils had a discussion on their own, without the teachers, to air their views on the "trustworthiness of the older generation when dealing with the history of the recent past". A short talk between a radio reporter, some of the pupils and the conference leader, Dr. Vogt, was tape-recorded by the schools service of Radio Hesse and broadcast in a program at 12.12 p.m.

From our point of view as teachers, the chief outcome of the conference was the realization that beneath the level of more or less superficially acquired knowledge about the recent German past (knowledge which is more extensive and probably sounder than might be deduced from the well-known Neven-Dumont television program), there are many deeply-seated relics of National Socialist thinking — sometimes merely scattered scraps of ideas — lying hidden, above all notions of a "social Darwinist" type; and beyond this, that an uncertainty concerning truth and justice can be detected, although this is doubtless only a reflection of the widespread uncertainty among adults on these points. These young people display a kind of passionate fervor in warding off propaganda in any form and however well meant. The slightest expression of comment is regarded as propaganda. They want to form their own opinions from the sources themselves, the records and documents. The commentary accompanying the film mentioned above was almost unanimously rejected, for instance. The undoubted effect produced by the documentary photographs was partially destroyed by the sound track text, which the pupils felt was intended to impose a specific opinion on them. The same applies to the volume of documentary records, Der Nationalsozialismus, compiled by Walther Hofer (Fischer-Bücherei, 1957), which is often used as a basis for discussion in the upper classes of high schools. Hofer's interpolations are regarded as superfluous and irritating. This hypersensitive, defensive attitude towards comment of any kind can almost be called allergic; it is a factor to be taken into account in all our teaching unless we wish our efforts to be in vain. One welcome sign was that certain pupils, who had arrived at a clear and firm position of their own, stood up for their views and struggled to convince the others in the debate. Most encouraging of all, however, was the fact that no one maintained an absolute inflexibility, all of the participants being prepared to listen to the views of others and meet them halfway.

Training Instructors for the Teaching of Social Studies [1]

The future of the teaching of social studies in secondary schools depends on whether it will be possible to obtain the necessary number of teachers with adequate training for this purpose. Strictly speaking, teachers of this kind are as yet not at all available. The teaching is carried on by teachers who have acquired the necessary knowledge through their own studies and through extension courses.

Such courses are held in almost all *Laender* of the federation and last anywhere from a number of days to four weeks. They are an emergency measure which will not by any means suffice, however indispensable it may be for the moment. The social studies will not be able to flourish alongside the classical subjects in the secondary schools unless the teachers assigned to teach them have been no less properly trained than the teachers of those other subjects.

Theoretical training for teachers in secondary schools devolves upon the universities, and particularly upon the departments of political science that have been established in them or are proposed. That may be difficult to understand on the basis of non-German ways of thinking and therefore requires explanation. This explanation is at the same time an introduction to the purpose and objectives of social studies as they are developing in the Federal Republic. It will consequently have to go farther afield.

First of all: In the Federal Republic, the social studies serve the goals of political education. This conception of their objectives ensues from the very simple fact that Germany has no consolidated democratic tradition of the kind natural to the traditionally democratic countries and that the body of social knowledge and modes of behavior capable of sustaining a democratic polity must first be developed. The failure of the first attempt to establish a German Republic (1918—1933) and the Nazi dictatorship (1933—1945) are experiences that do not facilitate a task of this kind and therefore make it especially urgent.

In order to understand this situation, it must further be kept in mind that in the Federal Republic, Systematic Politics has developed into a science dealing with the organization of the body politic in its entirety. Accordingly, it embraces what is called "social sciences" in the Anglo-Saxon countries, including sociology. The expressions "politics" and "political education" must be understood in a comprehensive sense. The ancient Greek use of the term "politics" (Aristotle) comes closest to this meaning.

In the traditionally democratic countries, social science and the fields of knowledge relegated to it are based on a democratic comprehension and democratic behavior habits. The latter consequently do not have to be subjected to contemplation in the same manner as in Germany. Therefore, the expression "political education" also includes social training and science. Neither the French expression *"éducation civique"* nor the English "citizenship" coincides at all fully with that of "political education" in the German sense.

Without these premises, neither the plan of the present inquiry concerning the Federal Republic nor the development and objectives of the social studies in that

[1] From *Mitteilungen* of the *Akademie fuer Politische Bildung*, No. 3, April 1960 (Containing a study concerning political education in the Secondary Schools in West-Germany and West-Berlin — a UNESCO project).

country's secondary schools are completely intelligible. That might well be kept in mind with respect to the following portions.

On January 6, 1954, the West German Rectors' Conference issued recommendations concerning political education and training at the institutions of higher learning. One year later, on January 22, 1955, the German Committee on Training and Education published a comprehensive appraisal on the same subject, referring with respect to the institutions of higher learning in Chapter IV, Section 8, to the recommendations of the West German Rectors' Conference. They complement one another most favorably and have meanwhile come to be acknowledged and adopted as something like the "Magna Carta" of all these endeavors in the Federal Republic.

These most important documents are in the form of appraisals and recommendations, and not of directives. That is an expression of two factors. The first of these is that under the constitution, the *Laender* in West Germany are independent in the realm of cultural and educational policy, including school policies. As a result, they are not subject to any central, federal legislation or directives. The autonomy of the institutions of higher learning has its counterpart in the autonomy of the *Laender* in matters of cultural and educational policy. Utterances by federal German bodies may be presented to the Laender only in the form of recommendations. In order to obtain a survey of the existing conditions, it is therefore necessary to inquire into the measures, directives and programs of study at the individual schools and institutions of higher learning and into their actual implementation. The second and underlying reason why the most important West German statements on this subject are in the nature of recommendations is the following: In its present conformation, political science is a young field of scholarship. The subject of instruction correlated to this science is not one of the classic school subjects. It has not yet even been introduced as a distinct subject in all of the *Laender*. Lastly and most important of all, the inherently functional character of political education and training entails the necessity for these efforts to take into account the political reality within which they are being undertaken, including the history of that people which they are intended to serve. Yet on the other hand, the Federal Republic is a young democracy — a democracy in trend, not in secure proprietorship. Moreover, Germany as a whole is divided into two regimes, one of which is totalitarian. This situation explains the experimental character which social and political education and training have and for a long time will continue to have in Germany. In this respect, we consequently cannot rely on dependable modes of thought and behavior, which would represent the scope for this task and would need only be given an ethical foundation, an informal content and scientific soundness. The task in Germany is unparalleled: It is elementary in every sense.

Training the teacher to give instruction in politics is one correlative of the task awaiting him in school. It will therefore be necessary to speak first of all about the task at the school level.

There are two realms which must be distinguished in this regard. Neither of them can be forgone, and training at the institution of higher learning will have to keep both of them in mind. Political education is treated firstly as a general principle of instruction in every subject and in every type of school, and secondly as a distinct body of knowledge in a separate subject or at any rate in separate lessons. The main effort is apportioned differently in the individual *Laender* of the Federal Republic. Implementation in both realms is not only very diverse among the

Laender[2]), but even among the schools of the same *Land*. However, the necessity for both realms is universally acknowledged in principle.

"Principle of instruction" means in the first place that the bearing each field of instruction has upon society and government is portrayed. In addition, it means that on the basis of the topics of instruction, the insights concerning the essence and structure of social and political life to be gained from them are made explicit. To forgo elaborating them would imply overlooking an important aspect of the individual subject-matter field and hence failing to do it full justice. It would also imply neglecting a method of political science that is particularly effective because the political aspect in this instance is fitted into a total reality. In the teaching of history and literature, for example, this reality strikes deep roots and affords an opportunity not only to gain a knowledge of subject matter but also to gather (secondary) experiences.

The objectives of social studies in the school are:

Interpretation and supplementation of the practical observations the pupils themselves make and of the perceptions accruing to them from all subjects.

Conscious realization of the social environment.

Exlporation of the political reality facing them in which they will have to prove their merit.

Preparation for social and political maturity and of political judgment, without which no free political system can exist permanently, surmounting political and economic crises. They include the presentation of objective information, orientation and the development of standards of practical political behavior. The teacher who is expected to be equal to these tasks must receive preparation for them. An impressionistic, unmethodical training will not suffice.

In regard to proper training for the teacher, the following consideration is significant: To educate a person politically means opening his eyes to the total context. Any one-sided approach will not be equal to this task, regardless of whether the depiction is presented in geographic, economic, sociological, socio-psychological, ethical or historical categories. If the young person is to be led to grasp the wide range of human and social relations and of political structures, this will only be possible in a sort of fused program of instruction, that is, by overcoming the view based on isolated subject-matter categories to attain a program of instruction in which all of these diverse viewpoints are interrelated. A program of instruction on these lines is especially difficult for the secondary schools, since their characteristic methods are dictated by specialty thinking.

This reveals that the teacher assigned to instruction in social studies in school must, it is true, have undergone training in political science. Yet he need not specifically be a political scientist, a specialist among specialists. On the one hand, the schools need teachers who are alert to, and interested in, social and political matters; who — though they teach history, German, geography or languages — have learned to see things from a social and political point of view; understand how to detect and interpret the correlative social and political values of their subject fields; and hence are able to treat social and political education as a principle. On the other hand, the schools also need teachers with a thorough scientific training who are able to present the periods of instruction stipulated in the program of studies and to direct group activities. Still, they must not conceive of political education as a mere specialized goal, but as a fusion and as a synthesis among the categories of the political sphere.

---

[2]) See survey, PART II B 5.

Following this sketch of the schools' needs, it would be appropriate at this point to proceed to answering the question as to how these needs are being met by the institutions of higher learning. In this respect, it should be kept in mind that the portrayal to be presented does not depict the actual situation in all institutions of higher learning. Matters are in the process of development.

There is no doubt that in the training of teachers for the social studies, the most important role devolves upon the departments of political sciences at the institutions of higher learning. Hence it is to be desired for this elementary reason that the 1954 recommendation of the Rectors' Conference will soon be complied with in every respect by all institutions of higher learning and that such departments will everywhere be considered no less appropriate than, let us say, the department of pedagogy.

The function of these departments in the training of teachers is being accomplished through two channels corresponding approximately to the two different realms of political science in school that have been outlined above.

1. The departments train those students who have selected Systematic Politics as a minor course. Systematic Politics has not by any means been recognized as a minor course of study in all *Laender* of the Federal Republic. The necessity for such recognition is also disputed by a number of teachers and particularly school administrations — moreover for very diverse reasons. The teachers have definitely gathered experiences in this respect and have with some justification shown a reaction in the face of a task whose scientific foundations appear incomplete to them or for which they simply do not have the scientific prerequisites. Anyone who has observed the fate of the social-studies field and of political education in general since 1945, and is aware of the teachers' reaction, cannot help considering the establishment of political science as a minor course to be significant for the success of well-founded, defensible political science at the school level.

That means that Systematic Politics must also be included in the examination system. That is not very easy to arrange under the conditions prevailing in Germany. The German *Studienrat* (secondary-school teacher) has a much heavier teaching load than the *professeur* in the French schools, that is, 24 to 26 or more hours per week. He has at least two and in some *Laender* even three specialties, compared to the one specialty of the *professeur*. Systematic Politics as a minor specialty happens to be an extreme example of a "short-range specialty": That means that it appears with a very small number of hours on the school program of studies. The result is that the *Studienrat* with political science as a minor is hard to "load up" even in large schools, and it is impossible in the many small ones.

That is the chief reason why in the principles for the scientific examination for the position of teacher in secondary schools drawn up on June 26, 1952, by the Permanent Conference of Ministers of Culture and Education, political science is listed only as a "supplementary field". This means that the student is supposed to be able to elect it as a supplement to his other two or three major and minor courses. Consequently, the field is not to be appraised as a regular component of the program of training and of the examination. The contradiction between this arrangement and the establishment of social studies as a regular course of study is apparent, since any such course is obviously contingent upon corresponding requirements for the program of training and the examination of the teachers who are supposed to offer it. For this reason, Baden-Wuerttemberg, for example, has classified Systematic Politics among the examination subjects of the philological and historical field. As a result, the student is now able to elect Systematic Politics as a regular minor course.

The requirements of this examination include:

A survey of the elements of political theory.

Ability to interpret the classical authors on the subject of politics.

Knowledge of comparative government and of the institutions of constitution and administration in present-day Germany (including the political parties).

Ability to analyze problems of world politics.

A survey of the elements of theoretical sociology.

Familiarity with the implements of Systematic Politics. These requirements for a minor field cannot be termed excessive. They circumscribe rather precisely what is absolutely necessary for teachers of this subject.

2. In whatever measure the departments of political science have a view to the schools, the goal just portrayed is only one realm. Of equal importance, and in some respects even more urgent, is their goal in regard to all of the other students preparing for the teaching profession. It has already been explained what is involved in the principle of instruction. For many teachers, the "principle" may merely reflect an evasion of the commitment to social and political education by and large, or at any rate of their specific aspects in the here and now. Yet it would be dangerous to fail to realize that this attitude reveals a very fundamental fact: The hypothesis of a purely contemplative concept of education, including German Idealism's concept of education, has suffered a loss of impact as a result of the social and political revolutions and changes of the past few decades, the hypertrophic development of technology and the supremacy of social and political factors in modern society. In a free society and a free polity today, the field of political education is an indispensable component of education in its full sense, and is in fact probably an integral component of any education. The danger of a revulsion into totalitarianism inherent in this conception of education must be recognized. It does not, however, relieve us of the duty manifest in such an imperative of our times. In fact, it is the very thing that makes this duty's full urgency evident.

At this point, it becomes apparent that the purposeful equipment of teachers to instruct the social studies in the schools converges with the broader task of revising our entire educational structure, to which the institutions of higher learning, being agencies of education, cannot consider themselves any exception. Although general studies must be looked upon as a failure in a number of the forms tried, the task was genuine and continues to exist.

Transposed into institutional terms, the remarks made above mean that the departments of political science must offer lecture and seminar courses intended for students of other disciplines and particularly for future teachers. Such courses must be confined to the elementary, fundamental aspects of the political sciences and devote special attention to establishing correlation with the professional studies wherever it exists, thus supplementing them. This has frequently been requested by the student governments themselves, and it is being done here and there. These lectures and seminars are intended to satisfy a pronounced need. If they really meet it and if they are good, then the experience has been that they are attended.

This phase of the study of political science should also include an optional qualifying examination binding upon the department of social studies for students with two majors.

This examination differs from that for the student with political science as a minor in that it does not so much cover examinable items of knowledge as it does the acquisition of the classificatory and methodological prerequisites for further individual study in this field, which is to be expected at a later time if the examinee is assigned the subject of social studies as a teacher.

Programs and Materials for Instruction in Social Studies from the Point of View of "Political Education"

In the light of the preceding explanations, critical observations are possible without running the risk of misunderstandings concerning the term "political education" as it is comprehended in the Federal Republic. In all of the social sciences, including those of the descriptive kind, the object is in the last analysis the purposeful organization of human beings. As free persons, which they are by nature, human beings cannot be organized according to arbitrarily established ends and making no allowance for their demand for liberty. The model of animal "governments", for example does not provide us any conceptions for human social organization. Purposeful, suitable organization of human beings, applied to society as a whole and to the state in which the society becomes capable of action with respect to necessary common decisions, is politics. This is the sense in which the expression is used in conjunction with the word "education".

If a people has had to undergo historical experiences like those of the German people in the years from 1933 to 1945, and if during this period, and as a result of its consequences its entire historical order, as well as its social order, has been subjected to cataclysmic upheavals, then a mere detached, descriptive knowledge of social phenomena is no longer sufficient. Such a people must be put in a position to identify the elements of a stable and free new social organization, in order to be able with substantiated insight to find its way, to make decisions and to act upon them. One aspect of this is that training and education, including the efforts of the schools, should be related to the organization of the whole, to whatever extent they are of a more than individual nature. In social training, this must be done explicitly. This reference to the whole is expressed in the term "political education".

Of course, there is a great deal of "social"-studies' subject matter that must first of all be treated in its own right. That applies especially to the lower age groups, that is, to the lower and intermediate grades of the secondary schools. Beginning with the upper grade, however, the overlying aspects must be elaborated very clearly, because a large number of pupils terminate their schooling upon completion of two years in the upper grades. Throughout this two-year period, social studies is dedicated entirely to the acquisition of "organizational knowledge", and hence to "political education".

How are these objectives of social studies reflected in the programs and materials for instruction and in the lively pedagogical discussion?

When the social studies were introduced in a number of *Laender* after 1945, a flood of social-studies expositions, information aids and textbooks began to appear. The subject matter they presented corresponds approximately to what is understood by the term "social sciences". Yet an uncertainty very quickly arose in regard to these publications. Not only was it hardly possible to keep abreast of the large volume of instructional materials offered, the problem of selection becoming insoluble, but a major portion of these publications were popularizations of the relevant scientific disciplines. What was lacking was the discriminating principle of selection which, as in the case of all instructional materials, can be found only in the answer of the educational purpose of a given sphere of instruction. Mere collections of material are almost worthless for educative teaching. Mere "studies", that is, knowledge which does not lead to perceptions and insights, are sterile.

In the programs of education and of studies that have been issued in the past few years by the *Laender* Ministries, the imprint of the pedagogical discussions conducted in periodicals, published works and numerous meetings has become quite evident. The programs counter the merely descriptive sociological approach, especially the pure study of institutions and any timeliness dictated by chance events of the day or social developments. They demand the elaboration of principles of social and political organization by means of which the ability to form judgments can be educated. For many years, there has been discussion concerning whether the mere concept of partnership could be the supporting idea of social studies, or whether training for the "community" — that is, modes of behavior and forms of association that have a strongly personal and sometimes emotional coloration and in most cases a predominately moral denotation — is sufficient. This discussion has in the meantime been resolved definitely in the sense that the idea of partnership is to be joined by that of society and that a "science of the structure and order" of society and state is indispensable. According to a formulation by the Committee on Citizenship Training in Baden-Wuerttemberg, the social studies are intended as a "prerequisite for comprehending politics". Still, this comprehension will continue to be imperfect until the static, institutional approach is supplanted by a treatment adequate to the dynamics of social and political developments, and until the phenomenon of power in social and political relationships receives a suitable appreciation in the teaching of social studies. This demand has been being advanced for a long time by educators like Weinstock, Weniger, Litt and others, but it is satisfied in only a small number of programs of study. A portion of the teaching profession adheres to the German Idealistic tradition of education and considers power to be the very embodiment of evil. For this reason, the same teachers are in danger of failing to oppose it with sufficient resistance when it is evil. They have little inclination to attribute to this aspect the weight that it actually carries. "A balanced relationship of sober sense of reality and unbroken moral purpose" (Erich Weniger) will not result unless the spheres of political and of social activity are experienced as fields of necessary power controversies, though of course under democratic rules of the game. Social studies would deny the pupils a realistic image of the social and political world as it is if they were confined to teaching procedure and to the use of the implements of a democratically constituted social and political life. They must "bend efforts towards a comprehension of the situation of tension between the social conditions achieved and the elements of the age speeding ahead of them". "They must arouse awareness of them, analyze them, and in recording antitheses, seek to arrive at new syntheses" (Fritz Jonas). According to the appraisal by the German Committee on Training and Education mentioned before, the social studies must gradually develop the sense of relationship between justice and power, liberty and education, ideas and interests, and thus provide preparation for political action on the basis of personal responsibility and decision".

In the programs of studies, which in fact have the character of directives, this conception of the social studies is to be found sometimes in greater and on occasion in reserved clarity. It is understandably difficult to ascertain to what extent this conception is being followed in the schools.

Yet it can, for instance, be determined that there is a considerable degree of compliance with the recommendations of a number of programs of studies not to teach social relationships as a static subject, but instead to provide opportunities to experience their dynamic character in the form of personal inquiry in the community, administrative institutions, plants, and social and economic establishments of the immediate and more distant environs. In a number of schools, it has been possible to accomplish this in ways ranging up to a sort of sociological field investigation. The reports in this respect disclose that such forms of personal activity are unusually educative and stimulating to the pupils' sense of the arrangements, relationships and developments in social and political life.

Equally positive comments cannot be made concerning all of the textbooks as were made in regard to the programs of studies. Many of them are confined in scope to the presentation of subject matter and to the study of institutions and behavior from the standpoint of testable items of knowledge, on the obviously illusory theory that the material acquired through learning will convert itself automatically, so to speak, into ability to form judgments and decisions, or in fact into proper social and political action. With few exceptions, the conception of the social studies established in some programs of studies has not yet gained admission to the textbooks. Instruction based on such books will afford the pupil no enlightenment concerning the contradiction between an idealistic "science of harmony" in regard to society and politics and the harsh realities, which will then inevitably be disappointing. This is extremely dangerous to the creditability of social-studies instruction. "Social myths" have no educative effectiveness. This applies to the observation that a number of books basically envisage a pattern of patriarchal social relationships, to which some modern corrections are then attached. Perceptions of decisive importance for comprehension of the age and its problems — such as that of the sociologist Alexander Ruestow concerning the connection between the deficient integrating force of the Weimar Republic and the "hyperintegration" of Nazi dictatorship — have apparently not yet become sufficiently respectable for the schools.

It will take many more years before a uniform clarification of the objectives of the social studies in the secondary schools can be formulated and can take its proper place, and before a clarification of this kind will then be implemented both in the planning of instructional aids and in actual school practice. In the meantime, the social studies will remain in the stage of experimentation.

Political Training as an Objective
of the Schools in Present Day Life [1]

By Ernst Matthewes

If at the present time there is general mention of the necessity for political training, and if political training is, without hesitation, equated with training for democracy, then on the basis of experiences in the past, there is an inclination to detect therein an objective of political powers which would like to win the minds of the younger generation in order to maintain their dominating position. It is therefore understandable that in the demand for political training, there is here and there a fear of an encroachment of alien intentions upon the educational mission incumbent on the schools.

Now, there can be no doubt that the political training of youth would be justified even if democracy were felt to be nothing more than the form of political life appropriate to our age and our situation. It happens to be a part of the school's mission to prepare young people for life, including the task that awaits them as members of the body politic. The thing that makes this task a vital matter is that not only our nation, but the entire world is at the present time engaged in a controversy that permits no one simply to wait and see as a bystander. The will to take political decisions must now be demanded of everyone, including those who have located the focal point of their human existence in non-political fields.

In order to perceive the pedagogical benefit of political training and its place in the general mission of the school, it will not be permissible to judge democracy exclusively according to whether it copes with the political issues of daily life, and if so, to what extent. Instead, the question must concern the image of man upon which it is based, and it must be investigated whether this image is in keeping with what our era, and hence the school, has to accomplish in order to educate human beings.

Of course, it must not be overlooked that in the actual course of history, democracy is formed more powerfully by the claim to power of the groups rising from below than by the intention of implementing any specific conception of man in the political sphere. The cognition of democracy and of politics as a whole would be led in an erroneous direction if it were to be denied or to be reluctantly admitted only with a bad conscience that political action is associated with the will to power. Yet democracy's claim to represent an adequate political system can be justified only if it is possible to answer in the affirmative the question whether its pattern for the formation of political opinion and volition is sufficiently well-founded in the intellectual and anthropological senses.

One aspect of democracy is that it does not honor the claim of any one person or any one group of persons to have sole possession of the proper insight concerning what is to be done, though they may be distinguished by ancestry, property and education, or by power. Instead, democracy presumes a multiplicity of political tendencies and a constant interplay of forces among them as a necessity for arriving at a realization of the proper course.

---

[1] Excerpts from: *"Politische Erziehung als Auftrag der Schule in der Gegenwart."* Hamburger Lehrerzeitung (Teachers' Magazine). Vol. XII, No. 13, 10 September 1959.

This conception upon which democracy is based — that a realization of the proper course can be found only through a multiplicity of opinions — reveals an essential characteristic of political training. Because democracy not only permits a variety of possible interpretations, but requires and demands them, and because as a result the individual in a democracy cannot arrive at valid inferences from thought processes alone without his fellows, political training (if it is training for democracy) trains the pupil to develop his thinking constantly on the basis of contact with other conceptions. Consequently, in political training, the encounter with other conceptions originates not only in an obligation to admit the tenability of other opinions, but in an inherent objective necessity to do so. It is the perequisite for obtaining results.

Yet the distinction between democracy and non-democratic systems of life must not be limited to a distinctive way of thinking. That would be neglecting the historical derivation of democracy and its inherent reality in favor of a formalistic approach. The historical volition of democracy arises out of the demand by the lower classes to assign to themselves the same share in decisions as higher ones.

A political theory has no intrinsic value as a truth. Its validity depends upon the extent to which it elicits a volitional tendency on a large scale. It is a mistake if it does not prove its mettle in the eyes of the common man, even if it is flawless in its train of thought.

There can be no doubt that the great controversy between East and West, by whose issue the future of mankind will be determined for a long period of time, will in the end be decided in favor of that side which succeeds in meeting the expectations of the common man in life which come out of the depth of human existence.

Political training will not be able to fulfil its actual missions unless it is perceived on every level, that political thinking aims at decisions and can arrive at political realizations or political behavior only in conjunction with the will to choose. The view of political training is not that of observation and does not originate in the intention to gain familiarity with institutions, interrelationships and political conceptions, but results instead from the will to make a choice.

Of course, the young person should not himself make decisions at this early age. He lacks the necessary experience and maturity of judgment. But such a decision should be the goal of his political training. All his thoughts should tend in the direction of decisions. The pupil must realize that the citizen's task does not only consist in fitting into the community, preserving rights and fulfilling duties, but in finding a political volition and gaining political convictions, because everyone is subject to responsibility in the eyes of the history of his times and none can be excused from it. In no case may social studies, study of the constitution or study of general ethics in associating with others, be permitted to supplant training for political volition, on the assumption that the inclination towards politics comes about of itself as soon as an adequate knowledge and a decent social behavior has been acquired.

Anyone who has ardently come to grips with dictatorship as a personal experience is able to identify the essential characteristics of totalitarian rule. Anyone who is moved by the social needs, of his time acquires a feeling for the underlying social forces of his era. Anyone who is struggling to institute a national state, will comprehend what forces are inherent in the national impulse of emergent nations. Anyone who in the field of politics has suffered his way with tremulation through the tension between

A Meeting at the Europa-Haus at Marienberg

Photo: Bundesbildstelle Bonn

Pupils at the Visitors' Gallery of the Bundeshaus (Federal Parliament) in Bonn

Photos: Bundesbildstelle Bonn

power and ethics, will recognize the significance accruing to this polarity. On the other hand, anyone who maintained the attitude of "wait and see" during these controversies, under the impression of being able to trace relationships more clearly by not taking sides, will not acquire the systematizing power to separate essentials from non-essentials and movements from the welter of marginal phenomena. He will face the infinite multiplicity in helplessness: Political interrelationships can only be recognized through the will to take the side of the good cause. Yet in school, the pupil is supposed to acquire a body of knowledge without being given the power of orientation necessary in order to assimilate the subject matter and analyze it thoroughly.

The pupil must be aware that it is unworthy of human beings to "wait and see" how matters develop. He must be aware that the individual can meet the test of his mission in the world only if he seeks the path to what is right and just among the events of his age, and is also willing to follow it, and if he especially senses the obligation to come at all times to the aid of those who are in distress. But the must acquire the power to carry out this mission of his within the given circumstances of this world. He must not ease his task by seeking to see reality other than it really is.

Even though democracy recognizes the multiplicity of conceptions and in fact considers them necessary, it still does not as a result become the realm of unbounded subjectivity, inhibited only by ethical requirements. That is precluded simply by the fact that the politically conscious individual refrains from professing a certain conviction for purposes of lending expression to his personal inclinations and characteristics. Instead, he pledges loyalty because he is in favor of the cause and strives to achieve a just solution for it which he believes serves all men and thus goes beyond his personal sphere. This affirmation of objective validity in politics evokes the question of where political toleration must draw the line beyond which a tendency of political volition loses entitlement to recognition.

The gauge for toleration or rejection arises solely out of the demand that man should be the end and purport of political volition and must not be misused as a means. A political volition in which man is merely a tool, a thing and an apparatus excludes itself from the scope of political toleration.

Without undue restriction of the breadth of possible political tendencies, it can specifically be said with respect to the present that any political view may exercise a claim to a right of being recognized only providing that it serves the free self-determination of the human being, peace and a just social system. Within this framework, all political tendencies must be given the liberty to compete with one another as to the best solution, and it must be left to each individual to choose the tendency he favors.

Understanding with respect to political issues must come from below, and that means from within, out of the little fellow's sphere of life and out of his relationship to the events and forces of his era.

The school consequently cannot arouse political volition by making the pupils imagine what they would do if they were Minister or Mayor. All of the material prerequisites for doing so are lacking. Instruction would deteriorate into capriciousness and neglect the obligations binding on every individual. Instead, the question must be what the inconspicuous individual must do in his own little sphere, using his limited resources, in order to do justice to his responsibility in the light of the trend of events. The desperate question of many Germans as to the element in which their own guilt for the collapse consists, leads to the crux of political training. The answer often heard: "I did not know: I was not in favor of it", is a subterfuge because it intends to admit the validity of a historical guilt only on the part of the ruling circles, but is not willing to acknowledge the responsibility of the individual and of everyone.

The individual enters history through political reflection and decision. Political training awakes the pupil's sensitivity to the impelling forces in the events of his era. He receives an inkling of the responsibility to which the individual is subject in the eyes of history as a whole. Yet this responsibility can only be taught if he realizes the way in which daily existence is inextricably bound up with overriding decisions, and if he is aware that a feeling for major decisions can only be discovered on the basis of the contingencies of daily life. Political training must be rooted in concern for everyone's right to live, and it must teach comprehension of the fact that the individual's expectations from life can only be fulfilled in an arrangement of the whole.

This interlocking of immediate tasks with decisions oriented to the whole, gives political training sound roots and morally binding character at the same time. It keeps the pupil both from wanting to satisfy urges of the moment through politics and from considering it a process that does not affect him in his everyday life. He will learn that the individual is called upon to avoid rejecting his era's demand and that there is no calamity in history that is not due to a failure by man.

It is amazing how rapidly a school class that is consistently trained to examine political convictions as to their tenability in everyday life, and to regard issues of the day in the light of their significance for the whole, develops a sound, incorruptible feeling for what is valuable and what is inferior, and how surely it can distinguish blatherskites from serious persons, impostors from believers, and half-truths from truths.

In political training, the class finds the field in which to pursue its longings for a life of fulfilment, provided they are not unclear, vague promises, and to develop enthusiasm for a cause that raises them above the immediate ends, and yet, provides an answer to the needs of the day. In political training, the young people become aware that there is no Golden Age in which all worries and distress are eliminated, but that on the other hand human existence is more than a meaningless groping from instant to instant. They come to realize that it is subject to an order of growth that joins all men of good will together and provides the footing and direction of all aspirations.

Through political training, the young person can be shown in an impressive way that every era seeks the fulfilment of its own meaning, that the fulfilment of meaning emanates from the matters immediately at hand has to prove its worth in them, but that the seriousness, on the basis of which all individual decisions are made, is in the last analysis, determined by an obligation indicating a timeless entity and finding its foundation there.

It is a fact, proved by experience, that individuals who have found their way to political volition articulated in this manner are shaped for life and are distinguished by a particular responsibility in non-political spheres as well.

What Does "Digesting the Past" Mean?

Report of the

Conference of Educators of November 6 and 7, 1959

in Wiesbaden

arranged by the

German Coordinating Council

FOREWORD

The German Coordinating Council is putting this document, embodying a report on its Conference of Educators of 6 and 7 November 1959, in Wiesbaden, in the hands of the public because of the realization that in all parts of our country, a growing number of teachers are concentrating more and more attention on the search for vived depictions of the recent German past and for fundamental, practical guidance concerning effective programming of the relevant instruction. At the same time, this record is intended to serve as a principal basis for continuing the work of the Coordinating Council and its Committee of Educators, particularly in view of our firm intention to convene educators' conferences of this kind in 1960 and the following years as well.

May the record presented on the following pages be read in the spirit of the message expressed recently: that especially in this field, knowledge is very necessary in order to be able to alert men's consciences and keep them alert.

German Coordinating Council of
Societies for Christian-Jewish Cooperation

Frankfurt-on-Main

What Does "Digesting the Past" Mean?

By Theodor W. Adorno

The question, "What is meant by digesting the past?", requires explanation. It originates in a formulation that has made itself highly suspect during the past few years as a slogan. By "digesting the past", it is generally not inferred that the past is processed in earnest and its path is cleared through lucid awareness. Instead, the desire is to relegate it to a dead file and perhaps even to erase it from memory. The gesture indicating that everything should be forgiven and forgotten ought to be reserved to those who suffered injustice; but instead, it is practiced by the partisans of those who inflicted it. During a scientific controversy, I once wrote: The skeletons ought to be left in their closets; otherwise there will be resentment. But the tendency toward an unconscious and not so very unconscious defense against guilt, associates itself with the idea of digesting the past to such an absurd degree, that it is sufficient grounds for contemplations concerning a sphere that even now radiates such horror, that one hesitates to call it by name.

There is the general desire to get away from the past. This is on the one hand justified, because it is impossible to live at all in its shadow and because there is no end to horror, if guilt and force are perpetually supposed to be repaid only by guilt and force. On the other hand, it is unjustified, because the past which it is intended to escape, is still highly vivid. Nazism lingers on, and to this day we do not know whether it is lingering merely as a specter of something that was so monstrous that it did not actually die when it met its death, or whether it even failed to meet its death — whether the willingness to inflict indescribable horror persists in human beings as it does in the conditions that surround them.

I do not intend to take up the question of neo-Nazi organizations. I consider the lingering existence of Nazism within democratic life to be potentially more menacing than the lingering existence of Fascist tendencies counter to democracy. Infiltration specifies an objective reality. The only reason why penumbral figures stage a come-back to positions of power, is because conditions are favorable for them. In contrast, the continuing existence of extreme right-wing groups — who moreover actually suffered a smarting rebuff not long ago at the hands of the electorate in Bremen and Schleswig-Holstein — seems to me to be only a surface phenomenon.

It is an uncontested fact that in Germany, it is not only the so-called "incorrigible" quarters that have failed to master the past. In this conjunction, there is constant reference to the so-called "guilt complex", often with the intimation that it was in fact only created as a result of contriving a collective German guilt. Incontestably, there are neurotic factors on a large scale in respect to the past. There are gestures of defense at points where there is no attack; vehement emotions at places that hardly justify them in reality; lack of emotion in regard to the most serious aspects; and not rarely, simple repression of what is known or half-known. For instance, in our group experiment, we have frequently observed that in recollections of the cruelties of deportation and mass-murder, mollifying expressions and euphemistic circumscriptions are chosen, or that a vacuum of speech forms around them. An evidence of this tendency is the generally accepted, almost good-natured idiom "Kristallnacht" (night of breaking glass) for the pogrom of November 1938. There are a very great number of people who said they knew nothing about the occurrences at that time, although Jews were vanishing left and right and although it is hardly to be assumed, that the people who observed what was happening in the East, always maintained silence concerning something that must have been an unbearable burden for them. It is probably permissible to imply that a proportion exists between the gesture to the effect of "having known nothing about it" or at least vague and fearful indifference. At any rate, the dedicated enemies of Nazism were very precisely informed from the very beginning.

We are all acquainted with the additional inclination at the present time to deny or to minimize what was done — as difficult as it may be to grasp that human beings should not be ashamed of the argument that it really was at the most five million Jews who were gassed, and not six million. Another irrational response is the widespread balancing of guilt, as though Dresden had been recompense for Auschwitz. In the advancement of such equations, and in the haste to excuse oneself from personal reflection through countercharges, there is from the very outset, something inhuman; and combat operations in war — whose model was moreover Coventry and Rotterdam — are hardly analogous to the administrative murder of millions of innocent persons. Even this innocence, the simplest and most plausible thing of all, is contested. The enormity of what was committed speaks for itself: The naive mind consoles itself by saying that a thing like this could not have been done unless the victims had provided some cause or other, and this vague "or other" may then run rampant according to the individual whim. Blindness shrugs off the glaring disproportion between highly fictitious guilt and highly actual punishment. Sometimes the victors are made into originators of what the losers did at a time when the latter themselves were still on top. Those who tolerated Hitler's seizure of power are supposed to be responsible for his crimes, and not those who cheered for him. The senselessness of all of that is actually an indication of something that has not been mentally mastered, an indication of a wound, though the idea of wounds ought rather to apply to the victims.

What with all of this, however, the mention of a guilt complex has something untruthful about it. In psychiatry, from which it has been borrowed and whose associations it drags along with it, it means that the feeling of guilt is abnormal, out of keeping with reality, "psychogenic", as the analysts call it. By the use of the word "complex", the impression is conveyed that this guilt — the feeling of which so many people are fending off, are trying to overcome by activity and are contorting by rationalizations of the most foolish kind — is no guilt at all, but exists only in them and in their psychological constitution. The horror of the past is euphemized into a mere whimsy in the minds of those who feel affected by it. Or is guilt itself, in fact, only a complex? Is it abnormal to burden one's mind with what is past, whereas the healthy and realistic individual merges with the present and its practical ends? That would infer the moral from the verse, "And it is the same as though it had never been", which was written by Goethe. However, the verse is uttered at a decisive point in *Faust* by the Devil in order to reveal his inmost principle, the destruction of memory. Those who were murdered are now to be cheated of the sole thing our powerlessness can bestow upon them: recollection. Of course, the callous attitude of those who want to hear no more of it would be in harmony with a potent historical tendency. On several occasions, Hermann Heimpel has spoken of a shrinking consciousness of historical continuity in Germany, a symptom of the same social tendency towards weakening the self which

Horkheimer and I have already tried to trace in *Dialektik der Aufklärung* (Dialectics of the Enlightenment). Empirical observations of the order that in many cases, the younger generation that no longer knows who Bismarck and who Kaiser Wilhelm I were, have confirmed the loss of history.

The German development did not become flagrant until after the Second World War, but it corresponds to the American people's divorcement from history, which has been evident since Henry Ford's pronouncement, "History is bunk" — the horrifying prospect of mankind without a memory. It is not simply a product of degeneration, not a form of reaction by a mankind that, as it is said, is inundated with stimuli and can no longer cope with them. On the contrary, it is inevitably bound up with the progressiveness of the middle-class principle. The middle-class society is universally subject to the law of barter, of tit for tat in calculations that are precise and actually have no carry-over. By its very nature, barter is timeless, like logic itself, just as the operations of mathematics in accordance with its pure form preclude the factor of time. In the same way, the specific element of time is hence disappearing from the process of industrial production as well. In an increasing measure, the latter follows identical, ramming and potentially simultaneous cycles, and hardly requires accumulated experience any longer. Economists and sociologists like Werner Sombart and Max Weber, have relegated the principle of traditionalism to the feudal forms of society, and that of rationalism to the middle-class ones. Yet that means nothing less than that recollection, time, and memory are being liquidated by the advancing middle-class society itself, as a sort of irrational carry-over, in a similar manner as the advancing rationalization of industrial production systems reduces categories like that of the period of apprenticeship along with other carry-overs of artisanry. If mankind is divorcing itself from recollection and exhausting itself short-windedly in adaptation to whatever happens to be current, then it is thus reflecting an objective law of evolution.

The forgetting of Nazism is, in fact, to be understood far more properly on the basis of the general social situation, than on that of psychopathology. Still, the psychological mechanism in the defense against embarrassing and unpleasant memories serves purposes highly suited to reality. Those applying this defense betray the purposes themselves when, for example, they point out practical-mindedly that the unduly specific and persistent recollection of past events might be detrimental to Germany's standing in the outside world. Zeal of this sort cannot be well reconciled to the saying of Richard Wagner (who was nationalistic enough himself) to the effect that being German meant doing a thing for its own sake, unless the thing itself is intended *a priori* as a business deal. The eradication of memory is more probably an accomplishment of the unduly alert consciousness than its weakness in face of the overweening power of unconscious processes. In this forgetting of what is hardly past, there is an accompanying note of rage over the fact that before it will be possible to make the others feel they are mistaken, it will be necessary to convince oneself of the erroneousness of something that everyone knows.

It is certain that the impulses and patterns of behavior I have cited, with which all of you are unquestionably familiar from countless observations, are in themselves not directly rational, since they distort the facts to which they relate. Yet they are rational in the sense that they exploit existing social tendencies and that anyone who reacts in this manner is sure to be in harmony with the spirit of the times. A response of this kind is directly enhancing to advancement. The person who avoids having useless thoughts, does not throw a monkey-wrench into the works. It is advisable to talk in the same vein as the one which Franz Böhm so penetrantly called "non-public opinion". Those who conform to a morale, that, it is true, is held in check by official taboos, but merely possesses all the more virulence as a result, show at one and the same time that they "belong" and that they are independent men. After all, the German resistance movement failed to find any mass basis, and such a basis has hardly been conjured into existence by the defeat. It is of course permissible to hope that democracy has struck deeper roots now than following the First World War. In a certain sense, Nazism, which was anti-feudal and quite middle-class, even paved the way for democratization against its will. Both the Junker caste and the radical workers' movement have disappeared. For the first time, something like a homogeneous middle-class situation has been brought about.

Nevertheless, in Germany, democracy came too late — that is, it did not coincide chronologically with the peak of economic liberalism — and it was introduced by the victors. It is hardly likely that this will fail to have any effect on the people's relationship to democracy. This fact is rarely voiced straightforwardly, because for the time being, everyone is too well-off under the democratic system and because it would be counter to the community of interests with Western democracy (especially America) institutionalized in political alliances. Yet the bitterness against re-education speaks distinctly enough. It is probably possible to say that the system of political democracy is, it is true, accepted in Germany as what is called "a working proposition" in America, that is, as something that functions and so far has permitted, or in fact, brought about prosperity. But democracy has not been assimilated to the point that the individual really identifies himself with it as his own cause and has an awareness of being an active participant in political processes. Democracy is felt to be one system among many, as though there were a choice on a sample-card between Communism, democracy, Fascism and monarchy.

It is not, however, felt to be identical with the nation itself as a manifestation of its political enfranchisement. It is assessed according to its success or lack of success, in which the individual interests then participate, but not assessed as a unity of individual interest with the interest of the community. Moreover, the delegation of the will of the people to the parliament in modern mass states makes this amply difficult. In Germany and among Germans, one often encounters the peculiar saying that the Germans are not yet mature enough for democracy. An ideology is made out of one's own immaturity, not unlike the adolescents who, when they are caught at any kind of acts of violence, place the blame on their characteristic of being teen-agers. The grotesque nature of this line of argument indicates a serious inconsistency of mind. The individuals who play upon their own naïveté and political immaturity in such unnaive fashion, are aware, on the one hand, of already being politically enfranchised and of the fact that it is up to them to determine their destiny and institute their society in liberty. On the other hand, they are brought up short by the fact that hard and fast limits are placed on such action by circumstances. Because they are not able to pierce these limits with their own ideas, they ascribe the impossibility that in reality is inflicted upon them to themselves, to the big-shots or to the others. It is as though they were splitting themselves once again of their own accord into a participant and a bystander. Aside from that, the definition of the ideology prevailing at the present time is that the more the individual is at the mercy of objective configurations in circumstances over which he has no control or over which he believes he has no control, the more he subjectivizes this powerlessness. In keeping with the slogan, "It is just up to the individual", he attributes to the individual everything that results from the circumstances. Consequently, the circumstances remain unaffected in turn. In the language of philosophy, it might well be said that the self-estrangement of society is reflected in the people's foreignness to democracy.

Among the objective configurations, perhaps the most urgent one is the development in international politics. It seems to be providing a belated justification of the aggression Hitler committed against the Soviet Union. Since the Western world as a unit makes its dispositions substantially on the basis of defense against the Russian menace, there is the appearance that the victors of 1945 had destroyed the proven bulwark against Communism only out of foolishness, in order to build it up again just a few years later. From the readily accessible, "Hitler always told them so", a quick path leads to the extrapolation to the effect that he was also right in other respects. Edifying Sunday orators are the only ones who might be able to skip over the historic portent of the fact that in a certain sense, the conception that once prompted the Chamberlains and their following to tolerate Hitler as a jailer against the East has survived Hitler's downfall. That is really a fateful development, for the threat on the part of the East to devour the piedmont called "Western Europe" is in deadly earnest. Anyone who fails to resist it makes himself literally guilty of repeating the Chamberlainian appeasement. The thing that is forgotten is merely — merely! — the fact that this very threat was only provoked by the action of Hitler, who brought down upon Europe precisely the thing he was supposed to prevent by means of his war of expansion. Even more so than the fate of the individual human being, the fate of the political network, is an inter-relationship of guilt. Yet resistance against the East has an innate dynamism arousing factors that are things of the past in Germany. This is true not only in the ideological sense that the slogan of the struggle against Bolshevism has from the very beginning provided camouflage for those who have no more use for freedom than does Bolshevism itself. It is also true in terms of reality. According to an observation made during the Hitler period, the organizational impact of the totalitarian systems forces something of their own nature upon their opponents.

So long as the economic gradient between East and West persists, the Fascist variety has greater chances among the masses than does the Eastern propaganda. On the other hand, of course, it is not yet considered urgent to adopt the Fascist *ultima ratio*, either. Still, the same types of individuals are susceptible to both forms of totalitarianism. It would be an altogether false judgment of the character types dependent upon authority if they were to be formulated on the basis of a particular politico-economic ideology; neither are the well-known fluctuations by millions of voters between the Nazi and Communist parties in the period before 1933 any coincidence from the point of view of social psychology. American investigations have revealed that this conformation of character is not so extensively equated to politico-economic criteria. Instead, these types are defined by traits such as thinking in terms of power and powerlessness, a certain rigidity and incapability of reacting, conventialism, conformism, inadequate personal reflection, and finally, an altogether inadequate capability to observe. They identify themselves with actual power as such, in priority to any particular content. Fundamentally, they have only a feeble ego and therefore require identification with large collective groups and support by them as a surrogate. The fact that at every step one re-encounters figures of the kind presented in the film, "*Wir Wunderkinder*", is contingent neither upon the vileness of the world nor upon alleged peculiar qualities of German national character, but upon the fact that those conformists who *a priori* have an instinct for the levers of all machines of power are identical with the potential followers of totalitarianism. Moreover, it is an illusion to think that the Nazi regime meant nothing but fear and suffering, although it did mean that even to a large number of its adherents. There were countless people who were not at all badly off under Fascism. The brunt of terror was aimed at only a few groups, which were defined relatively precisely. Following the crises undergone in the period before Hitler, the predominating feeling was that, "it will be taken care of", not merely in the sense of the ideology of "Strength through Joy" excursions and flower-boxes in factory rooms. In contrast to *laissez-faire*, the Hitler system actually did protect its own to a certain degree against the calamities of society to which the individual was abandoned. It was a violent precursor of the present control over crises, a barbarian experiment in the governmental management of industrial society. The much-cited integration, the all-embracing intensification of the social network, also provided security against the universal fear of falling through the meshes and sinking. For countless persons, the frigidity of the condition of estrangement seemed to have been abolished by the warmth of togetherness, regardless of how it was manipulated and turned on. The national community of the unfree and unequal was also a lie that at the same time was a fulfilment of the middle-class dream, though of course of a dream that had from the beginning been a bad one. It is quite true that the system offering such bonuses contained the seeds of its own destruction. The economic prosperity of the Third Reich was to a large extent based on armament for the war that brought on the catastrophe. Yet that weakened memory of which I spoke balks at taking in these arguments. It tenaciously glorifies the Nazi phase during which the dreams of power were fulfilled for those who were powerless as individuals and did not consider themselves to be anything at all except in the form of a collective power of this kind. No analysis, regardless of how lucid it may be, can retroactively do away with the reality of this fulfilment and the impulsive energies that are invested in it. Even Hitler's gamble was not so irrational as it seemed at that time to the average liberal intelligence or seems today to historical hindsight concerning the failure. Hitler's calculation to exploit the temporary advantage of intemperately forced armament with respect to the other states was by no means foolish in the light of what he was after. Anyone who pictures to himself the history of the Third Reich, particularly of the war, will constantly feel that the individual moments when Hitler was the loser were coincidental, and that the only thing that was inevitable was the course of the whole, in which the greater technological and economic potential of the rest of the earth, which did not want to be conquered, in fact did carry the day — to a certain extent a statistical inevitability and by no means a logical series of moves and countermoves. A persisting sympathy with Nazism does not actually have to expend too much sophistry to persuade itself and the others that it could just as easily have turned out the other way round at any time, that there were simply some mistakes made, and that Hitler's downfall was a coincidence of world history which the spirit that moves the world will possibly correct at some future time.

In the subjective direction, that is, in the psyche of the individual, Nazism heightened collective narcissism — to put it in plain language, national arrogance — beyond measure. The narcissistic impulses of the individual, which the hardened world promises less and less satisfaction, but which continue in existence without

diminution as long as civilization denies them so many things, find surrogate satisfaction in identification with the whole. This collective narcissism was maimed in
the extreme by the collapse of the Hitler regime. Its impairment occurred in the
realm of mere actuality, without the individual having made himself consciously
aware of it and thus having mastered it. This is the meaning, accurate from the
point of view of social psychology, of the term "unmastered past". Even the specific
panic which according to Freud's theory in *Mass Psychology and Analysis of the
Ego* occurs when collective identifications break down, failed to materialize. Unless
one abandons the great psychologist's instructions, there is only one inference
remaining: that those identifications and the collective narcissism were not
destroyed at all, but continue to exist in secret, smouldering unconsciously and
therefore with particular power. Inwardly, the defeat has been ratified with just as
little completeness as after 1918. Even in the face of obvious collapse, the collective
body integrated by Hitler held together and clung to chimerical hopes, such as
those secret weapons, which, in reality, the other side had in its possession. From
the point of view of social psychology, the expectation could be appended that
the maimed collective narcissism is lurking in hope of being repaired and grasps
at anything that first of all brings about harmony in the conscious mind between
the past and the narcissistic desires, but if possible even goes so far as to model
reality in such a way that the impairment mentioned before is cancelled out. Up
to a certain point, the economic recovery, the consciousness of "how efficient we
are", has brought this about. But I doubt whether the so-called "economic miracle"
— in which, it is true, everyone participates, but about which everyone at the same
time speaks with a certain mockery — actually reaches so deep in the socio-
psychological sense as one might think in times of relative stability. For the very
reason that hunger continues to prevail on entire continents, although it could be
abolished by means of technology, no one is quite able to enjoy prosperity. On
the individual level, for example, in films, there is malevolent laughter when
someone is having a good meal and tucks his napkin into his collar. In the same
way, humanity grudges itself a comfort which it most profoundly detects to be paid
for even now at the price of shortages. Resentment burdens every good fortune,
even one's own. Satiation has become a term of deprecation *a priori,* whereas the
only thing bad about it is that there are people who have nothing to eat. The
alleged idealism which particularly in today's Germany so automatically assaults
the alleged materialism owes the thing that it often considers its profundity only
to repressed instincts. Hatred against comfort causes discomfort about prosperity
in Germany, and the past mellows into a tragedy in the light of this discomfort.

Yet the latter by no means comes only from murky springs, but in turn from much
more rational ones itself. The prevailing prosperity is one caused by a boom. No
one has confidence in its unlimited duration. If one seeks consolation in the fact
that occurrences like those of "Black Friday" in 1929 and the ensuing economic
crises can hardly repeat themselves, then there is implicit in this consolation the
trust in a strong governmental power which is expected to provide protection
even in the event that economic and political freedom do not function. In the
midst of prosperity, even during the temporary shortage of manpower, probably
the majority of individuals feel like potential unemployed persons, like recipients
of charity, and for this selfsame reason like bystanders rather than participants in
society. That is the entirely legitimate reason for their discomfiture. It is obvious
that at a fitting moment, it can be compressed in the opposite direction and abused
in order to renew the calamity.

At the present time, the Fascist ideal no doubt merges with the nationalism of the so-called "underdeveloped countries", which are no longer called such, but instead are being called "developing countries". Even during the war, sympathy with those who felt they had been slighted in imperialist competition and themselves wanted a portion, was manifested in the slogans about the Western plutocracies and the proletarian nations. It is difficult to distinguish whether this tendency has already joined the anti-civilizational, anti-Western undercurrent of the German tradition and if so, to what extent; or whether in Germany, as in other countries, a convergence of Fascistic and Communistic nationalism is assuming outline. Nationalism today is obsolete and up-to-date at the same time. It is obsolete because in view of the mandatory combination of nations into great blocs under the supremacy of the most powerful among their number, the form dictated simply by evolution in weapons technology, the sovereign individual nation, at least in advanced continental Europe, has lost its historical substantiality. The idea of the nation, which once embodied the economic unity of interests of the free and independent bourgeois in contrast to the territorial confines of feudalism, has now become itself a barrier to the obvious potential of society as a whole. At the same time, nationalism is on the other hand up-to-date in the sense that the traditional idea of the nation, which is eminently well-furnished from the psychological point of view and is always the expression of the community of interests within international economy, is the only one having power enough to harness hundreds of millions for purposes they cannot consider to be directly their own. Nationalism does not quite believe in itself any more; yet it is politically necessary, being the most effective means of causing people to insist upon conditions that are obsolete from the objective point of view. As a result — being something not quite good in its own eyes and purposely blind — it has now assumed traits of cruelty. Since nationalism was the heritage of barbarously primitive tribal systems, it has of course never been completely lacking in such traits; but they were restrained so long as liberalism confirmed the right of the individual as a condition for collective welfare, in practice as otherwise. The witch-trials did not take place during the flowering of Scholasticism, but during the Counter-Reformation, and hence at a time when the thing they were intended to substantiate actually was already undermined. Analogously, nationalism did not become completely sadistic and destructive until an epoch in which it was already toppling. Even the anger of the Hitlerian world against everything that is different — nationalism as a system of paranoid mania — was of this caliber. Today, the power of attraction of these same traits is hardly any smaller. Paranoia — the persecution mania that leads to persecution of those upon whom it projects the things it would like for itself — is contagious. Collective hallucinations such as anti-Semitism provide confirmation to the pathology of the individual who proves no longer equal to the world and is thrown back upon an ephemeral inner kingdom. According to the theory of the psychoanalyst Ernst Simmel, they may in fact excuse the individual semi-maniac from becoming a complete one. As openly as the maniacal aspect of nationalism is today revealed in the intelligent fear of renewed catastrophes, this aspect is equally conducive to nationalism's propagation. Mania is the surrogate for the dream that humanity will arrange the world humanely, which dream the world is persistently driving out of mankind's mind. On the other hand, sentimental nationalism is accompanied by everything that came to pass between 1933 and 1945.

The fact that Facism persists, that the digesting of the past has not succeeded to this day, and that it has degenerated into its caricature of empty, cold forgetfulness, is all a result of the continuation of the objective social premises that engendered Fascism. Fascism cannot essentially be explained on the basis of subjective dispositions. The economic order and, according to its pattern, economic organization, continues to assign the majority to dependence upon circumstances over which they have no power, and to tutelage. If they want to live, they have no choice but to adapt to the given situation and to fit in. They have to cancel the selfsame autonomous subjectivity to which the idea of democracy appeals and are able to survive only if they forfeit their self. Penetrating the interrelationship of the factors of mirage requires of them the effort and labor of perception, which they are hindered from gaining by the arrangement of life, notably the cultural products industry, which has expanded to the point of totality. The necessity of such adaptation — to the extent of identification with what exists, what prevails and power as such — creates a totalitarian potential. It is intensified by the dissatisfaction and the rage which the same compulsion to adapt produces and reproduces. Because reality fails to yield the self-determination and finally the possible happiness that the term democracy of itself promises, they are indifferent to it, unless they secretly hate it. The form of political organization is sensed to be inappropriate to social and economic reality. In the same way that the individual has to adapt, he wishes that the forms of collective life would adapt. This is all the more the case since such adaptation is expected to result in the streamlining of the polity as a gigantic enterprise in the by no means very peaceful universal competition. Those whose actual powerlessness continues cannot support anything superior even as an appearance. They would rather be rid of the obligation to exercise an autonomy which they suspect they cannot emulate anyway and throw themselves into the melting-pot of the collective ego.

I have been exaggerating the dark side, following the maxim that in today's world, exaggeration is the only medium of truth by and large. Do not misinterpret my fragmentary and often rhapsodic remarks as "Spengleristics", which themselves make common cause with calamity. It was my intention to characterize a tendency concealed by the smooth façade of everyday life before it washes over the institutional dams placed in its way for the time being. The danger is objective and not primarily located in the individual. As I said before, there is a great deal to indicate that democracy, together with everything that is associated with it, has a more profound hold on the individual than in the Weimar period. By stressing what is not so apparent, I have been neglecting what good judgment in fact must keep in mind: the fact that within German democracy up to the present time, the life of the society has been reproducing itself more fortunately than at any time in the memory of man, and that is the relevant aspect from the point of view of social psychology, as well. The assertion that German democracy (and hence the real digestion of the past) would not be doing badly, if it only had time enough and a lot of other things, would certainly not be unduly optimistic. The only thing is that the conception of having time implies something naive and at the same time detrimentally contemplative. We are neither mere onlookers of world history, who are at liberty to disport themselves more or less unhampered within their large-scale areas, nor does world history itself, whose rhythm increasingly assimilates to that of catastrophe, appear to grant its objects the necessary time in which everything would become better by itself. That points directly to democratic pedagogy. Enlightenment concerning happenings must particularly counteract a forgetfulness that is only too inclined to pair up with justification of what has been forgotten. This may, for instance, occur through parents who have to hear from their children the embarrassing question concerning what the Hitler business was all about. In order to absolve themselves, if for no other reason, these parents then mention the favorable aspects and say that it actually was not so bad at all. In Germany, it is in fashion to deprecate political instruction. It certainly could be improved; yet educational sociology even now has data that drastically prove that wherever this instruction is conducted with seriousness and not as a burdensome obligation, it does a lot more good than it is generally considered capable of doing. If the objective potential of a persistence of Nazism is however taken as seriously as I believe it must be, then this fact also indicates the confines of enlightening pedagogy. Whether this pedagogy be sociological or psychological, in practice it probably reaches only those who are accessible to it and therefore are hardly susceptible to anti-Semitism. Yet on the other hand, it is by no means superfluous to strengthen this group, too, through enlightenment against non-public opinion.

On the contrary, it could well be imagined that out of this group, cadres are formed whose activity in the most various spheres then does succeed in reaching the whole; and the chances for such a development are the more favorable the more conscious they themselves become. It is self-evident that enlightenment will not be content with only reaching these groups. The question as to the extent to which it is advisable during efforts at public enlightenment to take up the past, and as to whether the very insistence on doing so does not bring about balky resistance and the opposite of what it intends to produce, is very difficult and burdens us with the utmost responsibility. I intend to leave this question to one side. To me, it seems more likely that what is in the consciousness could never entail so much peril as what is in the unconscious, semi-conscious and para-conscious mind. Probably the essential point is the manner in which past events are projected: whether the mere reproach is the conclusion or whether horror is conquered through the power to grasp even it. Of course, this would require an education of the educators. Such action is prejudiced to the utmost by the fact that at the present time, the field that is called Behavioral Sciences in the U.S.A. is hardly in existence at all in Germany, and if so, then only on a very small scale. It should urgently be demanded that, at the universities, there should be an increase in a type of sociology synonymous with the historical investigation of our own period. Instead of expounding with secondary profundity on the existence of man, pedagogy ought to assume the very task whose inadequate treatment is made the point of such zealous charges against re-education. In Germany, criminology has not yet attained at all a modern standard. The thing that must particularly be kept in mind is psychoanalysis, which is being displaced now as before. It is either completely lacking or it has been supplanted by trends claiming to overcome the much-castigated 19th century, but actually falling short of the Freudian theory and possibly twisting it into its own opposite. Its precise and undiluted command is more mandatory than ever at the present time. Hatred against this theory is directly identical with anti-Semitism, by no means simply because Freud was a Jew, but because psychoanalysis consists in precisely the critical personal reflection that puts the anti-Semite into a burning rage. Though the possibility of carrying out anything like a mass analysis may be slight, simply because of the time factor, it would be equally curative, if strict psychoanalysis were to be given its institutional place and its influence on the intellectual climate in Germany, even if this influence consisted only in making it a matter of course to refrain from striking out at others, preferring to reflect upon oneself and one's own relationship to those whom the recalcitrant consciousness is accustomed to striking. In any case, endeavors to work against the objective potential of calamity by subjective means should not be content with rectifications that would hardly be able to overcome the inertia of the thing that is to be taken in hand. There is hardly much benefit in, let us say, references to the great accomplishments of Jews in the past, however true they may be. On the contrary, they smack of propaganda. But propaganda, the rational manipulation of the irrational, is the privilege of the totalitarians. Those who are resisting them should not imitate them in a manner that inevitably would only put them at a disadvantage. Encomiums for the Jews, singling them out as a group, provide too much for anti-Semitism themselves. The only reason why anti-Semitism is so difficult to refute, is because the psychological economy of innumerable individuals required it and presumably still requires it even today in a subdued form. Anything that is always done propagandistically remains equivocal. I have heard about a woman who, after she had attended a performance of The Diary of Anne Frank, exclaimed, but they should have at least let the little girl live. Certainly even this level of understanding is good as a first step. But the individual case, which was to represent the terrible whole, simultaneously became a substitute for that very whole, which the woman forgot. The exasperating thing about such observations was and is that it is not possible to advise against presentations of the Anne Frank play or similar things even for their sake, because their effect — regardless of how much one is dissatisfied with them and how much they seem to flout the dignity of the dead — in fact does accrue to the potential of the better. Neither do I believe that too much is accomplished through joint meetings, meetings between young Germans and young Israelis, and other friendship functions, however desirable such contact continues to be. In these matters, there is too much stress on the premise that anti-Semitism has some substantial connection with the Jews and could be combated through specific experiences with Jews, whereas the genuine anti-Semite is on the contrary defined by his inability to undergo any experiences or to heed any arguments. If anti-Semitism is primarily founded on the objective factors of society, in the mind of the anti-Semite, then in keeping with the Nazi joke, the latter would have had to invent the Jews, if there had been none at all. If it is intended to combat anti-Semitism in the minds of the subjects themselves, not too much should be expected of references to facts which they often do not allow to get through to them or which they neutralize by saying they are exceptions. Instead, the argumentation should be applied to the subjects who are being spoken to. They should be made aware of the mechanisms that cause race prejudice in their minds. Digesting the past as a process of enlightenment is essentially this type of application to the subject, reinforcement of his self-confidence and hence of his self. It should be coupled with the recognition of those indestructible propaganda tricks that are keyed precisely to those psychological predispoisitions whose existence in the individual mind we have to assume. Since these tricks are rigid and are limited in number, it causes no unduly great difficulty to isolate them, disclose them, and use them as a sort of protective inoculation. The problem of the practical implementation of this kind of subjective enlightenment could probably be solved only by a joint effort on the part of teachers and psychologists who do not use the pretext of scientific objectivity to sidestep the most urgent task facing their disciplines today. Still, in view of the objective force back of the persisting potential, subjective enlightenment will not suffice, even if it were attacked with an entirely different energy and in entirely different dimensions of depth. If it is intended to counter the objective danger by objective means, then no mere idea will suffice, not even that of liberty and humanity, which simply does not mean too very much to the individual in its abstract form, as has in fact been learned in the meantime. If the Fascist potential establishes a connection with his interests, however limited they may be, then the most effective counteragent will continue to be the reference to his interests, his immediate ones — illuminating because of its truth. It would be really making oneself guilty of woolgathering psychologism, to ignore, in the course of such efforts, that the war and the suffering it brought down upon the German population was, it is true, not sufficient to eradicate that potential, but still influences judgment concerning it. If the individual is reminded of the simplest fact of all — that overt or covert Fascist revivals cause war, suffering, and need under a system of compulsion, and presumably Russian domination over Europe in the end; in a word, that they amount to a policy of catastrophe — then that will impress him more profoundly than the reference to ideals or even to the sufferings of others, which, as the old Larochefoucauld was aware, are always relatively easy to cope with. In view of this perspective, the present malaise means hardly anything more than the luxury of a mood. Despite all suppression, Stalingrad and the bombing nights have not been forgotten to the extent that it would be impossible to make the connection between a revival of the policy that brought them about and the prospect of a Third Punic War understandable to everyone. Even if that is possible, the peril persists. The past will not have been digested until the causes of past events have been eliminated. The only reason why their spell has not yet been broken, is because the causes continue in existence. Anything aiming at arrangement of the whole in a form more worthy of human beings, whether it be theoretical or in the sphere of practical politics, is at the same time resistance against a relapse.

* * * * * * * * *

Question

What possibility do you see of reducing universal fear? In our group it was stated that by using rational means, it is not possible to make headway against emotions, and that it is necessary to differentiate between older and younger people, as this kind of fear is probably less prevalent among the latter.

Professor Adorno

I believe that irrationality, which actually arises from rational considerations, has always been a very dangerous thing, especially so, since mankind is not to be changed through rationalistic endeavors. Irrationality, which is to a certain degree rationally based, is exactly what I depicted in my short characterization of propaganda and through which an element of untruthfulness and ambiguity, which I consider very precarious, enters the work which we have at heart. Now, I would say, and I am in complete agreement with you, that it is not possible to overcome very powerful irrational forces simply by using rational means. In fact, I have said so again and again in my address. To put it in psychological terms, there are, simply on the basis of instinct, far too many powerful urges for something like race prejudice to allow for eliminating them by making the individual realize that Rothschild did not start the Battle of Waterloo and that the "Protocols of the Elders of Zion" are fabrications. By the way, the fact that the universal refutation of the "Protocols" has not had the slightest influence upon their effectibility is, in itself, a very interesting matter. Yet that does not condemn us to irrationality; instead, the conclusion to be drawn from this, is actually what I have tried to characterize as application to the subject. That means that care should be taken to be rational, not in the superficial sense of simply confronting with the truth the individuals who believe in some untruthful things for irrational reasons but in the sense of helping them to gain through reflection an insight concerning what they can do in this direction. And at any rate that would seem to me to be the very most important objective of a training beginning relatively early in childhood: rationality not in the sense of rationalistically harping on the facts, but rationality in the sense of bringing the individual to personal reflection and thus preventing him from becoming a blind victim of his impulses. Besides, I do not of course intend to speak in favor of a deadly, supercilious rationalism, but I am only of the opinion that the irrationality to which I am referring here as a very grave danger, is not in fact embodied in the circumstance that people have drives, passions, and so forth; but instead the irrational aspect — and perhaps I have not stressed that sufficiently — in the penetrating sense that I meant of being something negative, is those drive impulses and those emotions that have been repressed (I am simply compelled to speak in Freudian terms at this point), that ferment in the dark, and that then come out again in distorted, wrenched, altered forms as aggression, projection, and displacement together with all of these things with which we are so familiar, and which cause so much trouble. Accordingly, if I have mentioned that irrationality is to be resisted, I am referring to irrationality in the suppressed, wrenched sense which was first depicted by Nietzsche in very magnificent fashion and was then analysed by Freud in detail. Consequently, I do not mean that human beings should become merely cold rationalists and should have no more emotions and no more passions. On the contrary, if they have more emotions and more passions, then they will have less prejudice. I would like to say that if they allow for more of their emotions and passions in their own hearts, instead of exerting on themselves the same pressure that society exerts upon them, then they will be much less evil, much less sadistic, and much less pernicious than they now are.

Question

You have mentioned that the social circumstances in our country have changed only superficially. But have these changes not in fact had a more profound effect?

You said that objective social premises, were moreover, a necessary but not a sufficient cause of Nazism. That gives rise to the question as to what is to be considered the fundamental cause for the emergence of Nazism and whether an overcoming of Nazism is possible, if the objective social premises have remained the same.

Professor Adorno

I do not remember having said the necessary but not the sufficient cause. You probably have in mind that I said I did not consider Nazism a specifically German phenomenon. In this regard, I would therefore say that the adequate explanation in fact was probably the critical worsening of the economic and political situation in Germany, as well as certain theological traditions. In addition, I actually have the feeling that in contrast to the militant nationalism found at every step in the

Germany of the Weimar Republic, people have somehow become more harmless. Above all, certain traditions of a definite militant nationalism have become weaker. Now, that probably does have a bearing upon the fact that Imperial Germany plays only a very small part in the collective memory, as well as upon the objective fact that no one on the whole any longer seriously thinks that we can victoriously defeat France and that no one can any longer imagine that Germany can conquer the world, simply because of the realities. In this respect there is something that has already changed, I believe — that is, in the sense of a genuine personal relationship with America which I do not at all ascribe to the so-called American influence, but to the fact that in countless aspects the structure of German society is simply coming closer to the American one. On the other hand, I would say the decisive cause of Fascism — that is, the concentration of economic and administrative power on the one side and complete powerlessness on the other — has made decided progress upon the Germany of 1933. Yet I should at any rate think that this altered subjective potential can actually have just as much strength as it does in America. After all, America has for 50 or 60 years been the land of trusts and trust legislation — this enormous amalgamation of economic power — and in spite of that, the democratic rules of the game have functioned so well in America, that consequently the danger of Fascism at the moment in America is in any case very slight. I do not see any reason why at least a possibility of this kind should not apply to our country as well, which, as we know, is populated by "scorched children" in every sense of the word. Excuse me, the answer has turned out to be a little complicated and complex; but the world happens to be so complex, and it is not possible to bring these matters down to an unequivocal formula in every case.

The Treatment of Anti-Semitism -
An Example of Teaching Practice *

by Wilhelm Langenbeck

Our acknowledgement of political education as the decisive task of educational effort derives from the realization that we are, today, all ensnared in a universal net of correlated events from which there is no escape. The standpoint of man today reflects his position in the world.

However heartily all responsible teachers may agree in theory with this need of the hour, a very different picture is presented in regard to putting this into practice in the schools. Although the best minds of our times are untiring in their efforts to enlighten and warn us that "we are living in an alarmingly late hour of democracy" (T. Litt), this urgent call finds little response.

Among the many "red hot pokers" of historical and sociological teaching, the problem of anti-Semitism is one of the hottest.

---

*) From *Gesellschaft — Staat — Erziehung*, No. 4, 1960.

8

It does, indeed, need to be approached carefully. The recent anti-Semitic demonstrations in the Federal Republic and the keen reaction among the public, however justified and necessary this might have been, not only for the sake of our reputation in the world, but still more as a documentation of our democratic way of life, may help perhaps to evoke anti-Semitic sentiments among juveniles.

These apprehensions are based upon what every teacher may experience in the classroom today when he begins to talk about Jews in Germany. The very least he has to expect is the surprised question "But what is a Jew? Please show me one, single Jew".

The teacher must force himself to face the disturbing question: "Am I really acting in the proper sense of integrating the juvenile as a citizen of our modern society with its majority values, in selecting as teaching material this intellectually insubstantial subject of anti-Semitism, surrounded as it is by so many ideologies?" Does not the need of the hour call rather for political education which — to adapt a remark by H. Heimpel — "achieves a deepening of knowledge in one quarter, while remaining silent on what has not been understood"?

But the raising of this question involves the risk of very great danger.

I shall try to characterize this by quoting from three prominent historians:

"If we do not take a constructive view of the past, we shall be driven either to mysticism or cynicism... If the careful, intelligent, and highly-educated man does not succeed in drawing a lesson from history, this will be done for him by the unscrupulous and the impertinent"[1].

"Forgetting and suppressing has never been the way to recovery. It is not looking away from a thing, but looking at it which liberates the soul"[2].

"We are living in a state of chronic paralysis of memory . . . we forget history because we have lived through too much history . . . a barrier exists between us and the past . . . the barrier of guilt — guilt in the form of silent acquiesence and cooperation"[3].

Three prerequisites are to my mind necessary, if we are to combat the dangers of a wrong interpretation, both of the human relationship and of the matter itself, and not bring grist to the millers of the past.

1. The treatment of anti-Semitism must be dissociated from the exclusively National Socialist perspective, and looked at from the point of view of its relationship to the whole history of European intellectual tradition.

2. A comprehensive grasp of the subject cannot be gained primarily from the political aspect, but should be attempted rather from the psychological, sociological, and social sides.

3. If our educational aim with regard to these questions is to awaken moral impulses through the presentation of objective facts, then it would seem advisable, particularly in the treatment of the problem of anti-Semitism, to begin by "tuning in" to the subject. A realization of the extent of the Jewish catastrophy might be evoked in the minds of the pupils through certain definite demonstration material such as the Warsaw ghetto, the proportion of Jews among the population of some outstanding German town before 1933 and after 1945, The Diary of Anne Frank, etc.

---

[1] G. Barraclough, *History in a Changing World.*
[2] H. Rothfels, *Zeitgeschichtliche Betrachtungen* (Contemporary Observations), Göttingen, 1959.
[3] H. Heimpel, *Der Versuch mit der Vergangenheit zu leben.* (The attempt to live with the past). *Frankfurter Allgemeine Zeitung,* 25 March 1959.

It should be made clear, however, that these questions deal with a universal ethical problem, which presents a challenge to the free man as being responsible for the decisions which he voluntarily makes, and not only with a stimulating, but a fundamentally antiquated interpretation of the past.

The extent of the wholesale destruction which was the outcome of a preconceived ideological outlook cannot be impressed upon the consciousness of one's hearers just by giving dates and statistics; these facts can only be brought home to them by a direct appeal to them on the emotional level.

Once this basic realization has become firmly impressed on the minds of the young, the further treatment of the subject should be absolutely objective, sober and critical. It goes without saying that the most diverse legitimate methods of teaching may be employed in solving this task. Two of these, which have already been tried out in school practice, will be presented here for discussion.

In order to preclude any possibility of misunderstanding, it is necessary to begin with a clear definition of terms. What does the treatment of anti-Semitism as a phenomenon of the European intellectual tradition mean? Up to what point should the teacher try to support the postulate that anti-Semitism is the outcome of a historical process, and how can he significance of anti-Semitism in National Socialist ideology be objectively dealt with?

I think that one method of attack[4]) is to include this special question in the general treatment of the subject of ideologies, since the various motives which produced the old type of anti-Semitism as a common European symptom were of religious origin (Paul Tillich: *Antijudaismus*). With the progressive secularization of all spheres of life it also became a pivotal and focal point of the ideologies.

We thereby make a definite contribution towards the breaking down of ideologies, no matter what their type or content. Since, especially in recent times, ideologies in European history have been the cause of so much blood-shedding, tears, and the deepest humiliation of mankind, the working out of their origins, their effect, and the part they play in the social and community life of mankind gains in supreme importance.[5])

It should suffice to pursue the question of the significance of ideology in totalitarian systems of government in a limited form and with special reference to our particular subject. According to Jaspers, ideologies, as a system covering the whole field of knowledge, give mankind the illusion of wholeness, i.e. the possibility of achieving a basically sound world through his own efforts. This claim of ideology to wholeness seems to many people in a certain general human and social situation to be nothing more nor less than salvation. It is an "informational" system which contains ready-made answers to all sorts of questions, and concrete instructions on behavior, which bar mankind from venturing upon free action. By including reasonable emotions and wishes in this system of information, an ideology assumes the steering function in man's community life which is otherwise held by the social opinion of the world.

[4]) A second possibility, which cannot be followed up here, may be mentioned briefly. In order to do away with certain prejudices against the Jews, that they are afraid of work, hagglers, cowards etc., it should suffice to point to the enormous achievements of the State of Israel and the energy of its inhabitants. The existence of this state, which was created ten years ago, is constantly threatened by inimical neighbors. This demands from its inhabitants constant alertness and readiness for combat, to a far greater degree than could ever have been conceived by the spritual founders of the national state. (cf. Martin Buber, *Israel und Palestina*, Zürich 1950; Helmut Gollwitzer: *Israel und wir*, Berlin 1958).
[5]) The author wishes to acknowledge his debt to Klaus Kippert's *Unbewältigte Vergangenheit: Der Nationalsozialismus, Hessische Blätter für Volksbildung*, Vol. 5, 58.

National Socialism represents the racial-biological bridling of collectivism. The biological value becomes absolute, is promoted to the central value of the system, and becomes consolidated in the conception of race (intellect and consciousness being auxiliary functions of the biological). As in Bolshevism the individual becomes the exponent of his class, so in National Socialism he becomes the exponent of his race. The final ideological aim is the creation of a racial collective, a nation which is racially superior and thus designated for world mastery.

In Italian Fascism, the nation appeared as the central value of the system. The ideological basis and justification of the authoritarian and totalitarian state as a pure power organization derived from what was known as the "national cultural heritage", Roman, Latin, Italian.

After the supreme importance of the central value in the problem of ideologies has been made clear, the special nature of National Socialism should be investigated, starting with the basic question: "Was National Socialism merely the necessarily logical outcome of certain fundamental forces which had become established long before in German history? Are general European symptoms present in addition to the specifically German origins?" And finally the heretical question: "Can National Socialism in any way be said to derive from an intellectual tradition?"

In principle a warning must be uttered against the danger of over-simplification in attempting to find an answer to this question. If the scholarly literature on this problem is consulted, we find completely contradictory opinions, as presented by Friedrich Meinecke, Gerhard Ritter, A. Ruestow, Eva G. Reichmann, etc.

Within this framework of the totalitarian system of government and the special function of ideological conception, the appraisal and importance of racial collectivism as the final stage of a historical process of development must be understood and elucidated.

For this purpose a summary account of the treatment of the Jewish community in the medieval world may suffice.

To avoid repeating in a diluted form information which has been appositely and convincingly expressed elsewhere, I should like to refer here to a number of works devoted to this subject.[6]) The common features of these may be described roughly as follows:

There has always been a Jewish question in European history, because the Jews have always formed a foreign minority among other national groups. From the sociological point of view, anti-Semitism may be interpreted as an example of group tension. The Jews had preserved their medieval forms of life and even later lived in religious, cultural, legal, social, and local segregation.

Whenever a state of tension, pressure or injustice prevailed, Jewry was in danger and exposed to persecution. We only need to recall the major Jewish catastrophes during the Crusades, at the time of the Black Death, or at the end of the Reconquest in Spain.

The similarity of circumstances between these basically different events will become apparent to us if we recall the social situation out of which they developed.

---

[6]) Eva G. Reichmann: *Die Flucht in den Haß, Ursache der Judenkatastrophe (Hostages of Civilization)*, Europäische Verlagsanstalt, Frankfurt, o. J. — Kurt G. Grossmann, *Die unbesungenen Helden (The Unsung Heroes)*, Arani Verlag, Berlin, 1957. — Adolf Leschnitzer: *Er ist wie Du (He is Like you)*, from the early history of anti-Semitism, München 1956. In addition, contributions in *Gesellschaft — Staat — Erziehung*. Helge Pross: *Die ideologischen Ursachen des Antisemitismus*, Vol. 3, 1957. — Franz Böhm: *Über den Antisemitismus*, Vol. 6, 1958.

It was not just by chance that the expulsion of the Jews from Spain coincided with the abolition of the last remains of Moorish domination and with the discovery of America.

Even the plague in the 14th century, which was first regarded as an Act of God, against which man was helpless, coincided with economic depression in many parts of Europe, and produced an overwhelming state of fear, with an accompanying growth of hatred of foreigners. For this reason people were all the more ready to believe the assertion that the Jews, as alleged well-poisoners, were the cause of the disaster.

In spite of all the persecution of the Jews in the Middle Ages, there was never any suggestion of their annihilation, since this would have been incompatible with the medieval conception of the world which believed that "for reasons connected with the Divine scheme of salvation, the Jews must continue to exist until the end of all time"[7]).

Wherever, at the time of the Renaissance, Jews were distributed only sporadically among foreign nations, hate and aversion were directed against other minorities, which were then condemned to the same fate as the Jews.

A. Leschnitzer is quite correct in pointing out that the history of the French Hugue-nots from the Edict of Nantes in 1598 until its repeal in 1685, and the ensuing years of horror, in many respects resembled that of German Jewry.

Following upon the ideas of the French Revolution (Emancipation), the Jews were faced with the problem of assimilation, and the Jewish community was compelled to dissolve itself.

The anti-Semitic movement has not, however, been triggered off by social problems alone. Economic grounds and purposeful subjective steering were also required. In the course of the 19th century tensions surrounding the position of the Jew in society lessened, but at the same time there was a growth in collective aversion, which was fed from other sources.[8])

The bitter competitive struggle in free trade economy resulted in the development of malice against the Jews among the victims of this struggle, principally artisans and wage-earners, since the Jews possessed a particular business ability for free competitive trade and acted everywhere as the pioneers of capitalism.

Further stages in a retrogressive trend which counteracted a genuine integration of the Jewish and non-Jewish elements of the population, were Nationalism, Roman-ticism and the control of politics by interested groups of persons. The nation came to take the place of humanity. One's fellow-men were no longer looked upon as brothers, but only as the members of a nation-wide family. Anyone who wished to free himself from his moral obligations towards the abstract idea of humanity, in favor of an instinctive preference for his own race, professed to embrace Romanticism.

Nationalism, above all in its more radical form of expression, contains the danger characterized in the well known words of Grillparzer as the development "from humanity to bestiality through nationality".

The result of the Industrial Revolution was that religious values depreciated con-siderably on the continent. The secularization of many spheres of life led to dis-

---

[7]) A. Leschnitzer *loc. cit.*, p. 161.
[8]) In an essay entitled *"Staat und Judentum"*, Walter Rathenau criticized his co-religionists very sharply: ... "closely linked with one another, strictly secluded from the outside world, they live in a voluntary ghetto, not as a living branch of a nation, but as a foreign element within its body".

belief and doubt in the average man, and produced in him an increasing perplexity. He was torn between diverse spiritual and moral possibilities, and sought for a mainstay. In a century which worshipped science, this mainstay was afforded by education, but in many cases it was an incomplete education, which left people open to the attacks of propaganda. All too easily did man become the victim of pseudo-scientific delusions.

The century of emancipation was, however, not only the century in which life became more complicated and the old values were replaced by new, it was also a century which saw an enormous growth in population, principally among the lower proletarian classes.

According to the strictness of his sense of responsibility, the politician was more and more tempted to desist from the use of reasoned arguments upon his voters. In regard to the exploitation of anti-Jewish slogans by political organizations and individuals in the last third of the 19th century, attention may be drawn to the book by Paul Massing: *Rehearsal for Destruction. A study of Political Anti-Semitism in Modern Germany*[9]).

With reference to Germany we can say that in the first two decades of our century a spontaneous anti-Semitism existed only in a mild form, but that there was a latent anti-Semitism which could be aroused at need.

It is true that Jews were still *déclassé* in the German social scale, as recognized with sorrow by Walter Rathenau in his essay *"Staat und Judentum"* (The State and Jewry). Walter Rathenau was one of the most prominent representatives of his race, who strove with every fibre of his being to bring about a synthesis between the fact of Jewish birth, and life as a German citizen.

> "During the youth of every German Jew there comes a painful moment which he remembers all his life: the moment when he first consciously realizes that he has been born into the world as a lower-ranking citizen, and that no merit and no proficiency on his part can save him from this position."[10])

It would be wrong to deduce from this, however, that active anti-Semitism was very virulent in Imperial Germany and under the Weimar Republic. In this connection it seems to me appropriate as a teacher of history to make some comments on an essay by *Professor Böhm*.[11])

While agreeing with the convincing basic attitude of the writer, I think I am right in saying that we shall not succeed in convincing our audience if we allow ourselves to be dominated by an impulsive attitude which is conditioned by painful personal experience.

Our task in the schoolroom must not consist in releasing counter-emotions; we should first of all attempt within the bounds of possibility to carry out an objective examination of actual facts of the case.

To tell the naked truth, is not the same in school as presenting one's own view of the case. In this way we shall never induce the young to master the problems of anti-Semitism intellectually and enable them to work out an objective criterion of judgment. This is, however, what is required if normal impulses are to be awakened in young people. These can never be supplied from outside by the teacher, but

[9]) Paul W. Massing, *Rehearsal for Destruction*, A study of political anti-Semitism in modern Germany, New York, 1949.
[10]) Quoted by Helmuth Boettcher: *Walter Rathenau, Persoenlichkeit und Werk*, Bonn, 1958, p. 70.
[11]) *Gesellschaft — Staat — Erziehung*, No. 6, 1958.

must develop spontaneously from the intrinsic morality or immorality of the subject under discussion.

If we present our own view of the case there is the danger of arousing prejudices against the sincerity of the teacher's opinion.

Every discussion in school always involves an initial risk, and the first steps along the path to truth are taken in the dark.

If we can accept the point of view that, for the first quarter of our century, the German people was the least anti-Semitic of the European nations, the following difficult question arises:

How was it possible that such excesses took place in Germany within barely a decade?

Both Eva G. Reichmann and Helge Pross are of the opinion that no adequate explanation is possible for the enormity of the Jewish catastrophe in the Third Reich, and that we are faced here with a phenomenon which cannot be unequivocably elucidated.

Perhaps we can approach closer to the heart of this problem, however, if we bear in mind that the National Socialist theory and practice of the annihilation of the Jews was considered as a commandment of Providence, as an essential prerequisite for the Nazi scheme of salvation, for the establishment of the "Thousand-Year-Reich". I am convinced that there is a concrete answer to the question raised above, but in attempting to answer it, we shall need to dig down to deep rooted causes which originate before the Age of Enlightenment, but which only in our century released the forces which would accomplish the monstrous.

Let us first of all recollect the universal process of secularisation, which, during its century-long course, detached more and more spheres of life from religious influence and proclaimed their autonomy, which would eventually lead to all forms of human life becoming independent, resulting in the complete disintegration of society.

The full extent of this process remained concealed as long as these disintegrating tendencies did not attack the conception of the Christian man.

In a deep-delving religious and sociological sketch entitled "Die Krise der Säkularreligionen" (The Crisis of the Secular Religions), Otto Heinrich von der Gablentz[12]) shows that, among the major secular religions, the "religion" of National Socialism can only be understood from the development of the state in the 19th century. He explains that the high priest of this religion was Jean Jacques Rousseau, who insisted that every man was nothing more nor less than a citizen, and who denounced as egoism any objection against this complete absorption in the civic function.

According to Rousseau there is no room for the individual, no res privata.

With regard to the further shaping of National Socialism as a substitute religion, it should be remembered that the legitimate princes, who ruled by the appointment of God, had been attacked by the heir of the French Revolution, Napoleon, and that in the struggle for liberation against Napoleon the slogan had been "With God for King and Fatherland". What was more obvious than that these words should be understood in the inverted form, that what was done for King and Fatherland was also done for God.

---

[12]) Die Krisis der Saekularreligionen in Kosmos und Ekklesia, Festschrift fuer Wilhelm Staehlin, Stauda Verlag, Kassel, 1953.

This attitude led to the sanctification of a national war of liberation, to a crusade. (E. M. Arndt: "It is no war of crowns, it is a crusade, a holy war."). In the next generation this led to all national wars being sanctified.

In the 19th century Nationalism was at first a secret religion, but was proclaimed quite openly. The catchword *sacro egoismo* points to the switchover.

National Socialism was the first to elevate the nation publicly to a sacred position. "A nation cannot be national, it must be nationalist with all the vehemence which extremity contains". This statement of Hitler's was made possible after the prophet Heinrich von Treitschke, as the proclaimer of the national power state, and Houston Stewart Chamberlain, as the race ideologist, had preceded him.

The time for such ideas had already become ripe at the turn of the century, when — at least theoretically — the long-maintained European claim to sovereignty over the planet, collapsed.

The social revolution of the classes and all the problems arising from it could no longer be kept under control by political means. Social progress, the development of social and political organizations, could no longer keep pace with the rapidity of technological development. Conditions of anarchy developed out of this incongruence, and the oppression of rising and sinking social classes of the population and of national and religious minorities.

The results were agitation, discrimination, oppression, and progroms.

After 1938 we can observe in National Socialist despotism an ever stronger tendency to transfer the stress upon the cult of the nation to the cult of the Leader. There is no more talk of the eternal nation, but of the "Thousand-Year Reich", the myth of "Blood and Soil" was replaced by the myth of Adolf Hitler. In other words, the prolitarian religion of "the nation" becomes a religion of "history", and it becomes clear how much has been borrowed from Jewry and Mohammedanism, the antitype of which it gradually evolves.[13]

National Socialist *Weltanschauung* was a loose collection of inconsequent ideological elements, each of which fulfilled a special function of wishful thinking.[14]

The broad mass of the population had received a very much diluted and distorted version of German intellectualism. Of the ideas presented to them, they had absorbed merely the crudest, mostly easily understood parts which made the greatest appeal to the instincts.

This process is basically the same in all countries. But what distinguished the education of the German masses from the education of those neighbors who shared the intellectual heritage of the West, were the elements of education which were fed to them by their teachers.

"It makes a difference whether children and juveniles are brought up in an atmosphere permeated with Christianity, or whether religious instruction is merely one more school subject ranking somewhat arbitrarily alongside the others; whether the spirit of the school is inspired with a readiness to help the weak and the abased, or whether the law of the jungle, which is practised in the school playground, is

---

[13] Two and a half thousand years ago, at an earlier stage of their development, the Jews did away with the sacrifice of animals, and set prayer in its place. In the 20th century it became possible for the heirs and successors of that small Isrealite group which has meant so much in the history of human civilization, to become first of all enslaved, and then to be offered as human sacrifices to the Nordic gods (A. Leschnitzer, *Saul und David*, p. 174).
[14] We are here consciously taking as our model ideas which Eva G. Reichmann has developed in the work of hers already cited, because out of the mass of possible motives these seem to us to be the most convincing.

acknowledged as the decisive rule of life. It makes a difference whether the natural love of one's own country and one's homeland goes hand in hand with the recognition of freedom, equality, and fraternity for all mankind, in acknowledgement of individual national characteristics, or whether it rests upon the sub-structure of the claim to dominate the world as the *Herrenvolk*.

It makes a difference whether the instruction is permeated with respect for the joy of responsibility, clarity of understanding, civic freedom and progress, or for the cult of a "deep emotion", which "is hard to express in words", but which "never lets one down", for blind obedience, which does not criticize, for the cult of the State, and the "God-willed sub-ordinations" of a fancifully-depicted medieval class system.

Although we are far from succumbing to the delusion that the recognized ideal conceptions of the West have succeeded in shaping people in accordance with these high demands, we are all the same certain that the constant striving to approach these standards represents an educative factor of the first rank.

If this is neglected in education of youth, the resulting gap can never be filled.[15])

National Socialism found the expression for fear, envy, and hate, and so enjoyed the success of the unscrupulous demagogue. No longer did appeals to popular mass feeling serve a moral purpose. Even the idealistic embellishments of National Socialism were taken exclusively from the primitive amoral sphere.[16])

National Socialist propaganda took pains to give expression to these desires of the masses; it may be said that the first conception of National Socialism lay in such mass wishes themselves. The slogans and symbols were to make the masses feel that they were understood, and to appeal to their secret longings.

Which mass instincts did National Socialist propaganda try to satisfy?

1. The demand for work and bread.

Hitler was not able to supply these at once, but he relieved the weary, the despairing, and the downtrodden from all the burdens troubling their souls. He led them into the paradise of irresponsibility and childlike belief. He cut out conscience altogether.

2. For those who were weary of thinking and assuming responsibility, Hitler supplied an attractive substitute for thought: National Socialist dogma.

In order to prevent the revival of critical reasoning, Hitler surrounded his doctrine with all sorts of attributes, which he had learned from the hated, but also secretly admired Catholic Church. He created a pseudo-religion, in which he himself posed as Christ. But as well as feast days there is the workaday world with its troubles, and this might start people thinking again as to why the promises of salvation had not been fulfilled. An effective counter-symbol was therefore necessary, a devil.

This counter-symbol was the Jew.

The Jew was admirably suited as an anti-symbol against renouncement of thought and belief in authority; he was looked upon as a typical intellectual, an enemy to authority, a critic and agitator.

The masses felt the need of some guilty person they could accuse and hate. Their hate was not systematically conducted against the representatives of the old régime, which was gradually regaining a certain amount of sympathy, another outlet had to be found instead. It is true that there were other objects of hate as

---

[15]) E. G. Reichmann *loc. cit.*, pp. 219—222.
[16]) cf. Thomas Wolfe, *You Can't Go Home Again.*

well as the Jews; there was the "disgraceful Treaty of Versailles", the "enemy league", the Catholic monasteries, the communist regime, and several others.

But it would have been impossible to pillory former enemies or the Catholic Church or the socialist and communist workers as enemy No. 1. That would have resulted either in complications abroad or political commitments at home which could not be afforded. There was no fear of this with anti-Jewish agitation.

Anti-Semitism fulfilled three functions in National-Socialist propaganda: a) it supplied or illustrated the symbols, with the help of which mass instincts were to be satisfied; b) it made possible an opportunist appeal to all interested parties; c) it served to divert attention from real problems.

The fact that in March 1933, 44 % of the German people gave their votes to the NSDAP, should not lead people to draw the conclusion that this 44 % thereby declared itself in favor of an active anti-Semitism.

The question of whether the success of the poll was due to anti-Semitism, cannot be answered with yes or no.

At that time people had to a great extent lost the will to make up their own minds, and vacillated between a sense of inferiority and arrogance.

It may be assumed, however, that the greater proportion of the party hangers-on were subsequently converted to anti-Semitism. Even in the years when crowds rushed to join the party, acts of violence against Jews were rare, and the boycott of Jewish shops did not catch on.

> "Even those who in those years of crises professed to be anti-Semitic stated decisively that they were not against "the Jews" as living persons whom they knew, but they were against "The Jew", a mysterious and sinister figure, whom propaganda had succeeded in representing to them as the cause of all their ill luck."[17]

> If the masses had indeed obeyed, would not the bloodiest pogrom in all Jewish history, a second Massacre of St. Bartholomew, have taken place at once in 1933?

> "It is amazing that this pogrom had to be organized and took place by order — but not until November 1938."[18]

Let us try to sum up:
The anti-Semitism of the 20th century in Germany was primarily an exaggerated political anti-Semitism, which drew its special driving power from racial collectivism as the central element of National Socialist ideology.

Even though the trend towards a one-party state and the call for a "strong man" can be shown to be a European symptom which appeared early in the century, the particularly inhuman form, which the totalitarian system assumed in Germany, was made possible because, for the reasons shown above, the process of democratization had already been denaturalized and corrupted in its initial stages. Here we are thinking less of the growing power and significance of organizations and institutions — however powerfully their usefulness threatens the existence of the human individual — than of the structural changes which our industrialized age brought about, in the course of which the human factor has become increasingly submerged.

---

[17] E. G. Reichmann loc. cit., p. 280.
[18] A. Leschnitzer loc. cit., p. 153.

110

The most alarming symptom of this change is the slackening of moral energy.

May the lesson to be learned from the grievous experience of the persecution of the Jews in Germany not only awake feelings of shame and of active repentance, but still more, an unreserved readiness not alone to grasp the deep-rooted moral impulses behind human actions, but still more to apply this knowledge in dealing with present day situations.

No one can relieve us of the responsibility for our behavior in our own eyes and in the face of history. The truth remains, even where the Christian point of view, that man's existence is bounded by creation and the Last Judgment, is no longer accepted.

Jewry and Education [1]

"Jewry and Education — the presentation of Jewry in teacher training and in the classroom"[2]) is the title of a book published by the Ner Tamid Press, Munich, for the Federation of German Students' Organization, which has included the publication in its official series. The work consists in the main of material prepared by well-known experts who were brought together early in June at a conference in Bergneustadt to discuss the presentation of Jewry in teacher training and school teaching. The Federal President, Dr. Heinrich Luebke, referred to the publication when speaking on the occasion of the "Week of Brotherhood, 1960."

A preface written by Dietrich Wetzel, chairman of the Federation of German Students' Organizations, comments on the premises and conclusions of the work. The book analyzes, from the angle of their presentation of Jewry, the textbooks for history, German, and religion used in schools. A further chapter deals with teacher training in universities and teacher training colleges. A critical bibliography of 100 works already published on the subject provides suggestions for further study of the general problem. An attempt is made to define more closely the suggestions made so far for the presentation of Jewry in the teaching of history, religion and civics, and to provide guidance for the requisite revision of textbooks. Proposals are also made on arrangements for continuation of the work.

As a consequence there is no final adoption of a position, but rather an indication that there is a task to be performed which it will take some years to manage. The Federation of German Students' Organizations hopes that by publishing this work they will have provided practical suggestions and help for school and college teachers and for the students. It is also intended to arouse the interest of a wider public , as it deals with a subject that goes far beyond mere techniques of teaching.

---

[1]) From the *Bulletin des Presse- und Informationsamtes der Bundesregierung*, 20 Oktober 1960.
[2]) *Erziehungswesen und Judentum — Die Darstellung des Judentums in der Lehrerbildung und im Schulunterricht*, Ner Tamid Verlag, Munich, published by Verband Deutscher Studentenschaften, 1960.

Instructional Materials for the Social Studies *

Abundant instructional materials for the social studies are available for the teacher's reference and for use in school, in the form of books, pamphlets, periodicals, project folders, etc. There is above all no lack of information material for teachers and pupils. The initiative of individuals, agencies and publishers has found a broad field of activity in this respect during the past 10 years. Another factor is that besides printed materials, an increasing amount of tape recordings, records, slides, and films have been produced and have been employed in the schools. They provide detailed, universally understandable presentations concerning the aim and necessity of social studies; the purpose and limits of sociological perception; family, society, and state; community, Federation and *Laender*; justice and law; and economics and technology. Moreover, they generally take into account the alteration of the social system in the area of Soviet domination and the evolution from the national state to the community of nations. There is an abundant supply of explanatory pictures and statistics serving to illustrate procedures in society, politics and economics. International issues and relationships are presented. In these publications, there is an ample amount of practical aids to instruction, material on methods, and presentations concerning principles involved in the path from social and civic training to political education proper, from the condition of more or less interested citizenship to that of informed political awareness.

There is a special journal of social-studies teaching that offers papers on fundamental aspects, teaching examples, reports on practical observations and book reviews, and reflects developments in this entire area of teaching.[1]

For purposes of social-studies teaching, the journal of the German Society of Teachers of History, *Geschichte in Wissenschaft und Unterricht*[2] *(History in Research and Teaching)*, presents papers from the field of contemporary history and about important present-day social and political developments, as well as teaching examples.

It is not possible within the scope of the present study to list and appraise individually the textbooks used in the secondary schools of the *Laender* for the field of social studies. Since jurisdiction for education rests in the *Laender* and there is consequently no central, Federal Ministry of Education, the diversity of textbooks is unusually great, though most of the books are accepted in all of the *Laender*. Among the favorite topics are the rights of man and the position of the individual in community and society (in accordance with the definition by Toennies). A number of books examine the great social and political ideals influencing history and schemes for a perfect governmental and social system. The problem of freedom in and from the state and the ideals of equality, of partnership and of social and political justice are treated.

In most of the books, a great deal of space is devoted to the study of the constitutional system and of institutions: the organs of the state; the community; larger and smaller governmental sub-districts; government at the Federal and

*) From *Mitteilungen* of the Akademie fuer Politische Bildung, No. 3, April 1960 (containing a study concerning political education in the secondary schools in West Germany and West Berlin — a UNESCO project).

[1] *Gesellschaft — Staat — Erziehung.* Published by Messrs. Messerschmid, Minssen, and Seitzer. Verlag Ernst Klett und Moritz Diesterweg.

[2] Published by K. D. Erdmann and F. Messerschmid. Ernst-Klett Verlag, Stuttgart.

Laender levels; structure and function of parliament; the political parties; electoral law and systems; justice and administration; the churches; the labor unions; and the insurance arrangements. In the field of law, there are even occasional presentations of individual problems taken from civil law, criminal law, and criminal proceedings. The problems concerning the individual in the economy are uniformly dealt with in detail: work and profession; the purpose and the forms of economy (economic systems); protection and security for the gainfully employed; the enterprise and the trade associations; the problem of a just wage; capital; international economic interlocking; market and prices; economics and culture, etc.

Less frequent are, on the other hand, presentations concerning mankind in the strained situations created by politics, such as "Berlin, Island of Liberty", "The Revolt of June, 1953", "Reunification in the Western and the Eastern View", and "The Present Status of the Unification of Europe".[3])

Another type of textbook for the social studies that should be emphasized is the one whose aim is to provide source material for the pupil's use in forming his opinions. For instance, *Freiheit, unser höchstes Gut (Liberty, Our Most Precious Possession)*, is the title of a reader for the graduating classes of the Hamburg schools. It contains among other things comments on the idea of liberty in the ancient world, narratives by Pushkin, sayings (e.g. of Abraham Lincoln), and evidence given by resistance fighters under totalitarian regimes. Various Ministries and the Federal and *Land* Organizations for Civics also make important materials for the teaching of social studies currently available. These include particularly treatises on specific social, economic and political topics, and issues. In this regard, special mention should be made of the newspaper *Das Parlament*, issued weekly with a valuable supplement by the Federal Organization for Civics. However, it is difficult to determine the extent to which teachers and pupils make use of this informational and instructional material.

In the light of "social studies as a principle of instruction", the question arises as to the manner in which textbooks for the teaching of German, history, geography, biology and languages have absorbed social-studies subject matter. An examination of the relevant books does not provide a uniform impression. The requirements of the individual subject are of course in the forefront. Neither the possibilities of broadening into the social-studies scope offered by the body of knowledge nor those that would readily result if there were an honest desire for application of the social-studies principle are perceived in all instances. Yet the actual teaching practices cannot be deduced simply from the contents of the books. One of the concomitants of the principle is that the opportunities are grasped where they arise. In this regard, a great deal depends upon the teacher's readiness, academic horizon, pedagogical ethos and mental alertness. In teaching German, let us say, prose readings or dramas may be treated as mere tributes to esthetic literary culture, neglecting or omitting the social and political purports contained in them. That would be in contradiction to the social-studies principle. The pupil editions and readers do not indicate anything of this kind. Moreover, it is unmistakable that among the authors of textbooks, understanding for the necessity of social sciences is growing. For instance, the selection of prose readings in some books shows that the intention was to acquaint the pupil with the problems involved in situations of social conflict, with the condition of the younger generation following the war or with the inhumane nature of the totalitarian state. In geography

---

[3]) Examples taken from *Freiheit und Verantwortung*. Ernst-Kett Verlag, Stuttgart. (A study and exercise book on the Community, for pupils; one volume of the *Politische Bildung* series).

books, world economic problems are treated in the light of social and socio-political aspects, and the social and political problems resulting from geographic and biological factors are illustrated. In all of the history books, issues of contemporary history are treated in a manner appropriate to the respective age levels.

The tape recordings, records, slides, and films employed in the schools are mostly interpretations of documents of contemporary history, taken chiefly from the period of the Weimar Republic and from the Third Reich.

The entire field of the social sciences is dealt with by the educational broadcast sections that have been established at all radio stations and collaborate closely with the schools. Both in individual broadcasts and in entire program series that sometimes extend over long periods of time, the school broadcast schedules offer an abundance of subjects from all relevant fields. In this way, the school broadcasts have acquired a leading position with respect to both the principle and the subject of social studies. Nonetheless, observations permit the deduction that this modern auxiliary for the school is used most of all by the primary schools and least of all by the secondary schools. The reasons for this are numerous. It is easier to use the school broadcasts in a type of school where each class has its own teacher than in the secondary schools, which are characterized by the subject-teacher system. But the underlying reason is to be found in the conservative basic character of the German secondary schools, which have more difficulty in adopting modern methods of teaching and teaching aids, as well as modern subject matter. In fact they consider them to be prejudicial to their mission of education. This conservative character of German secondary schools is also evident in many textbooks, in which the predominating image of society is stamped by a social pattern that would be more appropriate to horse-and-buggy days than to the atomic era. There has been mention of the "Pickwickian milieu" that is sometimes still cultivated in those schools. Yet in this fields as in others, there is a development in the secondary schools favoring a gauged influx of social-science subject matter.

New German Textbooks [1]

The notes below are extracts from a dispatch by Terence Prittie,
Bonn Correspondent of the *Manchester Guardian*, 20 February 1960

History books, which I have read, and which are normally those most read by young Germans in the two to three years before they leave school, make, on the whole, a fair effort to explain the Nazi past. There is, for instance, *Die Neueste Zeit*, Volume 5, which is currently used in Lower Saxony (education is in the hands of the *Laender*). It devotes a whole page to the Nazi persecutions of the Jews, and gives a figure of four to five million Jews murdered (proportionately not so wide of the mark. The correct figure is around six million).

---

[1] From *Wiener Library Bulletin*, XIV, No. 1, p. 9.

Ten lines of print are accorded to the concentration camps. The book gives an honest account of the Hitler-Stalin Pact, and of its implications. It even explains the the 1917 Treaty of Brest-Litowsk, perhaps the most brutal peace ever enforced by a non-Nazi German Government and conveniently forgotten by 99 Germans out of every 100.

Grundriss der Geschichte, Volume 4, is used by the higher classes in secondary schools in several *Laender*. It is the work of a Dr. Herzfeld and a Dr. Dittrich-Gall-meister. The book has to cover a lot of ground but finds room for nineteen lines on the persecution of the Jews and the concentration camps. In a statistical sense, its authors are elusive but not untruthful — they are content with writing that "Millions died in the gas chambers." The book, admittedly, makes a slashing attack on the trials of German war criminals as being "contrary to international law", and devotes what might be thought a disproportionate amount of space to the expulsion of Germans from their homes at the end of the war and after it.

Evasive

In Bavaria, *Aus der Deutschen Vergangenheit* by Benedikt Nett is in use for boys and girls of 14 and 15. Its treatment of the Nazi persecutions is unsatisfactory. It devotes seven lines to them, and adds that "hundreds of thousands of the imprisoned Jews lost their lives." This is, to say the least, evasive.

Am Fliessband der Zeit, in use in *Land* North Rhine-Westphalia and written by Herr Wilhelm Aretz, does little better; it, too, gives only seven lines to the persecutions and the concentration camps, but agrees that "several million" Jews were "murdered". Here, at least, is an operative past participle.

Roughly equivalent treatment of these subjects is given by *Grundzuege der Geschichte*, Volume 7, which has been approved for use in the higher classes by Berlin and seven *Laender*. This book, too, notes that "several million Jews were murdered", but it finds room for only six lines of print about it. On the other hand, its references to the brutal expulsion of Germans from their homes is a triumph of moderation.

Quite outstanding in its treatment of the Nazi past is *Weltgeschichte im Aufriss*, Volume 3, which is widely used in West Berlin and has been compiled by Dr. Hermann Meyer, Dr. Wilhelm Langenbeck, and Dr. Siegfried Sterner. This book devotes a whole chapter to "Why the Democratic Experiment failed after 1919", a solid page and a half to Nazi persecutions, another page to pre-Nazi anti-Semitism, and valuable extracts from *Mein Kampf*, Leon Poliakov's *Harvest of Hate*, and Frau Eva Reichmann's *Hostages of Civilization*. Any young German who reads this book has an excellent idea of what really happened, and what views about it are held by a number of people eminently suited to judge.

There is, however, one curiosity about all of these history books, with the exception of the last and, surprisingly, *Aus der Deutschen Vergangenheit*. This is that German attacks on small and friendly European neighbors — Belgium in 1914, Holland, Belgium, Luxembourg, Denmark, and Norway in 1940 — are treated simply as facts, and no reference is made to their neutrality. Benedikt Nett does, indeed, mention that these countries were "peaceful" and rightly attributes England's entry into the First World War as being due to the guarantee of Belgian neutrality (other history books suggest that it was entirely due to the desire to maintain the "British plan of a balance of power"). Wilhelm Aretz "explains" the German attack on Yugoslavia as having been "made necessary" by Mussolini's "ill-fated Albanian campaign". *Die Neueste Zeit* writes that Hitler occupied Norway only because the Western Powers were planning to do so.

Here is something for the German historians to straighten out, and as soon as possible. For there can be no point in prating about international law in connection with war-crimes trials, when unprovoked aggression by the German nation on so many others is lightly passed-over. But as far as Hitler and his works are concerned a fair start has been made.

*

Other textbooks are mentioned in the *Frankfurter Rundschau*, 13 January 1960. *Wiege der Völker* ("Cradle of the Nations"), Vol. IV, is stated to be disposing of the Nazi crimes in the following two sentences: "The worst of the Party's record was the persecution of the Jews. Shops were looted, and the Jews themselves sent to special annihilation camps". Says the writer: "Not a word about the millions of dead, the gas chambers of Auschwitz and the inhuman suffering of the tortured".

They are Better Than Their Reputation.
Experts examine German History Books [1]

Raymond King, headmaster of Wandsworth School, London, and expert on school textbooks on the British UNESCO Commission, gave his German colleague, the Brunswick history professor, Georg Eckert, a hearty handshake as he assured him, "I am glad to be able to say that your school books are better than their reputation". He smiled as he added, "That does not mean to say that they could not be still better."

Eckert, who has won international fame as head of the International School Book Institute and "decontaminator" of European history books, might well be pleased at this statement. For three days, five British historians and German experts on school textbooks jointly examined about a hundred history textbooks. At the request of their German colleagues, the British historians are to investigate whether foreign criticism levelled in recent months against West German history books is justified.

In December 1958, wholesale criticism began in the Soviet Zone press. This was followed, first in Poland and later in Britain, Norway and France, by the assertion that the portrayal of the National Socialist era was getting milder in West German history books from year to year.

This criticism was based mainly on a history book in use in Hesse *(Man in the Changing Eras)*. A comparison between the 1950 and 1958 editions, it was said, showed clearly that the sections on the Hitler regime, the persecution of the Jews, the resistance movement, and the concentration camps, had been considerably abridged in the course of the years.

---

[1] From *Die Welt*, 27 February 1960.

Lecture Room, Bundeswehr-School for Internal Leadership

Midshipmen at the Marineschule, Flensburg

Photos: Bundesverteidigungsministerium

Youths' Art Exhibit on the Theme "Germany Indivisible" in Bonn

Photo: Bundesbildstelle Bonn

The Anglo-German Conference of Historians, now being held at Brunswick, took less than twenty minutes to discover that this contention was based on an utterly irresponsible misunderstanding. "In this case, editions have been compared which simply do not bear comparison" Eckert remarked. While the 1950 edition presented the individual chapters in the form of little anecdotes, the 1958 edition tended much more to a narration of facts. "It is completely absurd to attempt in such a case to work with quantitative comparisons and say that the chapter entitled "The History of the Hitler Regime" formerly covered 41 pages, whereas it is now dealt with in 13 pages.

His British colleagues agreed with him. "Such a comparison simply does not hold water", they declared unanimously, and thus destroyed, at least in this one concrete case, the legend about the allegedly increasing tendency to judge the Third Reich more leniently. Nor did an examination of the other school books produce any indication that the presentation of the recent past in West German text books was unsatisfactory.

This fact cannot, however blind us to the realization that deplorable deficiencies still exist in the numerically excessive West German school books. One elementary school book, for instance, was judged to be "totally unsuitable" by both delegations, because it almost completely omits any discussion of National Socialism. The book presents merely a series of facts (Hitler abolished unemployment, built the autobahn network, and annexed Austria) without interpreting what lay behind those events.

"It is possible that I myself would not have criticized that book so harshly a year ago", Eckert admitted, "Today however", he went on, "after the swastika-smearing incidents, I fully share the opinion of my British colleagues that the analysis of those historical events cannot be left to the discretion of the teacher, but must be included in the text books."

However frankly the British historians rejected the all-over accusation that recent German history had been inadequately dealt with, they unequivocally criticized a textbook which stated that the gassing of the Jews was "a mistake on the part of Hitler". "In my opinion", said King, "that was not a 'mistake', it was a crime!"

In the view of Brunswick School Book expert Eckert the School Book Commissions in the various *Laender* should in the future apply rather stricter standards in licensing school books, for "So far, the licensing procedure has been handled in too lax and liberal a manner."

The Changing Picture of European History [1]

By Georg Eckert

Narrow nationalism in the presentation of history overcome by an all-embracing synthesis

Europe is for us no mere geographical concept, not just an economic area or a constellation of political powers, but first and foremost a community with a historical background, a colorful bunch of peoples and of cultures, checkered and variegated, with subtile differences and startling contrasts, yet in the last resort united by the bond of a thousand years of common history and by all those values which we have in these centuries accepted, despite all our misdeeds, as binding on us.

Deeper points of unity among the European peoples

The historical research of recent decades and the experience of the present generation have roused our understanding for the deeper points of unity among our peoples; they make it easier to burst the narrow nationalist framework which cramped the picture of history at the end of 19th century and to substitute for it a European, nay, a worldwide view.

It is perhaps one of the finest tasks of the teaching profession in Europe to let this changed view of history leaven the young people growing up in our midst. In this period of utmost danger, when the awareness of history and the people's understanding both of themselves and of the world is of historic importance, it will not be the least of our tasks to ensure that the practical work of teaching is promptly imbued with the lessons learned from research.

To our quickly moving and insecure era it cannot and must not be a matter of indifference whether an interval of years, decades or generations separates the concepts of research from the ideas held by the peoples of the different countries. To bridge this gap in schoolbooks, or at least to reduce it as far as possible, appears to me to be one of the most particular tasks of the Brunswick Institute.

Similar efforts everywhere

When more than twelve years ago pioneer groups from among the teachers of Germany made a start on the work, which was to lead to the foundation of our Institute, their spokesmen had far more limited, far more modest objectives: they aimed at the reform of history teaching at home, at training the young people of Germany to think critically and to be tolerant, to be conscious of a human solidarity which embraced all nations; these young people were also to be brought up to strive, today and in the future, for the fulfilment of the human traditions of our European history as well as those of the truly great periods of our own country's history. After the frightful experiences of the most recent past this reform was for us no theoretical, purely academic problem, but one of the essential preconditions for the revival and the security of renascent democracy in Germany.

When the representatives of the German teaching profession got down to this task, which included the recasting of textbooks and of all the other media concerned, they rapidly came across similar experiments, similar attempts of which most German educationalists had never heard during the years of dictatorship, the years

---

[1] From *Meet Germany*, published by Atlantik-Bruecke, Hamburg, 1960.

of intellectual isolation. They came across the Casares Resolution adopted by the League of Nations in 1926, the efforts made by the Historical Association in Great Britain to bring about cooperation among the history teachers of Europe. They came across the splendid action undertaken by the historians and history teachers of the five Nordic states, which since 1928 have shown so much common sense and had such noteworthy success with their agreement to work together on a voluntary basis.

But their main discovery was the admirable work done by their French colleagues — teachers in primary schools and history teachers in secondary schools — who under the leadership of Louis Dumas and George Lapierre had set a fine example for the teachers of Europe.

The work of the International Schoolbook Institute

German teachers felt especially indebted to these pioneers among their French colleagues who had striven with such success against chauvinism and pettiness in the textbooks of their own country; these Frenchmen have served as examples which the Germans have endeavored to follow during the last twelve years. In the course of this endeavor the work of the International Schoolbook Institute of the Brunswick Institute of Education, and of those teachers connected with it, has experienced three stages of growth which overlap both materially and in point of time.

In the early years which formed the opening stage, our first aim was to present the political and cultural relations between Germany and its neighbors in as objective, fair and balanced a manner as possible and to revise textbooks and the teaching of history in the spirit of understanding between the nations. From the start this work had to be looked at from two angles. We had first to take up arms against the mass of misunderstanding, misinterpretations, and ill feeling which, in the century of nationalism and of conflicts between national states, had bedevilled the understanding of the various peoples — thanks in no small measure to the influence of textbooks and classroom. We had at the same time to tell the history of the other countries and states which were linked with us in a common fate, to present their peculiarities and their particular values, accepting where possible their own interpretation of themselves, all in so balanced a manner that young people would be enabled or at least assisted to make critical comparisons and so to appreciate the various points of view.

In short, we set out to overcome the tradition of purely nationalistic thinking inherited from the 19th century and, where necessary, to make use of an entirely fresh division of material, of entirely new structures and emphasis, in order to ensure that other states and peoples did not only appear in textbooks when they influenced or shaped the fate of our own people, our own country, for better or for worse, in war or in peace.

Congresses and Symposia

In the second stage, when our work was decisively influenced and assisted by the action of the Council of Europe in organizing textbook congresses and history symposia, we tried to draw attention to the things that were common to us all, to the joint foundations of our history, to the permanence with which our national cultures are woven together. In this stage too we first endeavored, for practical reasons, to make clear the cultural give and take which existed between our country and its neighbors.

We attempted — to give but a few examples — to trace the fruitful influence of French thought and of the French religious spirit. At several meetings we tried to throw light on the reciprocal influence of cultural development in Germany and Italy and to obtain a balanced picture of the political, economic and intellectual relations which in the Middle Ages formed so close a bond between England, northern Europe and the Hansa League.

We hope that we will in future be able to continue this work on a broader and really European basis. We are planning discussions on the survival of Antiquity and the various phases of the Renaissance. We are planning a symposium on the Imperium of the Middle Ages and on the birth of national states; even more important will be the series of meetings and studies concerned with problems of recent and very recent history and how it should be handled in class.

At our future meetings, therefore, we shall be less concerned with the relations between the nationalist states in Europe than with the cultural substrata which link us, with the political, economic and social phenomena which are common to all of us or to the main groups of European peoples.

Concrete Results

The Brunswick Institute must thank its many friends and helpers in the various countries of Europe if, already during the second stage, and on the threshhold of the third stage of its development, it can point to a series of concrete results.

In collaboration with organizations of teachers and history teachers, with national committees in UNESCO and with groups of historians from 15 European and — to count only our specially active colleagues — 8 non-European states, more than 1,000 textbooks for the teaching of history, geography, and languages have been examined and an appreciable number of the consequent expressions of opinion have been made available through the technical press and by means of special publications, to those who are interested in education.

An increasing number of publishing houses has begun to submit the manuscripts of newly written textbooks and the teaching aids of foreign experts for a statement of views before printing. In various works which have appeared in recent years writers and publishers have made special reference to this voluntary cooperation in international self-control by the writers of textbooks and the teachers of history.

In a total of 31 bilateral meetings of historians, specialists from Germany have discussed debatable periods and problems of common history with colleagues from Austria, Belgium, Denmark, France, Great Britain, Italy, Jugoslavia, Luxemburg, the Netherlands, Norway, and Sweden. Most of these meetings dealt with problems of the 19th and early 20th century, with conflicts and rivalries during the period of national states, with the events leading up to the first world war, with policy in the 1920's, and similar difficult problems which worry the peoples of our countries.

Six volumes of the "International Yearbook for History Teaching"

At meetings with colleagues from Austria, Belgium, Jugoslavia, Luxemburg, the Netherlands, and Norway recent, even very recent, history has been outlined in a form that is as restrained as it is frank, and first provisional recommendations have been drafted.

With colleagues from Denmark, France, Italy, the Netherlands and Sweden there have also, as already mentioned, been discussions on medieval history, particularly on cultural relations between the different parts of Europe. The recommendations jointly formulated at these meetings have so far been issued in six volumes of the *International Yearbook for History Teaching* and in many other special publications; particularly in the German-speaking countries they have been made available to publishers, writers of textbooks and a large number of teachers. In this connection it should perhaps be mentioned that the theses worked out in the Sorbonne and in the Institute for European History with the help of Droz, Herzfeld, Renouvin, and Ritter, theses covering Franco-German relations from 1789 to the end of the first German Republic, have so far appeared in 18 publications.

In order to familiarize history teachers in Germany with the ideas and views of their colleagues abroad, the Brunswick Institute has published lengthy translations from the schoolbooks of European and extra-European states — including a volume which presents the last century of German history by means of long excerpts from the textbooks used in various European countries. This volume in particular, which has been consulted by many teachers, has helped them and their pupils to subject their own traditional point of view to the critical test of views held by other European historians and teachers.

Personal Friendship and Contacts

Perhaps even more essential than all these works, to which further examples could be added, are the personal links and friendships which have arisen out of the many meetings at the Council of Europe, at UNESCO and in the Brunswick Institute. That it is just historians and teachers of history, people more especially bound up with the cultural heritage of their own country, who should so quickly and unreservedly have understood and accepted each other in a spirit of joint responsibility, is very definitely one of the most encouraging signs for the growth of common solidarity in Europe.

These meetings were not merely occasions on which work was done for Europe, they were themselves part of the living Europe — a community of people with a common point of view, who felt the rightness of George Lapierre's exhortation that "only the man who binds his future to that of mankind at peace is really of service to his own country".

We teachers of history believe that we will best do justice to this legacy of Lapierre if we can bring up our young people to four degrees of loyalty: to love and devotion for their own locality, for their country, for Europe — and also for unity and active solidarity with human beings throughout the world, in line with Tolstoi's phrase: "The nearer men come to truth, the more tolerant are they — and vice versa".

A generation which is to manage the problems of a united world must learn to understand the growth of Europe in the broad context of a universal history which embraces all peoples and all epochs. Here the checking of traditional values and feelings would seem to be more essential than the gaining of new knowledge; a new basis must be found which will do justice not only to Europe but also to the other cultural regions of our world.

To the carrying out of this task, which has been taken up so vigorously by UNESCO, the Brunswick Institute hopes, in the third stage of its development, to make a modest but a concrete contribution.

The Presentation of Jewery
in Teachers Training and in the Classroom [1]

By Ekkehart Krippendorff

1) Teaching of History

A) Textbooks on History

In the various attempts to criticize the status of political education in the Federal Republic, the discussions have always centered around the teaching of history and the history textbooks. This criticism has been mainly directed against the unsatisfactory presentation of recent history, the insufficient information on the crimes of Nazism, and, in this connection, also on the mass murder of millions of Jewish citizens, and against the fact that the discussion on the Third Reich appears to be softer in more recent textbook editions than in earlier ones. There has certainly been much truth in this criticism; often, however, these discussions have been polemic in an unfounded, precipitate, and distorted way, having a damaging effect rather than helping the matter. Instead of simply discussing whether the number of murdered Jews should be brought up and what statistics should be used, the discussion on Jewery opens a much broader field, and therewith puts the problem in another, a more fundamental, perspective.

An investigation of the most important textbooks used today in history courses in all types of schools shows that, in general, Jews are mentioned only on two occasions: (a) when dealing with ancient Oriental history and (b) in connection with the crimes of the Third Reich.

A student in the elementary school, for example, who uses the two-volume textbook published by Klett-Verlag: *Damals und Heute (Then and Today)* learns briefly some facts about the Israelites in 23 lines. The closing sentence reads: "Later on the Jewish people lost their independence and were dispersed all over the world" (Vol. I, p. 15). In connection with the Stein-Hardenberg reforms he then learns, without further explanation, about the emancipation of the Jews in 1812 (Vol. II, p. 24); next, under the — not unobjectionable — heading "Hitler Unifies the Germans in the Third Reich", he is given an account of isolated anti-Jewish actions, such as boycotts, etc., followed by the statement: "They put the Jews into camps by the hundreds of thousands, where they had to work hard. Through hunger, sickness, and torture, many of them died" (Vol. II, p. 137). Apart from the fact that it is neither methodically nor didactically justifiable to circumscribe the systematic extermination of five to six million Jews by using terms like "hunger, sickness, and torture", it is important for our discussion to know that the elementary school student learns nothing about the Jewish fate between 500 B.C. and 1933, and that he gets no explanation why the National-Socialists committed those tortures — maybe the Jews themselves gave rise to them by their own conduct?

Similarly the elementary schools student is left ignorant about Jewery and anti-Semitism when using the two volume textbook *Unsere Geschichte (Our History)*,

---

[1] From *Erziehungswesen und Judentum (Education and Jewery)*. Published by the Verband Deutscher Studentenschaften (Association of German Student Organizations). Ner-Tamid-Verlag, Munich, 1960.

published by Schwann-Verlag. Six lines of the first volume are devoted to the Jewish people — here their merit of having given to the world the Old Testament and the belief in one God is mentioned (Vol. I, p. 21). Then the Jews appear again in connection with Hitler's attitude towards them who "blamed the Jewish citizens of having drained the nation and of having been responsible for the inflation and the economic depression" (Vol. II, p. 14). The persecution up to the *"Endloesung"* is mentioned in nine short, concise lines, this time mentioning the number killed. Whether or not Hitler might not have been right with his accusations, as many children learn from their parents, remains uncertain.

This basic pattern of discussing the Jews has been applied in history textbooks not only for elementary schools, it also underlies — with some deviations though — the textbooks for intermediate and high schools. By deviations we mean that some books *(Diesterweg und Buchners/Mittelstufe, Klett/Oberstufe)* mention briefly the role of the Jews in medieval towns or in the early capitalistic economy, without linking those facts with the general economic and sociological structure or with the religious struggles between Christians and Jews of that time. Such relationships cannot be analyzed since history is interpreted here as a series of political actions rather than sociological changes in leadership. In the second volume of Diesterweg's textbook for intermediate schools *Vom Frankenreich bis zum Westfälischen Frieden (From the Franconian Empire to the Peace of Westphalia)*, the Jewish Ghetto in the medieval town is mentioned and one reads that the citizens "because of super-stition and religious intolerance... saw in them (the Jews) the cause of their afflic-tions." (p. 79). This remark is not only insufficient, as an isolated statement it is also futile; even more so since the following remark, that hate was increased by the fact that only Jews were allowed to lend money, stands without further explanation. Only such an explanation, however, could give some insight into the medieval social and economic structure. Moreover, mentioning the role of Jews in German history in such a brief form may even lead to a strengthening of the prejudice: "they have always been disliked".

Another deviation from this basic pattern, i.e. the dealing with only ancient Israel and the persecution of the Jews, consists of mentioning individual personalities of Jewish descent without explicitly explaining this background. The latter is by no means considered objectionable. Assembling all textbooks for the eighth grade and up, the individuals mentioned are: Heine, Boerne, Marx, Lassalle, and Rathenau. Only rarely does one find a proper appraisal of a distinguished personality such as Rathenau as, for instance, in *Geschichtliches Unterrichtswerk (Textbook on History)* for grades 8—10, where 15 lines are devoted to him (Vol. IV, p. 144). In the textbook for grades 10—13 by the same publishing company, this part is missing (Vol. III, p. 85). But also the other names appear without referring to the social and philosophical history of the 19th century and the role of the progressive middle class, which would have been the only way to create an understanding for the historical importance of those persons.

Finally, in some books, Jews are talked about in a third connection. In Klett's text-book for upper grades, it is said of Lessing, "the advocate of humanitarian ideals", that his *Nathan* is a powerful plea for prejudice-free humaneness towards the Jews (Vol. II, p. 133). Only in one other textbook, *Geschichtliches Unterrichtswerk* for grades 8—10, published by Schroedel-Verlag, can a similar remark be found (Vol. III, p. 107). Others mention Lessing in a general way, many not even that. However it is precisely this Age of Reason with its ideas of tolerance, equality, and humanitarianism, which presents itself as a, not only very handy, but even very necessary inroad for the understanding of the philosophical and sociological preparation for the dissolution of medieval feudalism which leads to the establishment of the middle-class democracy, that found, for the first time on the European continent, its realization in the French Revolution when also equality for Jews as citizens had been explicitly formulated.

Only three of the presently used major textbooks report on anti-Semitism and racism, both of which are only indirectly related to Jewery, although of great importance for German history. In Volume 4 of *Europa und die Welt (Europe and the World)*, a Schroedel-Verlag textbook for grades 8—10, we find a 26 line sub-paragraph on "Anti-Semitism in Germany and Austria", with a brief and concise article on Gobineau, Chamberlain, Stoecker, Lueger, and the Schoenerer-movement.

It says that these anti-Semites had only a few followers, that this development, however, "grew disastrous for the future" (p. 96). In Klett's textbook for upper grades it reads that "the extermination of Jews" had been "one of the terrible consequences" of Gobineau's and Chamberlain's racial theory, with which the nation had been indoctrinated by mass-agitation (Vol. III, p. 120). Finally, in *Erbe des Abendlandes (Our Western Heritage)* from Schwann-Verlag, we find at least some mention that there were certain forces in society which sponsored this ideology: — "also anti-Semitic middle-class groups were formed in parliament: *Deutschsoziale* (German Socialists), *Deutsche Reformpartei* (German Reform Party), but they did not any gain influence" (Vol. III, p. 212). But nowhere do we find a reason given for those tendencies as to why it was that anti-Semitism became so violent, and by whom and for which social interests that mass-agitation had been arranged. However, answers to those questions "why" are indispensible for a historical and sociological education which should be built upon more than simply a superficial knowledge of facts. Even the most objective extract of Hitler's racial theories, as can be found in some books, still leaves unanswered the question about their truth; it leaves it up to the student to conclude that they are nonsense and only serving agitating purposes.

The new nation of Israel is virtually not mentioned in textbooks for elementary schools, with one sentence at most in high school books and only very briefly in college textbooks. In most cases one must be contented with only the registration of the founding of the nation in 1948 in a "Survey on World Politics". A gratifying exception is the *Geschichtliches Unterrichtswerk (Textbook on History)* for grades 8—10 put out by the Schroedel-Verlag. In as many as 44 lines it reports on the year 1948, the Israeli-Arabic War, the immigration, and the reparation treaty with the Federal Republic of Germany (Vol. IV, p. 181 ff.). Of the textbooks for grades 10—13 only the one published by Klett-Verlag goes beyond the usual one sentence, devoting 11 lines to the Balfour-declaration, Palestine under the League of Nations, the relation between the persecution of Jews and immigration, war and the founding of Israel (Vol. III, pp. 133 and 201).

Let us finally look at the history atlases which are being used extensively in classrooms. Volker S. Siegesmund wrote about them in *Die Zeit* on 4 December, 1959: "... In *Zeissigs Neuer Geschichtsatlas* of 1956 I was struck by a map which was not to be found in the first edition of 1950: 'The Germans as settlers and cultural pioneers in Eastern Europe.' I don't feel at ease when looking at such a map, because it may again lead to nationalistic one-sidedness. It suspiciously uses the term 'Kulturpioniere' (cultural pioneers) regarding the 19th century ...

"From its 72nd edition on, 'Putzger' has included a series of new maps in order to illustrate 'Turning Points of World War II' (Invasion and Stalingrad) which may

124

be helpful towards a better understanding. Of doubtful value, it seems to me, however, is the little map in this series 'Bombing Damages of German Towns'. Whoever believes that those damages have to be illustrated should be objective and, at least, on the war-map, mark the bombing of Warsaw and Rotterdam, the 'erasements' and 'Conventrieren'. In 'Putzger' even the names Rotterdam and Coventry are missing. It is also no different in the *Staatlich-Bayrischer Grosser Historischer Weltatlas (The Great Historic World Atlas for Schools in the State of Bavaria)*. Again there is space for a little map: 'German Towns Under Air Raids' where destructions of church buildings are carefully listed; but the Cathedral of Coventry, the churches in London and Rotterdam are conspicuously missing . . .

"In the Great Historic World Atlas (pp. 194—195) the same symbols are being used for murder and expulsion. As a result — willingly or unwillingly — the map illustrating the population-movement after 1944 is given a much stronger effect; the Jewish fate looks comparatively less chequered and less moving. The Nazi terror against their own countrymen is not portrayed at all. And towards Hitler's brutality, map no. 194b: 'Temporary European Population Movements' proves a surprising considerateness by using the following nuances in the text: foreign workers were 'brought' to Germany; Poles, Frenchmen, and Serbians were 'resettled by force; later the Germans, however, were 'deported by force'. . ."

B) The Curricula

Textbooks are, in general, realizations of the demanded curricula, which had been worked out by the State Cultural Ministries. It would be fruitless, at least with regard to our subject, to look for any directions in the current plans which have not been taken into consideration by the textbook authors. On the contrary: it has to be pointed out that, in some books, far more is being said about the role of Jewery than has been prescribed.

In general, a discussion on our problem is demanded only twice. In connection with:
   1) ancient Israel
   2) the persecution of Jews under Nazism

The argument that the Ministry's plans can only give a few general recommendations and cannot discuss details is of very limited value. Because other detailed directions are given, in which the discussion of Jewery in German history is at least of equal rank. A few examples from Hesse may illustrate this: In *Zeittafel fuer den Geschichtsunterricht an Volksschulen (Table of Dates for History Courses in Elementary Schools)* it says:
   1933 Hitler takes over power
   1939—45 World War II
   1945 the collapse, Potsdam Treaty, expulsion of the Germans, first atom bomb (Hiroshima)
   1949 Founding of the Federal Republic, the Constitution

One would expect that here, in connection with the expulsion of the Germans, the mass-murder of 6 million Jewish civilians would be mentioned.

The same is true for the treatment of National-Socialism in the 8th grade of the elementary school:
   The great recession
   Hitler takes over power

Nazism leads to World War II
World War II ends with total defeat
Blitzkrieg — Stalingrad — Africa
Invasion and air raids
The 20th of July 1944
Unconditional surrender
The Potsdam Treaty
Expulsion of the Germans from Middle-Eastern Europe

Also *Bilder aus der Geschichte (Glances from History)* for the 5th and 6th grades should be critically investigated. In *Aus der Neuzeit und der Gegenwart (From Recent and Present Times)* the following directions are given:

Life in a castle 200 years ago
Farmers under serfdom
How the potato came to us
The age of technology begins
The exploration of the world comes to a close
After the lost war
Exiled from home
New homes and factories rise from ruins
Relatives and friends in the Soviet Zone

The *Geschichtliche Einzelbilder (Selected Topics in History)* does not even go as far as the present time. The series which begins with cloisters and knights' castles ends with Frederic the Great and Maria Theresia. If selected topics are to include the crusades, the medieval towns, and the peasants' revolt, a description of the medieval religious fanaticism should also be considered educationally valuable. For the 8th grade of the elementary school in Baden-Wuerttemberg "Concentration Camps and Persecution of Jews" is a topic that is included in the treatment of the Third Reich, however, it sounds less offensive and less concrete than "Millions of Germans Must Leave their Native Homes", which is suggested later.

For upper grades in Baden-Wuettemberg high schools, an abundance of "Selected Topics", "Points of Views" and "Suggestions for the Cross Treatment (of History)" are given. However, among those there is nothing which even indirectly touches the Jewish problem (as would, for instance, rationalism and Lessing's *Nathan*, anti-Semitism and chauvinism in the 19th century).

Let us repeat: The treatment of Jewery has been laid down only for ancient history and in connection with National-Socialism. With the latter, one notices a certain tendency towards suppression because of the stronger accent on the exorcising of Germans from the east in 1945. In the ordinances issued by the State of Lower Saxony the consequences which have been drawn from very thorough educational studies are characteristic for this tendency. There, in regard to students in the 5th and 6th grades, it says: "Their experience in life has now begun to include the formation of groups, and conflicts between the groups as well as between the individual and his group." The history course should "help to clarify and strengthen the self-understanding of the German people." "A history course which does not lead to the most recent past therefore misses its goal." However, the only topical direction given to this end reads: "Special emphasis should be given to Eastern studies." The systematic study on group-psychology particularly would have offered an almost ideal starting point for the treatment of anti-Semitism, which can hardly be said of "Eastern studies".

Special emphasis is given to Jewery in the "Provisional Directions for Political Education at Berlin Schools". There, a lengthy paragraph "Additional Topics in Contemporary History and Reflections on Contemporary History in History Courses" brings an abundance of suggested topics. For example for the 9th high school grade (practical branch):

"The Importance of Jews for Germany: Mendelssohn, Heine, Marx, Lassalle, Liebermann, Paul Ehrlich, Albert Neisser, Siegmund Freud, Heinrich Hertz, Rathenau, Fritz Haber, Max Reinhardt, Hugo von Hofmannsthal, Einstein, Stephan Zweig and others."

The same again for the 10th grade and in addition:

"Anti-Semitism before 1919, Nuremberg Laws, The Jewish-pogrom of 9 November, 1938, concentration-camps versus reparation."

Among the recommendations for the scientific branch of high schools we find for the 9th grade:

"Lessing and the Jews (Nathan the Wise) — Hitler and the Jews (gas-chamber execution in Auschwitz and other camps). The duty of reparation."

And for the 10th grade:

"Jewish fighters in World War I — their treatment under Hitler. Darwinism, Selection — Eugenics, Extermination of human beings (euthanasia program, extermination of Jews). Resistance against these pogroms, based on Christian and ethical philosophies."

But those directions also have objectionable aspects since repeatedly the following recommendations appear:

"Persecution of Jews and Christians in ancient Rome and under Hitler, Persecution of counter-revolutionaries in communist countries. The destruction of Jerusalem — the murder of Jews in Auschwitz." (7th high school grade, technical branch).

"Persecution of Jews during the Crusades and under Hitler" (religious and racial anti-Semitism)." (8th grade of high school, technical branch).

"Execution of the Jews defeated by the Assyrians, Execution of Jews, Poles, and Russians by Hitler" (7th grade of high school, scientific branch).

Similar recommendations for historic comparisons are suggestions like:

"Genghis-Khan, Hitler, Stalin." (8th grade of high school, scientific branch).

"People of the Renaissance (Borgia) — SS. NKWD." (12th grade of high school, scientific branch).

Little explanation is required to see that such comparisons, when taken as historic parallels, represent the most destructive nonsense in history education. And the authors of those directions had never meant them to be used in that way, since it says in the introductory remarks: "The student shall not get the impression that history is a chain of cruelties to which the crimes of Nazism and Bolshevism are simply continuations; he shall rather recognize that the 20th century with its highly developed technology has also created forms of society, the inhumanity of which has surpassed everything experienced so far."

Theoretically this puts a stop to possible misuse, and the seeming historic analogy should lead to the realization of the inadmissibility of such a comparison. But doesn't it look different in practice? Isn't just the un-anotated grouping a temptation to find mutualities between Cesare Borgia and Himmler or between the Assyrians and Hitler? Isn't it asking too much of a teacher — and even more of a student — first to demonstrate the politically and morally so comfortable parallel, and then to explain, in rather general terms, that just the contrary is meant? Must we not —

unfortunately — assume that the general tendency moves in the direction of suppression, i. e. towards a historic relativity, which the Berlin program, though worked out with the best intentions, rather strengthens than prevents?

C) Recommended Curricula

After this stock-taking we shall now try to suggest matters of instruction, problems to be taken up in history courses and textbooks.

(The now following paragraphs represent in essence the results arrived at by the history committee under Professor Dr. Anton J. Gail and Dr. Willy Jaitner at the *Bergneustadt* conference. They deal with: Ancient history, the Roman Empire, European Medieval history, the 17th to 19th century, Weimar Republic, and National-Socialism, and conclude with methodical reflections. (Our limited space does not permit us to report these suggestions in detail. — Ed.)

D) Conclusion

A comparison of Jewish history as presented by our present textbooks with the recommendations of teaching matters and methods which we outlined here shows an almost insuperable discrepancy that is not surprising. This discrepancy did not emerge from a well-meaning "pro-Semitism" demanding a stronger consideration of Jewish history as expiation for moral injustice. The claim for presenting Jewery as part of our history rather becomes a question of the structure of our historic thinking.

If one agrees with the thesis that the history of the Jewish people represents a necessary part of our history teaching — not least because the German citizens of Jewish belief have taken an active and suffering part in the life-history of our nation — one must also admit that this claim can hardly be realized within the frame of a historical picture as drawn by today's textbooks and within a course of history as presented therein. Because their attitude towards history favors the "Policy-of-the-strong-hand" aspect and is of "etatistic" nature: The driving forces in historic developments are the political leaders and statesmen, the "great powers". Elaborate descriptions of Bismarck's treaty system, for instance, and the "creation of the Reich" by means of policy-of-the-strong-hand, are considered worth knowing, while social, economic, inner- and party-political problems are only mentioned on the side. Klett's textbook for grades 8—10 *Um Volksstaat und Voelkergemeinschaft (For the People's Government and the Community of Nations)*, for instance, has 23 pages on Hitler's foreign policy and the war (pp. 165—196) (although one page is devoted to the uprising on the 20th of July, 1944), but there are only six and one-half pages on the National-Socialist program and the establishment of the dictatorship (pp. 159—165) and again only sixteen and one-half pages on the Weimar Republic (one of which, amazingly enough, shows a full-page picture of Albert Schweitzer) (pp. 142—158). This quantitative analysis alone makes the tendency apparent. It is the policy-of-the-strong-hand aspect, the "etatistic" attitude, which prohibits a deeper insight into the laws of society, which implies, by its accent on the "policy-of-the-strong-hand", the belief in an inherent historical drive, and which, at least in the course of German history, has led to an anti-democratic undervaluation of the individual's responsibility towards history and society. However, teaching of Jewish history cannot convince, unless history is understood and explained as social history and goes beyond pure "national history". Simply adding Jewish history or teaching it only excursively would assume an apologetic character within the structure of our present textbooks. It would neither be factually convincing, nor would it make apparent the interplay of Jewish, German, and European developments. Instead, by using the Jewish fate and position in society, one would show exemplarily the status and change of sociological structures. This, of course, is not only possible by using the example of the Jews, but since the German catastrophe is so clearly linked with the nation's guilt towards the Jewish people, it is necessary to use just this in German history teaching. Although the roots and the driving forces of Jewish history are predominantly of a religious nature, there is still an anthropological and sociological task in teaching it; and this not primarily because of the Jews, but, above all, because of our responsibility towards our own history and our social and moral education.

The Invasion of Jugoslavia and Greece on 6th April 1941

An example of National Socialist film propaganda during the Second World War. Published by the State District Pictorial Office, Hamburg, and the Curatorium for Civic Education, Hamburg.

Introduction

The "special report" of the "German Newsreel" on the German attack on Jugoslavia and Greece on 6th April 1941 is an enlightening example of National Socialist war propaganda. The scenic order gives a good impression of the existing state of the film and propaganda technology in the Third Reich. The National Socialist regime handles the mass influence of the people by press, radio, and film with such cleverness that its effect — and that means also its historical importance — can scarcely be stressed strongly enough. To analyze the methods of this propaganda is therefore an important task for research and instruction. In doing so the following comments may be of assistance.

When showing the "special report" to schoolchildren and youth groups, there is undoubtedly the danger that the suggestive powers of National Socialist propaganda material is still effective even today. Some observers may still be "carried away" by the scenes of war incidents. However it is the suggestive power of National Socialism, which is just the phenomenon which creates the greatest difficulties for the comprehension of those who did not themselves experience these happenings. If one eliminates it from one's observation of the historical happenings, one achieves little. The evaluation of the propaganda material must of course be carried out carefully. The suggestive effect of that shown, not that shown itself, is the actual object for study. It is recommended that other film and pictorial material the contents of which clearly show the brutal reality of National Socialism, should be shown along with this "special report".

The "special report" begins with the official government declaration on the morning of 6th April 1941 and then shows scenes of the fighting during the first days in Jugoslavia and Greece. The political, military, and economic backgrounds to this campaign are not shown, in fact, not even mentioned. The report, however, can only be properly assessed when one compares what is shown with the actual historical happenings. Therefore, in the second part of this booklet a short summary of the previous history and the course of the campaign is given. The texts of the official commentaries have been added as in them can be seen typical instances of National Socialist propaganda.

Night and Fog*

Commentaries and hints for its evaluation by Guenter Moltmann

The film shows scenes from German concentration camps, punishment and annihilation camps of the National Socialist regime. With the help of the camera the observer experiences a tour of a deserted and dilapidated camp. That is the framework for the presentation of original pictures and film strips from the National Socialist period. One sees mass deportations, prisoner transports, arrival and classification in the camp, clothing, parading, accommodation, dormitories, sanitary installations, forced labor, food, registration, treatment of the sick, medicinal experiments, gas chambers, crematoria, piles of corpses, mass graves, utilization of remains of bodies, etc.

The film is accompanied by a commentary of unvaried tone, objective and informative, and conservative background music. The presentation is tactful. One perceives the endeavor to let pictorial documents speak for themselves. The choice is limited to typical examples. Certainly the naked facts visually demonstrated arouse feelings which approach the limit of endurance. This must be borne in mind when using the film for instructional purposes. It is only suitable for demonstration to the upper school classes. A simple routine inclusion in the history instruction curriculum cannot be justified. Careful preparation and evaluation must be made in order to assist the pupils to "digest" the experience. Only then can the film fulfil its purpose as a "Warning to the Living".

"Misused"

A documentary on the "Hitler Youth" for the enlightenment of youth

from *Allgemeine Wochenzeitung der Juden in Deutschland*, 21 Oct. 1960

Misused is the title given to a film which recently had its première in Duesseldorf. This 35-minute film, which deals with the youth movement of the National Socialists and has been graded "good" by the Film Education Office in Wiesbaden, has been put together by Eduard Bungter of the Citizens' Cultural Office of North

---

*) Published by the State District Pictorial Office, Hamburg, and the Curatorium for Civic Education, Hamburg.

Rhine-Westphalia and the young Munich director Peter Schamoni, from 25,000 meters of news-reels and other German and foreign material.

After a silent lead-in dedicated to the many unknown young people who struggled against National Socialism, the development of the Hitler Youth is shown by shots of groups marching to mass meetings and of Nazi leaders delivering their speeches. We see the whole story, from the enthusiasm to play a part in a new age and right through to the bitter end, of the "misuse" of youth under the National Socialist régime. The accompanying text is used simply to explain what is being shown and avoids expression of opinion. The film is to be shown in schools, youth organizations and cultural institutions.

At the première in Duesseldorf the Land Minister of the Interior, Josef-Hermann Dufhues, pointed out that the youth of Germany had realized only after 1933, when it was too late, that its natural enthusiasm and readiness for sacrifice had been misused. Dufhues stressed that to be right the work of civic education must give guidance and enlightenment on everything which "threatened our existence from the right wing or the left wing or through underground activities."

Youth Wants to Know How it All Came About [1]

There is a gratifyingly great interest in films on the Hitler era

Hamburg youth shows great interest in the events and developments during the Nazi regime in Germany. This is evident from the statistical data available to the State Picture Agency on the lending to schools of films on contemporary history as well as from the fact that the Swedish-made documentary film *Mein Kampf*, shown at the Studio Cinema near the *Binnenalster*, attracts young people as the greater part of the audience.

In a circular letter to all schools in Hamburg, Landesschulrat Ernst Matthewes of the Hamburg School Department expressly suggested that the students in Grade 10, and also in Grade 9, if they are mature enough, be given a chance to see this film during normal school hours. It is the opinion of the School Department that this film is excellently suited to create among the young people a deep impression of what Nazism means.

"For this reason the film should not be discussed at school, neither before it is shown nor afterwards, but it shall have its effect as an experience and should only then be discussed, if among the students themselves, there is a desire for a clarifying debate", (stated in the circular letter issued by the School Department). The annual statistics of the State Picture Agency (from 1 April, 1959 to 30 March, 1960) reveal the following information: 28 films on contemporary history were given out to schools 1,053 times. The concentration camp feature *Nacht und Nebel (Night and Fog)* was the most in demand, followed by *Der Prozess des 20. Juli (The Trial of July 20)*, *Berlin, Schicksal einer Stadt (Berlin, Fate of a City)*, and *Politische Reden 1930/1932 (Political Speeches 1930—1932)*. The distribution figures are about the same regarding sound tapes on contemporary history.

[1]) From *Die Welt*, 23 August 1960.

Political Science (Civics, Sociology, etc.)

in the Schools of the Federal Laender*

Status — Fall 1958

(In West Germany political education is treated firstly as a general principle of instruction in every subject and in every type of school, and secondly as a distinct body of knowledge in a separate subject or at any rate in separate lessons. Ed.)

I. BADEN-WUERTTEMBERG

1. Primary school:

Civic education as a principle throughout all grades, especially in local studies, history and geography. The four or five lessons devoted to history, local studies and geography form part of the 12 to 15 lessons devoted to "German language and general knowledge".
The program of study envisages:
Grade 5: community living
Grade 6: social institutions, the community
Grade 7: local government, the *Kreis* (county), trade, the professions
Grade 8: the Federation, the *Land*, the law, employment.

2. Middle school:
As principle of education, especially in history and geography.

3. *Gymnasium* (High School):
As principle of education in all subjects, especially history, geography, German, modern languages, science subjects. Local studies is generally taught by the history teacher. Voluntary study teams are run in addition to the compulsory lessons.
The study program envisages:
Grade 10: general view of state and society, basic facts (starting from current events), the Federal Government
Grade 13: organization of society, principles of government, the present system of government, the Federal Government, problems of world politics.

4. *Berufsschule* (Vocational School):
As a subject and as principle of teaching. Grades are entered on the report card.

II. BAVARIA

1. Primary school:
As principle of teaching in all grades, especially in the subjects local studies, general knowledge, German, arithmetic. No special lessons before Grade 8. In Grade 8 civics are given increased consideration, especially in geography, history and nature studies.
Grade 9: Grade 9 only exists for the present in the larger towns. Here the entire school teaching centres round social history and civics. Seven lessons a week are devoted to sociology for boys, and 6 for girls. Teaching is given in study teams, and the social side is emphasized.

---

*) Compiled from statements of the *Landeszentralen fuer Heimatdienst* (Central and Organizations for Civics) and related institutions by Dr. Walter Tormin, Secretary to the Curatorium for Civic Education in Hamburg

2. Middle school:
Teaching of sociology is combined with that of history. Special attention is to be given to the treatment of sociology in the light of current affairs. It is also a teaching principle, especially in geography.

3. *Gymnasium* (High School):
As teaching principle in all subjects. Special lessons in Grades 12 and 13 form the conclusion of these efforts. Themes: Man in his various social relationships, the present structure of our society.

4. *Berufsschule* (Vocational School):
Starting from the vocational standpoint, the subject forms an introduction to conditions of social life today, as well as to civic rights and duties.

III. BERLIN

The school system in Berlin is different from that of the other *Laender*. The names of the various schools do not therefore apply to Berlin, and are given only by way of comparison. As from 1 April 1959, history and civics are to be taught as separate subjects in the top grades.

1. Primary school:
As teaching principle, especially in history and geography. These subjects are taught by the home-room teacher. In many schools history and civics are taught as separate subjects. In Grades 7 and 8 special themes are set in order to introduce civics into the history lessons. In Grade 8 current events is an obligatory subject. In Grade 9 themes of recent history since 1945 are envisaged with special emphasis upon the civic point of view.

2. Middle school:
(High school Technical branch)
Civics and history as in Grades 7 and 8 of the primary school, taught by the history teacher. As teaching principle. In addition special school events (lectures by the local burgomaster). Program of study at present under revision.

3. *Gymnasium:*
(High school — Humanities and Science branch)
Civics and history partly as separate subjects, in which case one third of the lessons devoted to civics. In Grade 13 study teams. As teaching principle, especially in history. In the *Abitur* (Final examination before graduation from high school, and entrance to university) civics are examined jointly with history. New program of studies at present being worked out. School events as in the Middle School.

4. *Berufsschule* (Vocational School):
Civics taught by specialized teachers. As teaching principle. Study program in course of being worked out. To come into force Easter 1959.

IV. BREMEN

New programs being worked out for all types of schools, to come into force Easter 1959.

1. Primary school:
As teaching principle in as many fields of teaching as possible. Civics taught by the home-room teacher. No grades entered on report. This subject is intended to coordinate and utilize the stimuli deriving from its application as a teaching

principle in the other subjects. In addition several subjects may be temporarily combined for the teaching of civic themes.

The study program envisages:

Grade 7: the family
Grade 8: the parish
Grade 9: the path to working life.

Taught in general by the home-room teacher. Questions of school life are discussed jointly. In addition school parliament.

2. Middle school:

As teaching principle. Special lessons as in primary school. The natural fundamentals of government.

3. *Gymnasium* (High School):

Teaching principle. Special lessons as in Primary and Middle schools. In addition:
Grade 11: Our social system today
Grade 12: The Federal Republic. The Free Hansa City of Bremen; the treatment of current events.
Grade 13: The task which Europe sets us; cooperation between the nations; current events.

Questions concerning civics are sometimes asked in the *Abitur*, but grades are not entered on the reports.

V. HAMBURG

New program being worked out for all types of schools, which will shortly be completed.

1. Primary schools:

As teaching principle. Teaching is given by the home-room teacher. At present no special lessons in civics. The following civic themes are envisaged as follows:
(Grades 5 and 6: 9 lessons, Grades 7—9: 11 lessons)
Grades 5 and 6: family, school, community, world of work
Grades 7 and 8: the city state of Hamburg, questions of economy.
Grade 9: Special emphasis is given to current events.

The new directives which are to come into force in 1959, envisage special lessons on "Civics, History, and Geography". Number of lessons: Grades 7 and 8, 3 lessons; Grade 9, 3.

2. Middle school:

As above, in addition Grade 10: Current events, the community, world of employment, political geography.

3. *Gymnasium* (High School):

As teaching principle, especially in history and geography. Current events are prescribed for grades 10 and 13. In Grade 13, 4 lessons weekly are devoted to history (otherwise 2). The 2 additional lessons are to be devoted to political education, including sociology and economics, from the point of view of problems of the day. In Grades 12 and 13 study teams may be formed. After Easter 1959 some Hamburg *Gymnasia* are to introduce civics as a special subject experimentally. One Girls' *Gymnasium* takes sociology as a special subject: extra lessons in sociology.

4. Berufsschule (Vocational School):

In addition to civics as a subject, political education is a principle of teaching, especially in technical subjects. Teaching is given by the home-room teacher or by a specialist. The number of lessons varies according to the type of school and external circumstances. Some study teams have been formed. In general each school has its own plan for this subject. Grades are entered. An older program is being revised.

VI. HESSE

1. Primary schools:

Great emphasis is laid upon this as a teaching principle throughout the school, particularly in history and geography. Of the 4 or 5 lessons weekly devoted to world affairs, 1 lesson is given to history and 1 to sociology in Grades 5 and 6, and 2 lessons to history and 1 to sociology in Grades 7 and 8. In Grade 9 (not yet introduced everywhere) the 6 lessons in political science are to be divided between 3 for sociology and history and 3 for geography and economics. Teaching is given by the home-room teacher.

The program envisages:

Grade 5: individual examples of social institutions (the class, the home, the parish)

Grade 6: school, one's neighbors, the parish

Grade 7: the family, employment, the parish

Grade 8: rights and duties, the Land, the Federation, supra-national organizations

Grade 9: the professions, the economy, the law.

2. Middle school:

The teaching plans describe political science and/or sociology as the "characteristic subject" of the Middle school. As a teaching principle in all subjects, especially history, geography and English. Lessons are given by specialized teachers, as far as possible combined with history and geography as "Political Science". Grades are entered on report cards.

The study program envisages:

Grade 5: the class, the working world immediately around us

Grade 6: the school, the community

Grade 8: social rights and duties, basic rights, Land and Federation

Grade 9: economy, social questions

Grade 10: the professions, the law.

In addition, one lesson shall, as far as possible, be reserved for discussing questions of class and school government.

3. Gymnasium (High School):

As teaching principle in all subjects, especially history, geography, classical and modern languages. Should only 1 lesson a week be devoted to one of these subjects, this shall be a double-period; and a course of lessons devoted to each subject. Teaching is given by specialized teachers. In Grades 5 and 6 the period devoted to sociology may be used for class purposes and is held by the home-room teacher. In the senior grades lectures are given on the professions and problems of public life and study teams are formed. The subject is examined in the Abitur.

The schedules envisage:

Grade 5: the immediate environment of the child (class, workaday world)

Grade 6: the school and the community

Grade 7: work and the community
Grade 8: social rights and duties, basic rights. the Federation and the *Land*
Grade 9: the economy, social questions
Grade 10: employment, the law
Grade 11: the economy, currency, autonomy, basic rights
Grade 12: production, the constitutional state, law and justice
Grade 13: economic order, forms of government, communism, social theory.

4. *Berufsschule* (Vocational School):

Sociology as a subject in all branches, also in the examination. New plans are being worked out.

VII. LOWER SAXONY

1. Primary school:

As a principle of education in all subjects. In the first four grades civic themes in the local studies lessons. After Grade 5 special lessons, given by the teacher who deals with related subjects. No grades entered on reports.
Study program envisages:
Grades 5 and 6: the class as a community, the working world in the immediate environment.
Grade 7: the parish
Grade 8: the State, social conditions, employment
Grade 9: the State, social conditions, employment (not yet introduced everywhere).

2. Middle school:

As a principle of education in all subjects. Special lessons by a specialist teacher. From Grade 10 on grades are entered on reports, in some cases jointly with the grade for history or geography.
Study program envisages:
Grades 5—7: Themes of Grades 5—6 of the Primary School in a more advanced form
Grade 8: Themes of Grade 7 of the Primary School as above
Grades 9 and 10: Themes of Grades 9 and 10 of the *Gymnasium.*

3. *Gymnasium* (High School):

As a principle of education in all subjects. From Grade 10 grades are entered on reports, in some cases jointly with the grade for history or geography. Teaching is generally given by the history or geography teacher. Instead of one lesson a week a double period once a fortnight may be given, or a course of lessons planned.
Study program:
Grade 5: the place of the individual in his environment, community life, franchise, introduction to the economy
Grades 6—8: reference to civic themes in the directives for various subjects
Grade 9: place of the individual in his environment, juvenile law, commerce, local government
Grade 10: choice of a profession, Germany today, Lower Saxony, the Federal Republic, the eastern areas
Grade 11: European economy, European union
Grade 12: world economy, supra-national organizations
Grade 13: law, parliament, dialectic materialism, situation of world politics today.

4. Berufsschule (Vocational School):
As principle of teaching in all subjects. Grades are entered on reports. Themes are treated from the professional standpoint. Study program envisages:
1st year: the world of employment, business, legal status of juveniles
2nd year: family, society, state
3rd year: social, political and economic basic questions of today
Trade and continuation schools
Individual plans on the lines of the plans for the *Gymnasium*.

VIII. NORTH RHINE-WESTPHALIA

1. Primary school:
As principle of teaching from Grade 3 on. Special lessons in the last two years to sum up what has already been learned. Of the three periods devoted to history and civics, one is to be devoted to political science. Teaching mostly given by the home-room teacher. Grades are entered for "history and civics". Study program envisages: a survey of the most important community institutions, especially in local and national government.

2. Middle school:
As principle of teaching, especially in history, geography, German, foreign languages and religion. Each school decides for itself whether special teaching shall be given in addition, and how many periods shall be devoted to this. Teaching is given by the history teacher. Grades are entered jointly with history.

3. Gymnasium:
As principle of teaching in all subjects, especially in history. Not a special subject, but three weeks of the history and geography lessons are devoted to political science, in Grades 10 to 12 at the end of each half year, in Grade 13 at the end of the first half year and at some other time. Grades are entered under these two subjects, which are taken into account in the *Abitur*. In addition working teams. Study program envisages:
Grade 10: history, ancient and modern forms of government, social questions
Grade 11: history, autonomy, the judiciary system, international and supra-national institutions
Grade 12: history, the State and the Churches, human rights, economic forms
Grade 13: history, socialism, the modern state
Grade 10: geography, the division of Germany, the European idea
Grade 11: geography, undeveloped areas, man in the life of the community
Grade 12: geography, economic systems, changes in world pattern
Grade 13: geography, population problems, the great powers.

4. Berufsschule (Vocational School):
As principle of teaching in all subjects. In addition special lessons, the material for which is taken from the direct environment of the employed juvenile, leading up to the comprehension of cosmopolitan relationships and interlocking factors.

IX. RHINELAND-PALATINATE

1. Primary school:
As principle of teaching in the first four grades, in all subjects in the senior grades. Grades 7 and 8 as a special subject. The study program envisages: concentric circles: leading from the play community to the class community, the family, the parish, the *Land*, the Federation, to supra-national communities.

2. Middle school:

As principle of teaching. The study program envisages:

Grade 7: the class community, the school, the family

Grade 8: the employee, the parish, the *Kreis*, the *Land*, the Federal Government

Grade 9: the individual and the community (from the class to the Federal Republic)

Grade 10: basic rights, Germany as a part of Europe in the world.

3. *Gymnasium* (High School):

As a principle of teaching in all subjects, especially in history. In the Junior classes the experience and practical world of the pupil is taken as a starting point, in the senior classes emphasis is given to a more conceptual consideration. The study program envisages:

Grade 7: school and family

Grade 8: family, profession, the parish

Grade 9: trade, the parish, the *Kreis*, governmental institutions

Grade 10: law, the economy, autonomy, the State

Grade 11: more intensive consideration of the foregoing, employment and economy, basic political conceptions

Grades 12 and 13: employment and economy, the parish and the State, humanity.

4. *Berufsschule* (Vocational School):

As principle of teaching in all subjects. Special teaching centres round the professions and is further related to daily events. The study program envisages:

1st year: man in the community, the family, his profession, the parish.

2nd year: the economy, basic conceptions of national economy.

3rd year: the State and legal institutions.

Trade Schools: two periods a week are envisaged for 2 or 3 terms, in which the following material is to be dealt with:

1. man and the community (family, the parish, the State)

2. man and his profession

3. the economy

4. culture.

X. SAARLAND

1. Primary schools:

No special lessons before Grade 8. In Grade 9 (final year), within the framework of the entire school program, 12 periods for Catholic pupils and 13 periods for Evengelical pupils are earmarked for themes dealing with the obligations to the community. These centre round everyday life: the family, the world of employment, the parish, the nation and the State. Taught by the home-room teacher.

2. Middle school:

At present political science is not taught as a special subject. A new study program is being worked out, in which it is planned to devote at least one period a week to sociology. Taught by the home-room teacher.

3. *Gymnasium* (High School):

It is not planned to teach this as a special subject. In the senior grades political science is given consideration as a voluntary subject "Introduction to Philosophy". As a principle of teaching in all subjects. New study programs and directives are envisaged in the proposed revision of all study programs.

4. Berufsschule (Vocational School):

As a principle of teaching, especially in Business Training. Civics are taught by the home-room teacher or by a specialist. Grades are entered on the reports.
Study program at present under revision.

XI. SCHLESWIG-HOLSTEIN

1. Primary schools:

Civics is not taught as a special subject. In Grade 9 the study teams pay increased attention to civic themes. The principle of teaching is that social education should be the underlying foundation of teaching in all subjects. This applies in particular to history and geography.

2. Middle schools:

As principle of teaching. In nearly all schools civics is taught in connection with history and by the history teacher. Certain schools with specially favorable school conditions allot one additional period to civics. In some Middle Schools working teams for civics are formed. The subject is not included in the examinations. The working out of the directives is not yet concluded.

3. *Gymnasium* (High School):

As principle of teaching, especially in history, geography, classical and modern languages. In Grade 10, the four periods allotted are to be divided between 2 for history, 1 for current events and 1 for geography. In Grade 13 current events is a separate subject taught by a teacher qualified in history or geography. Grades are entered on report. In the *Abitur* current events is an obligatory subject, jointly with history. In the sociology branch this subject is taken in addition. In Grade 13 working teams may be formed.
The study program envisages:
Grade 13: Nature and practice of democracy. From the German breakdown up to the present (the Federation, the "DDR" (German Democratic Republic), the *Land* and the parish), Europe and the world.
Grade 10: the same subjects adapted to the age of the pupils.
In addition, the Sociology branch in the Girls' *Gymnasia* devote 2 periods a week to sociology in Grade 11, and 3 periods a week in Grades 12 and 13.
The study program envisages:
Grades 11 and 12: domestic science, family and juvenile aid, child psychology
Grade 13: introduction to sociology.

4. *Berufsschule* (Vocational School):

As teaching principle, especially in such subjects as history, national economy, geography etc. The subject is termed civics in the *Berufsschule*, science of politics and economics in the engineering school and sociology in the training centres for social workers. The subject is mainly taught by a specialist. Grades are entered on the reports. The subject is included in the examinations. A skeleton plan exists for the teaching of civics in the trade schools. Under this plan each school works out its own study plan.

A Study of the Present Situation Regarding Contemporary History Instruction in the High School of Land Hesse [1]

By Helmuth Leichtfuss

In the recent past, the daily press, as well as radio and television, repeatedly dealt with the problem of the history and political instruction provided for the youth of West Germany. The "insufficient knowledge" of the juveniles with respect to the most recent past was frequently deplored. It was emphasized again and again, that for the political education of the citizens of tomorrow a thorough examination of the history of the 20th century and, in particular, of the theory and practice of the totalitarian state, was required. This task, it was stressed, would have to be primarily accomplished in the final grades of all school types.

In the effort to investigate to what extent this public criticism of contemporary history instruction in the high schools was justified, the diaries kept by the top grades of all high schools (Oberprima) in the year 1958—59 were examined by the Hesse Ministry of Education. The entries on the topics listed as subjects of instruction were to provide an idea of the degree to which contemporary history had been discussed in the history classes of the top grades.

Since, however, the instruction subjects of history and of civic education classes partly overlap in the top grades, in line with existing education plans, and since, moreover, the fact was known that some chapters of contemporary history were also being dealt with in civic education classes, also the entries in the grade diaries referring to that subject were examined. Of course, the applied method which is bound to be superficial and unprecise cannot help being characterized by certain deficiencies. In the first place, the diary entries only list the subjects dealt with in the class, but provide no information regarding the plan underlying the instruction and the specific way in which it took place, nor do they indicate the actual results effected by it. Consequently, no reliable findings can be obtained in this way as to the extent to which this history instruction fulfilled its task in the sense of the education programs, and whether or not it achieved essential political education results in addition to the supplying of factual information. Therefore, a definitive verdict on the type, method, and success of history instruction cannot be obtained in this fashion. All the same, in spite of these reservations and provisos, the examination of the top-grade diaries provided some insight into the practice of history instruction in the top grades of the high schools.

The results can be summarized under the following four main aspects:

1) Observations regarding the methodic set-up of history instruction;

2) Periods dealt with;

3) Observations regarding the practice of history instruction;

4) Cooperation between history instruction and civic education.

[1] From *Gesellschaft — Staat — Erziehung*, No. 7, 1959.

140

The methodic structure of history instruction

The education plans leave it to the discretion of the history teacher to shape his instruction in whatever way he deems fit in order to do justice to the specific tasks with reference to the concerned age group. He has four characteristic procedures at his disposal:

1) a vertical historical cross section, as seen from a specific angle;
2) the scrutiny of a certain epoch in its central phase as to the formative forces and elements;
3) the study of historical structures and interrelations seen from a certain characteristic date (turning point); and
4) the elaboration of a universal and graphic historical picture of a specific smaller region.

The diary entries demonstrate clearly that hardly any beginnings were made to shape the history classes along the lines of these method suggestions of the education plans. As a rule, the chronological way of dealing with the subject was used. One might say at best that the so-called epoch surveys were granted preference because in this manner chronological points of view can be considered most easily. It has to be noted, however, that these epoch surveys were given in a rather narrow framework so that essentially only the political formative elements were examined.

Periods dealt with

The fact that the chronological procedure was granted preponderance helps in providing a clear picture of the periods with which history instruction in the top grades of the secondary schools had dealt. In 60 % of the grades, history instruction for the top grade started with the Era of Enlightenment or with the French Revolution; in approx. 30 % of all grades with the year 1815 or 1848, and only in approx. 10 % of the grades with 1870—71.

The examination of the diaries established the definitive fact that with a starting date around 1789, it had only been possible in very rare cases to place special emphasis, in line with the binding regulations of the education plans, on contemporary history, i.e., the era beginning approximately in 1917. As stated above, this is true for the majority of all top grades. One fourth of the above listed 60 % had not proceeded beyond 1900 at the time of the written examinations for the high school diploma (Abitur) at the beginning of February; another fourth had not proceeded beyond 1919. This means that less than half of the grades had not yet started, at the beginning of February, to deal with that period of history to which this particular grade had been meant to accord special attention.

The situation at the time of the written examinations for the high school diploma was as follows:

17 % of all grades had reached the year 1900,
18 % had reached the end of World War I,
22 % had reached the time of the Weimar Republic, and
43 % had started discussing the National Socialist period.

This state of affairs brought it about that in not quite 20 % of all top grades, due to lack of time, the time after 1919 was not dealt with at all or, at the utmost, was only briefly outlined in one or two lessons in the form of a summary survey. It could not be ascertained, however, to what extent problems of the totalitarian state had already come up in the civic education classes for the grades below the top grade, as the education plans suggest (*Der totale Staat*, p. 500). The time after 1945 appears to have been discussed hardly at all in the history classes for the top grades.

Observations regarding the practice of history instruction

The discussion of political history appears to have been granted priority. The course of revolutions, the resulting war hostilities, alliance systems, treaties and agreements, political crises and wars were frequently listed in the diaries: e.g., six hours of "World War I", as compared to one hour of "National Socialism". It can be seen from the diary entries, on the other hand, that only rarely the attempt was undertaken to examine the formative elements which had shaped events in the sphere of art and literature, economics, the social system, and the legal sector. Romanticism and Liberalism, e.g., were primarily dealt with isolatedly as political phenomena. The isolated discussion of the Weimar Republic, seen from the nationalist angle, is a specially striking fact. The events of national history in this period were hardly incorporated at all into a system of world-wide interrelations.

Cooperation between history instruction and civic education

It happens relatively seldom that both subjects are being taught by the same teacher. In such instances, there exists in most cases — but definitely not always — a close relation between the two subject matters. If, however, the said subjects are taught by different teachers, they remain isolated in most cases and there is not much evidence of that integration procedure which is prescribed by the education plans.

A Survey on the Most Important Ordinances Issued by the State Cultural Ministries

During the Period 1 Feb., 1959 — 1 Oct., 1960[1]

Baden-Wuerttemberg

In accordance with the Cultural Ministry Ordinances, directions for the teaching of contemporary history were issued during the period 1 Feb.—30 April, 1959. Through these ordinance it was ordered that at the latest four weeks after the beginning of the school year 1959—60, instructions on contemporary history should be taken up in elementary, middle and high schools, even if the curriculum in the foregoing classes had not been completed. By this, assurance is given that every student who leaves school will have been thoroughly instructed in the history of the most recent past. In an Ordinance of November 1959 teachers of history and civics were also requested to discuss the cruelties which had been committed during the dictatorship by its leaders who ignored even the most fundamental human rights. A bibliography is also included.

---

[1] From *Erziehungswesen und Judentum*, pp. 132—134.

In the Ordinance of 5 Jan. 1960 for vocational schools, it has been requested that recent history must be discussed thoroughly in graduating classes.

For high school teachers, university seminars on political science will be held. More emphasis was given to continual teachers training. The libraries of teachers' colleges were supplied with more books on civics and political science. Every two or three months instruction bulletins are worked out giving suggestions for the treatment of recent history. In history- and civics-teachers' conferences, which are held in each county, opportunities are being offered to discuss teaching methods and new teaching-aids.

Bavaria

On 17 Feb. 1959 the Bavarian State Ministry of Education and Culture issued a new curriculum for the teaching of history in high schools which strongly emphasized the treatment of contemporary history. The department for secondary schools is asked to watch closely the history courses in grades 8, 9 and 13 of high schools, where contemporary history is taught. It is its special duty to check whether the history of the 20th century is being taught effectively.

In the Bavarian four-grade middle school, contemporary history is being taught for the whole of the fourth year.

Also in elementary schools a history course for one full year is devoted to recent and contemporary history.

Berlin

For some time an ordinance has been in effect which requires that in graduating classes, the history course has to begin with the year 1912, and to be continued under all circumstances up to very the present.

In addition to already existing ordinances and directions the Minister for Education in Berlin, in September 1959, had organized a contemporary history seminar for interested high school students.

Bremen

In December 1959 the Minister of Education issued new instruction plans for primary and secondary schools which allow ample time for the teaching of contemporary history. Curricula for high schools, for instance, require that in the 9th grade the year 1850 should be reached, so that in the 10th grade the present time could be dealt with.

History courses in graduating classes must be devoted entirely to the 20th century and especially to the period from 1917 until 1945.

Hamburg

In an Ordinance of 28 September 1959 for elementary, middle, and high schools, the Hamburg School Board requested that for graduating classes history courses must be centered around contemporary history. In addition, an Ordinance of 8 Jan. 1960 rules that in all schools recent anti-Semitic incidents have to be discussed from the 5th grade on.

Hesse

Within the framework of the Hessian study-plans an Ordinance issued in the spring of 1959 referring to the evaluation of inquiries made earlier at the schools, directs that the recent past be treated in the schools, particularly in the higher grades. An Ordinance of 8 January 1960 further directs that all schools from the fifth grade upward will discuss the recent anti-Semitic incidents.

143

Lower Saxony

On 15 Oct. 1959, the Minister of Culture called the attention of all school super-intendents in the State to neo-Fascist youth organizations and ordered that the State officials must counteract the beginning of such organizations. On 23 Nov. 1959 he requested all high school principals to see to it that the Lower Saxony State directions for political education are followed. Also superintendents were asked to give tests on contemporary history in the graduating examination for high school students and to report on the results. As in previous years the Cultural Ministry together with the State Committee on Civic Education organized for the summer of 1959 and winter of 1959—60 courses on contemporary history and problems of political education as part of the teachers continuation training program.

North Rhine-Westphalia

In addition to the instruction plans of 1957 and directions on political education for various types of schools, elaborate study plans for elementary schools were issued in 1959. In these plans it was requested that in graduating classes history courses must be devoted entirely to the period from the Congress of Vienna until the present time.

The Cultural Minister repeated in an ordinance his request that teachers in middle and high schools discuss the period of National Socialism in history classes.

During the last months school faculties of this State have organized more high school teachers conferences on the teaching of contemporary history.

Rhineland-Palatinate

An Ordinance of the Minister of Culture issued on 14 July 1959 requested that the number of hours per week in grade 13 be increased to two hours for civics and three for history. During the second half of the 13th grade, approximately 45 hours should be devoted to the teaching of contemporary history (1917 till today).

In the graduation examination a sufficient number of students have to be tested on their knowledge of contemporary history and civics.

In the 10th grade at least 20 hours should be devoted to the teaching of con-temporary history. In the presence of the principal an examination on this subject matter has to be held before the passing of students to the 11th grade is discussed in the faculty meeting.

In addition the ordinance mentions all available teaching aids including those for teachers' continuation training.

Schleswig-Holstein

The Minister of Culture ordered in late fall that the most recent past must be more strongly emphasized in history and civic classes in primary and secondary schools.

Teaching Recent History in German Schools

From *Bulletin* of German Federal Government Press and
Information Office, 18 February 1960.

At its session held in Hamburg on 11—12 February 1960, the "Permanent Conference of Cultural Affairs Ministers" of the States in the Federal Republic of
Germany adopted the following resolution on the teaching of most recent history
in German schools:

"The special events of last year were not needed to induce the school authorities
to take the necessary measures for the political education of our young generation.
The Permanent Conference of Cultural Affairs Ministers established principles on
political education in schools as early as on 15 June 1950. These principles are
based on the experience which the various State Cultural Affairs Ministries had
gained previously.

"These principles were taken into consideration by the Cultural Affairs Ministers
of the German states when drafting their instructions for the curricula of the schools
under their jurisdiction. For example, a decree of the Cultural Affairs Ministry of
Lower Saxony of 1951 demands that in the higher grades of all types of schools
the historical background of the last 100 years be covered in detail, and that
current affairs be included. In 1953, the Cultural Affairs Ministers' Conference
adopted principles for the teaching of history. These principles define the task
and goal of teaching history, as well as the beginning and scope of these lessons.

In 1955, the opinion on political education adopted by the German Committee
for Educational Matters resulted *(Deutscher Ausschuss fuer das Erziehungs- und
Bildungswesen)*. Finally, the Cultural Affairs Ministers' Conference emphatically
pointed (during its 71st plenary meeting, held in Munich in April 1959) to the need
for constant checking of the demands made in the various decisions and decrees.
"The Ministers also pointed out, however, that the work of the political education
of the young generation can be done by the schools only when parents and the
public assist the teachers in their difficult and responsible task.

"In its statement of 30 January 1960, on the anti-Semitic outrages, the German
Committee for Educational Matters made the necessary remarks regarding the need
for cooperation of all those responsible for the education of children and
adolescents. The Permanent Conference of Cultural Affairs Ministers has noted
with satisfaction that this statement has been given due public attention.

"At the plenary meeting on 24—25 September 1959, the methods regarding the way
in which the directives and decrees shall be implemented and how the implementation can be controlled, were once again discussed. It was also decided to review
the textbooks on history and geography now being used. The constant activities of
the Cultural Affairs Ministers' Conference during the last ten years induced the
school administrations of the states to review on a continual basis the guiding
principles for political education. The extent to which this work is being done is
evident from the voluminous collection of all decrees and guiding principles for
history lessons and civic education.

"In order to render the decrees of the State Ministries and the resolutions of the
Permanent Conference of Cultural Affairs Ministers still more educationally effective
than they have been to date, the Cultural Affairs Ministers' Conference adopted

the following resolution at its 75th plenary meeting in Hamburg on 11—12 February 1960, as being binding for all states:

I.

"1. In the course of their examinations the candidates for all types of schools must prove that they are acquainted with the elements of a political system based on law (basic rights, human rights, international principles of law), and that they have a knowledge of German history of our century. They must prove that they are aware of the main facts which during the Nazi era led to the destruction of the political system based on law, and that they have formed an opinion on the cause and effect of the division of Germany. Whoever wishes to qualify as a teacher of history must have a particularly thorough knowledge of this subject, independent of the field of studies in which he concentrated.

"2. The Cultural Affairs Ministers will work toward the placing of an emphasis on the establishment of additional university chairs for political sciences. At all colleges and institutions at which teachers are trained, chairs and/or lectures shall also be provided for the didactics of political sciences and history.

"3. During his training period, between the first and second state examination, every teacher must be introduced to the methods of civic education (as a principle and as a subject). Every teacher must learn during his training period to understand, and to establish, the interrelations of his special field with contemporary history and civic education.

II.

"1. It is agreed which issues and facts from the Nazi era shall be dealt with in detail in the higher grades of all schools throughout the Federal Republic. This agreement applies also when it is planned not to treat history chronologically in the higher grades of secondary schools, but to concentrate on specific issues.

"2. Libraries for teachers and students must include the basic works on most recent history. The official gazettes of the Ministries shall carry increasingly more references to, and reviews of, scientific and methodic works, as well as literature for classroom reading, on recent history and civic education. Insofar as this has not yet been done, the State Picture Agencies shall receive a fair supply of audio-visual equipment, while the teachers shall be trained in the handling and methodic use of such equipment.

"3. The findings of the review of textbooks, decided upon at the plenary meeting on 24—25 September 1959, shall foresightedly be evaluated by the School Committee in order to be able jointly to give advice to the publishers of textbooks for the scrutiny and improvement of their books.

"4. All efforts aimed at raising the standard of teachers in regard to political education must be encouraged. Their effectiveness will be improved if personalities of public life, especially also of political life, would offer their assistance to such efforts more than has been done up to now.

"5. The board of the Cultural Affairs Ministers' Conference will deliberate with the leading organizations of the teachers in regard to joint projects related to political education.

"6. Efforts must be made to have greater amounts included in the State budgets for political-education projects, for the promotion of the work of the Land Organizations for Civics — Landeszentralen fuer Heimatdienst — (and/or political education), and to assist projects planned by teachers' associations.

"1. History lessons must be planned in all grades with a view to their political and educational aspect and as a preparation for the coverage of most recent history. The School Committee is instructed to draft guiding principles for civic education, such principles to supplement the policy on history lessons.

"2. Mutual confidence within the school community, and teaching methods based on confidence between teachers and students, are prerequisites for successful teaching. Cooperation with the Parents'-Teachers Associations at the various schools, and also with the self-administration of the students is of major importance for political education.

"Historical and political facts can objectively be passed on and discussed at school. In those years when young people are particularly receptive to education, prejudices can most easily be overcome. The teachers must not "editorialize" in their lessons. However, they must determinedly support the democratic state and the social order based on law, as the basis of our intellectual, economic and political existence. In their lessons they will then be able to lead to issues of political ethics, to encourage responsiveness to such issues, and to train the students for proper conduct in political life.

"The teachers share in their turn responsibility for the education of young people as guardians and defenders of the political order based on law. The Cultural Affairs Ministers' Conference is convinced that the teachers realize this responsibility and their duties for political education."

Education for Citizenship today [1]

By Walter Jacobsen

Education for citizenship today means, for us Germans, more than just a general training to be responsible and politically mature citizens of a democracy; for us it includes making ourselves more actively aware of the fact that in the eyes of the world, the German people are saddled with an extraordinarily heavy moral burden drawn from the very recent past, and that for their own good Germans must keep this fact particularly in mind. No German, however free of blame he may feel, can escape from this joint burden, can claim the privilege of being free of any degree of responsibility (unless he wishes and is entitled to claim that he has no further connection with the German people). No German can escape — for even persecuted emigrants as they were helped by kindly citizens of the country that took them in, will have sensed the silent reproach: "It is your country which is persecuting you, your people who have brought this misery upon the world". Can anyone say today, "I am not one of these people"? When someone feels a glow of pride at an athlete from his country "bringing home" a gold medal, how can he suppose

---

[1]) This paper was written after an Advisory Council of Experts had been convened by the Federal Minister of the Interior as a result of the wave of anti-Semitic and National Socialistic acts committed at the end of 1959 and beginning of 1960.

that he can cut himself off from the disgrace, the shame, and the moral obligation to make a personal effort to repair the monstrous things done in the name of his people, by a government unreservedly applauded by the masses?

Yes, one might answer, but what then was the point of categorizing the Germans in the five grades of culpability or exoneration during de-nazification? For reasons of internal policy, and in part for reasons of foreign policy too, this action was a necessary, an invitable measure (though another form, other methods might have been used), and arguments of individual psychology required a distinction to be made between those who bore a personal share in responsibility and those who did not. But this sort of thing could never destroy the concept and the reality of the unit known as the "German people" and replace it with a multiplicity of individual persons or independent closed groups; whether we liked it or not, we were still all in the same boat. As a political community, the German people were still, and continued to be, a unit whose fate was indivisible; as such, it remained indivisibly responsible for its deeds — and not even the subsequent division of the country could alter this in any way.

In education for citizenship it is just this task of making Germans conscious of the moral burden resting on their country which is of special importance today, for a tendency has remained — and is becoming increasingly evident — which points in the opposite direction, the tendency in the individual to dismiss lock, stock and barrel any share in moral responsibility, even as a nation to feel to a large extent exonerated and so to behave in a way that can only damage the community; this reaction is psychologically explicable, but it is also possible, given a reasonable arousing of consciousness, to influence it.

This particular task of arousing consciousness is two-dimensional: there are the points which one comes to realize through external influences, and those which come from within. It is just in such a case as this that it is not enough to note only the external, objective facts and to evaluate them with more or less objectivity, but an essential part of the process is that awareness should penetrate through to the inner inhibitions which have a habit of blocking any honest review of one's conscience, any real grappling with a problem and so preventing, in the long run, an attitude of good will and of "tact". When someone is so psychologically cramped, nothing can be done till this cramp has been cured, least of all in the effort to educate him to be a citizen who will be called upon to play a responsible part in democracy not only with his intellect, but with his heart and his conscience — and who must be made capable of playing that part. On this depends not only success in building up a democratic state, which assumes inner participation by its citizens, not only the increase in the confidence felt in us by the "free world" which is our ally, but also our success in resisting a hostile Great Power with a great talent for the use of propaganda weapons.

The reasons making it necessary to take just this aspect of education for citizenship much more seriously than has been done in the last fifteen years are, then, of great importance. It is part of the whole business of coping with our recent past, of which so much is heard today. The convening of a special advisory council of experts shows that the Federal Government has recognized that this is a matter which must be tackled.

What are the disciplines in which the twelve experts specialize? All but one, who is the scientific director of the Armed Forces' *Schule der Inneren Fuehrung*[2]) (a

---

[2]) A school which trains personnel to take care of the morale of the Forces. See II E 4.

**Advertising the Unification of Europe. A Special Train Exhibit
Promoting European Unification Tours Germany**   Photo: E C A

DIE BUNDESREGIERUNG SORGT FÜR DIE

Photo: B. B. Bonn

Exhibit on Wheels. This Special Exhibit Inside Railroad Coaches on the German Federal Republic is Carried to Remote Areas by Train

Exhibition on the History and Persecution of the German Jews. Visitors Listening to Tape Recorded Speeches of Hitler and Göring. Göring's photo (right) was taken at the Nuremburg Trials

specialist in psychology) are university professors, some of them retired; they include three historians, two theologians, two lawyers, two professors of education, and two representing philosophy, sociology, and political science.

Which, then, are the most difficult or the most pressing of the problems in this tricky task of popular education which has been given to these professors? Are they to be found in the scale, the selection and the presentation of contemporary history? Is the problem to find the best way of continually admonishing people to remember the duties placed upon them by their religion? Is the main need to have additional enlightenment and instruction on questions of international or constitutional law? Or are they having to deal with technical problems of teaching methods, which are causing special difficulties for political training in schools, peoples colleges, academies and universities? Or is the problem that of right and safe "reception" of all these efforts at popular education made in a society which, for many psychologically understandable reasons, either remains to a great extent unresponsive to "political" education, admonition, interference in matters of conscience, words of advice or any other actions which disturb the privacy of the individual, or else tries to evade them (in favor of more acceptable external stimuli).

I think there can be only one answer. It is that all the various disciplines mentioned must work together as a team; but the ultimately decisive and, at the same time, most difficult problems are in the last of the groups cited: for unless a satisfactory answer were found to the question of how we can accurately and successfully "put over" the partly ethical, partly intellectual efforts at education, these efforts would in most cases show but poor results. This particular set of problems falls into the field of psychology with its special branches of social psychology, folk characterology and depth psychology. Social psychology must tell us what processes before and after Hitler's seizure of power led to the great "follower urge" in its many forms, and today still leads to many manifestations of undemocratic conformism.

From studies of folk character we should learn what national peculiarities may perhaps predispose us Germans to certain politically significant attitudes (or omissions); we might also learn whether we have certain weak spots in our psychic make-up to which education for citizenship should pay particular attention. Depth psychology must reveal to the teacher — it is the first thing he needs to know — what complicated psychological processes are possible and common, especially in cases of inner conflict such as the one we are dealing with, and prevent the individual from facing the unpleasant, indeed distressing task represented by the requisite "working up" and from fully accepting "all the same" what is put to him. All these three branches of psychology overlap naturally; the last mentioned inhibitions or "cramps", for example, can very well have their source more in social psychology than in conflicts of discordant motivations or ideologies within the individual (in other words in genuine and strictly personal conflicts of urge or conscience).

Many foreign visitors have come to Germany seeking a picture of Western Germany's political thinking; amongst them there have been journalists and representatives of the international Anti-Defamation League and professional psychologists from America who saw in the 1960 International Congress in Bonn an opportunity for making studies in this field. Again and again one could hear at the end of their interviews an undertone of doubt which might be summarized thus: "We applaud the good intentions, the efforts and the multiplicity of methods which the competent authorities are employing in the endeavor to make good democrats of the Germans and to make them appreciate the gravity of what has been done. But has anyone yet made any systematic effort to find out what effect all this has had on the broad masses of the people? Is no one worried about the possibility that much of the work is a waste of energy? Has any effort been made to find out why? Have the scientists been asked to find ways and means of surmounting the obstacles and inhibitions?" Probably none of those who were interviewed was in a position to give a satisfactory answer to these questions. Our friends from abroad were not just putting random questions; as they travelled round they had been systematically making a great many observations and had talked with people from many sections of the population in Germany.

All this should serve as a pointer to the type of study which the Advisory Council of Experts is likely to put forward as the most urgent. Only the most thorough scientific studies will be able to give an indication of what will enable those working in all sectors of the broad educational front to have greater success than has so far come their way in changing the views and attitude of the many who still manage to shut their eyes to a more correct appreciation of National Socialism so long as a fully thought out, appropriate psychological alternative is not offered them. Here psychology is facing a new task on a political scale such as it has probably never before encountered.

Members of the Advisory Council:

Theology:	Prof. Hahn	Heidelberg
Philosophy:	Prof. Hirschmann	Frankfurt
Political Science and Sociology:	Prof. Bergstraesser Prof. Horkheimer	Freiburg Frankfurt
History:	Prof. Huebinger Prof. Rothfels Dr. Krausnick	Bonn Tuebingen Munich (Institut fuer Zeitgeschichte)
Education:	Prof. Litt Prof. Wenke	Bonn Hamburg
Law:	Prof. Peters Prof. Kaufmann	Cologne Heidelberg
Psychology:	Prof. Moebus	Koblenz (Bundeswehr School for Internal Leadership)

Political Education Commission to Call on Chancellor[1])

The Commission set up by the Federal Minister of the Interior to improve political education will be received by Federal Chancellor Adenauer on Monday.

Federal Minister of the Interior Schroeder had appointed the Commission in particular to work out directives for the teaching of civics in the schools. The Commission is composed of scholars and educators of repute, and its formation was the outcome of the anti-Semitic outrages in the Federal Republic of Germany last spring.

---

[1]) From *Die Welt*, 7 November 1960.

C. Political Education in the Universities

The Universities and the Reform
of Higher Education in the Federal Repubilc [1]

By Juergen Fischer

I.

The universities and other educational establishments of university level in Germany are all State instutions. They are supported financially by the State and come under its jurisdiction. The link with the State is, however, coupled with freedom from State control: Article 5(2) of the Basic Law in the Federal Republic guarantees "freedom of research and of teaching", and this means in effect not merely that a teacher is free to teach what he wants and to carry out what research he wishes without instructions, regulations and State planning, but that the constitution provides protection for the freedom of the university itself. In this way the State, which supports the universities financially, has through its constitution removed them from the field of direct State activities and given them their freedom, thus observing the western world's principle that teaching and research shall be free.

"Teaching and research", as meant by the constitution, form one entity. The research scholar, the research scientist are teachers because they do research. The universities and establishments of university level in Germany are dedicated to this unity of research and teaching on the personal plane and in subject matter; it is the basis of their high standing and distinguishes them from the mass of other educational establishments in the country. The leading centres of education in the Federal Republic are:

1. The Universities of Kiel, Hamburg, Goettingen, Cologne, Muenster, Bonn, Marburg, Giessen, Frankfurt on the Main, Mayence, Saarbruecken, Freiburg, Tuebingen, Heidelberg, Munich, Erlangen, Wuerzburg, and the Free University of Berlin;

2. The Technical Colleges of Hanover, Brunswick, Aix-la-Chapelle, Darmstadt, Stuttgart, Karlsruhe, Munich, and the Technical University of Berlin;

3. The Institutes of university standing in Clausthal (Academy of Mining), Hanover (School of Veterinary Medicine), Mannheim (School of Economics), Nuremberg (School of Economic and Social Sciences), Duesseldorf (School of Medicine) and Stuttgart-Hohenheim (Agricultural College).

These 32 seats of higher education are members of the West German Rectors' Conference.

---

[1] From *Meet Germany*, published by Atlantik-Bruecke, Hamburg, 1960.

11*

II

As in all other parts of the world, the universities in Federal Germany have been running into very great difficulties. The number of students has been rising for a wide variety of reasons; among those put forward are:

The high birth rate of the years following 1935;

The demand, created by automation and the rationalization of industry, for graduates capable of working on their own and taking their own decisions;

The fuller acceptance in ever wider circles of the principle of popular education, with the result that more and more families are seeking to give their children a higher education;

The system of qualifications under which an academic degree is required for entry into various professions;

The spread of scientific method throughout the world, with the result that more and more extensive spheres are being subjected to scientific treatment.

In the winter term 1959—1960 the number of students attending the centres of higher learning passed the 200,000 mark, though these centres were only intended to take some 140,000 students. By 1964 the number of students is likely to rise by about 50,000 more.

In the midst of the endeavors they have been making since 1946 to adapt themselves to the changed social and political situation in the world without losing anything of their freedom, the seats of learning have been invaded by this flood of students. The State, already struggling with the reconstruction of a country in ruins, with social benefits for refugees, war invalids, prisoners, and other sections of the population, and also occupied with re-armament, was not in a position to expand these institutions fast and far enough to cope with this foreseeable rush of young men and women. The result is that there is a catastrophic situation in those branches to which society looks to meet its needs (technicians, teachers, scientists, and doctors). The excessive strain on the staff and facilities in these centres of higher learning may ruin all the efforts being made to attain a reform of higher education.

III.

In the Federal Republic this reform is essentially different from that in the Soviet Zone.

1. In the Soviet Zone there was never any doubt about the purpose to be served by a reform of higher education. The State plans the entire development of the country, and in particular its economic progress. Such planned progress pre-supposes the availability of given and calculable numbers of specialists with scientific training. As the traditional German university system only recognized the education of the individual and not the training of supervisory staffs for specific schemes, it was of little use for the execution of State policy, and had to be changed. In 1952, therefore, the reform was put through in the form of a law. The famous old Universities of Berlin, Leipzig, Halle, Jena, Rostock, Greifswald, the Technical College in Dresden, and the Mining Academy of Freiberg in Saxony, were dealt such a severe blow that they are hardly recognizable today.

Party, trade union, and youth officials moved in to the senates and faculties, and an end was made to academic freedom in the teaching staffs.

The Rector was given assistants in the form of pro-Rectors for the Social sciences, for the supply of new scientists, for students' affairs, and for research, the last-named alone being chosen for his academic ability.

The students' union lost its rights of self-determination, which fell to the "Free German Youth"; only officials of this organization can be elected to represent the students.

The students' work was subjected to strict controls. Constant examinations — unknown in the system of the free German universities — make it possible to "select" students on political and academic grounds.

The purpose of the university is no longer the unfolding of the intellectual abilities of the individual, it is broad popular education. Instead of freedom of research, there is a fixed system of research, instead of freedom of teaching, there are supervised lessons. The university has been turned into a school.

Higher learning is being turned into a higher school system. In order to produce the supervisory staffs required by economic plans, and also to break the intellectual superiority of the old-established universities, the State is setting up 22 specialist institutes endowed with all the rights of the old universities (the system with a Rector as its head, the right to confer doctorates, and the right of testing and approving candidates for subsequent appointment to teaching posts in seats of higher learning). Today the old universities are hopelessly outnumbered in the "Rectors' Conference of the German Democratic Republic", and in addition this body meets under the chairmanship of the Under-Secretary for Higher Education.

2. In the Federal Republic the reform of higher learning was entirely different. Between 1945 and 1948, at a time when the future form of the State and of German society was still uncertain, the universities and institutions of comparable standing shook off the rulings which rested on National Socialist legislation and then adopted new regulations which should prevent a repetition in any possible form of what befell them in 1934—35. They strengthened the sphere of their autonomous rights, they dissociated themselves entirely from the Prussian system of higher education with its strict supervision by the State and they acquired greater freedom than they had ever had before.

Here we have the key which enables us to understand the efforts made to reform higher education and the two events in which these efforts culminated, the conference held in 1952 at Hinterzarten in the Black Forest and the conference at Bad Honnef in 1955.

The principle of the freedom of teaching and research and of their unity emerged unquestioned from all the discussions.

The structure of the academic staff was subjected to scrutiny; it was recognized that the old system with its professors, lecturers, and assistants no longer corresponded with the increase in specialization or with the aims of education, and it was decided to introduce between the upper and the lower groups a further class of teachers, all of whom, however, were to have passed the tests for candidates to posts on university staffs, i. e. were to be suitable in principle for promotion to an established post. The regulations governing study and examinations, many of them out of date or distorted by National Socialism, were brought into line with current knowledge and their co-ordination was agreed on between the autonomous faculties.

Direct support for the students in the form of grants (the "Honnef Model") and indirect assistance by the provision of quarters (Mr. McCloy started the movement with his generous gift), of dining halls, sickness insurance funds, and students' homes, satisfied the social demands of modern times without sacrificing the old, high concept of quality.

Proposals were put forward for the education of the students in political matters.

The relationship between seats of higher learning and the public, which had been neglected because of the earlier provincial structure of the universities, was improved (press offices, further education, people's colleges, etc.)

The contents of the university entrance examination, which is taken at 18 and is being removed from the hands of the schools (but not of the universities), were recast in joint discussions with the State authorities.

Just as ideas and plans were in the air for

Grouping of the students,

Re-shaping of the university institutions (e. g. Senate, faculties, etc.),

Extension of the idea of teachers and students forming a corporate body that would support a homogeneous university,

Relief of the pressure on the universities through technical schools and technical colleges, and recasting of the completely antiquated system of remuneration for university teachers,

the flood of students burst upon the universities and turned the efforts at reform into measures of self-preservation.

IV.

The Federal Government, the *Land* governments, the institutes of higher education and business circles have co-operated in the forming of a German Council for the Promotion of Science and Humanities (*Wissenschaftsrat*). The purpose of this body, which recalls an English "royal commission", is to prepare a plan to cover the expansion of all universities and institutes of similar standing, and to put forward proposals for the financing of its long-term plan, which is to be published in the summer of 1960. The West German Rectors' Conference, the German Research Association, the German Students' Union, and the *Wissenschaftsrat* are all equally anxious that the concepts contained in the reform of higher education shall be incorporated in any expansion of the relevant institutions.

Generous Plans for the Universities[1]

Proposals of the *Wissenschaftsrat* (German Council for the Promotion of Science and Humanities) for the development of the German universities.

In the lofty regions of diplomacy, it has become customary to publish — as a documentation of one's own point of view — books taking their names from the color of their covers. The German Foreign Office has been granting preference to the issuance of "white books" and has now submitted to the public another volume of that color; a 535-page publication, *Recommendations of the German Council for the Promotion of Science and Humanities for the Development of the Academic Institutions — Part I: Universities and Technical Universities*. It is, however, not only a documentation of facts which in many respects are not very satisfactory, but also provides advice regarding the way to remedy these short-comings; it deliberately refrains from voicing new theories on an "ideal university", but endeavors to point out a road towards overcoming the much-quoted university crisis.

In approximately these terms the problem was defined by the President of the *Wissenschaftsrat*, Helmut Coing, professor of Roman and Civil Law and History of Law in Frankfurt. In a conversation he stressed: "Here we do not find ourselves in the sphere of mathematical truths; we do not believe to have found the Philosopher's Stone. But we believe in practicable possibilities which are being demonstrated here."

In view of the existence of 240,000 university students . . .

Two years elapsed, the public sometimes watching proceedings with impatience, before the *Wissenschaftsrat* finally submitted the first part of a plan for the universal re-organization of the promotion of science, after close scrutiny of the situation in all universities, technical universities, mining academies, academies of agriculture, forestry, social sciences, medical sciences, and the philosophical-theological academies in Bavaria.

What was the initial situation after 1945? A present total of 200,000 university and technical students, which probably will increase to 240,000 (not including foreign students), must be faced, as well as a growing tendency in the modern social mass state to acquire an education or, at any rate, a "professional training", a tendency which intensifies the already existing tension between the educational goal of the universities to open the road to learning and science to the students, and the goals of the state and of interest groups of all types for "trained" specialists. Since 1918, upheavals of a political and economic nature slowed down the steady growth of our academic institutions, finally bringing it to almost a full stop in certain periods, namely, between 1930 and 1949. Almost 15 % of the members of the teaching body of the universities existing in 1933 were removed from their posts by the National Socialists, or even compelled to go abroad. At the end of the war, approximately 60 % of the university buildings were destroyed or heavily damaged.

In the meantime, there have been some achievments, but as yet not enough. The *Laender* alone raised 1¹/₂ billion DM between 1949 and 1959 for building projects on behalf of the universities. 1952 chairs and approximately 6,000 positions for research

---

[1] From *Die Welt*, 26 November 1960.

assistants were newly established. However, at the present time a total of 200,000 students are facing a total of 3,160 full professors. And what kind of productive studies will be possible in view of the fact, e.g., that at the huge university of Munich, only 15 professors of law are available for a total of 2,626 students of law, and only 2 professors of English for 689 Students of that subject?

Consequently, what can be done? Part B of the *expertise* attempts an answer to the problems of the students as well as of the teaching body; it also includes an analysis of the development of the various university departments.

Any type of a *numerus clausus* is being rejected. Professor Coing declared explicitly that, in the true spirit of independent studies and of the freedom of research and teaching, the possibility ought to be granted to each university student to attend already in his first semester, if he wishes to do so, the lectures of a Nobel Prize winner. On account of these considerations, the question of a special "research university" with a, so to speak, "elite" character is regarded with some reserve.

Instead, the attempt is made to solve the problem of the large number of students with the help of a reorganization or further division of the faculties and departments. This will require the establishment of 1,200 new chairs and of new academic institutions (three universities; one technical university; moreover, in order to provide some relief to the overcrowded medical departments, also new medical academies). The establishment of new universities appears to be appropriate in certain areas, e.g., Upper Bavaria, Northern Germany, North Rhine-Westphalia. Specific locations have not been named, however.

The initial building costs for each of these planned objects are estimated at 250 million DM. The financing problem of these plans has not been clarified as yet. The result of the effort to relieve the existing universities of part of their burden will only assume noticeable proportions four to five years after the foundation of the respective new university.

On the other hand, such new foundations offer increased incentives to the younger generation to enter professional careers, the prospects of which so far had been judged with scepticism by many professors. For the time being, the increase of the number of chairs has to be effected simultaneously with a reform of the *Kolleggeld* system (by which a certain portion of the student's tuition is payable to the respective professors), so that an equivalent will be created for the individual professors who, instead of having an audience of 1,000 students in the main lecture will only have half as many or even less under the new system. Second, a speeding up of the appointment procedure by the departments and, third, a strong numercial increase of the "faculty members of intermediate rank", i. e., the group of the assistant professors, is required. The number of the *Wissenschaftliche Raete* will have to be augmented, and in the institutes budgeted positions for *Abteilungsvorsteher* have to be created (both types of position to be held by faculty members with tenure, who in Germany do no hold departmental chairs). Finally, the establishment of positions for *Studienraete im Wissenschaftsdienst* (high school teachers temporarily assigned to universities) is being envisaged through which these teachers will be given a chance to work in universities for certain periods of time.

The said projects have the purpose of easing the burden of their teaching activities of the full professors; at the same time, however, the faculty members of intermediate rank, too, are definitely meant to be granted an opportunity of engaging in research work of their own. Also, the assistant professorships without tenure are to be increased in number to the point that they will finally come up to one third of the existing chairs. Ultimately, also the total of the more or less technical staff has to be raised.

A big step forward

In the opinion of the *Wissenschaftsrat* it will not be possible to expand indiscriminately the number of members of the individual departments, e. g., to one hundred or more full professors, if the corporative self-administration of the departments is to be maintained. By the same token, sensible and productive research and teaching activities are no longer feasible if more than approximately 8,000 students attend one university. This is the basis of the idea to effect a further division of the faculties into academic departments and to establish new universities. The thought, specified by definite proposals, to create "points of strength for research" *(Forschungs-Schwerpunkte)* in certain universities offering suitable conditions, is meant to serve the same purpose.

The entire enterprise of this over-all plan — two additional expert's opinions referring to the learned societies and academies and to the research institutes (government-supported institutions, Max Planck Society, etc.) will follow — constitutes not only an organizational problem but also a financial one. These aspects are outlined in Part C. According to those data, the development of the university body will require a minimum of 360 million DM per year; the completion of the building projects now under way or being required up to the year 1964 will necessitate expenditures of 2.6 billion DM. The recommended supplementation of the equipment of institutes and colleges — including the libraries as well as the various appliances and implements — will cost another 83 million DM per year. While the Federal Government and the *Laender* will jointly allocate the funds for the building program, the personnel costs will remain a burden of the *Laender* alone since under the federative system these have exclusive jurisdiction over cultural affairs.

The *Wissenschaftsrat* neither has the authority nor the intention to insist upon the implementation of an over-all plan with the help of this expert's opinion. It only wants to show up possibilities and to offer suggestions regarding the system that might be adopted. It wants to respect the jurisdiction over cultural affairs of the *Laender* as well as the autonomy of the university departments. This consideration of manifold aspects has its disadvantages but also its positive points; Professor Coing called attention to this fact. For that reason, e. g., "model departments" are being described in the *expertise* so that a margin for initiative of its own is left to the individual university department, in line with the specific conditions characterizing it. The idea is to make suggestions, not to decree.

If the *expertise* will be understood correctly, a big step forward will be made. The *Wissenschaftsrat* adopted it unanimously; the Ministers of Education of the *Laender* approved of it. With regard to certain fields, views were coordinated with the Rectors' Conference. Prof. Coing stated that with the drawing up of its *expertise* the *Wissenschaftsrat* had not yet passed its first test; this would only be the case after the plan had become reality. Its realization is now up to the Federal Government and the *Laender,* as well as to the universities, university departments, and university administrations.

Political Science in Germany

A Survey by Jost Riedel[1]

Scientific concern with politics in Germany goes back to the 18th century. Men like August Ludwig von Schlözer, Friedrich Christoph Dahlmann, Lorenz von Stein and Robert von Mohl are examples of the active influence of scientific thinking on political reality combined with the endeavor to cope constructively with this reality. However, whereas since the end of the 19th century, politics in France, England, and the USA have been the subject of teaching and research, the scientific treatment of politics in the authoritarian state of the German Empire came to a standstill which was only overcome after the First World War.

The establishment of the German College of Politics (Deutsche Hochschule fuer Politik) in Berlin in 1920 was to create a "point of crystallization for the mental and spiritual reconstruction of Germany". Until 1933 the German College of Politics was able to carry out its work successfully as a civic school whose students comprised representatives from all professions, and it achieved international recognition. It regarded its object as being the education in political knowledge and relationships of people who were already in professional life and who were desirous of obtaining an insight into politics in addition to and for the purposes of their profession.[2])

The science of politics only became a specialized subject in academic professional training at the universities of the Federal Republic and West Berlin after 1945. A number of the teachers at the old College of Politics in Berlin who while emigrants, had made a name for themselves between 1933 and 1945, as teachers and research workers in political science, commenced, in conjunction with college teachers of various faculties and academicians who had hitherto been engaged in practical occupations, the development of the science of politics as an independent subject of study with politics as a profession at its conclusion. Of considerable importance in this respect, has been the knowledge acquired through National Socialism and war, that politics on a free democratic basis can only retain its character and realize its objectives, if groups become effective on the widest social plane, which armored with sound practical knowledge, are prepared to participate in the political formation of the state. Hence arose the task for German universities, not only to concern themselves as in the past with politics within the scope of jurisprudence, of economics, and sociology, but to combine in one seperate science, with its own object, the political aspects of all spheres of modern life. A conference convened in 1950 by the German College of Politics (which was re-established in 1949) on the subject of "Science within the Framework of Political Education" and in which the professors of political science in West German universities took part, described the subject of political science as "the forming of public life". This science "has to concern itself in particular with the acquisition,

[1] This short survey has been published by the Bundesanstalt fuer Arbeitsvermittlung (Federal Agency for Labor Exchange), Nuremberg, for the information of future students of Political Science. (Original title Politologe). Excerpts from it have been reprinted here as at present there exists no up-to-date comprehensive study on the subject. However, such a study is about to appear at this writing, December 1960): Denkschrift zur Lage der Soziologie und Politischen Wissenschaft by Rainer Lepsius. Dr. Lepsius got a research grant from the Deutsche Forschungsgemeinschaft to do this study. He is a political scientist at the University of Munich.
[2] See Ernst Jaeckh and Otto Suhr, Geschichte der Deutschen Hochschule fuer Politik, from the series of publications by the Deutsche Hochschule fuer Politik Berlin, Vol. 7, Berlin, 1952.

the use, and wastage of power, with civilization and corruption. This includes dealing with the politically decisive problems of the collective era, of inner political organization, of international relations and the application of the results of political daily practice. Present German reality demands for this political science the establishment of its own research centres, professorships and study groups in all academic educational institutes and the development of political science in independent colleges. These should also be available to a large circle and at the same time devote themselves in research and teaching to the education of the coming generation in politics."[3])

The differentiated uncertainties of modern political life — and particularly of the German situation — accentuate the necessity to master them by means of political science which deals with the nature of political matters — power, formation (of the way of life), and law.

The "joint treatment" of political science in conjunction with other specialized individual sciences must now be regarded as inadequate, when one realizes that the extensive material of the other sciences when added to that of political science makes the penetration with the necessary intensity into the political depths impossible, as well as ruling out a comprehensive survey of political associations. This fact does not represent a contradiction of the conclusion that political science requires the backing of philosophy, history, jurisprudence, economics, and other fields of study. Political science, by means of its research and teaching activity, does not only fill a gap in the ranks of the sciences but also contributes towards enabling scientifically trained persons to take up professions in public life in the field of politics, who, in addition to their suitability of character, also have expert knowledge of the subject. The increasing requirement for people with this training has led to *Politologe* being trained at thirteen universities in the Federal Republic and West Berlin, who, on conclusion of their studies, will take up professions in the various spheres of political life. It must be mentioned here that *Politologe* is a general definition of a profession but does not represent a title which is backed by any law. West Berlin is an exception, however, and the graduates of the Otto Suhr Institute at the Free University of Berlin, (formerly the German College of Politics) are entitled by decree of the Senator for Public Education to assume the academic degree of *Diplom-Politologe*, a description comparable to the degree of *Diplom-Soziologe* or *Diplom-Psychologe*.

According to the nature of its structure, democracy does not offer any patent solution for mastering the manifold problems which arise from the existence of the modern state in our specialized and differentiated society. A great number of social forces are pursuing their own objectives with subjective conceptions of the formation of the state. The struggles of differing intellectual tendencies, economic interests, conceptions of law, and religious beliefs lead, through the endeavors of individuals and entire groups, to impose their principles of order with the aid of intellectual and physical mediums of power against the resistance of other groups with other objectives, to a dynamic process. Power distribution and power concentration, judicial circumstances and varying conceptions of how things should be done, decide the political order of the state. The existence of democracy is thus dependent upon the maintenance of democratic rules within our social life. For this the prerequisite is the continual present consciousness of the individual so that with all the opposing opinions and interests, the struggle to assert claims to power, the main-

---

[3]) *Ibid.*, p. 41 f.

tenance of positions of power already attained and the administration of power must be bound to a specific political culture which sees in its opponent also its partner and in its adversary also the individual who exists in the same political sphere of decision. Such an attitude is, in addition to an appropriate suitability of character, to a large extent a question of knowledge of the objectives and methods of those who think different politically and also of knowledge of the entire structure of the institutions and organizations within whose framework the political life in the democratic state is carried on.

Necessary and desirable as the political education of adults on the broadest scale is, there also exists the growing need for technically trained replacement personnel qualified by their special training to take over political functions at all social levels in the professional framework of our society. The consolidation of the democracy recently established in the Federal Republic, the existence of which is threatened by totalitarian powers, poses the *Politologe* the great task in all professional spheres of activity of establishing the connections between the theoretical and practical matters of political life. Both spheres affect each other mutually and are interdependent. In the same way as practical politics creates facts which politologists make the subjects of their research and the basis of their teaching, the politically active individual receives analyses, suggestions and directions for his actions from the theoretical sphere of politics. The exclusive emphasizing of theory means the schematizing of associations of events and leads to dogmatism, i. e., the domination of rigid tenets. The one-sided assertion of the practical on the other hand, is accompanied by the lack of knowledge of important fundamentals of political aspects and their effects and the result is pragmatic dilettantism.

The activity of the *Politologe* extends over a number of groups of professions which appear at first sight to have little in common. Thus, for example, could the reviewer of an institution of communal self-government, an official of the foreign service, a newspaper or radio editor and a teacher of social science all have graduated with the same politological professional training. Special suitability and inclination result in varying professions being adopted after completion of the studies which sometimes renders supplementary training necessary. Whereas one individual is inclined towards political journalism and finds his sphere of activity in press or radio, another will become a scientific assistant at a university in the field of political science.

Professorships.

There is a chair at each of the following universities and colleges in the Federal Republic and a scientific institute or seminar for teaching political science:

Bonn	Chair of political science at the faculty of philosophy.
Technical College, Darmstadt	Chair of political science at the faculty of cultural and state sciences.
Frankfurt	Chair of political science at the faculty of economic and social sciences.
Freiburg	Chair of political science and sociology at the faculty of law and state sciences.
Goettingen	Chair of political science at the faculty of jurisprudence.
Hamburg	Chair of political science at the faculty of economic and social sciences with participation in the faculty of philosophy.

160

Heidelberg	Chair of political science at the faculty of jurisprudence with participation in the faculty of philosophy.
Kiel	Chair of science and history of politics at the faculty of law and state sciences with participation in the faculty of philosophy.
Cologne	Chair of political science at the faculty of economic social sciences.
Marburg (Lahn)	Chair of political science at the faculty of philosophy.
Munich	Chair of political science at the faculty of state science.
Tuebingen	Chair of political science at the faculty of philosophy.

No special final examination can be taken in political science at any of these colleges.

Political science is, however, an examination subject in each case (major subject, first and second minor) in

a) examination of the candidates for the position of teacher at high schools;
b) examinations (diploma and state examinations) in the faculties listed;
c) graduation to doctorates of philosophy, law, political science and political science (econ.).

The Otto Suhr Institute at the Free University of Berlin (formerly the German College of Politics) offers more extensive training. The teaching establishment has 10 chairs of political science at the faculty of jurisprudence, economic and social sciences and philosophy, which comprise the foundation for a comprehensive and intensive study of political science:

1. Faculty of Jurisprudence
   State law and politics
2. Faculty of Economic and Social Sciences
   a) Science of politics with particular emphasis on the theory of politics.
   b) Science of politics with particular emphasis on the teaching of economics.
   c) Science of politics with particular emphasis on internal politics.
   d) Sociology with particular emphasis on political sociology.
3. Faculty of Philosophy
   a) Science of politics, particularly theory and comparative history of political forms of rule.
   b) Science of politics, particularly theory and history of foreign policy.
   d) Science of politics with special emphasis on political theories.
   e) Science of politics with special emphasis on history and theory of parties and interest groups.

Political science is taught at the Otto Suhr Institute at the Free University of Berlin as an independent academic subject of study. The studies last at least four years and conclude with the academic degree of *Diplom-Politologe (Dipl.-pol.)*. The first four terms until the interim examination are devoted to the acquiring of basic knowledge of history and geography, political jurisprudence, political economics and internal politics. In addition, the student must acquaint himself with the political, social and economic affairs of one world power or of a group of countries. Then in the subsequent terms a build-up of important phases ensues. The candidate can concentrate, according to his professional interest or scientific inclination, on a main field of political science, namely political theory, political empiricism (political jurisprudence, political economics and sociology, internal politics) or supranational politics and foreign policy. One of these fields is also the main subject in the final examination. The candidate is also tested in the two other fields as secondary subjects. There is also in addition, a supplementary subject from the field of philosophy, economic and social sciences or jurisprudence, which must be closely related to political science. The diploma of the Otto Suhr Institute is regarded as the prerequisite for a degree in the main subject of political science in the philosophical and in the economic and social sciences and jurisprudence faculties, whereby supplementary subjects from the final examination (e.g. recent history, public law, economic law, political economy, journalism or sociology) can on the other hand be chosen as a second main subject or as a secondary subject for the graduation examination.

In addition to the colleges with chairs of political science, the College of Political Science in Munich (Hochschule fuer Politische Wissenschaften, Muenchen) offers politological training. The training staff of the college consists of professors of Munich University and of persons commissioned to teach who are engaged in practical professions. The subjects of instruction in the college comprise: 1) Philosophy of communal life; 2) Law and State (political science and political law, international law); 3) Economy and Society (political economy, political economic policy and sociology); and 4) History and Geography (recent and contemporary history, political and economic geography).

The studies last eight terms for high school graduates. After passing the final examination the candidate receives a certificate bearing the inscription "Diploma".

Possibilities and Limitations
of Political Education at the University [1]

by Juergen Fijalkowski

The reason for concern after 1945 regarding the tasks of political education at universities, was the memory of the let-down by the intelligentsia before the beginning of, and during the Third Reich. In the general opinion which set in after 1945, some said to themselves, "The academicians provide a society with its main leading personnel. If there had not been so many among them whose basic attitude towards democracy was negative anyhow, for whom politics were not refined enough, who, according to a questionable "German tradition", steadfastly opposed at the outset any dictatorial authority and who were convinced of the rightness of Bismarck's motto, that the best politics were a good administration, if, in a word, there had not been so many who also unnecessarily and all too quickly withdrew into silence, when they should have made themselves loudly heard, perhaps some things would have happened differently.

It is not our task here to investigate whether it would really have come about otherwise, but the justification of the demand that the universities should also en-

---

[1] From *Gesellschaft — Staat — Erziehung*, No. 4, 1959.

courage political education cannot, in the light of this reflection, be repudiated. The university is, in fact, an institution which produces important leaders of society such as technicians, business men and scientists, judges, barristers and civil servants, teachers and doctors. Whether the university wants to or not, it has a public function to fulfill, for which it bears a corresponding public responsibility.

If one recognizes this responsibility, the task of political education at the university can easily be deduced. It means, however, that a new visualization of the university must be agreed upon or at least, a reform of the old one. We know the traditional ideal of the university: freedom of teaching and of research — the scientific profession responsible only to truth — in addition to which, free self-education of the personality in the cosmos of *universitas litterarum et scientiarum* — the wealth of humanistic inner nature as an indication of the educated. That is a beautiful picture of the mission of the university, but it is that of the 19th century, and has not been representative of the truth for quite a long time. Freedom of research and teaching does in fact still exist, but unity of research and teaching has become dubious. As regards free self-education of the personality in the cosmos of the arts and sciences, we had better say nothing: the majority of university graduates are, at best, specialists. We shall mention here only something in respect of the ideal of humanistic inner nature. Some reserve is now advised towards this ideal as it cannot be disguised that behind the picture of the humanistic personality only a kind of class-conscious academic self-conceit is often concealed. There are such academically educated personalities whose education consists mainly of the shamelessness with which they pursue their privileged existence. That has little to to with humanism, but still occurs as a product of the education of our universities. There are humanistic personalities whose humanism consists only of sadly looking down upon the present "age of the masses", and of disassociating themselves from any participation in public affairs as politics does not appear to be clean enough. If we agree upon a new form of university we must recognise the public responsibility of the university and its task also in the political education of its students. The university should impart to its students the ability to perceive with critical faculties, the relationships in society and politics, and it should teach them to feel a democratic joint responsibility for the organization of public affairs.

If one now considers the present reality of German universities and their students, one could perhaps distinguish three types of varying political behavior. Unfortunately we know nothing of the quantitative distribution of these types. A sociological investigation of these which was commenced at the instigation of the Committee for Political Education and Training from the Institute for Social Research at Frankfurt University appointed by the West German Rectors' Conference, could, unfortunately, not be carried to a conclusion. However some revealing qualitative differences could be determined with the assistance of this valuable investigation. There are, to begin with, those who regard all public affairs with estrangement. They are devoid of understanding, as their conception of the world and people takes its bearings exclusively from their inner and private values. For them the only real world is the world of their private life or of intellectual life. They have only a vague awareness of that which is happening outside in society and in public. What they know of it is known to them in the same way as tales of travel in distant lands which they listen to rather apathetically, rather wonderingly or rather anxiously. Information from the field of public affairs remain without any association with the life which they themselves live. The field of public affairs is regarded at best as a continuation of private affairs; the tension-filled relations between social groups are rendered understandable in that the moral relations between individuals are simply put into the plural. They like to orientate themselves with differentiations such as "internal" and "external", "actual" and "non-actual". Social differences and political contrasts belong all too easily in the world of external and non-actual and pale completely before the differences of intellectual morality and of the individual moral character. This type feels private moral responsibility but no public or political responsibility and his concern in the happenings in society and politics remains disinterested.

A second type is constituted by those who intentionally and consciously disassociate themselve from public affairs. They can have quite an understanding of political relationships and more especially of social differences as they are able to distinguish very well according to their own fashion between private and public events, but they intentionally take no part in public affairs. The information received and the inevitable actions in the field of public affairs are often gladly and hurriedly recoiled in their striving after private social progress. They disassociate themselves from democratic joint responsibility and political participation for reasons which individually differ considerably. Some are "too refined" socially to deal with political matters as these are beneath their presumed dignity. To others who act in the tradition of anti-political educational humanism, politics appears offensive for intellectual and esthetic reasons, as profane and sordid, demoralizing for the character. Others again whose attitude is found particularly often among students of natural science, find politics simply burdensome and refrain very soberly from concerning themselves in public affairs as they prefer to devote themselves in their spare time to their own private cultural pleasures. From the type of the politically unrelated and the type of the politically disassociated, a group stands out in contrast finally as the third type which, being immediately concerned in public affairs, showing itself usually to be well-informed, often already politically organized and in any event appearing to be well integrated in its thinking and acting in the field of public affairs. Here are the followers of very different and often very contrasting political lines of policy, which have in common, however, a lively engagement in public affairs. Some have amazingly intimate detailed information and great knowledge of persons in politics, some have made political activity their entire private life. None however would deny that this group represents a minority among German students. In the connection in which we are interested, we should first, however, be clear in our own minds about what we should actually expect from political education.

Political education and political concern need not necessarily mean actual political activity. Politically organized and being active in the political organization, constantly collecting political information and being "mixed up" in everything need not be proof of political education and democratic responsibility. We know the rather dubious type of the genuine student functionary or of the functionary of the political student groups, who can't find the way back to his studies and, who, also in politics, can sometimes no longer differentiate between the important and the unimportant.

Political education and political concern do not consist either of having formal knowledge of the organization of the political institutional system or of having the habit of procuring information from news sources. It is obvious that it is not possible without that. There is also, however, an attitude of formal democratic fellow-travelling. Such democratic fellow-travellers may even have made quite a study of civic science and still only be democrats because they happen to live in a democracy. If an emergency arose when they were needed, democracy could not count on them with certainty. There is also a kind of shallow "consumer" attitude which is to just as small an extent a potential of readiness to accept democratic responsibility. Press news, as everyone knows, is just as quickly forgotten as it is read. The habit of following public events by radio does not, therefore, necessarily prove political concern. On the contrary, the political and social awareness of the pure news "consumer" is shapeless and dissolvent. This type knows today what is of actual topical interest, but has forgotten what was topical yesterday, and he really hasn't any opinion regarding it, unless it is that, which is just fashionable. With this type of democrat one can, after all, solve all public problems by not writing about or reporting on them for a while. What should be expected of political education and political concern, is thus more than, and different from, constant political activity, formal civic knowledge, and a non-committal knowledge of current affairs. It is peculiar to observe, as the Frankfurt Institute for Social Research did, that the feeling for one's own political responsibility and the readiness to show political initiative on critical occasions do not necessarily depend upon how well-trained and differentiated the conceptions of society and the execution of training of the political will, are. Observations show, rather, that people with good civic knowledge do not take part in politics and, vice versa, people with little political information have quite a ready basic attitude of responsibility on which one can count. This difference between knowledge and attitude is a very significiant one.

It goes without saying that knowledge and being well-informed, clear conceptions of the distribution of social forces and interests, of the organization of the political institutional system, and of the carrying out of political events are indispensible. But something more is also necessary. Political education and political concern demand a basic attitude to politics and to public affairs which permit one to keep the larger relationships under observation and to have a close feeling of democratic joint responsibility, not only to have a political opinion but also to bring it to bear when necessary.

Whether and in what form this basic attitude exists, depends upon many factors which can hardly be influenced by the university, as they lie outside its scope of influence. The basic attitude to politics and the conception of society as it is and as it should be, are, for example, impressed on the individual to a large extent by family influences. The basic attitude of the children cannot fail to be influenced by whether they originate from a rising or declining family, whether they are intended to become "something better" than their parents were, or are once again to attain that which their social and individual fates took from their parents. How their relatives think about politics and social differences is imparted somehow directly or in reactions to the children also. In addition, there are deeply impressive experiences which can imbed themselves in the basic attitude: the experience of expulsion or of flight, the denazification of the father or even the treatment which the student working his way receives at the hands of his colleagues. Finally, the influences cannot be overlooked which school and the church exert. The concrete "how" of these influences will not be discussed here but they exist just the same.

Students, when they come to the university, thus bring certain basic attitudes with them, indefinite as they may be. As far as young people are concerned, however, it is only in the rarest cases that these basic attitudes are already firmly fixed. Other influence can thus be exerted upon them. Certainly only the imparting of political knowledge will be insufficient. If a serious influence is to be exerted upon the basic attitude it will have to be much more in the nature of training, i.e. arising from an intensive personal acquaintance with the subject. One should distinguish between education as a means of imparting knowledge, and training as the shaping of the individual. But what happens with the normal student at the universities today? He is offered knowledge, which he acquires more or less laboriously and critically in pursuing his professional studies. Apart from his studies, however, the student is either left to his own devices or he is under the instructional influence of student communities in which the student associations impose the most intensive instructional discipline upon their members. Training towards awareness and a feeling of democratic joint political responsibility is thus either non-existent or in a form about which doubt may often enough be permitted. The university has in any event handed over to a large extent its possibilities of instructional influence on its students.

One can now ask oneself whether political education by the university is at all desirable, whether a university which tries to train its students politically does not represent something very dubious. There are in our society various factions and political tendencies which are in conflict with each other. Such tendencies represent differing basic attitudes towards politics and society. Even the self-comprehension which academicians have of themselves and their place in society is controversial. There are class-conscious, pluralistic, elite-conscious, and solidaristic models of society from which the political attitude can be fixed. If the university is now declared the place of political training which political tendency will this instrument adopt? Will the university not be torn into parties and made the object of political argument to an intolerable extent to the detriment of science and teaching?

Here is undoubtedly a limit of political education and training. It must be categorically laid down that the university must remain a place of free research and teaching, a place to be kept aloof from the immediate vicinity of political and social conflicts of interest, a place where sound reason has an opportunity to postpone decisions time and again for the sake of renewed criticism and rational consideration. The university must not become the instrument of political indoctrination, otherwise an end will soon be put to freedom of teaching and research as well as to democratic freedom in the state.

Nevertheless that is the thesis here, if agreement can be reached on some basic values which could be upheld beyond inner-democratic party antagonisms and established as standards of political education and training. These are the fundamental values of democracy itself. They can be distinguished by several fundamental questions of which only a few are chosen here for the sake of example.[1])

The opening question was in regard to the limits and possibilities of political education at the university. The thesis can after all be defended with good reason that the university has the public mission of imparting a feeling of joint political responsibility and a knowledge of the organization of society, and of the execution of political power. It will thereby be able to follow the way of political education in addition also, however, to the way of political training. Political education can be achieved without the university becoming the dreadful sight created by political indoctrination. From a practical point of view, some courses must be followed on which the first steps have already been taken.

All measures are important in this connection, which have as their objective the elimination of the unbalance between the shortage of lecturers and the superfluity of students. Of importance too is generous aid to students granting them material and latitude of time which they require for free self-development. These are the

---

[1]) The examples have been omitted.

166

general conditions. Of importance for the particular purpose of imparting political knowledge and the faculty of political judgment would be an increase in the professorships of sociology and politics. Still, it has been shown in several places that where a university lecturer devotes himself with considerable intensity to the task of imparting political knowledge, even the widespread lethargy of the students disappears to a striking extent and a deeper need for orientation and training arises. This result is obviously dependent upon the quality of the appropriate lectures. And political education can be cultivated not only in special political science and socioligical lectures by university teaching staffs but also at professional lectures and professional seminars, where various opportunities exist to pursue problems to the full extent of their social and political associations.

For political training in its narrower sense, there are some hopes of a program to be followed energetically for the erection of students' hostels and housing settlements if a second measure can be combined with it, namely the systematic enlistment of tutors to carry out pedogogic work there. These tutors should be persons who have the knowledge and feeling of democratic-political joint responsibility to a marked extent without being bound to an all too narrow party line or being just a meeting-manager. Their most important faculty would be, as open-minded, scientifically interested, and well-informed personalities in all public affairs, to translate pedagogically their own democratic spirit, with all the many possibilities which one has, when one can cultivate a more intensive acquaintance with people of the same neighborhood.

If, in addition, all the methods, which are now being practised successfully, are continued — joint responsibility of students in the self-administration of their universities and institutes, systematic and selective encouragement of the communal life of students, political forums of the students' representatives, etc. — than some opportunities still present themselves within the task of political education of democratic universities.

The Influence of High School and College
on the Political Awareness of Students *

By Juergen Habermas

"No room has been found in the educational curricula of the high schools for the major political and social problems of the times. Politics had first to become history in order to qualify as instructional material. Thus in the 19th century the high school became a center of the cultivation of non-political education which has characterized the entire attitude of the German middle classes. This is one of the main reasons for the political failure of the German cultured class." This diagnosis, which has the authority of eminent people, was cited once by Georg Picht[1] with the addition of this thesis: "The non-political attitude of the High Schools is so deeply imbedded

---

*) *Gesellschaft — Staat — Erziehung*, Vol. 8, 1959.
[1] Georg Picht, "Ten Theses on the High School", from *Frankfurter Hefte*, December 1958.

in its conception of education, that it can only be overcome, if we make up our minds to re-examine our entire concept of education." This thesis provokes a number of questions.

Firstly: Are the young people who leave high school actually then for the most part simply politicaliy indifferent? Nevertheless, political education has already taken on concrete form in the sociology classes of many high schools. Although political indifference can be confirmed in a specific form, even among the graduates of these schools, could that actually be associated with — and that is the second question — an unbroken tradition of humanistic culture? Nevertheless, school education has long since incorporated learning from other, mainly philosophical sources. If in the meantime this tradition is still in force, would it not rather associate itself — the third question — with very definite political tendencies instead of producing simple indifference? Nevertheless, the guarding against politics of which one accuses humanistic culture, the intellectual aristocrat tends to combine with the national-militant self-confidence in order to form, as it is called, a politically effective ideology of national citizenship. Even if we assume, moreover, for a moment, the thesis to be true, there remains one question, which appears to me to be the cardinal one: whether then a determined reorientating of school educational objectives, according to the so-called functional requirements of society, would now guarantee effective political education?

An investigation carried out in the summer term of 1957 by the Institute of Social Research with students of the University of Frankfurt[2]) leads to conclusions, some of which also appear useful in the assessment of these problems. Students represent that type for which high school education is still primarily fashioned.

* * *

1. In conversation regarding a number of concrete problems, the majority of the students questioned, showed certain signs of a mutual mentality which, at bottom, is ambivalent: it is imprinted by a retreat into the sphere of inner feeling to the same degree as by a pragmatic adaptation to so-called external necessities.

The attitude towards the political past is, as it were, bookishly estranged. The attitude of the neutral authority on the subject, moreover, is bewildering: only rarely is history treated as a process in which the past takes part in the determination of the present: recent history has already been filed away. This corresponds to a neutralization of events almost unencumbered, however, by the resentments of the first post-war years; events, which, from the point of view of national self-love, are offensive. The de-politicalization of political events is shown then in a particular form in the example of the 20th July 1944. In the assessment of this coup d'état, the abstract discussion of conceptions of duty take the place of political pros and cons: political questioning is moved into the "moral level" and is unintentionally converted into one of the "purely human" decisions of conscience.

The unhistorical and, at the same time, moralizing attitude towards history which tends to dissolve objective processes into the biographical, graduates, of course, into powerful pragmatism as soon as questions arise — such as military service, — which immediately affect one's own life. Rearmament is supported — certainly only on the basis of the situation which has now been established — by the over-

[2]) The report in question refers only to excerpts of a study to be published shortly in book form entitled *Student und Politik* in the series of *Frankfurter Beitraege zur Soziology*.

whelming majority of the students. The typical turn of phrase, "I believe I share the opinion of the Minister of Defense", reveals how they let officialdom speak first, and then afterwards, interpret their own situation accordingly. Lastly "voluntary enrollment" is discussed, but in such a way that one sees therein an identification with the force of circumstances rather than with the circumstances themselves. The half pragmatic, half reconciled resignation to the facts, remarkably hampers every awakening of a Utopian impulse: those questioned live politically in a world without alternatives.

One cannot immediately dismiss this mentality as entirely unpolitical; but expectations of a political attitude, ready for action and intelligent, can scarcely be attached to it. The influence of sociological teaching obviously does not penetrate into the class in which this kind of attitude most often develops.[3]) This is substantiated by a comparison of those questioned who were taught sociology at school with those whose curriculum contained no such subject. The former are, as one would expect, more often well informed of the formal rules of the game of democratic system and thus of how a law originates, than the latter. Astonishingly, the proportions are reversed, however, when questions are asked on concrete subjects like that of the dynamic pension, which was under lively discussion at the time of questioning: those who have had instruction in sociology show themselves to be less well-informed in this case.

The equivalent of that which can be shown regarding the political information of those questioned can also be shown in respect to their political activity. Here, too, the effect of sociology remains superficial in a certain sense. As far as it concerns certain democratic rules of the game, those influenced by sociological teaching are far ahead of the other students. Thus, for example, 80 % of those who put particularly much effort into the students' self-administration are influenced by sociological teaching; also another 41 % of those who are at all active in the self-administration as against only 5 % of those who have participated little or not at all. This correlation permits the assumption that pleasure in their own parliamentary roles, as often practised in the sociology class under the influence of Oetinger, is one of the dominating motives here. On the other hand, no interdependency is at all shown between its influence and political activity outside the model example of the students self-administration, that is to say, in the form perhaps of participation in political demonstrations, election meetings or even political discussions. The small extent to which sociology "gets under the skin", so to speak, is shown also in another result of the investigation: a relationship between sociology and the deeper-lying structures of political awareness could not, in fact, be confirmed. We have tried to put these structures on record in a number of typical common conceptions of society.

2. Where there can be no question at all of conceptions of society, where the ideas of social life more or less unite under a central perspective and do not, ostensibly free from ideologies, crumble apart in isolated morsels of disconnected opinion, humanistic cultural motives, mutilated as they are, are now in fact at work.

Certainly that almost now venerable school of thought, which, up to Ortega and Jaspers, combines educationally conservative criticism of culture with the apology of a presumed decadent academic middle class, is no longer very widespread in the minds of our students. They all know this protest against the *nouveau*

---

[3]) That too, requires certain limitations which, in connection with this report, however, are neglected. Here we refer again to the forthcoming publication of the entire study.

riche, against the traditionless classes, whose position is said to depend purely on business success without being able to distinguish itself by culture or bearing. The apology refers to the academicians, who allegedly substitute "class" by character and culture and who are still secretly regarded even today as being the actual representatives of society. Society appears to be split, as it were, into two camps, on the one hand, those who, by virtue of their quickly acquired wealth, comprise the leading class, and, on the other hand, the academicians; certainly not the academicians by profession, but the academicians by calling who represent intellect as opposed to money, culture as opposed to television receivers, and Goethe's educational journey to Italy as opposed to mass tourism. One student demonstrates the comparison in an impressive formula: the nobility of wealth versus the nobility of mind. But this conception is shared only by 5% of those questioned.

More important, rather, is a conception of society of inner values, which loosens the humanistic cultural motives from the conflict of social groups and translates them, so to speak, into a contrast of types of character. The protest of culture against "materialism" has become, with this type, a mental attitude which is no longer bound socially to one location. The conception of society thus becomes a moral conception of the world, which has as its theme the socio-psychological problems of the mind's power of resistance against the temptation of wealth, which is no longer culturally legitimate. One student expressed this as follows:

> This affects the entire problem of the revival of the economy, of the living standard. Everything adjusts itself to the conception of earning money, whether academician or non-academician, everyone does it (!). On the intellectual side — I mean here not expressly academicians but people . . . that is difficult to say, I mean people who strive after an ideal although they need not be particularly well qualified intellectually. The other thing is not good at all, it is hectic and probably not durable. The values of society thus become lost.

Differentiation according to income and prestige, profession and influence, are regarded from this standpoint of inner feeling as irritating, if not altogether as irrelevant. And as the newly-won wealth has detached itself from the class of the newly rich, so, in the eyes of this type, culture has, in its "deeper" sense, detached itself from the class of the cultured. The two groups, that with a need of a living standard and that with a need of culture have "cut right across each other". The academicians are envisaged rather as the prototypes of the "intellectual", as "academic idealists", who rise out of the body of the academic proletariat. One political economist stated:

> That is something which is just up my street, the "intellectualizing" of the economy. The academician has this responsibility by reason of his greater discernment, by his learning and his occupation with intellectual values.

Usually, of course, culture and civilization undoubtedly contradict each other to such an extent that self-realization of the mentality in the place of business, in the social sphere generally, does not appear possible, not even in the form of an "intellectualization".

> Compared with previous times, the position of the academician has changed, because the well-known manager type has emerged alongside of him who may also possibly be an academician, but who cannot be regarded as such

170

and who in economic life draws everything under his own influence and organizes everything. That is the abasement of culture to civilization.

Intellect is often incompatible with power, with social efficiency; only so-called "nominal academicians" can achieve anything in the highly exposed and rugged reality of economic life. The extent to which intellectuality has first of all been elevated in its own bearing to the criterion of a real academician and person, is shown by this mistrust of academicians in influential positions.

Where, however, the hierarchy of inner values, — the cultured at the top and below, the mass of the uncultured, — is directly portrayed in the social sphere and made the standard for the grading of social rank, another social conception evolves, that of the intellectual elite. Those of this type who were questioned regard the masses as being only a primitive level of mankind. Their sole anxiety is that of the "levelling ideas of enlightenment":

> I believe the worker desires the leadership of the academician. But if the emperor makes himself the equal of the subject he has lost the right to be emperor. The academician must not allow himself to be degraded. He must maintain with dignity the position to which he is entitled, he must have the courage to rule.

The "functional academician" appears to be the quite logical representative of this modern elite: he is still enough of the academician to be able to show the insignia of the intellectual, of a cultured individual: on the other hand, he has also enough of the manager to be able to cope with the conditions of the apparatus of rule. The academic manager of this type at the same time transforms humanistic culture into the province of the technician of power, retains from the one, his good conscience, and obtains from the other, a perceptive intuition for the "politically realistic". The social differences between the class of culture, called by virtue of its inner intellectual attitude, morality, character and way of life to the elite on the one hand, and the broad mass of the uncultured on the other, have, according to this model, grown "naturally", even although not quite without receiving their own deserts. And thus everything falls into its proper place. And where conflicts nevertheless ensue, they appear as artificially exaggerated antitheses. Then the cause is mainly the inferiority complex of the masses:

> Those with little education, states a student of law, always have inferiority complexes towards those who have more education. They, therefore, do not strive to catch up with the other person, but say to themselves, "what I am, is all right". Thus the contrasts arise, which are accentuated from underneath.

Another group of those questioned considered in rather the opposite way, this antithesis of inner feeling and externalism, or rather, the un-actual world. In this conception of society of social equality, the differences are regarded as being just as external, as cumbersome. People should not make themselves different and unique, but rather take up a basically equal position within society. Where conditions of special inequality prohibit people from developing is a case, according to the opinion of those questioned, of definite differences with grave consequences but still of differences, which in the end are "imagined" in both senses of the word, just as fictitious as snobbish:

> I believe they are artificially maintained by some circles, said one philosopher, they are all, nevertheless, human and must live alongside each

other and one cannot simply over- or underestimate them according to their extraction or education.

Now academicians are neither personally nor socially any better, but their education enables and obliges them to be initiators of progress. Even in this model of equalization, the tradition of humanistic culture asserts itself also: the academican can never be only a specialist.

> They have the opportunity to obtain an insight, even in a political respect. If somehow, the things of life, the sacred and even necessary things of life, are in danger, then the intellectually active must stand up and fight since they would be the first to realize the danger. They have, therefore, a kind of protective function. By the things of life, I mean freedom, equality, and such values.

More than half those questioned share the model of humanistic culture in one version or another. (Of these, the "elite" conception of society is undoubtedly the most widespread, actually among nearly a quarter of the students.) With a further quarter, on the other hand, one finds forms of a quite different, a "realistic" awareness. Some of those of this type questioned, know precisely isolated facts of social life, but nowhere do these splinters combine to form a mosaic, however. They lack the tendencious perspectives, above all, that suggested by humanistic culture of an antithesis of intellect and wealth. Where something in the nature of a conception of society is thereby portrayed, it reflects the neo-liberal characteristics of a mobile and completely levelled middle class society in which the academicians distinguish themselves by nothing unless it is a better professional training and correspondingly good chances of advancement.

3. One could easily suppose that in contrast to this "realistic" awareness, the conceptions of society orientated from humanistic culture, are encouraged in the first instance by the parental upbringing in houses in which an academic tradition exists. That, according to the results of our investigation, however, is not the case.[4] The investigation shows, rather, that the High School and, to a certain extent also, the college, give the impulses as the imparting medium. The conceptions of society, orientated from humanistic culture, are actually relatively most frequent among students who, either in Classical High Schools or later in the Philosophical Faculty, have obviously been more under an cultural influence of this kind, than among others questioned, particularly those who have attended a Technical College or have studied philosophy or industrial management.

The more both institutions are orientated according to the traditional cultural objectives (this goes to a marked degree for the Classical High Schools and Philosophical Faculties), the more they appear to contribute to the articulation of the culturally humanistic conceptions of society referred to. Sociological teaching, as far as the high school is concerned, is certainly not a participant. On the contrary, we have come to the conclusion that its influence remains formal and thus, on the whole, without consequence in the mastery of political reality, as it is absorbed by the conflicting influence of that humanistic cultural tradition which still determines particularly the teaching of German and history.

---

[4] This probably is connected with a change in the social structure of our students about the time of the First World War. Then the number of university students increased many times over and, in fact, the influx from the middle classes was so great that the percentage of students of university trained parents was halved. Nearly a fifth of the students questioned come from such homes of university trained parents their proportion is thus just as large as that of those who can show an academic tradition going back over more than one generation. With this "invasion", the tradition of humanistic culture is certainly also, as far as it is imparted by parental influence, disrupted to a large extent.

This, however, does not neutralize political bias altogether. Those questioned differ rather according to the type of their social conception, even in their attitude towards the democratic fundamentals of our state. This attitude was carefully ascertained with the aid of a battery of questions and complexes of questions. A comparison shows that, on the one hand, only the social conception of social equality is relatively often accompanied by a reliable democratic attitude, whereas, on the other hand, the conception of a decadent academic middle class and that of the intellectual elite are relatively often associated with authoritarian tendencies. In the middle, as it were, are found those with "inner" and also those with "realistic" awareness: they are relatively often pseudo-democrats and feel themselves only formally bound to our system, without identifying themselves bindingly with democracy.

4. The last result is revealing: it gives an indication of a hidden relationship of impulses of inner feeling with those, apparently contrary, of realism. Perhaps today a shrewd conformity to the forces of circumstances is endeavoring to hedge off on the good conscience of the values of the free and moral personality which are fetishistic in humanistic culture.

* * *

To summarize, the following standpoints from all this for the study of the thesis initially discussed:

Firstly, there exists a certain danger that the pedagogic effect of sociology is exhausting itself for the most part in enriching itself with mechanical knowledge and in habituation to a pseudo-parliamentary planning game.

Secondly, a deeper-reaching influence of sociology is apparently being intercepted by the still effective motives of a diluted tradition of humanistic culture in the other classes. This imprints to a large extent the structure of political awareness.

Thirdly, from the appropriately orientated social conceptions, not exclusively and not even primarily, follows, of course, indifference.

Fourthly, there were certain indications that where the curtain, as it were, of humanistic culture is torn aside, not a reflected, live and alert awareness becomes visible, but a kind of pragmatism with politically ambivalent consequences. Culture, in its traditional form, takes on an ideological character and still conceals impulses necessary to life: even those facts presented by the natural and social sciences lose some of their elucidatory power where they are not adopted in the medium of critical education capable of synopsis.

Students and Political Education [1]

By Dietrich Wetzel

This booklet emerged from an educational conference which was held from 31 May to 4 June 1960 at *Heimvolkshochschule Bergneustadt* under the sponsorship of the Association of German Student Organizations, the Friedrich Ebert Foundation, the International Schoolbook Institute, and the Institute for International Meetings. The principal theme of the conference was: "The Presentation of Jewery in Teachers

---

[1] Excerpts from the preface to *Erziehungswesen und Judentum* by Dietrich Wetzel, Chairman of the Association of German Student Organizations. See footnote p. 122.

Training and in the Classroom." Professors, schoolbook publishers, authors, representatives of the educational departments of radio stations, experienced educators and officials of state cultural ministries, representatives of Jewish congregations and of the National Conference of Jews in Germany, as well as university students from Germany and Israel, accepted our invitation. In five committees, headed by specialists, practical recommendations for various areas in the field of education had been worked out.

For reference, the results of five months of carefully conducted scientific research on the subject had been made available to the conference. With the help of the International Schoolbook Institute in Brunswick, textbooks on history and religion for various types of schools were studied and analyzed. Also courses and seminars at universities and teachers colleges, lecture series offered by adult education centers and teachers continuation training courses, educational radio programs, and teaching aids which are being offered by the Federal and State institutions for political education, had been investigated with regard to the subject. This research did not attempt a critical evaluation of the material, but through collecting extensive material it enabled the conference to base its objectives on exact data. However, this analysis cannot be considered complete, for this would have required many years of intensive research. In spite of the fact that the importance of our subject has frequently been stressed in the press, it has been found that, in the field of education, useful studies on either the subject as a whole or even parts of it have been lacking. However, the results of the research project which had been conducted by Dr. Krippendorff, were considered sufficient enough, by both the conference members and our organization, to draw well- founded conclusions and to make suggestions for further work in this field.

The reaction of specialists, of university circles, and the press were unusually lively and favorable. The mimeographed conference report was soon depleted. We have been repeatedly asked to print the findings of our conference and therewith make them available to the public. Although hesitant at first, we decided to publish them. This booklet is merely a contribution to a discussion and it does not pretend to be a thorough study of the subject giving a final answer to its problems. However, it aims at more than simply an appeal to the public in a general, noncommittal way, since it contains detailed suggestions for textbooks and teachers training programs which are being based upon findings derived at by making use of well-founded analyses. The Association of German Student Organizations published this book with the above mentioned restrictions. It is obvious that individual statements and answers to particular problems cannot represent the Association's opinion; but the Student Organizations gladly assume responsibility for the message and problems contained in this work.

That the Association of German Student Organizations picked this task to deal with the presentation of Jewery in the field of education did not happen accidentally. As an organization which partakes in the responsibility for political education in Germany and which represents the majority of future teachers, we felt entitled to do so.

When in 1926, during the Weimar Republic, the German students were challenged to make a political decision, the majority of them failed. The Prussian Minister of Culture, Becker, made a generous bestowal of rights upon the student councils dependent on the outcome of a referendum, which he requested to be taken by the Student Organization, on an issue which was fundamental for the Organization's future policy. The issue was: "Shall membership in the German Student Organization be made dependent on certain Germanic Characteristics which can be derived from the concept of a German culture or from 'racial' concepts?" The German Student Organization voted for "racial characteristics", excluded Jewish students from membership, and, even before an influence of National Socialistic doctrines was evident at German universities, favored extreme anti-Semitism. Here Nazism could easily make use of already implanted prejudices which turned out to have dreadful consequences. Soon afterward the public burning of books and the dismissal of Jewish professors followed. The Student Organization even decided to demand that Jewish scholars should not be allowed to publish anymore in the German language. Only Hebrew or other foreign languages were to be permitted. Except for a few, the majority of students remained silent while this happened.

The students of that time are our professors of today, our lawyers, teachers, journalists, state officials, and parents. This statement does not mean that we want to create suspicion or demand that the past of individuals be investigated. It points to the fact, however, that we cannot keep silent with regard to those problems, that we, as students, have taken a firm position, that we cannot leave the past, and that we expect an answer from the older generation. If, in individual cases, silence means adherence to fiendishness and expression documents stubborness, we may even find it necessary to make it quite clear that our universities and schools have no room for professors and teachers who have been unable to learn from the consequences of the German catastrophe. The year 1945 was not the year "zero". The collapse was brought about from the outside. But what happened can only be digested intellectually step by step. Those forces in our nation which influenced our recent history are still alive. This obliges us to examine carefully each step and each development towards the reconstruction of our education.

Today, in 1960, young people who study at our schools and universities seem to have the similar prejudices that their counterparts had during the Weimar Republic. Investigations by Juergen DuMont, Belinde Buetow, and Walter Haehnle made in elementary and secondary schools have given rise to such apprehensions. The establishment of a "League of National Students" at our universities, which is not national but stubbornly nationalistic, makes it evident that the poison of the Nazi myth, that of a Germanic race, has not yet lost its power. This poison, emerging from stupid emotionalism, may bring about new political danger.

Confronted with this potential danger we took the initiative to contribute to the combating and resolving of such prejudices. Already in November 1957 and in Ocober 1958 the Association of German Student Organizations in two German-Israelian discussions attempted a study of teaching and knowledge of Jewish history in various areas of education and journalism. These discussions led to the suggestion to hold a conference on the subject where, on the basis of exact investigations, useful recommendations for educators could be worked out. The anti-Semitic occurrences at the turn of last year proved the urgency of such plans, which call for more than the claim that "more contemporary history should be taught".

Therefore this booklet, as a contribution to a discussion and as a recommendation for further studies, is indeed of a political nature. We believe that such studies should belong to the urgent tasks of a university.

"It is impossible to avoid new political catastrophes, if scholars fail to learn to fulfill their humanitarian duties as citizens of the nation: and a university which withdraws its power from this task, may find itself one day facing blind subversion, instead of practical reform plans." We find this statement in the "blue survey" on the university reform plans of 1948. It remained a program, but a program more valid today than ever.

The fact that the recently published study has been worked out by university professors and students gives reason to hope that the university will realize this task.

But the result of this book has also shown that there is still a tendency to suppress historic facts and the historic conscience in academic teaching and research. While the press takes up Jewish issues and anti-Semitism with great interest and engages in careful journalistic studies on the subject, academic research and teaching, on the other hand, is strikingly reserved when it comes to these problems. The only chair for Jewish studies, at the Free University in Berlin, has been vacant for years. At our universities there is not a single institute which engages in collecting and studying the material relevant to this subject. Within our academic system such a specialized aim of an institute would, by no means, be unusual. Let us summarize that, with this booklet, recommendations have been made which are also in the scientific interest of our universities, since we can no longer allow ourselves to neglect the problems of Jewery and anti-Semitism, because of our duty towards historic truth.

The conference in Bergneustadt could not fully answer the abundance of questions and problems, nor can this book. For this our time was too limited and we would have needed more specialists. We therefore believe that a permanent commission, similar to the German Commission for Teaching and Education, should be established. Such a commission could present intelligent programs and detailed recommendations as a result of long-term work. The commission, of approximately twenty permanent members, should be established for one year at first. It should first concern itself with the procurement of expert opinions on particular questions. Recommendations for the presentation of Jewery and anti-Semitism in our text-books and in teachers training should be part of its most important tasks. Together with textbook authors and publishers as well as university officials these recommendations should be realized.

We also recommend the establishment of a university institute for Jewish studies which should engage in research and, on this basis, develop complete courses on Jewery.

Both recommendations make it possible to go beyond general appeals to the public and to change the present situation in our education. Since we are not interested in covering up obvious deficiencies through pat phrases, we consider it our duty to examine all practical suggestions and to realize them.

I tried to make it clear that this booklet represents the beginning of a necessary work which we must take up. Removing the ignorance of the dangers of today will help to prevent that tomorrow we shall have to ask for belated forgiveness

D   Political Education Activities

Political Education Activities
Outside of Schools and Universities *

By Hans W. Kuhn

After the establishment of the Federal Republic of Germany, a special branch of general educational work developed in West Germany: those political education activities which take place outside of the schools, universities, and academies. Partly this work went back to the traditions of youth and adult education prior to 1933; partly it had its basis in the initiative as well as the — in many cases considerable — financial and material assistance granted by the occupying powers of those days. Also today it is still possible in many cases to recognize from the density and the organizational structure of these institutions, the influence previously exercized by the respective occupying power within whose sphere of jurisdiction they had been set up. In the following decade, the said institutions — although occasionally the subject of disputes at the time of their formation and initial phase — were extended and supplemented by a large number of German activities that found the support of Federal as well as *Laender* authorities. No comparable development had taken place in the time of the Weimar Republic, if we leave aside civic education activities within the Adult Education Program of those times. Everything that had been done in the field of independent political educational work in those years, however, had neither requested nor obtained governmental aid.

The present way of financing the work of the said political education activities, primarily out of public budgets and only to a smaller extent from the funds of large organizations and with the help of private contributions, is proof of the fact that today this effort is regarded, by the governmental side as well as by the leading groups in the sector of social and economic politics and also by the churches, as a desirable supplementation of government- and community-sponsored educational activities and is being recognized as deserving financial assistance. This fundamental recognition has been due, to a not inconsiderable extent, to the attitude introduced and practised by the occupying powers, by the *Bundeszentrale fuer Heimatdienst* and the *Landeszentralen fuer Heimatdienst* and by the Federal Youth Plan; it is primarily a result, too, of the continuously increasing realization that the cooperation of educational elements outside of the schools and universities is indispensable for the formation of a civic awareness of the democratic and constitutional principles as well as for the creation of the ability of political judgment in the Federal Republic. The high quality of the work which was achieved under the given circumstances fully justifies this recognition.

The progress made by political education activities took place in close connection with the discussions and disputes regarding the incorporation of political education into the curricula of the schools and universities and, as far as the practical outcome was concerned, soon could outdistance those efforts due to their greater

*) From: *Die europaeische Bildungsarbeit in der Bundesrepublik — Gutachten fuer das Bildungswerk Europaeische Politik e. V.*, pp. 4—9.

flexibility and adaptability to the educational policy situation. The more the introduction of political education as a curriculum subject in the schools was delayed and, in many cases, remained unsatisfactory, the more the activities outside of the schools and universities were challenged and promoted. In view of the evident demand for this type of work they were faced, right from the start, by a vast scope for the application of their efforts. In the recent past, an increasing number of cases exist in which entire school classes have been making use of these institutions.

On the other hand, the slow establishment of professorships for political sciences in the universities and academies brought it about, that political education institutions outside of the schools and universities frequently had to complain about a lack of qualified teachers, which even today has not been completely remedied. The availability of teachers from the younger generation is being complicated by the fact that the durability of the said educational institutions depends on the favorable aspects of the political as well as financial situation, so that in this field of educational activities, no job security exists. With regard to the fields of the Adult Education Program and the institutions of the trade unions, the economic institutes, and the churches the situation is more favorable, though.

It is true, that in the meantime, the conditions regarding political education in the schools underwent a radical change in most *Laender;* however, the tasks of the other educational institutions did not decrease. The new subject in the school curricula will have its repercussions upon public life only after several years and, consequently, will require supplementary activities outside of the schools still for a long time to come. This is particularly true, too, for the advanced studies of the teachers. Moreover, adult education is still less affected by the modified school education measures and in view of the rapid political development it appears to be still more urgent that a continuing information of large population groups will be possible.

The institutional structure of the political education activities outside of the schools and universities is extremely multifarious. It includes the institutions of citizenship education, of the trade unions, the economic associations, and the churches, of the centers maintained by the Federal Government, and the *Laender* as well as a large number of private institutes and organizations. This variety and lack of uniformity is largely responsible for the fact that this type of political education in its entirety, and also its interrelations and repercussions jointly with the political education in the schools has not as yet been granted much public attention.

The Principle of Equality in Political Education

However the term "political education" may be defined in detail — there is one principle which all definitions are bound to accept equally: there can only be one political education. It must be the same for all citizens. Of course, educational work always has to adjust itself to the respective age groups and professional groups, but these differentiations are exclusively due to requirements of a didactic and pedagogic nature. They must not violate the principle of equality. This is true for the schools, academies, and universities as well as for the youth and adult education of the denominations, for the socio-political and economic-political organizations, and for the private educational institutions. The laborer needs the same political education as the director of a bank, the trade union secretary or the academician. It is a matter of course, that beyond this basic education, the various professional activities require special knowledge of a varied nature also in the political field. But the ability of political judgment as such and of methodical political thinking which everyone should possess, combined with an adequate political general knowledge, is the basis of any professional and social function. It ensues from the principle of equality that political education has to refer to the individual in his capacity of citizen (and not in his capacity of functionary of an organization, member of a political party, gainfully employed person or member of a denominational group). It does not supply knowledge concerned with organizations or professions but, instead, provides general political knowledge. It wants to place the individual in relation with the general situation and to teach him to form for himself, in line with his justified and clearly realized personal interest, his own opinions and verdicts as a result of taking into consideration the democratic and constitutional principles as well as the entirety of the network of political interrelations. In this respect, it is also necessary to understand which position and function is lawfully being occupied by the political parties and organizations in the democratic state structure, as well as to give a neutral and comparative description of their political objectives and platforms. The dealing with special subjects directly linked with certain professional activities can also be regarded as political educational work, provided that it serves the purpose of unbiased information with due regard to the general ability of judgment and to the general educational level, and does not grant consideration to any group interests.

Political Instruction

Wherever things are being handled differently and where political education is turned into a vehicle for party policy aims or group interests, or where a one-sided ideological interpretation is being given, this constitutes an abuse for the purposes of political indoctrination or propaganda. There is no doubt that ideological instruction and propaganda are lawful and necessary. However, the differentiation as to the tasks and methods must not become blurred, instead, it has to be made especially visible. As experience tells, propagandistic undertones rapidly deprive political education activities of their hoped-for effects.

The recently developing attitude of the political parties to claim public funds for the purpose of political education activities of their own is posing a series of problems which at the present time are as yet not fully discernible. On the part of the educational institutions, this development is being watched with concern. In particular, the idea that the political parties have a "claim to educate" is being contested; attention is being called in this respect to the instruction of the party followers which is a natural obligation of the political parties and which should not be financed from the funds accumulated by the taxpayers' contributions. Moreover, it is being feared that the reputation of impartiality, which the political education institutions enjoy in general, and which must be realized to carry a publicity appeal as well as the power of conviction, may get lost in the process, and that the widespread antipathy against party politics might also turn against the educational institutions, as soon as the political parties claim, that their indoctrination and their publicity efforts toward soliciting new party members also amount to political education activities. The argument is advanced, moreover, that the political parties are in no way in a position to carry through political educational work — however unselfish it may be meant to be — since they do

179

not have the necessary teachers at their disposal and, in addition, fail to arouse the necessary interest within the population. Finally, it is being stressed that the interest of the political parties in political education activities might, in the long run, lead to a reduction of the funds allocated to the other types of educational institutions. These fears to which also general misgivings of a constitutional law nature are added definitely have to be emphasized.

Work in the Public

A special form of public political activities which, so to speak, lies halfway between education and indoctrination, as well as halfway between information and propaganda, is what might be termed public relations activities. These have to be mentioned here because some educational institutions (e.g., also the *Europa-Haeuser)* have taken on this task in addition to their other work. Public relation efforts of this type have to be understood as the attempt to render concrete, with the help of elucidation, information, and appeals, — independent from specific party and group interests — individual political issues of particular importance to the public; thus, a definite political will is meant to be called into life. Such efforts are being made, e.g., by the *Europa-Union* with reference to the unification of Europe, or by the *Kuratorium Unteilbares Deutschland* with respect to the reunification problem. The borderlines between political education and public relations activities, on the one hand, and public relations activities and political indoctrination, on the other hand, are fluctuating. A criterion is always the absence of party and group interests as well as the extent of the information which is being disseminated, i.e., the level of the knowledge passed on.

The Topical Unity of Political Education

Political education is a factual and topical unity. The world-wide interdependence of international politics and the interrelation of domestic and foreign policy make it impossible to talk about citizenship education only, or isolatedly about European education. However fascinating definitions like "education towards Europe" or "Europe as an education idea" may be at a first glance, they are dangerous because they give rise to the misleading thought that this education might more or less exclusively be placed at the disposal of the European unification idea.

Any limitation of this type of the educational horizon would not only reduce the general ability of political judgment but also would anticipate — with the help of an "education idea" (which then frequently turns out to be nothing but a substitute for a nationalistic way of thinking) through the reduction of political knowledge and, so to speak, via the "education channel" — those political decisions which have to be left to the discretion of the individual. Such an education would always try to preserve the concept of a world centered around Europe — anyway existing in the eyes of the public — instead of leading towards an attitude of world-wide receptiveness. The spreading of European civilization and technology throughout the world prohibits a recourse to European "culture". There exist indications of the fact that now already the concept of a "little Europe" is becoming an idea limiting the imaginative forces of the population.

The citizen is incessantly confronted with politics in the form of a global process. His judgment must refer to this entirety. He can only be placed into a position of doing so if political education includes everything that is required, with respect to knowledge and normative understanding, for independent judgment regarding

Exhibition on the History and Persecution of the German Jews. Shown on
Opposite Sides of the Main Room a View of the Auschwitz Annihilation Camp
(above) and 50 Portraits of Famous German Jews of the Past and Present
(below)

A Group of German "Halbstarke" at a Jam Session   Photo: Maage — Bavaria

the affairs of domestic as well as international politics as far as these are of importance for the respective political decision. Only an adequate formation of knowledge, consequently, can provide the prerequisites for the responsible participation in the general process of the formation of political will.

Present-day Education or General Political Education

In many cases, the educational institutions cannot afford so comprehensive a program, in other instances they were established with the explicit purpose to place special emphasis on individual problematic issues of our times, e.g., European Unification or the East-West conflict, because these topics appear to be particularly urgent as a political education subject.

These priorities are typical of the entire political education work which must see its task in providing its special type of support to the formation of political will in the public. Naturally, its main topics, being the present-day subjects of the general formation of will, are particularly exposed to controversial discussion and also to the changing political developments. This situation brings it about that the activities of the institutions of political education have acquired a definitely political importance, characterized by a state of productive as well as problematic tension with reference to the political controversies of the day. The ability of adjusting to the changing development of politics is, moreover, determined by the necessity of condensing the extremely heterogeneous material into the proportions required for short seminars and conferences and — last not least — also depends on the directives issued in relation to the public budgets. This adjustability undoubtedly has some advantages over the school education system with its rigid adherence to long-term instruction plans; this fact, too, underlines the indispensability of political education activities outside of the schools.

The decision to grant priority to this or that complex of questions within the education program, does not amount to partiality in the sense of a party political attitude; at the same time, however, it is undoubtedly the expression of a clearly defined political will. Whoever, e.g., is undecided with respect to European unification, cannot choose this subject as a topic of instruction; whoever is opposed to it, will refrain, too, from selecting it because he must expect a discontinuation of the allocation of public funds (within the framework of political educational work), if he frankly expresses his opinion. The same considerations would be valid with regard to the reunification issue.

Parliament and government have an understandable interest in the topical actualization of political education activities. The disadvantages of this attitude are sufficiently severe, however, to deserve attention; for any actualization must be effected at the expense of a general political education and, thus, is bound to neglect important sectors of political life which happen not to be in the limelight of public interest. Due to this situation, the "German perspective" — to which the participants in the courses are accustomed, anyway — and fashionable topics easily obtain preponderance. Some topics are dealt with, too, after having long since been superseded by world political developments, either because funds continue to be allocated for them or because the public as yet has taken no notice of the latest situation.

The granting of topical priority on the part of the various political education institutions has led — without explicit plans and arrangements to that effect — to

13

a sort of distribution of the tasks. But this enforced distribution undeniably amounts to a danger to the factual topical unity of political education. It is a requirement of first-rate importance, consequently, that also individual problems will be taken up as subjects of instruction with due consideration to their world political context. There is another disadvantage to the distribution of tasks. As a rule, it prevents the basic consideration to what extent a topical actualization is really necessary and permissible. Of course, there exists no alternative between present-day political education and general political education. Actuality and general knowledge are in a continuous state of reciprocal relation. Nevertheless the planning of the instruction programs is always again confronted with the necessity of a decision to grant priority either to the one or to the other side.

Political Education in the Youth Associations [1]

By Dieter Geldschlaeger

In 1949 fourteen youth associations voluntarily united to form the *Deutscher Bundesjugendring* (German Federal Youth Ring). According to the membership figures given for 1959, the size of these associations is as follows:

1. *Deutsche Sportjugend* (Athletic Group) .... 2,459,705 members
2. *Arbeitsgemeinschaft der evangelischen Jugend Deutsch-lands* (Evangelical Study Teams) .... 1,431,000 members
3. *Bund der deutschen katholischen Jugend* (Catholic Youth Group) .... 1,033,844 members
4. *Gewerkschaftsjugend* (Labor Unions Youth Group) (DGB) . 776,460 members
5. *Bund der deutschen Landjugend* (Rural Youth) .... 163,000 members
6. *Deutsche Jugend des Ostens* (Youth from the East) .... 160,000 members
7. *Jugend der Deutschen Angestellten-Gewerkschaft* (Union of Employees Youth Group) .... 132,718 members
8. *Sozialistische Jugend Deutschlands —* (Socialist Youth Group) — *"Die Falken"* .... 120,000 members
9. *Ring deutscher Pfadfinderbuende* (Association of German Scout Group) about .... 116,000 members.

In addition, and in the following order, come those associations with a membership of under 100,000 — the *Deutsche Wanderjugend* (Hikers), the *Naturfreunde-Jugend Deutschlands* (Friends of Nature), the *Jugend des Deutschen Alpenvereins* (Youth Group of the Alpine Club) — the *Deutsche Schreberjugend* (Young Gardeners) and the *Ring deutscher Pfadfinderinnenbuende* (Association of German Girl

---

[1] Excerpts from *Bericht ueber die Probleme und die Versuche der politischen Bildung unter jungen Menschen in der Bundesrepublik Deutschland*. (Report on the Issues involved and the Attempts made at Political Education among the Youth of the German Federal Republic, prepared during the summer and fall of 1960 — a Manuscript.)

Scouts Groups). The latter is the smallest association, with 28,153 members. As well as these associations there are five political youth associations, which are united in the *Ring Politischer Jugend*. These associations are connected with the political parties of the Federal Republic, but their membership figures are far below those of the associations which belong to the *Bundesjugendring*.

The total membership of the 14 youth associations in the *Deutscher Bundesjugendring* in 1959 amounted to 6½ million. According to statistics, in which all persons under 25 years come under the head of juveniles, there were at this time 19,100,000 juveniles among the population of the Federal Republic. A comparison of these figures shows that about one third of all juveniles belong to a youth group. Deductions must be made from this figure for double membership, since it is obvious that some are members of several groups (for example members of a religious group may also belong to a sports group, etc.). If it is considered, however, that it is not very probable that children become members of youth groups under the age of 8 or 10, and if it is further taken into account that all youth groups state unanimously that after the age of 20 people cease to attend the events of the youth groups, the membership figures for the youth groups appear fairly high.

The question may be asked regarding the way in which their aims are stated inside the youth organizations. Are they so formulated as to express political consciousness on the part of the youth associations? The Minister for Youth and Sport in Berlin and the Berlin *Land* Youth Ring have published a booklet which is intended to encourage young persons to join in the work of the youth associations on graduating from school. Ten of the youth associations named publicize their organizations in this booklet. What do these autographic accounts reveal in the way of political activity? The labor unions group points out that they can be of use to young persons, especially in workaday life; the Employees Union youth group writes in a similar strain, particularly emphasizing the possibilities of trainee continuation courses. The scouts lay stress on hiking, comradeship, and "good deeds", as the characterstics of their group. In regard to their political attitude they say: "The association of German scout groups is entirely non-partisan, but this does not preclude active participation in political events. The leaders of the association are not permitted to hold any leading position in a political party". The *Falken*, the German socialist youth group, begins by outlining the normal program of a youth group, but then expresses a decided political opinion: "For us all these questions which affect the development of the young person are basically political questions. We think it more sensible to cultivate Jazz than to march in new uniforms. We want to train ourselves to become free individuals who can think independently and who are conscious of their responsibility. We are opposed to war, and every conscientious objector in East and West Germany will receive unanimous support from us". The Evangelical Youth Group describes the characteristic features of their work as "giving ear to one another, discussing with one another and living side by side with one another", but also remarks in passing that attention should be given to "special questions . . . . . including matters of state". The sports group aim at relaxation and recreation through cheerful companionship, there is no mention of political education. The German Catholic Group describes itself as "a team for education and action" and declares further, "Catholic youth is in touch with the times and open-minded! We, therefore, form opinions on all current issues, support all government measures which serve youth, and work together with all democratic youth organizations". The *Jugendwerk der evangelischen Freikirchen* (Youth Movement of the Evangelical Free Churches) expresses itself similarly to the *evangelische Jugend*; the friends of nature lay particular stress upon friendship, and among some 20 groups with diverse interests, the young gardeners' group is the only one which mentions a "democratic education". This then is a picture of the programs of the youth groups, not a very encouraging affair. In the same area, also in Berlin, the *Falken*, the German socialist youth group, was the only one which mentioned political subjects as the content of events, in a joint program issued for one month by all the groups. These events included lectures and discussions on such subjects as "Soviet Democracy", "Fascist Ideology", "The Basic Program of the German Socialist Party", and indeed two courses in basic political science were announced, to be continued weekly. The programs of all other groups are entirely lacking in similar subjects in the course of this one month.

The fact that the *Falken*, of all youth groups, develop a specially lively political activity is shown for example by the fact that in November 1959, 500 members of the German socialist youth group went on a journey to the former concentration camp of Auschwitz, which lies in Polish territory. At Easter 1960 a second journey was made to the same place, in which 700 members took part. These figures alone show that this was a conscious demonstrative act on the part of the *Falken*, an impression which was confirmed by the laying of wreaths and the speeches made on this occasion, as well as by the statements made following their return. It is understandable that these journeys have also made an impression on the people of Poland. Other youth groups obviously lay more importance on showing a sense of political responsibility through their actual behavior. For example one single number of the newspaper *Deutsche Jugend* contained the following list of activities of diverse groups: 200 girls belonging to the Catholic youth group gave their services in hospitals in Dortmund, and in Freiburg 400 girls followed their example. The labor union group in Giessen undertook to sponsor a school for the blind in Ghana. Youth groups of the Catholic youth movement in Bavaria collected 26,000 DM for the aid of lepers. Another unspecified youth group in Essen collected relief parcels for Algerian refugees. 135 young miners, between the ages of 14 and 21, collected 18,000 DM to build an orphanage. The pupils of a *Gymnasium* in Cassel undertook the care of a cemetery where former foreign workers were buried.

The relatively slight amount of political information within the youth groups may in part be due to the fact that there are fairly abundant opportunities to acquire political information and form political opinions outside these groups. We have seen that relatively few political subjects appeared on the programs of the Berlin youth groups in the course of one month. In the same month, however, the municipal youth movement announced a large number of events connected with political education. These included such subjects as "Stresemann, an Important European", "Radio in a Democracy", "The Path to Tolerance", "What can Berlin Youth do towards Reunification?". The films *Die Machtergreifung* and *Nacht und Nebel* were to be shown and discussed; lectures to be given on "Youth and Current Events" and "Do You want Total War?", and a radio program composed by juveniles alone was to be broadcast. Another showing of and discussion upon the film *Die Machtergreifung* was announced, and a week-end discussion on the subject "Young marriages — young families". There was a week-end course in political responsibility under the titles "The Freedom of Man" and "The Power of Bureaucracy", a lecture on the separate treatment of the Jews under the Third Reich, a week-end course held by the youth organizations jointly with the Society for Christian-Jewish Cooperation.

In the central committees of the individual youth groups no doubt at all exists as regards the necessity of political education in general. To take another example, a booklet published by the Federal Central Organization of the Employees Union Group (DAG) says: "A group which does not take part in politics fails in its mission ... Some youth groups have a different conception of their work. They say that the fact of community life alone is a factor which has political influence and which is itself political ... The DAG is one of the consciously political youth groups ..." These remarks are followed by a list of special subjects, including "coming to grips with communism", "a knowledge of the legal basis of life in the German Federal Republic", "Efforts towards an economic and political European Union". In another booklet intended for the leaders of the DAG youth groups, suggestions are made of subjects for political events for the purpose of political education. Among a long list of subjects are the following: "The Individual between Democracy and Dictatorship", "The 17th of June", "The Path to Europe", "How is a Law made?", "What led up to the 30th January 1933?", "Behind the Scenes in the UN". The annual conference of the DAG in 1960 also concerned itself with these questions. The following subjects were described as specially important politically, and their significance emphasized by the remark that they were just as important as the social efforts of the DAG youth group: "Interest in Germany's recent past", a clarification of the facts connected with the reunification of Germany, the combatting of a new German right-wing radicalism, the attitude to the federal army, international contacts etc. Moreover political education in the youth groups of the individual youth associations is stimulated by collecting and publishing discussion aids for local use. The *Arbeitsgemeinschaft der evangelischen Jugend Deutschlands* (Working team of the German Evangelical Youth Movement) has recently brought out a detailed study of the following subjects: a periodical for Evangelical youth which appears in Bavaria brought out two special numbers devoted to a comprehensive documentation and description of dialectic and historical materialism. Other Evangelical youth periodicals, which have a circulation all over Federal territory, have printed an extensive documentary and critical account of issues of the National Socialist dictatorship. There is no doubt that one of the main difficulties in the way of handling political subjects in the youth groups is the lack of suitable assistants. While it is a widespread complaint among the youth groups that it is very difficult to find enough educated and able persons to handle the work of the groups, these difficulties become immensely magnified as soon as the issue is one of political education, which always demands a considerable amount of specialized knowledge. It is true that a certain amount of help can be given by pointing out material which has appeared and assembling sources of information which are difficult to get hold of, but it is doubtful whether this is sufficient.

In judging political education in the youth groups of the larger associations, one must come to the conclusion that this activity could with certainty be enormously increased without these youth groups needing to lose their original characteristic features. The central organizations display remarkable readiness to undertake political education, indeed an urge towards it. The difficulties which political education has to face, especially in the individual groups, are obvious. It is

185

equally obvious that in many youth groups in which political information and opinions are lacking, there is a tendency to cultivate a certain political attitude, the encouragement of a cooperative spirit, which it would be very cynical to underestimate. One of the real difficulties under which political education in the youth groups also widely suffers is the fact that this political education takes place during leisure hours, so that it is hard to bridge the gap between the information so gained and the habits of thought formed, and the world of everyday life, especially in the field of work.

In this study of the youth associations we have neglected one activity to which we shall draw attention in the following. Most of the larger youth movements have associated to form Youth Rings, at the local level, the *Kreis* level, the *Land* level and the Federal level. We must now discuss the political activities of these Youth Rings.

The Work of the Youth Rings

When, after the German capitulation in 1945, new democratic associations needed to be built up, youth rings and youth committees began to be formed in various places in the three western zones, sometimes with the cooperation of the juvenile welfare officers of the allied occupying powers. At the beginning of October 1949, scarcely a month after the German Bundestag met for the first time, the union of the various youth associations and youth rings in the *Deutscher Bundesjugendring* (German Federal Youth Ring) was effected. Critics of the youth association system and the Federal youth plan today should particularly note this sequence of events, for some youth rings were already in existence before the Federal Republic was constituted, in any case long before the announcement of the first Federal youth plan, which took place in December 1950. The associations and *Land* youth rings, which united in the *Bundesjugendring* entirely of their own accord, declared their aim to be to encourage the individual associations to become familiar with one another, and so to foster a growth of sympathy for each other, indeed possibly to stimulate an exchange of information and a benefiting from one another's experience. In this way would not only other young persons become attracted, but also these movements would be able to come out in public with opinions on issues affecting youth, and also to adopt an attitude to other and more general questions from the point of view of the youth associations. From the very beginning the *Deutsche Bundesjugendring* stated its aim to be "in the interests of youth to prevent with all its power the revival of militarist, nationalist and totalitarian tendencies".

The usual procedure in the youth rings is that in all important public decisions the delegates must vote unanimously, failing which no public statement of policy is made. After the anti-Semitic smearing incidents at the turn of 1959/60, a number of *Land* youth rings issued appeals. Thus the Schleswig-Holstein *Land* Youth Ring appealed to its member associations to devote an evening in the course of the winter in all groups to the disastrous part played by the swastika in German history; the Bavarian *Land* Youth Ring urged the youth associations belonging to it to contribute money towards the building of a new youth hostel in Israel, to be named after Anne Frank. The Berlin *Land* Youth Ring condemned "these events in the strongest terms. It disassociated itself both from the isolated actions of politically abused young persons, as well as from those adults who were politically incorrigible. The *Land* youth ring sets its face against exaggerated importance being attached to these isolated events, but it is of the opinion that the sharpest action should be taken against these beginnings". On 8th January 1960 the Berlin *Land* Youth Ring organized a protest demonstration against the incorrigibles, in which some ten thousand young Berliners took part, not by any means all members of youth groups. The chairman of the Berlin Jewish community said: "the Jewish population of Berlin has confidence in the youth of Berlin".

It is however not the case by any means that the *Deutsche Bundesjugendring* or the *Land* youth rings only began to busy themselves with the "the unmastered past" when these events first attracted the public gaze to German youth. As early as November 1951, for example, the 5th plenary meeting of the *Bundesjugendring* in Hannover expressed its "growing concern" at the increasing number of foundations of veterans' associations, rejected the formation of youth groups belonging to these associations, and criticized the reintroduction of war decorations. At the 14th plenary meeting of the *Deutscher Bundesjugendring* in 1956 in Oberursel, the youth associations once more unanimously condemned new totalitarian tendencies which had been manifested in Germany. At that time the plenary meeting of the *Deutscher Bundesjugendring* drew up appeals to teachers, journalists, writers, film-directors, judges, politicians, official departments dealing with juveniles and German youth as a whole. The youth rings were urged by the plenary meeting "not to accept as members youth organizations which followed nationalist, militarist or neo-Fascist aims, and to use their influence with the committees for juvenile welfare and other official bodies, that such youth organizations should not be countenanced or given any encouragement". The *Land* and *Kreis* youth rings have followed this line in innumerable cases, by constantly rejecting repeated applications put forward by small extreme right-wing youth groups, which were frequently repeated under various names.

The youth rings have, however, by no means restricted their attention to issues of the recent German past, other political questions are constantly being dealt with. The 3rd plenary meeting of the *Deutscher Bundesjugendring* in October 1950 in Berlin chose as its main theme "Youth under the democratic system — youth under totalitarian dictatorship". It was then decided to collect and evaluate material on extreme right and left wing youth organizations, which has continued to be done ever since. The 7th plenary meeting of the *Deutscher Bundesjugendring*, which again took place in Berlin, discussed, among other things, the subject of "The situation of youth in the Soviet occupied zone". "What does the democratic state expect from its young people? What do the young people expect of a democratic government?" was the subject around which discussion centred at the 9th plenary meeting in Hamburg, a discussion to which the Federal Minister of the Interior, among others, contributed. The 11th plenary meeting of the *Bundesjugendring* in November 1954 chose as its central theme: "Indivisible Germany, a responsibility of the whole nation". The youth groups were particularly concerned with the question of whether possibilities existed of forming contacts with young people in the Soviet occupied zone. The main theme of the 12th plenary meeting of the *Deutsche Bundesjugendring* in 1955 was: "Against a revival of militarism". The general question of "the political education and training of youth today and tomorrow" formed the core of the discussions at the 13th plenary meeting of the *Bundesjugendring* in November 1955. The 16th plenary meeting also, which was held in Upper Franconia in March 1957, discussed the question "Youth and political responsibility". Dr. Gerhard Schreeb, from the League of German Catholic Youth, who presented the main report, demanded, among other things, that young people should be given chances to help with the work of parliamentary democratic institutions, even though they had not yet reached the usual age of 45 years. At the 18th plenary meeting of the *Bundesjugendring* in March 1958, a resolution was adopted on the problem of the German Jewish citizen. The 19th plenary meeting, which met in October 1958 at Homburg in the Saar, discussed problems connected with East-West issues, including the situation of youth under these conditions of stress.

A critical biographer of the German *Bundesjugendring,* is therefore justified after these ten years of work, in coming to the conclusion that this committee showed decisive leanings towards the political side, which dominated to the exclusion of cultural activities. (Martin Faltermaier).

The *Land* youth rings and the *Bundesjugendring* suffer from the same difficulty which is shared by other bodies of our public life. They cannot say with a good conscience that they speak on behalf of all juveniles, since they know that only about one third of all young people belong to the associations they represent. The youth rings on the whole are quite clear on this point. They deliver their proclamations not as coming from "German youth" as such, but as unanimous declarations of the associations represented in the youth rings. All the same it should be remembered that they are the legitimate representatives of that part of German youth which is prepared to take an active part in the associations. Martin Faltermaier, the historian of the *Deutscher Bundesjugendring* already mentioned, writes in a summary appreciation: "the actual outcome of all these discussions, suggestions and events cannot be put into attractive figures. It may be that the public and many politicians take no notice of them at all. It has become a matter of course that the *Deutsche Bundesjugendring* should undertake to fight against extreme left and right wing tendencies, and it has become a matter of course that the youth associations should carry on the work of political education on a broad basis. Many efforts, it is true, do not alwyas suffice to cope with the dimensions of the task. But this commitment is not a matter of course". Certain journalists, who work very swiftly but not always very thoroughly, and who moreover become very irate, consider it the smart thing to work up excitement over the officialdom, over State support for the independent youth associations and over the Federal plan for youth. Irresponsible critics of the youth associations ought to take the trouble to read through what less superficial observers have discovered in the course of their investigations. Thus Helmut Schelsky comes in the course of his examination to the conclusion that there could be no question of escaping out of the impersonal complicated organizations of the body politic as they exist today, into smaller and more intimate cells. Schelsky then continues: "... it therefore seems to me that the youth organizations of today, dependent as they are upon a large-scale system of associations, and the bureaucratic officialdom which this, in part at any rate, involves, are more suited to fulfill the task of the political education of youth than all the traditionally 'youthful', small-scale and intimate youth movement community groups". And Walter Grosse-Hartlage and Karl Rauch, after examining present-day trends among the youth of Germany, come to the conclusion that most young people are not prepared to follow any inner or outer compulsion, but that they are very ready to absorb a great deal of information and to test it critically.[1]) The two writers deduce from this that "the official and semi-official organizations for youth welfare will also have to take this very carefully into account in the measures they undertake, including the important field of financial support and furtherance. The growing generation of today needs financial subsidies, not only for the buildings, which are constructed with an eye to their practical requirements, but also for all their efforts and plans. In contrast to former notions of independence they consider this their due right, but they are not under any circumstances prepared to make any concessions in their opinions which would compromise their liberty and independence".

Many Discussions on the Unmastered Past [2]

After the winter program of the Bavarian Youth Associations — which were already planned prior to the desecration of the Cologne synagogues — the young people in all the youth groups and in many youth hostels are at present concerning themselves intensively with the subjects and problems of the "Unmastered Past". More of the available literature is continually being demanded of the publishers; the brochure "The Seizure of Power" of the Land Organization for Civics (Landeszentrale fuer Heimatdienst), for example, has been so much in demand that a reprint must now be issued. The same applies to film material. The copies of the films Night and Fog (Concentration camp atrocities) and Seizure of Power are continually in circulation. The country youth is also concerning itself with this subject at its meetings and home evenings. For example, in this connection, in the young farmers' school at Untergrainau recently youths and girls criticized "the impotence of large circles to provide a sober and objective portrayal of information on historical events". It is indeed necessary to expedite in the schools the work of education in good citizenship but it must also be "made more attractive". It has also become problematical in some youth associations because "it is often carried out in a too dry and school-masterly manner and not clearly enough", as quoted in an announcement by the Bavarian Young Farmers' Association. Finally a warning is given not to go to the other extreme and still only "act in the unmastered past".

Instructional Aid for Youth Leaders [3]

As the youth associations on local, provincial, Land and Federal levels established the Youth Circles as platforms for their joint work, they intended to keep their meetings free from the influences of all totalitarian ideologies and from organiza-

[1]) Zwanzigjaehrige haben das Wort; Paul List Verlag, Munich, 1959.
[2]) From Informationsdienst of the Landesjugendring Bayern, February 1960.
[3]) Foreward from a Guide for Youth Leaders in the Provincial and Town Youth Circles. Published by the Deutscher Bundesjugendring (German Federal Youth Circle).

tions, which have undemocratic tendencies of this kind, in their intellectual background. This desire is a joint foundation of the work and has often found its expression in the statutes of the Youth Circles. In the statute of the German Federal Youth Circle, which in this question has very often become an example for the formulation of statutes of Youth Circles on Land and local levels, Article 4 quotes in this respect:

"Basic conditions for admittance and membership of the German Federal Youth Circle are:

1. The recognition of the Federal Republic of Germany and these basic rights laid down in the Basic Law:

Freedom of Conscience

Freedom of the Person

Freedom of the Community

in purpose as well as in practical work.

In Article 3 the following is described as one of the most important tasks of the German Federal Youth Circle:

"To hinder with all force, in the interests of youth, a revival of militaristic, nationalistic, and totalitarian tendencies."

As with all the tasks of the German Federal Youth Circle, here too, political educational work is first of all necessary among its own ranks, and this in the Youth Associations and Youth Circles at all levels. Political education must particularly stress the study of German history, especially the period, and the events before and during the National Socialist regime. We wish that the experience gained from this period of dictatorship should be handed on to the young people and that a strong democratic consciousness may arise therefrom. Only then are we all able to resist the totalitarian dangers which threaten our state, also from the direction of right wing radicalism.

In addition, the necessity rises to maintain the Youth Circles themselves as free alliances of democratic youth associations, i. e., therefore to refuse admittance to undemocratic youth organizations. This is also accompanied by the task of coming to grips with the intellectual and political forces which lead or support such undemocratic youth organizations. Finally, this includes also approaching young people who have gotten into the slipstream of such organizations — intentionally or by accident — and to make our conceptions understandable to them in order to bring democratic awareness closer to them.

From our experience in the Youth Circle we know that youth organisations to which democratic thinking is not a matter of course, often would like to be admitted into the local Youth Circles in order to have themselves thus substantiated before the public as enjoying equal rights in the sphere of democratic youth associations. The local Youth Circles are often faced with the task of having to decide whether organisations which apply for admittance to the Youth Circle are democratic in their fundamental attitude and can thus be admitted to the Youth Circle. Such decisions are not easy for a local Youth Circle and place great demands on the sense of responsibility of the members. The consequences of thoughtlessly made wrong decisions can be very damaging. The German Federal Youth Circle wishes to provide here a guide, particulary for the local Youth Circles, to give them a basis for these decisions. This guide does not come to grips with communistic tendencies in youth work. It is limited intentionally to coming to grips with nationalistic, racially inflammatory, right-wing radical, militaristic, and so-called *Voelkisch* (ethnical) tendencies in youth work, and incorporates also the coming to grips with endeavors in youth work based on military traditional associations and organizations of ex-soldiers. This limitation is made as the German Federal Youth Circle often expresses elsewhere its opinions on the communist youth work.

Instructional Aid for School Magazines [1]

Anti-Semitism is in its nature, of a completely irrational character. For this reason, all the theories which purport to justify anti-Semitism must fail, which, on the other hand, does not deny the existence of such theories.

The aversion of our grandfathers along with that of our fathers towards a certain group of people became, in a metaphysical interpretation, a criminal offense. Regarded from the viewpoint of the present day, we can only speak of an absence of intellectual responsibility, that the theories of anti-Semitism were not taken seriously enough, that their consequences were not made known.

Anti-Semitic discrimination occurs then, when the Jew is endowed from the outset with every negative characteristic. To begin with, as a reply to this discrimination and persecution, the extreme Zionist movement grew stronger with the postulate of the Chosen People. Under the rule of National Socialism, the idea of anti-Semitism became gruesome reality. Even out of partly genuine fear of the idea of world domination by Jewry, one can hardly comprehend an action which did not even shrink before the murder of children in concentration camps.

What is left to us now about it all is a legacy: we have to study the theories, causes, actions, and consequences of anti-Semitism. Ideas have to settle with ideas, but people may not become enemies because of ideas, and because of these ideas, kill each other.

The documentation on National Socialism shown here contains mainly sources of a universally coordinated anti-Semitism propaganda. In this publication, press reports from local and regional newspapers of the North Hessen area, official party editorials and reports from *Der Voelkische Beobachter*, *Das Schwarze Korps*, *Der Stuermer*, *interalia*, and leaflets pro and con have been included in the collection of material. As some of it was available only in newspaper clippings, the date or name of the newspaper in question could not be ascertained in every case. These few undated press reports, which otherwise embrace the period from 1933 to 1944, will not however, detract from the general subject expressed.

May this documentation find a resonance in the newspapers of the youth press. For financial support of this publication, I thank the *Hessische Landeszentrale fuer Heimatdienst* (Hessen *Land* Office for Civics).

[1] From the Preface to a special edition of the *Digest of the Youth Press*, Hessen, for all member newspapers of the Youth Press in the Federal Republic of Germany and West Berlin.

Political Education of "Non-Organized Youth" [1]

By Dieter Geldschlaeger

During recent years four responsible bodies have concerned themselves with the political education of "non-organized" youth, in addition to a number of individual institutions which need to be specified. The four responsible bodies are the *Deutsche Volkshochschulverband* (Association of German Adult Education), the *Arbeitsgemeinschaft Arbeit und Leben* (Working team 'Labor and Life'), the *Katholisch-soziale Bildungswerk* (Catholic Social Educational Society), and the responsible Evangelical groups, in which joint work is done by the Evangelical Academies in the Federal Republic, the Young Workers' Movement of the Y.M.C.A. and the *Christliche Jugenddorfwerk* (Christian Youth Village Movement). Of these responsible bodies the *Deutsche Volkshochschulverband* and its aims can probably claim to be best known, since its history dates back to the end of the first world war. The *Deutsche Volkshochschulverband* is not bound by politics or religious confessions. The *Arbeitsgemeinschaft Arbeit und Leben* is an alliance between the *Deutsche Gewerkschaftsbund* (German Labor Unions) and the *Deutsche Volkshochschulverband*. This alliance is also the outcome of the remarkable urge towards education which has always existed in the labor unions, and it is obvious that the endeavors of *Arbeit und Leben* are closely connected with the labor unions, although they go further. The *Katholisch-Soziale Bildungswerk* and the *Evangelische Akademien* are institutions for adult education and discussion of the two main Christian Churches, in which an attempt is made to acquire spiritual and intellectual clarity on questions upon which decisions must be reached in social and political everyday life.

In addition to these four responsible groups there are a number of individual institutions which are, for the greater part, amalgamated in the *Arbeitskreis Jugendbildungsstaetten e.V.* (Working Team of Organizations for Education of Youth — a registered society). The organizations working in this team include those set up by the *Land* Juvenile Welfare authorities, the *Jugendhoefe* (youth retreats), the East-West Institute, the Europe Houses and similar institutions. In most cases these institutions do not belong to a larger association, they are often supported by registered societies, which have grown up around these youth education organizations.

It is necessary to draw attention to the fact that state-supported political education of the "non-organized" is carried out by the four responsible groups named above and the individual institutions, and not by a separate state institution specially created for this purpose. One should also point out that these institutions which receive state support for their work of political education are very different in regard to their standards of values. The conclusion must be drawn from this that if political education of those young people who are not prepared to become full members of a youth association is to be assisted out of public funds, our democratic government consciously and purposely refrains from setting up its own uniform

[1] Exerpts from *Bericht ueber die Probleme und die Versuche der politischen Bildung unter jungen Menschen in der Bundesrepublik Deutschland.* (Report on the Issues involved and the Attempts made at Political Education among the Youth of the German Federal Republic, prepared during the summer and fall of 1960 — a Manuscript)

official school system, preferring to support other institutions, in part of long standing and proven value. The meaning and estimation of political life are therefore not considered to rest with the state alone, so that these efforts represent the exact opposite of totalitarian political conditioning. Nor is it a case of one institution or another being one-sidedly supported; several educational institutions, which differ widely from one another in their aims, are aided, so that in the political education of "non-organized youth" care is also taken that the pluralistic system of our social order comes to the fore.

Who attends?

In 1958, a total of some 50,000 young people took part in the congresses, courses and classes of the four responsible groups; the largest share being taken by the Catholic group with 23,458 participants. This was followed by the Evangelical group with 15,949, the working team *Arbeit und Leben* with 12,082 and lastly the *Volkshochschulverband* with 7,481 participants. In 1959 the figures were higher, a total of some 60,000 young persons took part in the events of the individual institutions, which in 1959 amounted to 40,000, should be adde dto the above figure. In 1959, therefore, some 100,000 young persons took part in those measures of political education which were arranged for the "non-organized". As empirical value it may be assumed that about one tenth of those taking part were members of youth associations. This figure, however, does not mean too much. Membership of several youth organizations does not count as "organization" as regards the work of political education, for instance the athletic associations themselves confess that scarcely any political education takes place within them, so that as far as the work of political education is concerned members of an athletic group must be counted as "non-organized".

That the congresses, courses, and classes held form a distinct attraction to many young persons is shown by the fact that some 10 % of the participants often came again to political education events (this of course does not mean the repeated attendance at a course of classes, but a repeated attendance at major events). The statements of the responsible groups regarding the occupational analysis of the persons attending are as follows: In the Evangelical group 80 % of the participants were industrial trainees and young workers, and 20 % school pupils, clerical workers and other juveniles. The Catholic group names young workers and high school pupils as forming the bulk of their attendances. According to the *Volkshochschulverband,* the courses in adult education, as far as these are concerned with political education, are mainly attended by clerical workers. The working team *Arbeit und Leben* states the share of industrial workers to be 80 %, that of clerical workers 15 %, and school pupils 5 %. In an institute which is associated with the *"Arbeitskreis Jugendbildungsstätten",* it was found that 40 % were school pupils, 15 % students, 10 % industrial trainees, and the rest was made up of teachers, government officials and employees, industrial workers and craftsmen, social workers and professional workers. In almost all cases boys were more numerous than girls. Both the Evangelical group and the group *Arbeit und Leben* report 25 % girls, the Catholic group and the *Volkshochschulverband* report some 33 % girls, and only in one case, that of a *Jugendhof,* were almost equal numbers of boys and girls counted in the course of one year. As regards age, the groups most frequently found in courses on political education are those between 18 and 22 years.

Advertising Democracy [1]

By Eberhard Bitzer

There will probably be some lack of clear understanding of what is meant by the term "positive protection of the constitution", which the State Ministers of the Interior advocated at their conference in Kiel, Schleswig-Holstein. Even to people who have to do with politics every day, this term seemed to be something which is absolutely new, behind which there might be mysterious or possibly even dangerous motives. This is not so. Beginning about ten years ago, special institutes for the promotion of democratic ideas were planned, and set up, on the Federal level; and in the states, too, there has been positive protection of the constitution, as the counterpart to the "negative protection of the constitution" by the security agencies handling the direct defense against leftist and rightist radical infiltration. It may be a debatable issue as to whether the term "positive protection of the constitution" (reportedly coined by the Minister President of Hesse, Georg August Zinn) is an adequate term. In practice one meets it on rare occasions only. Even those institutes which are engaged in the practice itself use it seldom: — agencies such as the *Bundeszentrale für Heimatdienst* (Federal Organization for Civics) and the various state centers, all of which advertise the idea of parliamentary democracy by using films, booklets, periodicals, or even the more refined methods of modern public relations work.

For many an observer even this seems already like "propaganda" and like tutelage by a police-controlled state. It goes without saying that all of us have had more than enough of insincere phrases and stupid agitation. However, one must not fall victim to the false conclusion that democracy does not need advertising and the spreading of information at all. The Weimar Republic had to pay bitterly for such a mistake. It was a mistake of the German *Antiliberalen* who always believed that reasonable and clear and solid domestic and foreign policy would alone be sufficient to make the state resistant to crises.

The issue in the Federal Republic now is to find methods for political education which do not seem like stubborn propaganda, but are in line with the devotion of our young state to freedom. It is easier to say such things than to do them. Whoever studies the activities of the *Bundeszentrale fuer Heimatdienst* notices a still uncertain probing. A group of Bundestag deputies from all parties, as a board of trustees, makes sure that there is no place for party politics in this work. This alone does not yet guarantee, however, that the *Bundeszentrale* always finds the right tone and the appropriate medium. This problem has not been made easier by the fact that this institution — created along the lines of the *Reichszentrale für Heimatdienst* founded in 1917 and disbanded in 1933 — has been placed under the control of the Federal Minister of the Interior. It is true that at present grave political dangers hardly threaten it from the executive branch — for the reason that the opposition deputies would immediately sound the alarm — but bureau-

---

[1] From *Frankfurter Allgemeine Zeitung*, 15 June 1960.

cracy can nonetheless paralyze the best intentions. The *Bundeszentrale* employs intellectually active brains, not typical career civil servants, but chiefly pedagogues, publicists or *Politologen,* a terrible word now often used to describe political scientists. The Ministry of the Interior, being the supervisory institution, lives and thinks along other lines, however. This is not always to the benefit of the *Bundeszentrale,* the more so as its budget of 7.5 million DM (approx. $ 1.8 million) is not exactly sumptuous, measured by its tasks, and by the current price level in the advertising field. Many a good idea already has had to be buried because there were no funds available.

What does the *Bundeszentrale* do? Its name sounds somewhat vague. One cannot help thinking of something like an agency for the maintenance of monuments or for the conservation of nature. However, this name offers big psychological advantages. Many people notice publications of the *Bundeszentrale* — e.g., on a train or in their doctor's waiting room — without losing their desire to read as soon as they see the dry-cut name of a state agency. "Our work is done for democracy and not for our agency", this is the motto of the about fifty staff members of the *Bundeszentrale fuer Heimatdienst.* Indirect approaches rank first. Special appreciation must go to the *Bundeszentrale* for not having given in to the temptation of developing into a mammoth agency, when one bears in mind that every month it mails 800,000 copies of a political information sheet to teachers in all types of schools and to companies interested in it; that it publishes the periodical *"Das Parlament"* (circulation 80,000); that it supplies material for lectures to numerous organizations; that it arranges series of lectures; that it encourages theater performances; that it commissions scholars to do research work (e.g., about anti-Semitism, Communism or the roots of Fascism); that it organizes contests among students, and conducts tours to Berlin. The *Bundeszentrale* now employs almost the same number of people as eight years ago when it began operations.

It is also the sole Federal institution in which all democratic parties cooperate without hitches. Really, one cannot preach political fairness and do the opposite. "You have slandered your opponent, so you lose ten points!" This is, for example, one of the rules of a political game aimed at developing a sense of politics among school children. When playing, children often learn things more easily than through lessons on theory. In the course of time certain habits may develop. This is what the team, led by Dr. Paul Franken, a 55-year old man from the Rhineland, wishes to achieve: not only a minimum of knowledge and ability for political analysis, but also a positive attitude toward the democratic way of life.

During peaceful times little publicity is given to the work of the *Bundeszentrale.* However, as soon as the barometer of domestic politics points to bad weather, everyone is happy that there is "positive protection of the constitution", namely by the *Bundeszentrale* and its state-level counterparts. This was so five months ago during the anti-Semitic hysteria. Many a Minister sought its protection. However, one should not be satisfied with occasional praise only. The *Bundeszentrale* is still far from using all the chances offered by modern advertising techniques (which does not mean that it should advertise democracy in the same way as breakfast cereals are advertised). Certainly, the *Bundeszentrale* can hardly do more than it now does unless we give it broader opportunities.

Report on the Work of the Federal Organization for Civics [1]
Bundeszentrale fuer Heimatdienst

On the problems of

Coming to grips with the past
and
Conquering racial and national prejudices

A. Suggested books and pamphlets

B. Courses and conferences

C. Aids to teaching

D. Mass publicity

E. Films

F. Exhibitions

G. Supplement

A. Books and Pamphlets recommended by the Federal Organization for Civics

Aim: a strengthening of sympathy for the democratic form of government and the willingness to undertake democratic co-responsibility. Encouragement of the European idea.

I. Special list of publications by commercial firms on problems connected with anti-Semitism (1955—1959).

Walter A. Berendsohn	*Aufbauarbeiten in Israel*	Verlag Bernard und Graefe, Berlin
Stephan Spender	*Eine Reise durch Israel*	Steingrüben-Verlag, Stuttgart
Stephan Spender	*Israel*	Steingrüben-Verlag, Stuttgart
Gordon W. Allport	*Treibjagd auf Sündenböcke*	Christian-Verlag, Bad Nauheim
Michael Müller-Claudius	*Deutsch-jüdische Tragik*	Verlag Josef Knecht, Frankfurt/M.
Leo Baeck	*Dieses Volk — Jüdische Existenz*	EuropäischeVerlagsanstalt GmbH, Frankfurt/M.
Dr. H. G. Adler	*Theresienstadt — Das Antlitz einer Zwangsgemeinschaft*	J. C. B. Mohr (Paul Siebeck), Tübingen
Gerald Reitlinger	*Die Endlösung der Judenfrage*	Verlag Otto H. Hess, Berlin-Dahlem
Walter Ehrenstein	*Dämon Masse*	Verlag Dr. Waldemar Kramer, Frankfurt/M.

---

[1] Drawn up for the 16th International Congress of psychologists in Bonn, and the Conference of psychologists and sociologists of the SSIP (Sociological Study Team on International Problems) in Bonn, August 1960.

Alexander Weissberg-Cybulski	*Die Geschichte von Joel Brand*	Kiepenheuer & Witsch, Köln
Poliakov-Wulf	*Das Dritte Reich und die Juden*	arani-Verlags-GmbH, Berlin
Lucie Adelsberger	*Auschwitz*	Lettner-Verlag GmbH, Berlin
Dr. Ehrlich	*Die Geschichte der Juden in Deutschland*	Schwann-Verlag GmbH, Düsseldorf
Eva G. Reichmann	*Flucht in den Hass*	EuropäischeVerlagsanstalt GmbH, Frankfurt/M.
The Wiener Library	*Persecution and Resistance under the Nazis. Catalogue Series No. 1*	Vallentine, Mitchell, London 1960
Wolfgang Jäger	*Unsere jüdischen Mitbürger*	Juventa-Verlag GmbH, München
Kurt R. Grossmann	*Die unbesungenen Helden*	arani-Verlags-GmbH, Berlin
Paul W. Massing	*Vorgeschichte des politischen Antisemitismus*	EuropäischeVerlagsanstalt GmbH, Frankfurt/M.
Arno Scholz	*Bildband Israel — Land der Hoffnung*	arani-Verlags-GmbH, Berlin
Walter Sulzbach	*Die zwei Wurzeln und Formen des Judenhasses*	Kohlhammer-Verlag, Stuttgart
Hannah Arendt	*Elemente und Ursprünge totaler Herrschaft*	EuropäischeVerlagsanstalt GmbH, Frankfurt/M.
Hermann Levin Goldschmidt	*Das Vermächtnis des deutschen Judentums*	EuropäischeVerlagsanstalt GmbH, Frankfurt/M.
Wiener Library	*German Jewry, Catalogue Series No. 3*	Vallentine, Mitchell, London
Edgar Kupfer-Koberwitz	*Die Mächtigen und die Hilflosen*	Vorwerk-Verlag, Stuttgart

II. Series of publications by the Federal Organization for Civics. Special list of publications on problems connected with National Socialism and anti-Semitism (1954—1959).

Hermann Graml	*Der 9. November 1938 — Reichskristallnacht*
Gerhard Ritter	*Das Problem des Militarismus in Deutschland*
Peter Lotar	*Das Bild des Menschen*
Hermann Weinkauff	*Die Militäropposition gegen Hitler und das Widerstandsrecht*
Deutsche Gespräche über das Recht zum Widerstand	*Die Vollmacht des Gewissens*
Theodor Heuß	*Zur Wiederkehr des 20. Juli*
Erich Kosthorst	*Die deutsche Opposition gegen Hitler zwischen Polen- und Frankreichfeldzug*

197

Gerstein-Protokoll	*Dokumentation zur Massenvergasung*
Helmuth Krausnick	*Zur Zahl der jüdischen Opfer des Nationalsozialismus*
Josef Schneider	*Das Ermächtigungsgesetz*
Hans Rothfels	*Das politische Vermächtnis des deutschen Widerstandes*
Hans Rothfels	*Zehn Jahre danach*
Walter Jacobsen	*Lauter Vorurteile*
Edgar Kupfer-Koberwitz	*Als Häftling in Dachau*
Josef Wulf	*Vom Leben, Kampf und Tod im Ghetto Warschau*
H. G. Adler	*Der Kampf gegen die 'Endlösung' der Judenfrage*
Grete Salus	*Eine Frau erzählt*
Dieter Ehlers	*Die Methoden der Beck-Goerdeler-Verschwörung*
Verschiedene Verfasser	*Der Ausbruch des Zweiten Weltkrieges*
(Sonderreihe) Romano Guardini	*Verantwortung*

III. "Aus Politik und Zeitgeschichte" — Supplements of the weekly paper "Das Parlament". Special list of publications on problems connected with anti-Semitism (1954—1959).

B XXXXV	10. Nov. 1954	*Urkunden zur Judenpolitik des Dritten Reiches* 22,000 copies
B XXXXVI	17. Nov. 1954	*Urkunden zur Judenpolitik des Dritten Reiches Dokumente zur weiteren Entwicklung der national-sozialistischen Judenpolitik auf die 'Endlösung' hin,* 22,000 copies
B XXII	1. Juni 1955	*H. G. Adler, Die Rolle Theresienstadts in der End-lösung der Judenfrage,* 27,000 copies
B VII	15. Februar 1956	*Edgar Kupfer-Koberwitz Als Häftling in Dachau*
B VIII	22. Februar 1956	*1. Forts.*
B IX	29. Februar 1956	*2. Forts.*
B X	7. März 1956	*3. Forts. und Schluß in* 30,000 copies
B XXXV	7. Nov. 1956	*Karl Löwenstein, Minsk Im Lager der deutschen Juden,* 60,000 copies
B L	12. Dez. 1956	*Alex Weissberg, Die Geschichte von Joel Brand,*
B LI	19. Dez. 1956	60,000 copies
B XXXXII	30. Oktober 1957	*Grete Salus, Eine Frau erzählt,* 73,000 copies
B VIII	26. Februar 1958	*H. G. Adler, Der Kampf gegen die 'Endlösung' der Judenfrage,* 75,000 copies
B XV	16. April 1958	*Josef Wulf, Vom Leben, Kampf und Tod im Ghetto Warschau,* 75,000 copies
B 26	6. Juli 1960	*Walter Jacobsen, Die Vergangenheit mahnt. — Wille, Wege und Wagnis zur Bewältigung,* 75,000 copies
In Vorbereitung		*Walter Jaide, Die Einstellung heutiger Jugendlicher zur Politik*

B. Courses and conferences held by assocations and study teams

Since, towards the end of 1952, associations began activities in the field of reading papers, the subjects of anti-Semitism and neo-Nazism came to be included among those suggested for educational and training institutes. As is shown by the programs which accompany applications for assistance, all organizations which work in cooperation with our agency tended more and more to include such subjects in their educative schemes. If now and again for psychological reasons it did not seem advisable to designate the subject specifically, care was taken that when dealing with "The Constitutional State" or cognate subjects, anti-Semitism was intentionally indicated as a limitation or denial of human and basic rights.

The number of conferences to which assistance was given rose from year to year. In 1959 assistance in the form of a grant towards expenses and cooperation in the work was given to some 350 conferences organized by some 150 organizations (e. g. The German Association of Labor Unions with its Federal schools, the Catholic Women's Study Team etc.), as well as some 430 conferences arranged by some 50 educational institutions (e. g. the Evangelical and Catholic Academies, classes and institutes on European questions etc.). This assistance was only given provided the subject matter to be treated was such as might make a contribution to political education in the interests of democratic or European ideals. To a very large extent these subjects were concerned with problems connected with recent events in German history. Care was always taken to ensure that National Socialism and its evil deeds were always tackled in an honest and self-critical manner. With this in view private courses lasting several days were held in 1959, at which some 35,000 persons who play an active part in political education were supplied with the necessary information and practical suggestions.

Specialist conferences

As early as 1952 the Federal Organization for Civics began to hold specialist conferences regarding the best ways of conquering the remains of National Socialist ideas and racial prejudices. The insight thereby gained was a valuable aid to the entire work of the coming years. These specialist conferences were resumed in 1959. Arrangements were placed in the hands of educators who had been in close cooperation with the Federal Organization. The following are some of the subjects upon which papers were read at 5 different study conferences held since early 1959:

In the Europahaus Neuhaus (Schliersee):

Is there such a thing as a national character? — problems and results of research on prejudice in USA and Germany — Frustration and authoritarianism — how can authoritarian and nationalist attitudes be changed? — what is a national character — the nature and origin of national prejudices — how European nations appear to one another.

In the Heimvolkhochschule (Boarding Institute for Adult Education) at Bergneustadt:

Prejudice against minorities from the sociological viewpoint — psychological research on prejudice — prejudice in juveniles — national prejudice as a barrier to understanding between nations — the type of person swayed by prejudice — methods of political corruption in the Soviet zone of occupation — the part played by conformity — problems of mass psychology — the part of the fellow-traveller in National Socialism — dependence of the political judgement of the individual upon the majority and authority — the problem of independent thinking — on the problem of gullibility towards the incredible — on pathological traits in political thought.

In the Fridtjof-Nansen House in Ingelheim:

Authoritarianism and nationalism in Germany history — the attractive quality in National Socialist leadership principle — authoritarian personality — pattern of authoritarian behavior in modern collective society — social psychology research on the problem of authoritarianism, nationalism and anti-Semitism — susceptibility to nationalism and authoritarianism — the problem of authoritarianism and nationalism seen from the aspect of school pedagogics — attitude of youth, the school faculties and the educational authorities to the problem of authoritarianism and nationalism in education.

C. Aids to teaching

Aids to teaching in the form of information circulars, pamphlets, calendars, pocket books, and competitions were made available in abundant quantities also for schools and educational centres in factories. Some of these publications run into a million copies and more. Contemporary history with all its individual problems, which cover sociological, social-psychological and constitutional fields, is repeatedly introduced into the subject matter, since political education in relation to topical events would be unthinkable without this. Special study conferences for teachers — in cooperation with the ministries of education — serve to deepen the general pedagogic and didactic knowledge required for this field of education. Amateur dramatics in schools is also recognized to be a fit means of political education and has been correspondingly encouraged. This provides the possibility of a particularly striking presentation of facts which are sometimes difficult to deal with in the classroom.

D. Mass publicity

The Federal Center also maintains close contacts with the publishers of newspapers, periodicals and circulating magazine libraries. This makes it possible to bring important elucidatory articles on National Socialism and anti-Semitism into wide circulation — sometimes in the form of special numbers. A special role in this connection is played by the voluminous *Freiburger Rundbrief*, which appears quarterly and which presents detailed discussions on the subject of "Friendship between God's Chosen People of the Old and New Covenants".

E. Films

The great importance of the film as a means of education and training could be utilized with the somewhat limited means available in particular through encouraging the making of short and documentary films and, through lending such films, as well as entertainment films, free of charge. The titles of some films may be given here, which with the help of the Federal Organization have been made available to a large public:

1. *Nacht und Nebel*
Documentary film on concentration camps in the second world war.
2. *Land und Volk Israel*
Documentary film on the Jews of today and their State, which contradicts false impressions publicized by anti-Semitism.

3. Entertainment film *In jenen Tagen*
Contains a long episode showing how an elderly couple — the wife is a Jewess — were driven to suicide during the Third Reich by the Pogrom of November 1938 *(Kristallnacht)*, the commercial boycott and the withdrawal of the driving licence etc.

4. Entertainment film *Das Komplott*
combats racial prejudice.

5. Entertainment film *Die Angst vor der Gewalt*
contains an episode describing the fate of a couple that took refuge from the National Socialists in Switzerland. This has also been assisted in the commercial field throught financing the German synchronization.

6. Entertainment film *Lang ist der Weg*
deals with the fate of a persecuted Jewish family from Poland.

7. Documentary film *KZ-Schergen — Bericht über den Sorge Schubert-Prozess.*

8. Documentary film *Der 20. Juli vor dem Volksgerichtshof.*

9. Trickfilm *Es war einmal*
(Rise and Fall of the Third Reich).

10. Short film *Der Spielverderber* (Awarded the "Silver Bear" prize in Berlin 1960), shows the mode of action of the demagogue.

F. Exhibitions

Exhibitions may also serve to encourage the readiness and ability to review the past in a self-critical manner. With the aid of the Federal Organization these can be made available to a large number of visitors. They include:

1) An exhibition of books under the title "We Stand Uncompromisingly by the Resistance Fighters in the Third Reich". This was arranged by the Political Youth Ring in Berlin and is now on tour in the Federal Republic.

2) An exhibition with the title "Warning of the Past", which was first shown in the Congress Hall in Berlin, and later in the Town Hall of Charlottenburg. This has also been shown in various places in the Federal Republic.

3) A third exhibition with the title "National Socialism" is in course of preparation.

G. Supplement — July 1960

Books and articles:

Siegmund Kaznelson	*Juden im deutschen Kulturbereich*	Jüdischer Verlag GmbH, Berlin
Walter Poller	*Arztschreiber in Buchenwald*	Verlag für Politik und Zeitgeschehen, Hannover
Cyrill Bibby	*Rassen, Gruppen, Vorurteile und Erziehung*	Mosaik-Verlag, Berlin, 10,000 Ex.
Helmut Heiber	*Adolf Hitler*	Coloquium Verlag, Berlin
Wanda von Bayer-Katte	*Das Zerstörende in der Politik. — Eine Psychologie der politischen Grundeinstellung*	Quelle & Meyer, Heidelberg
Various Authors	*Überwindung von Vorurteilen*	Friedrich-Ebert-Stiftung, Bonn

In preparation:

A. Wiener/H. Krausnick   *Dokumentation zur Judenverfolgung*

Special supplements to Sports newspaper

Alexander Besser   *Der Staat Israel*

Films

Documentary film *Der Huppenkothenprozess*
Entertainment film *Mitgerissen*, on the fellow-traveller problem
Entertainment film *Meine Ehre heisst Treue*, about the activities of a restistance group against Hitler.

Publications

Various Authors   *Das Vorurteil*   (in preparation)

E The Bundeswehr

Dovetailing the Bundeswehr into NATO [1]

An interview with Defense Minister Strauss
By Adelbert Weinstein

In an interview with the *Frankfurter Allgemeine Zeitung* Franz Josef Strauss, the Federal Minister of Defense, declared that this year the Soviet Union had launched a psychological attack on the Federal Republic in general, and the *Bundeswehr* in particular. The German people's reaction to these attacks, most of which had been made by Mr. Krushchev himself, showed that they would not succumb to the communist propaganda campaign. The work done within the *Bundeswehr* to instruct servicemen on the meaning of communism would prevent a weakening of the morale of the troops. On the other hand, the positive results attained in resisting this psychological penetration should not make us complacent. The methods used to fend off such communist attempts at subversion must be strengthened and made more polished. Psychological defense merited our special attention when we remembered Lenin's maxim that it was the highest form of strategy to soften up the enemy's morale to such an extent that he was no longer capable of effectively using his material means of resistance. The ceaseless psychological attacks by Soviet Russia on the Federal Republic and its armed forces had to be looked at from this angle.

In their psychological warfare the Soviets pursued two distinct methods. When the Americans were still the sole possessors of nuclear weapons, in the Soviet Union, Stalin publicly minimized their effect while at the same time he used all the means of propaganda at his disposal to paint the apocalyptic danger in its most gruesome colors for the benefit of the western and neutral countries. Mr. Krushchev's forays against NATO and the *Bundeswehr* showed the same twist. The German armed forces were told that they were being abused as an instrument of "capitalism", colonialism and the monopolists, while on the other hand the Soviets would have the western countries believe that the German *Bundeswehr* was an army led by fascists, whose sole aim it was to start a war.

It would, said the Minister of Defense, be irresponsible to leave the young servicemen to their own devices in standing up to this sort of propaganda and attempted demoralization, the full background of which they could not be expected to grasp. Therefore, psychological defense as practised by the *Bundeswehr* was divided into two parts. First, there was psychological warfare. This consisted of thorough instruction in the characteristic features of communism. Secondly, the *Bundeswehr* provided its soldiers with psychological armament by way of intensive information on the methods and aims of the Bolshevik psychological attacks. In the fiscal year 1960, 1.12 million DM had been set aside for psychological warfare and 3.213 million DM for psychological armament.

Minister Strauss pointed out that the political and military authorities in the Soviet Zone of Occupation received some 30 million Marks per annum for the purpose

---

[1] from *Frankfurter Allgemeine Zeitung*, 19 October 1960.

of undermining the *Bundeswehr*. He said that the constant talk of the danger that the *Bundeswehr* might break away from its western alliance and embark on a military adventure of its own, was also part of Soviet psychological warfare. This had to be countered by ceaseless information and education.

Strauss repeated and emphasized the following points:

1. The *Bundeswehr* is an organic part of our democratic state. 2. It is founded on an unassailable basis of law. By providing German divisions, the Federal Republic is meeting its international obligations. The *Bundeswehr* is therefore the result of contractual commitments. 3. The leading military and civilian personnel in the *Bundeswehr* have been carefully selected and are of blameless character. 4. Within the *Bundeswehr* serious thought and action is devoted daily to the problem of finding new ways of military symbiosis in an international alliance. 5. Even in peacetime, all *Bundeswehr* units come under NATO. 6. The *Bundeswehr* has no independent operational staff. Each corps receives its operational orders direct from SHAPE in Paris. The Federal Ministry of Defense is in no way to be confused with a General Staff. 7. The Federal Republic has no self-sufficient armaments industry of its own and will not set one up. 8. One third of the supplies required in case of war are kept on German soil, whereas two thirds are stored in foreign supply bases; in other words, the *Bundeswehr* could fight on its own for just under one week, and even this would depend on supplies reaching us through pipelines which our allies could at any time bring under their control.

Minister Strauss stressed that NATO Supreme Commander General Norstad had only recently confirmed the fact that there is complete agreement between NATO and the *Bundeswehr* on the question of nuclear armaments. Nuclear armament was a term often loosely used — either through ignorance or by malice aforethought or with the clear intention to cause confusion. We had to distinguish between (a) the carriers of warheads, such as aircraft, rockets and guns, and (b) the warheads themselves. Without the warheads, the carriers were useless. But Germany had never asked for the possession or control of warheads. Under the terms of MC 70 (a NATO Document in favor of equipping the central European front with tactical nuclear weapons) nuclear warheads cannot and may not be held by any one national army. Germany's renunciation of them was an international obligation. The Minister said that he was following with great interest the ideas on the future of NATO which were being aired by the U.S. Secretary of State, Mr. Herter and others. It was true that on points of detail there were some differences between General Norstads' and Mr. Herter's concepts of the character of NATO's atomic force. The General was thinking of a *force de frappe* with atomic weapons on land, sea, and in the air, whereas Mr. Herter had in mind a predominantly naval atomic force for NATO. However, basically the two concepts were in agreement; if the Minister had understood the Secretary of State correctly, NATO was to become the fourth atomic power. Strauss, as the German Minister of Defense, had neither political nor military objections against this. The proposal to turn NATO into the fourth atomic power gained particular importance in connection with the further American proposal to increase the conventional forces of the U.S.A. The idea that an increase in the conventional forces would relieve NATO from the necessity of envisaging an immediate and automatic atomic strike, was in full accordance with the German view.

In German military opinion, too, a wide range of armaments might delay and perhaps even prevent the automatic use of nuclear striking power. These American

Personnel Strength of the German Bundeswehr

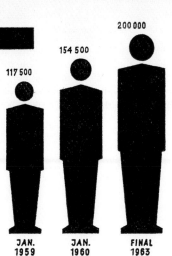

ARMY

JAN. 1957	JAN. 1958	JAN. 1959	JAN. 1960	FINAL 1963
42 400	87 500	117 500	154 500	200 000

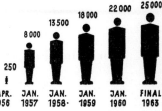

NAVY

APR. 1956	JAN. 1957	JAN. 1958	JAN. 1959	JAN. 1960	FINAL 1963
250	8 000	13 500	18 000	22 000	25 000

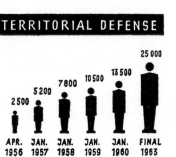

TERRITORIAL DEFENSE

APR. 1956	JAN. 1957	JAN. 1958	JAN. 1959	JAN. 1960	FINAL 1963
2 500	5 200	7 800	10 500	13 500	25 000

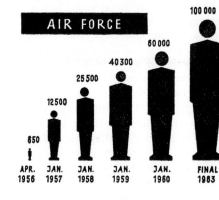

AIR FORCE

APR. 1956	JAN. 1957	JAN. 1958	JAN. 1959	JAN. 1960	FINAL 1963
650	12 500	25 500	40 300	60 000	100 000

TOTAL BUNDESWEHR

APR. 1956	JAN. 1957	JAN. 1958	JAN. 1959	JAN. 1960	FINAL 1963
5 200	68 100	134 300	186 300	250 000	350 000

205

thoughts, and the call for greater conventional forces, were the first conclusion drawn from the changes brought about in the strategic situation as the result of technical development. It was an attempt at making it possible to restore by political means the situation which would arise if the Soviets provoked an armed conflict. It would lift us out of the dilemma of either doing nothing or precipitating a catastrophe.

An Army Full of Surprises[1]

By Franz Woerdemann

The scene (it is nearly always the same, whether you visit a tank battalion in South Germany or an artillery unit up in the North): a bright, simple common room, strong wooden chairs, colored photos cut from a calendar and mounted in self-made frames, and some newspapers. The cast: young recruits of the *Bundeswehr*, volunteers as well as drafted men, spruced up in honor of the guest visiting their secluded world in the form of a reporter; maybe there will be an officer, sitting unobtrusively in a corner, but he is likely to disappear quietly after a short while. Finally, the play: a game of questions and answers, from which the visitor hopes to gain an impression of these young people.

Truly, a difficult job. The young soldiers feel embarrassed and the conversation drags along lamely. They find it difficult to explain why they have volunteered for service, or why they have obeyed their drafting orders without resentment and without fuss; thinking hurts, especially when you are 18 or 20; it hurts even more if it has nothing to do with the bore of an engine, the workings of a fourstroke motor, rifle-locks or bridge-building. There was little to be gleaned from their answers; one felt they vaguely understood that a State needs an army ... it always has and always will. But what do they feel, what do they think when they say: "the State"? Perhaps what has come out of these many labored discussions could be expressed as follows: to these young men the Federal Republic represents an order of things; there is scarcely the shadow of a doubt that the State and this order of things must be as they are and could hardly be imagined otherwise. The existing order has neither been sought nor established in battle — it has been accepted and has long become a matter of course. And the people are more or less contented with it. That, then, is the frame; but the picture inside it lacks color and contour. This State is accepted by its soldiers and to a certain extent it even enjoys their good will but the cool detachment of their attitude overrides all other feelings.

And yet, it is an attractive coolness; the absence, rather, of the romanticism of previous generations — the absence of high-flown illusions. The old concepts and the worn out phrases with which the ties that link the individual to the wider community are expressed are dead and lost on these youngsters. If the visitor's memory serves him well, only one of the many young soldiers he talked to uttered the word "fatherland". It was a word used by a lonely spirit. To the others, not

---

[1] from *Magnum*, No. 29, April, 1960.

even the word "nation" seemed to convey anything. It held no meaning for them. No longer did it arouse in them, as it had done in their fathers, any sacred or unholy sentiments. It is no longer the spark with which to set emotions ablaze. It leaves the young soldiers unmoved. Yet, and this is the reverse of the picture, this vacuum of thought and feeling which so clearly distinguishes them from their American, French, British, and Canadian fellow soldiers has been filled by a new community spirit. It is the feeling of comradeship which they have for the soldiers of the other NATO armies with whom they live and work; this feeling is perfectly natural and matter of course and by no means the result of any official propaganda. If the frontiers of national thinking have melted away anywhere since the war, they have done so in the minds of these young men.

But, of course, it is a difficult job to arrive at these conclusions in tidy barrack quarters, in bright common rooms or while having a beer in the nearest bar. One's first immediate impression of these young soldiers of the *Bundeswehr* was gained from an entirely different angle. Those of us who remember the barrack-square atmosphere of former days are left speechless at the ease of manner and the matter of fact attitude of these twenty-year-olds. The prescription for the build-up of the new *Bundeswehr* worked out at the conference table in Bonn was like an equation with several unknown quantities. The most important of these was the new generation of recruits; no one knew exactly what to expect. By now, several years of experience allow us to sketch some of the basic characteristics of our young soldiers. They are: frankness, frequently mixed with a dash of impudence; respect for practical achievements or personal superiority; hardly a trace of shy deference vis-à-vis mere authority or the hierarchic chain; noisy and very boyish, open-minded, and very matter of fact — that is a description of the young German soldiers. This generation hardly knows of the mortgage with which its elders have burdened the soldiering profession; they pass over it almost with a slight shrug of their shoulders. Square drill never raises in them the flood of evil feelings which cannot or will not subside in most of us. The recruits of 1936 and those of 1960 represent two entirely different worlds.

In the face of such undramatic, matter of fact, courageous and open-hearted youngsters, of whom only few admit the traditional concepts of unquestioning military obedience and discipline, the old type of barrack-square hell-hound has little chance of success, whether he wears the stripes of an NCO or the stars of an officer. Any officer trying to establish his authority exclusively on drill and intimidation will sooner or later have to declare his human bankruptcy before his soldiers (although it must be said that any slackness or timidity is as disastrous for an officer, because he loses his men's respect). There is only one way to success for the modern unit commander in the German army; he must combine ability with leadership. The former makes for respect and the latter allows confidence to grow. The generation of modern unit commanders is really a "generation of fathers". This term is not used frivolously, but results from a series of observations and many talks with young soldiers who are quick to say that their commanding officer treats them "like a son". They are a generation of fathers stamped by the war (or rather by that phase of the war in which human leadership outweighed mere command authority) but even more by "the twelve years". This is a phrase we hear again and again; the "twelve years" were decisive. After the last war our commanding officers of today were architects, teachers, salesmen or industrial managers. Each one of them had to make his way, and almost all succeeded. Their self-assertion seems to be based not so much on their wartime feats, on Iron

Crosses and other decorations, on their new military rank, on entries in their personal file or on their chances of promotion, as on the fact that they have once built up for themselves a civilian livelihood, that they have managed to give a good account of themselves in a free sort of life which to many of them must have seemed hostile at the beginning. They have learned to look upon themselves as members of a civilian society.

Memories of the old feudal officer class have faded since the social basis of that class was swept away. The mentality of the patriotic mercenaries who, after the First World War, found their way into the army of the Weimar Republic via the "Free Corps" has not survived the civilian struggle for life after the second collapse. The myth of the "people's officer" of the Third Reich was blown away with the storms of 1945. Our democratic civilian society no longer tolerates the social hegemony of the officer class; the officers know it and agree.

Yet it must be admitted that they have hardly any choice in the matter. The officers of the Weimar Republic and von Seeckt's army could say with some justification that it was thanks to their forces that the young republic had managed to survive at all; indeed they said only too frequently what von Seeckt had written down in the summer of 1919: "We must accept this State with revulsion in our hearts and a curse on our lips". A war had been lost, it is true, but so far as the soldiers of Weimar were concerned the regime which had lost the war had retained its moral integrity. Conflict with the new outward form of the State was almost inevitable. What about today? Every officer knows that his unit owes its existence to the State and not the oher way round. This is a simple fact but nevertheless a decisive one. The past no longer serves as a moral guide.

All that has been said so far, however, is no more than a frame within which there is much to be learned by experience. In these past years of the *Bundeswehr's* build-up almost each unit commander has had a wide and free scope in moulding the features of his unit despite the paper flood of regulations and decrees from above. It has been, and still is, exclusively a matter of the personality of the officer concerned and just as their characters necessarily differ so the picture differs which our modern army units present to the outsider. Yet, frequent visits to the *Bundeswehr* will strengthen the conviction that these brief notes on the group-character of modern unit commanders reflect reality in almost every battalion with, of course, varying emphasis and shades of difference from one to another. But this is only part of the overall picture because these officers, this generation of fathers, are waging a two-front war; there is, in the first place, the front of the "very old ones" which is mercifully withering away as those die or are pensioned off who were blind in the years after 1945 and who distrust and ridicule all that is new on the barrack-square or in the men's quarters. They look upon the world as upon a shelf of box-files for rules and regulations. Secondly, there is the line dividing the "fathers" from the very young men, who are growing into military life and their officers' boots without the experience of those "twelve years" — and maybe the boots will prove just a little too big for them.

The older generation of officers has a twofold educational function to fulfil: they must train and mould the rising generation of officers who will shortly have to face their coolly critical men unsupported by the proof of professional ability outside the army or by any civilian experience. Moreover, this father generation of officers must also train and educate (mainly in the political sense of the word) the young, detached and almost rootless recruits of our day. The *Bundeswehr* must needs take on a job our present schools and parents almost invariably fail to do:

to enlighten the young people about the true disaster of our history, and to make them into citizens of the new State. It is only in the barracks that these youths from factory or farm learn of the burden of our past and the chances offered by the present. For the first time they experience community life under the auspices of the State, and it is here that they meet the State in its reality; they sit in their classrooms, looking up to the officers who endeavor to explain a far away and strange world to them: How is a bill enacted? What is the difference between *Bundestag* (roughly: Congress) and *Bundesrat* (roughly: Senate)?

Among his notes taken during weeks and months of visits to *Bundeswehr* units, the writer finds one reflecting the thoughts of a Bavarian captain, who for many years after 1945 had been an elementary school teacher: "Citizens in uniform? — With all my heart, yes. But that presupposes the recruits being citizens when they reach us. The Bundeswehr has sufficient uniforms for citizens, but not enough citizens for these uniforms."

Army Education and Civil Responsibility [1]

"Handbook of Inner Leadership"

Something of what is hoped will be the new spirit of the German armed forces is presented in a *Handbook of Inner Leadership* and a number of Army manuals, published by the Federal Ministry of Defense.[2]) The Handbook (and, in a more popular form, also the set of regulations and official statements compiled by Otto Marcks) contains the guiding principles on which the other pamphlets — aids designed for the instruction of officers or the information of private soldiers — are based.

Repeatedly the officer is told in no uncertain terms that the purpose of a democratic army is to preserve peace not to wage war. The German myth of the "eternal soldier", of war as a law unto itself and a realm of absolute values, is forcibly rejected. The widespread legend that the German, even the Prussian, armies were always organizations built upon unquestioning obedience *(Kadavergehorsam)*, is effectively scotched by way of quotations from the works of Scharnhorst, Gneisenau and other early 19th Century Prussian army reformers, but also from the memoirs of more modern generals. In fact a bold attempt is made to build a bridge of valid tradition linking an enlightened conception of the past with all that stayed untarnished in the German story even under Hitler, far above the gulf of that moral and political degeneration which began with William II. An "internal leadership" informed by such a view of history will certainly embark upon a new experiment in German army organization.

The revolt of 20 July 1944, is frequently acknowledged as a symbol of true obedience to the mission of a German officer, and due stress is laid on the duty to challenge false and immoral authority — a regulation probably unique in any army manual. It seems a pity that, in this connection, the crucial matter of the soldier's oath is discussed in the turgid diction of the German theologian and moral philosopher which does little to render the naturally complex problem any less complex. A sharp distinction of course is drawn between the soldier's obligation to perform his civic duty under a democratic Government (however imperfect) and the responsible human being's obligation to fight evil. As for the things to be fought for, it is clearly stated, they are the liberties of Europe and not of Germany alone.

Officers are constantly admonished to treat recruits as fellow-citizens who are in the army to learn how to behave responsibly and independently. They are warned against mechanical drill methods, and frequent reference is made to the lessons to be learnt from modern industry for the efficient organizing of collective activity.

A distinction is drawn between useless military conventions, e.g., sticking to outdated uniforms and modes of saluting, and true tradition, which is stated to be efficient and thoughtful teamwork, both in the military unit and in the wider context of politics, of which the army is only an instrument.

With few exceptions, the textbooks of military education now used in West Germany seem to fulfil their purpose — to preserve the few things that were good in German military tradition, and to cut away the huge amount of deadwood and

---

[1]) From *Wiener Library Bulletin*, XIV, No. 1, p. 9, published in London, England.

corruption that had accumulated in the past. The authors of the *Handbook* are even aware that they have been given a unique opportunity, not shared by any other institution of West Germany society. Through the dissolution by the Allies of the entire German military organization, they were enabled to start from scratch. Indeed a veritable revolution has taken place in German military affairs, significantly one imposed "from above", like all German revolutions, not spontaneously grown, but a revolution nevertheless, lending strength to earnest hopes that for once an instrument of democracy has been created rather than another "State within the State".

²) *Handbuch Innere Führung. Hilfen zur Klärung der Begriffe.* September 1957. 191 pp.
Die Ersten Stunden. Hinweise für den Umgang mit Rekruten in den ersten Tagen. Reihe: *Erziehung Heft 1.* September 1957. 34 pp.
Gruppenselbstarbeit nach ZDv 3/1. Einweisung in ihre Methodik. Reihe: *Erziehung Heft 2.* March 1957. 30 pp.
Wiederaufstieg aus Trümmern. Der politische und wirtschaftliche Aufbau der Bundesrepublik. Reihe: *Bundesrepublik.* March 1957. 63 pp.
Bundestag und Bundesrat. Das Parlament der Bundesrepublik Deutschland. Reihe: *Bundesrepublik No. 2.* January 1958, 88 pp.
These five titles, all published by the Federal Ministry of Defense, are part of series entitled *"Innere Führung".*
Information für die Truppe. Hefte für staatsbürgerliche Bildung und psychologische Rüstung. Herausgegeben vom Führungsstab der Bundeswehr. 1959, No. 8. pp. 464—520. Containing an informative article on Israel by Herbert Schottelius.
Otto Marcks, *Die Bundeswehr im Aufbau.* Bonn. Athenäum Verlag. 1957. 110 pp. With 143 illustrations.

The Bundeswehr School for Internal Leadership [1]

When it was founded, the school was faced with the problem of whether it was more practical to commence immediately in an improvised manner or first to build up under careful preparation. Taking the needs of the units into consideration work was commenced immediately; in addition it was necessary to establish contact immediately with the officers of the units in order to keep closely in touch with the practical side of the operation.

Scientific Research and Training Staff (civilian lecturers)

a) When the organization is completely built up the following fields of study will be represented under the leadership of a university professor as scientific director:
Military Law (International Law, Public Law, Military Penal Law, Military Disciplinary Law, etc.);
Political Sciences (with public opinion research);
Sociology (Military Sociology);
Philosophy;
Pedagogy (group pedagogy, theory of method);
Psychology;
History (general and social history, contemporary history);
Study of foreign countries (West and East);
Theology (Protestant and Catholic);

¹) Excerpts from a report of the Federal Ministry of Defense.

Freedom is like the air we breathe. One first realizes that one can't live without it when one is deprived of it.

You are free
if you can...

... *express your opinion*
without fear

... *profess your Faith*

... *leave your country and*
return to it at will

...enjoy legal protection and invoke a magistrate without regard to his political party

...freely choose your own place of work and exercise the right to strike

...choose your own prefered sources of information

It is possible that you might lose all of these rights in one day, and it will take years to recover them. Or these rights might be slowly undermined without your being aware of it.

THE PRICE OF YOUR FREEDOM IS VIGILANCE

(taken from a *Guide for Servicemen*, used by the Bundeswehr; Ed. note)

15

b) The following are already active:
1 Scientific Director;
1 Pedagogue;
1 Historian;
1 Political Scientist;
1 Teacher of Law;
1 Theologist;
c) The library (including archive) which is now being set up is to contain the most important literature for the school's fields of study.

The Fundamentals of the School's Purpose

The Federal Military School for Internal Leadership is a military training establishment which, of its type, is without precedent in history. Its object is to convey to the Federal Military Corps of Leadership intellectual fundamentals and methodical understanding to enable them to master the task of leadership and training under the changed conditions of our time.

The unchanged purpose of military training is the brave, loyal, and disciplined soldier with excellent combat training. In addition to this, however, it is important, today more than ever, that the soldier consciously acknowledges the positive values of a free way of life and at the same time also becomes steadfast in psychological warfare.

It is, therefore, indispensable for the striking power of a modern fighting unit under heavy physical and moral stresses that the officers and NCO's establish for themselves the same conceptions of which they are certain in four large spheres which are described as "internal (as opposed to "tactical") leadership";
a) in the objective and responsible leadership of men;
b) in education in good citizenship and the training of its soldiers;
c) in the legal system of military service and in the application of disciplinary power;
d) in attending to the welfare of its soldiers on and off duty.

What has altered?

The Federal Forces, compared with the fighting forces of the past occupy an altered position in the State and in society. During their build-up a deep seated change has been taking place in the form of war and in that of combat. Techniques and politics are revolutionizing military technique to an as yet unforeseeable and tempestuous degree. Rearming is taking place in the field of tension of a psychological dispute which the totalitarian power-block forces upon the free world. Our Fatherland is divided. The Federal Republic belongs to supranational defense communities, WEU and NATO. In the social sphere we are confronted with a social reconstruction which presents new economic and social problems. The intellectual fundamentals are still insecure due to a past hardly overcome and to a painful loss of historical continuity in large circles of our people.

What does the new situation demand?

These altered circumstances must, just as in tactical leadership, be analyzed in a sober prejudice-free "assessment of the position". They demand of every military leader the learning anew of a state of preparedness, sound knowledge,

214

mental effort and an alert capability of assessment. This realization caused the leadership of the Federal Forces to establish a school in which commandants, general staff officers, and other officers make themselves acquainted in long-term courses and in free discussion with the spiritual fundamentals which enable them to cement the inner structure of the Federal Forces and to lead their various units in unified conceptions. The commandant courses at present last two and a half months.

In order to maintain immediate contact with the pulsating life of the companies etc., the company sergeant-majors are also instructed at the school in special courses. Instructional programs and the intellectual policy of the school have developed in long years of critical work which was carried out mainly by the sub-department of "internal leadership" in the Federal Ministry of Defense.

The present main tasks of the school

The present state of development renders as priority the treatment of the following among numerous individual subjects in spheres which are developing.
1. The moral and spiritual fundamentals of military service.
2. Objects and methods of military training.
3. Political training and training in good citizenship including coming to terms with the Bolshevist ideology.
4. Practical problems of leadership of men in peace and war.
5. Methodical instruction in troop welfare.
6. Personnel matters — Technique of assessment.
7. Military spiritual welfare.
8. Military Law: application of disciplinary powers.
9. International rules of war.
10. Work on behalf of the public.

In addition, the school has the following tasks:
a) Evaluation of the results achieved by home and foreign science in regard to leadership of men.
b) Evaluation of the results of the school's experience for the Federal Ministry of Defense.
c) Research tasks for the Federal Ministry of Defense.

From 1956 to 1960   133 courses have been held.
Participants: Officers: 3,097
                 NCO's: 952
                 Civilians: 1,030
                 Officials: 352
                 5,431 Persons

A selection from the subjects which at present comprise the school's training program.

1. Fundamentals of Internal Leadership.
2. Importance and function of the legal state. GG: Art. 2—18, 20, 25, 28; SG: Par. 6.
3. What is and what is not the meaning of the Fundamental System in Freedom? SG: Par. 8.
4. The Basic Law and its meaning.
5. Organization and tasks of the Federal Parliament. GG: Art. 38—49.

6. The military constitution of the Federal Republic. GG: and SG.
7. The primacy of politics and military power. GG: Art. 1, 17a, 45a, 45b, 59a, 60, 65a, 87a, 87b.
8. Military Law.
9. Military Conscription Law.
10. The soldier and the citizen in German history.
11. The position of the soldier in, and in relation to, the democratic state. GG: SG:
12. The Corps of Officers and its relationship to the state and society.
13. The preservation of fundamental rights in military service. SG: Par. 6, 7, 8, 10, 14, 15.
14. The political activity of the soldier and its limits. SG: Par. 15.
15. Ethical problems affecting the modern soldier.
16. Fundamentals of the soldier's responsibility today.
17. Military tradition.
18. What does the Fatherland mean to us today.
19. Why we are in military service.
20. The tasks and importance of internal leadership.

(GG = *Grundgesetz* — Basic Law (Constitution)

SG = *Soldatengesetz* — Military Law)

Information for Troops

1. The objectives of information for troops. SG: Par. 33.
2. Methodology of up-to-date and general information.
3. Political education within the unit. SG: Par. 33.
4. How does one read a daily newspaper?
5. The soldier and political parties. GG: Art. 21; SG: Par. 6.
6. The soldier and trade unions. GG: Art. 9.
7. Historical explorations.
8. Study of the homeland and of the garrison.
9. Awareness of history and the overcoming of our past.
10. The German soldier through the changing centuries.
11. Life portraits of great soldiers of the past.
12. The *Reichswehr* in the Weimar Republic.
13. Influence of treason and sabotage on the loss of World War II.
14. Why was World War II lost?
15. Hitler and the German soldier.
16. Resistance against the power of the state. (20th July)
17. Introduction into the ideology of Bolshevism.
18. Intellectual fundamentals of Bolshevism.
19. Introduction into the literature of Bolshevism.
20. Civilization of the Eastern World in its relationship to historical materialism.
21. Soviet education.
22. Dialectic materialism in its historical development and present form.
23. The Soviet interpretation of justice.
24. Soviet economy.
25. Working groups on dialectic and historical materialism.
26. Soviet Zone films.
27. Songs in the Soviet Zone.

28. Political schooling in the Soviet Zone.
29. The strengths and weaknesses of Bolshevism.
30. The responsibility of the Western world with regard to Bolshevism.
31. Europe at the end of the Colonial Age.
32. What does youth think of Europe?
33. The defense of the Western world.
34. The defense of Europe at the present time.
35. The integration of Europe.
36. Europe as reply to Bolshevism.
37. Our allies.
38. Our American allies.
39. NATO.
40. The experience of NATO.

Annual Report of the
Bundestag Commissioner for the Armed Forces [1]

Background

The idea of creating in Germany the hitherto unknown institution of a Commissioner for the Armed Forces to amplify parliamentary scrutiny of the armed forces arose in connection with the legislative preparation of re-establishment of the combat forces. Deputy Ernst Paul, who was forced to leave Germany during the Nazi reign of terror and found asylum in Sweden, became acquainted in the host country with the institution of the Swedish Royal Commissioner for Military Affairs. As a member of the former Bundestag Committee on European Security Questions (since 10 January 1956, the Committee for Defense), he proposed an analogous institution for Germany for the first time, late in 1952. The idea was taken up by the Committee and was actively promoted especially by its Chairman, Bundestag Vice-President Richard Jaeger, and the Deputy Chairman, Fritz Erler.

The Internal Situation in the Federal Defense Forces

In conjunction with the first Report, the Commissioner for the Armed Forces cannot forgo prefacing a number of thoughts concerning the political and legal foundation upon which the integration of the Federal Defense Forces into democratic government under law is based and which are determinative of the internal situation of the Federal Defense Forces.

Following the last war, there were no longer any soldiers in Germany for a period of 10 years. Then, as a result of political decisions, the re-establishment of an army became necessary. This development was achieved under unusual conditions.

The collapse following the lost war had altered the political visage of Germany from top to bottom. At the time when Germany was able to restore its political independence, it was prevented from incorporating its entire body politic and

---

[1] Excerpts from *Deutscher Bundestag, Drucksache 1796*, 8 April 1960.

territory in this process. Contrary to the will of the German people, Central and Eastern Germany remained under foreign rule. In view of the expulsion of more than 10 million persons, a social upheaval that had already begun after the First World War assumed dimensions that do not defer to the outcome of great revolutions in history. Even though they had nothing to do with the perversity of the Nazi reign of violence, intellectual foundations were overtaken by the maelstrom of history and rendered questionable. The continental development in the sciences, a comprehensive technologization and mechanization, the "dawn of the atomic age and space travel" are the essential characteristics of the intellectual image of our times.

In such an altered political and social environment, it was a difficult task to build up the Federal Defense Forces. The necessary psychological prerequisites for the re-establishment of an army were largely destroyed in consequence of the incriminations resulting from the recent past. Following the collapse, a rearmament of Germany had become inconceivable in the minds of large sectors of the population as a result of expressions of political intentions on the part of the Allies and of German internal controversies. Specifically, the unnatural division of Germany and the fact that the Federal Republic represented merely a provisional State confronted the people's will to defend themselves with problems and questions with which leadership doctrine in the Federal Defense Forces has to come to grips. For the first time, the Parliament created the political and legal foundations of the army in accordance with its will and in accordance with the laws of democracy. In this process, the negative experiences of the past were taken into account. It is insured that the army can no longer attain a position in which it can lead a political life of its own within our polity and — as it was termed by a well-known slogan — become a "State within a State". The primacy of the political authorities is anchored in constitutional law. The power to order and command is vested in the Federal Minister of Defense as a member of the Federal Government, which is accountable to the Parliament, whereas this power devolves upon the Federal Chancellor if the state of defense becomes operative. There is no independent military commander. Moreover, the army is subject to full parliamentary scrutiny.

The rights of an investigating committee have been conferred upon the Bundestag Committee for Defense, a constitutional agency. The institution of the Commissioner for the Armed Forces has been created for the protection of the Basic Rights and as an auxiliary agency of the Bundestag in the exercise of parliamentary scrutiny. Accordingly, all of the prerequisites for an unhampered integration of the Federal Defense Forces into the free democratic system of government under law are fulfilled.

In view of the proportions prevailing among the age groups, the Federal Defense Forces have to depend upon officers, non-commissioned officers, and enlisted men who had served in the war. These former soldiers had been occupied for a period of 10 years in the most diverse civilian occupation at all levels of society, or had spent long years in harsh prisoner-of-war camps. This period had broadened their mental horizon, a factor that was of benefit to the internal setup of the army that was to be organized. Respect for the fellow citizens with whom they had been dealing on the job and been living without having them at their "disposal" was taken over as a component of human leadership. These men had learned that the military profession was, in comparison to others, not a more valuable mission in life with special class consciousness and social privileges, as was the case in the past. Moreover, the post-war period did its share towards eliminating any over-estimation of the military career once and for all.

For the purpose of selecting the ranking officers to be taken into the Federal Defense Forces, the Parliament instituted a Personnel Screening Commission for the armed forces — composed of independent personalities of various occupations and political affiliations — which had the task of appraising the personal suitability of officers from the rank of Colonel upwards and proposing directives for the acceptance of officers from the rank of Lieutenant-Colonel down, of non-commisioned officers and of enlisted men.

The older officers accepted into the Federal Defense Forces not only have a great deal of professional experience; as a result of heavy burdens of the past, they have gained a wholesome conception of their profession. Their painful experiences and observations during the period of Nazism, collapse, and the aftermath of war enable them to perform their military task in an altered environment with a great deal of open-mindedness.

The officers of the intermediate age group — for instance, the battalion commanders and the older company commanders — belong to the generation that was still young enough after the war to undergo a professional training that opened the possibility of a new start in a civilian career and not, let us say, only in the sense of an auxiliary occupation. These officers have not infrequently given up a good position in civilian life in order to devote themselves once more to their original profession as soldiers.

The command of a large proportion of the companies is still entrusted to officers between 35 and 40 years of age with wartime service. The post-war group of officers is growing into the ranks of the company commanders only gradually. From the point of view of internal leadership, the older officers have the advantage of greater experience in leading men, an element that is significant particularly during the organizational period. Of course, it cannot be overlooked in this regard that on account of the war, these officers' training was short, and they consequently require careful guidance concerning the accomplishment of peacetime education and training. The young officers, unburdened by the past, apparently perform their task with a great deal of eagerness to serve, a high feeling of responsibility and youthful *esprit*. Some of them do, however, get beyond their depth and naturally require guidance and instruction. The latter are frequently not being provided to them in adequate measure as yet, on account of the overburdening or the insufficient experience of their immediate superiors.

In summary, it can be said that the officer corps of the Federal Defense Forces is devoting itself to its military task and to the modernization of the military profession with seriousness of purpose and consciousness of responsibility.

In contrast to the Weimar period, during which the officer corps of the *Reichswehr* was largely unable to arrive at any inward bond with the democratic Republic, the relationship of the Federal Defense Forces' officers to the democratic State is without reservations, because they affirm the foundations of our democracy: government under law and freedom. Apparently there is not as yet a universally sufficient familiarity with the forms of democratic representation and discussion. In this respect, the soldiers require a patient, confident program of education. It is only fair to allow the Federal Defense Forces the same amount of time for citizenship training as is required by our people in general. But on the whole, the beginning of the army's political integration into the democratic State can be considered successful.

Particularly during a period of ideological controversies between liberal and totalitarian systems, our free, democratic government under law must demand that the men, who are supposed to defend its integrity and are entrusted with such great powers for this purpose, affirm and advocate this form of government out of inner conviction. Only then will they acknowledge the rights of their subordinates as free men in the military sphere as well and further the soldiers in their awareness as citizens.

The present non-commissioned officer corps has a different structure than in earlier times. About 25 per cent of the non-commissioned officers have the opportunity to make the non-commissioned officer's profession their career. The rest of the non-commissioned officers are non-career soldiers whose period of service may vary in length, but amounts at the maximum to 12 years.

The present non-commissioned officer's profession cannot be compared with that of former times with respect to its mental and technological demands. In a completely technologized army, the non-commissioned officer is required to have a high degree of technical ability and therefore a well-trained mind. The days when stripes sufficed to establish adequate authority are over. A non-commissioned officer's authority can only be founded on personal and professional excellence. The legislative branch has made allowance for the increased demands upon the non-commissioned officer corps by freeing the non-commissioned officers from the analogy to the ordinary civil service officers and making them equal to officers of the intermediate civil service grades, and, in some cases, even equal to those of the upper grades. The difficulties involved in obtaining suitable recruits, who must be taken from the broad mass of the population, grow, of course, with the higher prerequisites.

In view of the short period of organization for the Federal Defense Forces and the diversified composition of the non-commissioned officer corps, with veteran and young non-commissioned officers, this corps has not yet had time to find its final, uniform approach. Among other things, uncertainty in gaining authority is to be detected not infrequently. The development of the non-commissioned officer corps will have to be observed with care and guided with deliberation. In the modern army, as in the past, the non-commissioned officer substantially determined the visage of everyday military life, and thus the atmosphere in which the principles of leadership doctrine are to take effect.

The negative characterization of the non-commissioned officer, which in the past was often pronounced with undue readiness, is devoid of any basis under present-day conditions. Certain recriminations of the non-commissioned officer corps dating from the past should gradually be removed in acknowledgement of the altered situation, with the sympathetic aid of superiors and public.

It is obviously difficult to obtain the necessary high-quality recruits for the non-commissioned officer corps. The reason for this seems particularly to be the present overburdening of the non-commissioned officers in their duty obligations; the risk in the choice of occupation (since entering the non-commissioned officer career does not immediately permit a decision concerning the final professional course of development); heavy responsibility as a superior; personal and family inconveniences resulting from separation, frequent transfer, etc.; and not least of all the deficient general appreciation of this career. Besides, the business boom often makes a position in private enterprise seem more attractive than the career of a non-commissioned officer in the Federal Defense Forces.

Careful consideration is required as to the means for imparting to the non-commissioned officer career a sufficiently attractive form to obtain an adequate number of high-quality recruits. In any event, the non-commissioned officer corps requires emphatic furtherance.

The internal situation in the Federal Defense Forces cannot be discussed without devoting a word or two to the young men who are supposed to perform their military service in the army or to enlist for extended service as volunteers. The changed conditions in the intellectual, social, political and technological spheres inevitably influence and stamp the younger generation most indelibly. Their objectives, their way of thinking, and their relationship to material and spiritual values and to the community are problems that affect the people as a whole and its destiny, but on the other hand are also for this very reason directly related to the internal structure of the army that is to be supplied by this younger generation for the most part. The present-day, younger generation awaiting military training is one that seems to differ from the generation of its elders by more than merely the difference in generations engendered by nature. Its attitude towards the heritage of idealism that may have meant a great deal to the pre-war generation — aside from the misuse of youthful idealism during the Nazi period — is largely objectivized and sobered. One of the characteristics of this generation seems to be scepticism. Nothing is any longer adopted without examination. Any false sentimentality meets with rejection. On the other hand, these young people are open-minded towards all spheres of life. Yet to some extent, their minds reveal greater instability and sensitivity. Respect for their elders is no longer a matter of course. Authority is acknowledged only in those instances where it is based on qualities of character and on performance. Yet it is confirmed all the more readily when it is justified because of example and trustworthy humanity. The younger generation requires human understanding and seeks guidance without tutelage.

The attitude towards earnings and money seems on the whole to be different than among the earlier generation. The young soldiers often consider military service from the standpoint of specific chances to earn. The altered attitude goes so far that they are inclinded to measure military service by the yardstick of the "job", something that of course can also be observed among the older generation at the present time. Still, it would be premature to give this phenomenon among the younger generation a negative evaluation. It would particularly be wrong to draw the conclusion that our younger generation no longer has any sympathy with altruistic service for the community. It has it in a sober sense contingent upon the necessity.

Among the young men who enter the Federal Defense Forces — whether as draftees or as volunteers — the question of further professional training or career advancement plays an essential part. In many cases, they expect a special furtherance of their civilian professional knowledge. The soldier drafted for duty has an understandable desire to derive the greatest possible benefit for his civilian career from the period of service required of him. The volunteer who intends to drop out after several years of service and return to a civilian occupation has an interest in profiting by his period of service to prepare for his future career and in acquiring the widest possible knowledge, which will stand him in good stead at a later time. A highly technologized army like the Federal Defense Forces has an abundance of opportunities to meet such wishes. It would be well if the induction agency were to realize this fact and have more of an eye than in the past to assigning the soldiers to branches providing opportunities of employing the young men in accordance with their capabilities and desires. The soldiers' performance and devotion to duty would be enhanced as a result. At the same time, it should not fail to be recognized that certain limits are placed upon such wishes by the requirements of service.

The different attitude of the younger generation towards military service is expressed among the soldiers in additional respects. In several cases, the Commissioner for the Armed Forces received communications in which the introduction of the 45-hour work-week was demanded for soldiers. In such instances, civilian standards are transferred to military circumstances without hesitation. This has a positive effect in the reaction to so-called "Yard-bird fatigue", where the superior uses up the soldiers' time in accordance with the once-familiar theory of "keeping the troops occupied", because he lacks imagination or the ability to organize and train the soldiers sensibly and rationally. The young soldiers no longer have any understanding for the old saying that "the soldier spends half his life waiting in line". From their experiences on the job, they are accustomed to rational activity and tight scheduling, and they are guided by the ambition to keep from frittering away their period of military service, which detains them from their professional training or job. Moreover, they express this in drastic terms. In everyday military life, there is certain to be some lost motion that cannot always be avoided. Although a fast-moving, rugged basic training is favored by the young soldiers, the subsequent period of service often leads to equally pronounced resignation and distaste. It therefore continues to be an urgent task for the company commander to schedule and prepare the duty in such a way that the time is employed purposefully and the detrimental effect of "yard-bird fatigue" on the internal structure is avoided.

The problem comes to light particularly with respect to guard duty. It is especially the mentally active soldiers who consistently react against being assigned to guard duty over a long period of time, because the feeling arises in their minds that the sacrifice of military service is demanded of them contrary to common sense. In individual cases, they overlook the fact that guard duty is not lost motion, but falls within the scope of military necessities. Yet the complaints seem justified when, for instance, a number of college juniors have to spend the rest of their military service, following basic training, in an airfield guard company.

Constantly and inescapably, the young men pose the question of what they are expected to defend in view of the fact that Germany is partitioned and the Federal Republic represents only a provisional institution. They take it for granted that they are living under the blessings of liberty. It is certainly one of the most difficult tasks of superiors to conduct discussions on this question earnestly and conscientiously. Of course, it must be recognized that the basic attitude towards these questions ought to be provided primarily by the home and the school.

The willingness to perform military service is present among the younger generation, but it does not lead to identification with the community, the people or the Fatherland founded on idealism or even tinged with sentiment. Instead, it rests principally upon the acknowledgement of a legal duty that on the other hand is perceptibly evaluated as a sacrifice. The feeling and experience of comradeship is considered to be a particular value of the period of service.

On the whole, the mental alertness of the young soldiers is a favorable phenomenon. They have grown up in an atmosphere that has furthered their free self-confidence. Yet not infrequently, they lack the sense of duty, obligation and sub-ordination. The result is that they often are not sufficiently aware of the serious requirement of military discipline. If a young soldier feels his rights have been violated or if he considers a command unjustified or contrary to common sense, he easily allows himself to be stimulated to resistance or even to disobedience. On occasion, this danger is brought about by superior's action contrary to regulations or lacking in skill. Failing to realize his duty to obey, the young soldier frequently is not aware that in doing so, he possibly commits a serious military offense that may lead to punishment. Consequently, the young men, who are often not ac-customed to subordination and discipline, require early instruction on the serious-ness of the soldier's duties and understanding guidance even at the beginning of their period of service.

These few references may suffice to show how greatly the internal structure of the Federal Defense Forces differs from that of earlier German armies. It is not diffi-cult to perceive that modern, progressive tenets are necessary for the leadership doctrine of this army.

It cannot be said that the intellectual controversy over these principles has already been concluded unequivocally in the Federal Defense Forces and particularly among the troops. Regardless of how much they may be disputed in theory, there is in almost all instances and among superiors of all grades the effort to observe the principles in practice and to implement them. Convincing proof of this is given by the cheerful, natural, unconstrained manner on the part of the soldiers in their dealings with their superiors. Anyone who thinks he is in a position to evade the application of the principles concerning leadership doctrine is forced by superiors, comrades, and not least of all by subordinates — to whom the channel to the Commissioner for the Armed Forces is now open, in addition to the usual chanel of complaint — to mend his ways. Not infrequently, a certain degree of insecurity in understanding and applying the principles concerning leadership doctrine is still to be encountered. It is heightened especially by misunderstanding or in fact distortion of the principles; for instance, under the impression that they permit or promote softness, unmilitary bearing or even breaches of discipline. Such con-ceptions naturally lead to difficulties and detriment to military esprit. Still, the Federal Defense Forces and their leadership corps will have to be granted a certain period of development before the principles of leadership doctrine have been evaluated correctly in all instances and have become the unquestioned, universally accepted style in everyday military life.

Must the Soldier Be Shrewder Than the Politician?[1]

Recent Past a Hindrance to Understanding between Army and Trade Unions

By Werner Veldmann

The workers' suspicion of the army and the contempt of many soldiers for the workers contributed equally to the downfall of the Weimar Republic. In order to avoid repetition of the formation of such opposing fronts, discussions on the relations between the worker and the soldier are organized today, particularly on the initiative of the trade unions. The following is a report of one such discussion.

No revolutionary fanfares filled the Friedrich-Ebert hall of the Trade Union House in Bremen. On the contrary, it was all very decorous at the discussion on topical problems of the Federal Forces which the young trade unionists of Bremen deserve credit for organizing.

"Barrack-room and Spit-and-polish — Slogans or Reality?" was the subject at the first meeting to which the trade unionists had invited the military men for discussion.

The soldiers came. They came in such numbers that at first one might have imagined that the home of all political interest was the Federal Forces. There they sat: artillerymen, privates, officers, non-commissioned officers, and other ranks — "citizens in uniform" — and waited for what was to come.

At first the hosts were in the minority. Among them was also many an old war veteran who, now in "civvies", reflectively scrutinized the uniformed guests.

Only gradually did the hall fill up with young trade unionists. A wide variety of trades was represented: apprentices, office clerks and shop-assistants, cheek-by-jowl with industrial and dock workers from the Bremen "Vulcan" shipyards, and stevedores from the overseas docks. Curious and interested, animated and dispassionate, sceptical and taciturn faces.

Then came the speakers. The spokesman for the Federal Forces was a captain of the Marines, slim, elastic, not nervous, but alert and keyed-up. He would certainly have preferred to be standing on the bridge of a motor torpedo boat than at the speakers' rostrum. The speaker for the trade unions was a representative of the German Trade Union Federation of Land North Rhine/Westphalia, middle-aged, a member of the "war-generation", with that air of confidence that comes from having successfully survived many a battle of words.

The prescribed subject was to be dealt with in the form of a questionnaire that had been formulated by the trade unions and previously delivered to the competent army headquarters. Both speakers had to answer the twenty questions or so, in turn — each from his own standpoint. Not exactly an ideal method as soon became apparent, but after all, the questionnaire seems to have become an indispensable requisite of our times.

Question 1: How can the danger of the Federal Forces becoming a "State within the State" be circumvented?

---

[1] From *Die Welt*, 20 February 1960.

The captain of the Marines enumerated the following preventive measures: legislative controls, cooperation with committees representing public bodies, ideological defense preparedness on the part of the entire nation, the development of a corresponding desire for defense among the public at large ... You see, the answer was "dry cleaned" in every way from the political angle; not even the German Trade Union Federation representative took exception to it. He did, however, reserve comment on the "ideological defense preparedness" and the "common desire for defense", but supported all the more vigorously the other arguments of his military predecessor. The latter's unquestioning acceptance of the historically dubious premises of the "State within a State" which — from the way in which the question was put — was tantamount to a belated accusation, came as a surprise. Did he want to maintain neutrality? Did he want to avoid exposing himself to attack? Did he not know about the frequently proven counter-arguments of neutral historians of the calibre of a Gordon or a Golo Mann?

Whatever the reason, the doubtful past was not discussed — a circumstance that possibly made the military members of the audience feel rather uncomfortable.

Next question: What does "a citizen in uniform" mean? This question aims at the heart of democracy. The Marine captain's reply proclaimed the educational aim of the forces to be the production of "soldiers acting out of conviction and prepared to assume co-responsibility". "Co-responsibility", let it be understood, not "co-determination". The trade union speaker commented rather sceptically, "It is to be hoped that this educational aim, with which I absolutely agree, will be attained. The question is only whether the Federal Forces is the right medium in this connection ..."

Question: Do you believe that the Federal Forces can train and form the individual during service?

Obviously this question was trying to establish an anti-thesis to the former thesis of the "school of the nation". The Marine captain by-passed the trap: "Generally speaking, yes! But of course only as a supplement to the school and family ..." The value of communal education was emphasized and acknowledged by the trade unions as well. "We regard the forces as an environmental factor, of course. Every environment has automatically a formative influence. But naturally not in the manner of my former Prussian-minded regiment where we were all mashed together into a uniform mass like cabbage in a pot, so to speak!" The Prussian tradition seemed to have made an impression on the trade unionist, who wound up with a flourish: "An eighteen-year-old, who is being taught how to kill, must be treated like an adult!" This declaration rang out accusingly like a warning loud and clear through the hall; there was no contradiction. The faces of the soldiers grew thoughtful, those of the eighteen-year-olds and older men alike.

*

Question: Should instruction in civics be carried out by officers or not?
This question did not seem to upset the Marine captain. "As far as possible by officers", he said, "insofar as they are capable of doing so (!). If civilian teachers are available they should, if possible, be consulted".

The trade union speaker was more explicit. "The teaching of civics should be left to specialists. Officers are primarily soldiers by trade! But this is not a question of principle", he modified his statement.

This gave one of the forces commanders present the following idea: "The assistance of civilian staff as a supplement is always something that should be gratefully welcomed, but on principle, such teaching is the task of the officers. To a certain extent ability for this is the crucial point for the modern, superior officer."

He, too, concluded with a flourish. "The one who is the leader in the fight for the common conviction must be able to explain the basis of that conviction."

The captain of the Marines looked slightly indignant at his aggressive comrade. The atmosphere in the Friedrich-Ebert hall had become decidedly warmer than that of the ocean brine. The mention of the "common conviction" had brought up the much discussed problem of "values worth defending" and therewith the unpleasant problem of defense preparedness. But it was not put to discussion. On the contrary, the young trade unionist, who was master of ceremonies, made it quite plain that today the trade unions are no longer concerned with "whether", but rather with "how", as regards the West German defense contribution.

The debate continued. The Federal Forces speaker continued to maintain his attitude of official, conciliating, well-covered defense. His debating partner was also making visible efforts to avoid touching on any sore points.

Only once did the picture of concord and harmony become considerably blurred, and that was at the question, "What is your attitude to the 20th July?", which called forth from both speakers an unequivocal profession of belief in the decision of conscience. But whereas the Captain confined himself to elaborating on the "genuine" conscientious decision — as opposed to pure opportunism — and for the most part disregarded the tragic conscientious conflict with regard to the principle of the soldier's duty to obey, the representative of the German Trade Unions Federation could not refrain from adding the polemic remark: "It seems to me that many of the wearers of the Knight's Cross and many generals among the resistance fighters only discovered that they had the courage to resist, when they noticed that the war was going to be lost." . . . At this juncture there was a short, but sharp protest from the military side. The *point d'honneur* had been touched and the cry of protest was clearly a warning signal that said, "Look out! A dangerous stretch of road ahead!"

The speaker managed by a quick adjustment of tactics to steer things into more peaceful waters. The taboo of the past had been touched but not disturbed.

Question: Do you consider war inevitable?

This last question threw into relief the bitter dilemma of a generation forbidden by its painful experience to have faith in its own long-cherished ideals. The audience listened with close attention to the military speaker's answer. "It is conceivable nowadays that the outbreak of war will be checked by the existence of nuclear weapons to such an extent that, in time, war as a 'political means' would be reduced to absurdity" — They listened hopefully and credulously. The danger developing proportionate to, and alongside, the growing destructive power of super-weapons, of "local conflicts" to be fought out with limited repercussions, was passed over. The problem of the changed status of war in the age of mass society and modern technology was not referred to.

Question-time brought a sudden and complete change of atmosphere. The speakers had up to that point endeavored to conciliate, to mollify, to avoid acrimony and conflict, and indeed to establish and emphasize identity of interests, but now it was evident that these tactics had not fulfilled the expectations of the large audience.

It was, however, soon to become apparent that not all those attending the meeting had come with the desire for information about the nature of the Federal Forces. Their interest in the set subject sprang from quite different motives. "The speeches — of military and trade union speakers alike — were insipid and unsatisfactory, for they have simply evaded the issue! I put a question of principle" — the speaker introduced himself as a secondary school teacher — "If we really and truly do not want war, do we need the Federal Forces at all?" There was no gainsaying a question presented with such dramatic emotion. All of a sudden the atmosphere in the room which until then had fluctuated between scepticism, indolence and laboriously cultivated interest, became electric.

The master of ceremonies begged everyone to keep to the subject. But the opposition attacked again. The speaker asked about Germany's war guilt documented in the Versailles Treaty. It was not clear what he was driving at. The meeting became increasingly restless. Questions were heard, asking about the speaker's political antecedents. When the teacher, at first hesitantly and then quite openly admitted to being a member of the International Organization of Conscientious Objectors, a sergeant-major attacked him in typical army manner: "Throw him out!" The latter had to swallow reprimand for intolerance of the political views of others, but the master of ceremonies, at the same time, reiterated his exhortation to keep to the subject.

At this point the opposition again launched a wholesale attack. "Federal Forces unsuitable as an educational means! Suppression of the individual's rights by soulless barracks life. Submersion of the personality by drab standardization!" "The Federal Forces sympathize with militant soldiers' associations; they keep revengeful policies alive!"

"Lack of integrity among high-ranking officers! Generals Speidel and Heusinger shared responsibility in the Nazi forces!"

These were the kind of arguments that were served up. They culminated in the assertion that "war was the eternal Fall of Man" and ended with the emotional declamation, "War — never again! Away with atomic weapons! Down with weapons! Thou shalt not kill'" —

*

The reaction in the hall had at first been one of half-amused, half-irritated astonishment, but now the temperature quickly reached the boiling point. Again the master of ceremonies tried to pour oil on troubled waters. And the desire for objective discussion finally prevailed. Questions were put to the military speaker who had to answer them impromptu. The very first question was a leading one:

"Do you think that the Federal Forces will be used against the trade unions to break strikes?"

The captain hesitated only for a brief moment. "That is a problem which — if at all — could only arise in a case of national emergency. Any decision about it would not lie with the forces but would be incumbent on the Federal Government. I recall the "primacy of the political authorities to which every military executive is subject".

This answer did not fail in its effect, but did not manage to satisfy the audience completely. The unexpressed argument of the "Christian Democratic Army" could be felt hovering in the hall, unmistakably perceptible to the more delicately attuned ear. Then came the next question, probably the most important one that could be asked, put by a nineteen-year-old, in a low voice but with impressive urgency:

"How would the army react if it was forced to the conclusion that an irresponsible policy pursued by the government was bound to lead to war?"

Dead silence fell in the hall. The question had to be repeated. Curious and expectant, as well as malicious glances were cast at the captain. His answer was short and quick. "The question is of a political nature. The answer is to be inferred from the relationship of the army to the State and thus from the position under constitutional law. It is the soldier's duty to obey, regardless of whether the individual soldier or the entire army is involved. The decision with regard to war and peace is in its turn subject to the primacy of the political authorities!"

*

The answer was correct. It was incontestible both de facto and de jure, but there seemed to be something missing. What was it? Somehow, everyone present — old and young trade unionists, officers and men, ready listeners and more or less well-trained hecklers (a large number of whom were present much to the affliction of the hosts of the evening) — somehow, they sensed that the taboo of the past had been by-passed in this answer, too.

Then one of the older generation took the bull by the horns, the commanding officer who had already intervened, if only briefly. He said, "Discussions like the present one are pointless unless they are conducted with complete frankness. And frankness means the courage to acknowledge the truth! In our position such frankness should never mean to tell the truth for the sole purpose of causing an injury. In politics such truths are only half-truths, for they do not analyze history, but only distort it into a black-and-white drawing, so to speak. When that happens we become a prey to slogans. And slogans are fatal!"

The audience sat up at this. Probably few of those present knew that the reference to the "fatal slogans" was a quotation from General von Seeckt, a member of the Weimar Reich Parliament.

What followed was a history lecture delivered to the meeting, which began with Clausewitz's philosophical dissertation On War and ranged from the relations between politics and war in the modern national states to the military opposition under Hitler, right to the heart of the conscientious issues at stake in the problem of the 20th July.

The speaker did not spare himself when he spoke of the disintegration of the military code of ethics under Hitler. This lent force to his arguments. But he did not spare his listeners either. "The Reich forces would never have become a 'State within the State', if the Weimar democracy had been a sound one, capable of providing the soldier with a spiritual backing! Men like General von Fritsch and General Beck resigned without comment because they did not wish to jeopardize the foundation of the army, i.e. discipline for private reasons. They realized that a political opposition of the generals from a sense of co-responsibility, as might have been conceivable under the Prussian monarchy, was simply out of the question in the age of politically hysterical mass-psychosis under the pseudo-democratic legitimation of the 'people's king', Hitler.

*

"Every student of history knows that the military opposition before the war was impotent because the weapon that would have given the military the primacy of the political authorities was struck out of its grasp in Munich in 1938! . . . It is unfair to demand retrospectively of the *Wehrmacht* that it should have been shrewder than the politician and overthrown Hitler in time. In 1933 there also existed the primacy of the political authorities that was manifested by the will of the majority . . . But during the war it was expecting the impossible to ward off the enemy from without, on the one hand, and on the other, to try and overthrow one's own government without possessing the necessary means of internal political power! . . .

"We must be careful not to flay each other in retrospect with mutual reproaches. On the contrary, we must finally acknowledge the truth of the realization of Count Moltke of the Kreisau Circle, viz., that National Socialism was bound to lead to its own destruction! . . .

"Once again the opposition tried to seize the initiative. "We are not prepared to serve under a General Heusinger or a General Speidel! Hitler's generals cannot be the representatives of German democracy!"

And the answer to that: "The decision as to the integrity of the German generals is taken by authorities who are backed by the free will of the German people — not those who are here claiming to be the protagonists of democracy while using arguments designed to destroy that very democracy!"

In vain the opposition tried to enlist the support of the trade unionists by dwelling on the reservations and resentment in the socialist camp with regard to the soldiers. The master of ceremonies managed to bring the meeting to a close before the discussion had passed from rapier parrying to "dangerous sword-play". And this he did, not omitting to pay tribute to defense preparedness. His concluding remarks established a common bond with the spokesmen of the military guests. They were to the effect that the actual subject of the evening had come off rather badly; the past had proved more powerful than contemporary problems. But it had become clear that nothing was capable any longer of causing disunity between them.

That was the net result of the "tough discussion". One wonders if guests or hosts were fully aware of this result as they wended their way home.

Service for the Protection of Freedom

The Chancellor of the Federal Republic on the Fifth Anniversary of the *Bundeswehr*

On the occasion of its fifth anniversary the Chancellor of the Federal Republic extended the following words of thanks to the soldiers and civilian members of the *Bundeswehr:*

To all the members of the *Bundeswehr:*

On 12 November 1960 our *Bundeswehr* will have been in existence for five years. On this occasion I devote my attention to the soldiers and civilian members of the *Bundeswehr*. He who has followed the building-up of our young troops with understanding knows what untiring work had to be produced before our present-day position of defensive readiness was attained. Precisely the last manoeuvers have shown that the *Bundeswehr* has been, and to an increasing degree will become, a remarkable and trustworty factor in the defense of the free world.

In spite of not a few obstacles, you, the officers, non-commissioned officers and enlisted men have applied yourselves to the task, side by side with the civilian members of the *Bundeswehr* and in good comradeship with the soldiers of the allied armies. In the beginning you had to depend on various improvisations but, in spite of considerable psychological stress, you have not allowed your confidence to be shaken. This determination earns our respect and our trust. You can be certain that your service for the defense of freedom has opened to you the hearts of our people.

We do not know what storms threaten our people. We abhor war and love peace, the preservation of which is our highest goal. The fulfillment of your military obligation is an irreplaceable contribution thereto. The future, too, will make high demands on you. Furthermore, the foundation for your work must be the conviction that, above all, a life in freedom exists for us which allows us to serve God and man, to mould our existence in our own decision, and to accept human values as the inalienable guide of our actions. In this spirit, the building-up of the *Bundeswehr* has been accomplished; in this spirit it must carry on.

I thank all soldiers, the civilian members of the *Bundeswehr*, and the chaplains for the self-effacing service performed during the years of the build-up in the defense of the freedom of our people and its allies.

III   Adult Education

Adult Education in the Federal Republic [1]

Views of the German Committee on Training and Education

By Hellmut Becker

Seven years ago a Committee of Experts, on the lines of a Royal Commission, was appointed by the Federal and Land Governments to provide a substitute for a Federal German Ministry of Culture. This Committee has just published a paper on the current situation of German adult education and the tasks ahead.

The paper shows that People's Colleges, People's Libraries, and also the adult education work of the churches, are essential to the working of modern society. People in this secularized world, having lost the support given by the old social order and its groupings, are in need of constant guidance, if they are to face the world of today and not become just material to be shaped to someone else's will. It is not surprising that, at a time when the expansion of adult education is only beginning, millions of men and women are already following the courses arranged by the People's Colleges.

Adult education is presented in this paper as a third branch of education which has the same standing as schools and vocational training.

The Committee does not try to make a depressing comparison between a past world supposed to have been in good health and a present world in a state of collapse, but seeks to enable people to cope with the world as it is. Adaptation to the world of today is considered just as important as having the individuality to resist it. In this way we are given a world of tension such as is normally found only in modern fiction.

Instead of adult education we ought to speak, like the French, of *éducation permanente*. Obviously, not all grown-up persons can follow all subjects equally in this education. The participants will be the lively minorities who, whatever their social or vocational group, are ready for a maximum of activity, and who in the last resort decide the character and action of their group. These active minorities produce the tension without which the free world would probably soon succumb to the yoke of sterile conformity.

The paper sketches a picture of our intellectual and social situation which shows clearly that we have to choose between a democracy, in which adult education is widely pursued, and a totalitarian mass state of, very probably, communistic character.

Nor does the Committee dodge the old question of the aim of education, the question of freedom and responsibility in culture. There can be no freedom without ties, and equally no ties without a free decision to accept them. Adult education as a clarification of consciousness is no longer in conflict with the possibilities of

---

[1]) Excerpts from *Die Zeit*, 8 April 1960.
[2]) *Zur Situation und Aufgabe der deutschen Erwachsenenbildung*, Ernst Klett-Verlag, Stuttgart, 1960.

faith. The second *Aufklaerung* which is put before us, the second age of Enlightenment, is not a fight against faith, but embraces faith. The paper expresses approval of the legitimate educational interests of the various religious and social groups and recognizes the educational possibilities of institutions in which the participants have a common tie.

For the State and the community, however, in fact for the public as a whole in a democracy, public and free adult education is the more important, for it is here that men and women of various elements of society with their special ties, Protestants and Catholics, mutually seek their education. Free adult education ought to become the force which brings together the active minorities in the various groups. It has been found time and again that these minorities, because of their more vigorous reactions, have more common ground with each other than with the more colorless members of their own group. The People's Colleges are not to be dominated by a religious or political concept that claims to be above church or party, but should enable people who have made up their minds in one direction or another to foregather in the freedom which is the common element of all European culture.

The Committee deals with the immense variety of tasks of adult education, from political education to the development of taste, from good manners to vocational training, from the first notions on the developing countries to the compositions of Alban Berg. There is a frank statement of the gap between the vast work that lies before us and the inadequacy of the staff, the buildings, the money so far made available. The paper ends with very specific demands on the Federal Government, the *Laender* and the local authorities for increased support to be given to People's Colleges and People's Libraries.

The views expressed by the Committee provide a basic program for the development of schools, universities, and adult education; its demands would slowly adapt the modest situation of these educational institutions to the scale of the tasks before them. For every one of us the paper gives a picture of our times, not with a recipe, not with a solution seeking the idealistic, but with all sorts of tensions and with a fullness of vigor to which we are no longer accustomed in the field of education.

On the present situation of adult education in Germany

Culture is not the same thing as understanding or courage or love, but without understanding and courage and love no culture is possible.

Our democracy will gain in strength when people in all social strata enjoy the chance of educating themselves, and active minorities in all groups make use of their chances.

Adult education lives by the spirit of constructive tolerance, on which our whole political order is founded.

Anyone who constantly endeavors to understand himself, society, and the world and to act on the basis of this understanding, is receiving adult education.

As science exerts an increasing influence on the outward forms of human life, adult education must familiarize itself more and more closely with science.

Men and women who seek to develop their personality in the world as we know it will have to adapt themselves to it at the same time as they stand out against it. One of the forces which can provide the means for the necessary adaptation while giving power to resist, is tradition.

In the democratic states of the Western world there is a tendency to steer people in the mass and to seek technical perfection; this tendency threatens to turn the forms of political life into instruments of domination and then to destroy them. If we in Western Europe wish to establish and maintain a free society, independent education must secure for us what in totalitarian systems is enforced by centralized methods of steering the masses.

In the society of today the democratic state and adult education are interdependent. In adult education the democratic state possesses one of the few centers of contact which rise above party and denomination, a center of democratic integration which can only exist in freedom.

A live community can be recognized by the importance attached in its budget to People's Colleges and People's Libraries.

(From the Recommendations of the German Commitee on Adult Education)

Ministers of Education Discuss Adult Education [1]

Last month the German Committee on Education and Training presented its report on the "Conditions and Aims of Adult Education" (cf. *Die Welt* of 22 April), which attracted considerable attention. The basic ideas in that report have now formed the center of a study conference organized by the Permanent Conference of the Ministers of Education of the *Laender* at Ulm. The Mayor of Ulm, Herr Pfizer, is Chairman of the German Education Committee.

The Conference, which lasted four days, was attended by representatives of the German Federal Ministry of the Interior, the Federal Ministry of Family and Youth Questions, the Federal Ministry of Defense, as well as of the education authorities, of top-level local government organizations, of the Adult Education Centers, and of the public libraries. "Urgent Questions for the Adult Education Centers", "Urgent Public Library Questions", "Adult Education and the German Federal Forces", "Adult Education — Radio and Television" — such were the subjects of discussion for the four study groups.

Herr Landahl, representative of Hamburg, opened the Conference as representative of the Conference of the Ministers of Education. He described adult education as "a necessary concomitant to collective industrial society". Although it was firmly ensconced in society, its importance, and indispensability have not been given nearly sufficient recognition. Herr Landahl demanded that in the future the generous and unselfish support of the Federation and the *Laender* for adult education and lending libraries. The local authorities are admittedly the initiators of this branch of

---

[1] From *Die Welt*, 19 May, 1960.

education, but they cannot possibly cope alone and unaided with the steadily in-creasing demands on them.

"One of the primary tasks of the Adult Education Centers is to bridge the ever-increasing gulf between experts and lay-persons", said Hellmut Becker, President of the German Adult Education Association. Furthermore, the mediating work of the Adult Education Centers was successfully counteracting the effect of the "edu-cational ghetto" idea, the typically German concept of the "exclusive nature of education" and the "qualification system".

In Herr Becker's view, the Adult Education Centers take on a particular significance in the field of political education. Especially the nonconformist element among the young people feels attracted by institutions in which — as in the Adult Education Centers — "constructive tolerance" is cultivated and "appreciation of other ways of thinking".

Herr Becker broached the subject of whether the "non-committal coming and go-ing" in the Adult Education Centers did not prejudice their being taken seriously.

Perhaps it would be advisable in future to issue "Proficiency certificates without qualification" to participants in the course, in order to set them a standard.

Herr Joerden, director of the Hamburg public libraries, speaking on behalf of the public libraries, called for better service, better librarianship training, a more ra-tional distribution of public funds, and larger subsidies from the Federation and the *Laender*. Their functions were, he said, not by any means confined to lending books. Lending libraries were also important educational centres, a connecting link between political and ideological groups.

According to Herr Joerden, the "index libraries", traditional in Germany, were dying out. They were being replaced by the "free access libraries" developed in the Anglo-Saxon countries; individual advice and the well-considered selection of books being retained, however. Herr Joerden said that it was not the number of readers registered or books borrowed, but the assistance proffered that was de-cisive in judging the work of the libraries. Nonetheless, the stocks of the public libraries in the Federal Republic had increased from five million to fifteen- and -a-half million in ten years.

"As necessary as our daily bread" and the "heart of all education" was the way journalist Walter Dirks (Frankfurt) described political education, if it is to prevent the almost inevitable cleavage between intellect and power in German history from occurring in the future. Democracy was an "adventure of reason" and was dependent "for weal or woe" on at least an active minority acquiring a fundamental political education beyond the level of purely factual knowledge.

At the present time, there are over 1,000 Adult Education Centers in the Federal Republic with roughly 4,000 extramural points. Last year they conducted more than 60,000 courses and organized 54,000 individual events; almost 1,7 million par-ticipants registered for the ten-evening courses, half of whom were under 25 years of age. The public libraries, which number more than 10,000, lend fifty million volumes annually — forty percent to children and young people under twenty-five years of age.

National Socialism and Anti-Semitism
in Study Plans for *Volkshochschulen* [1]

By Marianne Grewe

The interest on the part of the students in our Adult Education Centers in the fields which are circumscribed by "political education" — government, society, contemporary history, law, economics — is increasing. This is shown by the enrollment figures in these courses as they have been reported by the individual Federal States. From the total enrollment of about 1.6 million in 1958 and from the fact that according to the State statistics the percentage of enrollments in political education reached an average of 15 %, we may assume that 240,000 were enrolled in these courses. Not only the number of enrollments, but also the part that this shares in the entire adult education program has grown. This is made apparent by a survey on courses, lecture series and work shops offered in programs which have recently been prepared by the Educational Council of the *Deutscher Volks-hochschul-Verband.*

Five hundred programs had been studied. From this number 447 were from 1958-59. The remaining 53 from 1959-60 were used for comparisons although, at that time, a survey on the whole academic year was not yet possible. However a study of the 53 programs of 1959-60 shows clearly that especially *"Zeitgeschichte"* (contemporary history), which was started in 1958 under the theme "undigested past", has found much response and was in 1959 taken up more often and more thoroughly than previously in the programs of adult education centers. In the following, we present the results of our study of the 500 programs, which have been examined in respect to: the approach to National-Socialism, including the racism of the Nazi Government, and to Jewry in Israel today.

The 500 examined programs can be broken down as follows:

447 Programs for the Academic Year 1958-59 Offered
Activities Related to the Following Topics:

Topics	Courses	Lecture Series	Single Lectures	Total
Contemporary history, National-Socialism	36	1	42	79
Jewry, Modern Israel	9	4	55	68
Total	45	5	97	147

53 Programs for the Academic Year 1959-60 Offered
Activities Related to the Following Topics:

Topics	Courses	Lecture Series	Single Lectures	Total
Contemporary history, National-Socialism	24	—	4	28
Jewry, Modern Israel	7	—	4	11
Total	31	—	8	39

[1] From *Erziehungswesen und Judentum* pp. 134-9, see footnote p. 122.

The table shows an increase of courses in both fields in 1959. In connection with the topic National Socialism we should like to note that the showings of the film *Nacht und Nebel* (a documentary film on concentration camps) are not included in the figures of our table. In almost all adult education centers this film was shown by their film clubs; in some of them more than once, as, for instance, in Mainz where they had eight showings.

Most of the single lectures on modern Israel had been given by excellently informed officers of the Israelian foreign service. With the aid of short films and other documentary material they reported vividly on the development of Israel. These lectures were received with much interest.

We have picked two typical examples of how National Socialism was discussed in the program:

1) Adult Education Center Wuppertal, where three forms of programs are being offered to meet the various tastes of the participants: the seminar in connection with a department of the University of Cologne, the lecture series, and the work shop.

From the catalogue of VHS Wuppertal 1959—60:

Structure and History of National Socialist Totalitarianism.

A study group in cooperation with the Seminar of Political Science at the University of Cologne.

Chairman: Dr. Rudolf Wildenmann.

Beginning with the question: "What Does Totalitarian Dictatorship Mean?", the seminar will deal with: history of the NSDAP and the ideology of the Third Reich — problems of the Weimar Republic such as social and political development, the *Voelkisch* movement, soldiers unions, constitutional problems, the state of foreign policy, the role of the Communist Party — rise and politics of the Hitler regime — racism — the concept of mankind in the eyes of National Socialism.

The analysis will be completed by a series of studies such as: intellectual, social, and political conditions leading to totalitarianism in the 20th century — similarities and differences between National Socialism and Communism — freedom and justice, the problems of our time.

Under the Swastika. Germany from 1933 till 1945.

Lecture Series.

Chairman: Otto Roche.

Often we have to face the reproach of the "undigested past". Whether it is a true one or not, the happenings and the background of Adolf Hitler's dictatorship are not sufficienty known to the Germans in order to speak of a thorough understanding of the twelve years. However the past can be digested, if one first starts to study its sources — and this is the objective of the lecture series.

History of the Second World War.

Work shop.

Chairman: Hans Joachim Oehm.

The goal of this work-shop will be to offer an insight into the occurrences on the German and the Allied side during World War II.

236

Although a true evaluation is still impossible, since we have not yet been able to see this historic event from the necessary distance, and a complete survey on source material is still missing, we shall nevertheless try to recognize the factors which led to the catastrophe of 1945.

The subjects will center around Hitler's concept of an All-German policy, methods used by him for its realization, and the reasons why this policy had to collapse.

2) Weekend Seminars of VHS Mainz held in Schloss Dhaum. From the catalogue of VHS Mainz, Fall 1959:

Seminars on Contemporary History in Mainz

Chairman: Josef Rudolf

"Around the Brandenburger Tor"

(Documents and original recordings lead us through the turn of the century and exemplify German history through the fate of the capital Berlin).

"The Voices of the Deceivers"

(Tape recordings of speeches by Hitler, Goebbels, Goering, and others show how the German tragedy began and how it ended).

"The Enabling Act"

(Tape recording of the session of the German Reichstag on the Enabling Act of 23 March 1933).

"The Advent to Power"

(Film and sound documents, and other documentary material show how Hitler came to power).

"The Silent Revolt"

(Report on the resistance movement of the German people 1933—45).

Weekend seminars of the VHS centers in Mainz:

"Why Are They Against Us?"

(Discussions on youth problems of our time).

"The Silent Revolt"

(Report on the German Resistance Movement 1933—45).

As an example of the treatment of anti-Semitism we should like to mention the course offered in the VHS Hanover fall program 1958:

"Anti-Semitism"

Chairman: Dr. Dietrich Bronder

Racial theories from Gobineau to Guenther. Jewish contributions to German culture. European anti-Semitism and the Protocols of the Elders of Zion. Psychology and sociology of anti-Semitism. Its development from Adolf Stoecher to Adolf Hitler. The Ludendorffs and the "supra-governmental powers". "Induced insanity" through pseudo-scientific teachings.

Examples of the objective discussion on Jewry are found in the programs of the adult education centers in Worms and Berlin-Neukoelln.

From the catalogue of VHS Worms (Sept. 1958—March 1959). Special series on German-Jewish discussions.

"My Trip to Israel" (travelogue with slides by Mayor Voelker).

"The Jews of Worms" (Dr. O. Boecher).

Earliest beginnings, immigration and establishment of communities; Worms Jews in the beginning and the height of the Middle Ages; Jews in the late Middle Ages and the Renaissance; the period of Baroque and the Emancipation.

"The Voice of Israel"

(Recitations by Lotte Roettger with an introduction by Thillo Roettger).

"Jewish-German Writings in the Emigration"

Baermann-Steiner, Werfel, Wolfskehl, Lasker-Schueler, Zelan, Mombert, Sachs, and others.

From the 1959-60 catalogue of the Otto-Suhr-VHS Berlin-Neukoelln:

"Meeting Israel Again", by Anna Maria Johl.

The old prophets and the new life.

The Negev — land of the future. Cities and districts grow in the desert. Eliath — gate to the Red Sea; Israel and Germany.

What then is the status of contemporary history in comparison to the other subjects of political education?

A survey on the 447 programs of 1958-59, which are offered in the field of political education, answers our question.

Political Education:

Academic Year 1958-59

Number of programs:		447
Number of those not featuring political education:		113

Subject	Courses	Lecture Series	Single Lectures	Total
Contemporary history	120	5	107	232
Government	64	2	45	111
Civics	170	1	52	223
World Politics	110	7	130	247
Foreign Policy	9	2	17	28
National Politics	10	—	9	19
Reunification	39	2	56	97
Political ideas and their history	72	6	50	128
Economics and social politics	100	3	24	127
Jewry and modern Israel	9	4	55	68
Political propaganda	5	—	5	10
Under-developed countries	39	39	563*	641
"Europe", economic and political points of views	51	31	84	166
Total	798	102	1,197	2,097

* Majority of lectures with slides

From the above table it is apparent that contemporary history ranks second in the efforts spent on political education. It ranks after those activities which are aimed at immediate actions such as citizens' forums, women's forums, parent's forums, etc. We should also not forget that courses offered in political education which do not directly deal with National Socialism or Jewry often do mention these problems and that just in this way a clear and calm political thinking can be achieved which is an important prerequisite for counteracting anti-Semitism.

No one answer can be given to the question: what reasons account for the increase of enrollment in the field of political education. The adult education organizations of the States Hesse and Rhineland-Palatinate claim that this is due to the more intensive staff training, especially on the district level. The study of the curricula of those adult education centers which have been leading in this field suggests that also the employment of full time staff members and the extension of university seminar courses account for it. Finally we should not forget that the work shops and discussion groups established by full time youth leaders, who are paid out of funds of the Federal Youth Act, play a part in the increase of political education in adult education centers.

The European Education Work in the Federal Republic [1]

By Hans W. Kuhn

Foreword

In the spring of 1960, the *Bildungswerk Europaeische Politik e. V.*, commissioned an expert with the preparation of a critical analysis of the knowledge imparted by political education activities in the Federal Republic on the subjects of European politics and European integration. This assignment was based on the consideration that the political education activities — which to an overwhelming extent are being financed from public budgets — are called upon, in addition to the institutions of the governmental and communal education system, to prepare and promote the formation of political opinion and political will within large parts of the population, doing so by way of a dispassionate and suprapartisan assessment of the existing conditions with the help of information, discussion, and education. There is no doubt that all of this also applies to the questions of European politics.

The experiences of the last decade have proved the need for, but also the productiveness, of a large-scale youth and adult education program. In the face of progressing West European integration within a sphere of continuously changing world political relations and tensions, an enthusiastic attitude alone toward the European idea, however well-meant it may be, is not sufficient. Instead, a substantial information of the public on the problems and structures of the European Community, on the "big" as well as the "little" Europe, and the resulting challenge to the individual's ability of judgment and decision have the same importance as the examination of European questions under the aspect of their correct context and impact within their world-wide interrelations. Seen in this way, there exists no "European" education, but only a political education devoting due attention to European interests. For this end, also the concept of a world centered around Europe has to be overcome. Political education, if it is to do justice to the task set to it, always must be, in each one of its aspects, a contribution to a total, world-wide, political orientation.

There can be no doubt that up to the present, the manifold efforts — in many cases unknown to large parts of the public — of numerous institutes and organizations toward the promotion of the ability of political judgment have been successful. The fact must not be overlooked, however, that this work will produce the full scope of its achievements only after years of patient effort. In the recent past, more and more individuals and organizations have made their services available to educational activities of world-wide political scope.

This gratifying progress is in need of incessant public encouragement as well as of material and spiritual assistance. The herewith submitted expert's opinion intends to provide an idea of the multiformity and the proportions of what has been achieved so far. Wherever it points to shortcomings and problems, it does so in the effort to give some suggestions to the educational institutions with regard to a self-critical reappraisal of their activities.

* * * * * * * * *

[1] From: *Die europäische Bildungsarbeit in der Bundesrepublik.* Expert's opinion for the *Bildungswerk Europaeische Politik* e.V., Bonn (Manuscript).

The analysis is exclusively based on the material and the information made available by the educational institutions. I am especially grateful to all those who, by way of written or oral information, granted me far-reaching insight into their work.

The institutional structure of European educational work

The concise descriptions of institutions, which are presently concerned with topics of European politics and integration in the field of free political education — which in some cases borders on culture, education, and public works — should provide an idea of the diversity of these efforts.*) The survey is far from being complete. No mention was made, e.g., of the youth organizations, the *Amerika-Haeuser*, the former British information centers *Die Bruecke*, and the *Institut Français*, nor of the events and meetings arranged by the *Europa-Union* and its subgroups on *Land* and *Kreis* level. Also, the widely ramified activities of the *Internationale Buergermeister-Union fuer deutsch-franzoesische Verstaendigung und europaeische Zusammenarbeit***) can only briefly be referred to. On the other hand it was necessary to go beyond the group of institutions specially closely linked with the European movement and to grant consideration, too, to educational institutions which do not feel obligated to a specific program for the unification of Europe. With regard to some activities only characteristic examples could be listed.

The enumeration starts with the specific institutions of European educational work. It proceeds with those educational institutions which deal with European questions, among other things; next follow those societies which see their primary task in the cultivation of bilateral relations in the European area, and the organizations promoting international exchange programs. In conclusion, the educational institutions of the trade unions, the economic associations, and the denominations are listed. Wherever no specific remark to the contrary is added, the institutions concerned are privately founded organizations in the form of an *Eingetragener Verein (e. V.)* (registered association) which are working as non-profit institutions.

*) Cf. also Erich Ullrich: *Erziehung zu Europa* (published by Europa-Union), p. 11 seqq.
**) It publishes a monthly *Deutschland—Frankreich — Beiträge zur europäischen Einigung.*

The Europa-Haeuser

The *Europa-Haeuser* at Schliersee and Otzenhausen as well as the *Gustav-Stresemann-Institut* are members of the *Bildungswerk Europaeische Politik e.V.*, which was founded in April 1959. The *Europa-Haus* at Marienberg did not joint the latter organization. Compared to the Marienberg institution which has been in existence since 1951, they are relatively new installations. What they have in common is the objective of working towards a promotion of European Unification on a Federal basis with the help of youth and adult education. As far as topics are concerned, the work is centered on all questions of European politics and European integration which, with the inclusion of the East-West problem and the German question, are being examined within their world political framework.

With regard to the organizing of courses and study meetings, the *Europa-Haeuser* frequently cooperate with the *Europaeische Aktionsgemeinschaft e. V.*, and with the *Europa-Bildungswerk e. V.* Various non-institutional events arranged by the *Europa-*

Haeuser at Otzenhausen and Schliersee are jointly carried trough with the sub-groups on *Land* and *Kreis* level of the *Europa-Union*.

The participants in the courses come from all parts of the Federal territory and primarily are members of those organizations with which the *Europa-Haeuser* maintain partnership relations. In some cases also a cooperation with the Adult Education Centers takes place. Foreign citizens have been guests in all *Europa-Haeuser*, particularly in Marienberg.

The *Europa-Haus Schliersee e.V., Institut fuer politische Bildung und Oeffentlich-keitsarbeit* was founded in March 1958. In addition to the current educational work in these courses, three working groups exist which are concerned with European law and with the problems of social psychology and economics coming up in connection with European Unification. Recently, special experiences could be gathered from a training program for high-ranking local administration officials *(Landraete, Ober-buergermeister,* and *Buergermeister)* which, starting from basic seminars, extended over several months. The institute, moreover, assigned to a team of authors the task of writing a textbook *Unity and Unification of Europe in the Instruction on Social Studies* of which the manuscript already exists.

The *Europa-Haus Otzenhausen e.V., Institut fuer politische Bildung und deutsch-franzoesische Zusammenarbeit* (Saar), has been working since October 1959. Its location in the Saar has been conducive to a close German-French cooperation.

Out of the *Europaeische Jugendkampagne,* the *Gustav-Stresemann-Institut e.V. fuer europaeische Bildungs- und Informationsarbeit* developed. It held its constituent meeting at Bonn in February 1960, but actually had already been working prior to that date. It is attached to the International Association of the Institutes for European Education and Information Work. Due to the lack of a home of its own, the work of the institution is being carried on in various meeting centers throughout the entire West German Federal territory and also in the neighboring European countries and in Berlin. As the No. 1 issue of its series of publications *Europaeische Hefte,* the institute published *Ein Sorgenkind Europas. Das Beispiel Suedtyrols zur Frage der entwicklungsfaehigen Laender* (A problem-child of Europe. The example of South Tyrol with regard to the question of the countries capable of development), edited by C. E. Ortmann, 1957-59.

The oldest of the *Europa-Haeuser, Europa-Haus Marienberg, Informations- und Bildungsstaette fuer uebernationale Zusammenarbeit e.V.* (Westerwald), has been in existence since 1951 and started work as an education center in 1952. This spring it associated in a loosely organized working group with various other Europe Houses in Sweden, Denmark, Austria, and France. With the help of an international staff of assistants, the activities of this institute are predominantly concerned with international encounters. In continuation of the tradition of the international "Loreley Camp" of 1951, European summer camps are organized every year. The *Marien-berger Briefe* provide current information on the activities of the center.

Working in a style not exactly similar to that of the *Europa-Haeuser* but in the same spirit, the *Aussenstelle Berlin,* set up by the Secretariat General of the *Europa-Union,* is active in Berlin. Every month it arranges "European Work Conferences", extending over several days, for teachers, trade union representatives, women's organizations, and similar groups which are being held in various West Berlin meeting centers *(Haus der Zukunft, Wilhelm-Westkamp-Haus, Wilhelm Leuschner-Haus* of the German Federation of Trade Unions).

The Europa-Seminar Goehrde

Having developed from the regularly held *Europa-Lehrgaenge* (Instruction courses on Europe) of the *Heimvolkshochschule Jagdschloss Goehrde* which began in 1951 as well as from the *Europaeische Sommerschulen* (European summer schools) which supplemented the said courses and took place every year, the *Europa-Seminar* was established in 1957[1]). Acting upon instructions from the *Deutscher Volkshochschulverband e.V.*, and in cooperation with the Bonn office of the European Communities, it organizes advanced study and model courses on European topics for teachers at Adult Education Centers and schools. In addition, the *Europaeische Sommerschulen* are being continued with foreign participants; other courses are being held for various organizations and vocational schools; study tours are being organized. The *Europa-Seminar* regards as its main task the promotion of the introduction of the idea of European unification into all branches of youth and adult education. The experiences reaped so far found their expression in the publication *Die Behandlung europaeischer Themen an der Volkshochschule*[2]) (The Treatment accorded to European Topics by the Adult Education Centers) and in the article by A. Feickert *"Wie interessiert der Volksbildner seine Hoerer fuer das Europa-Problem?"*[3]) ("How does the educator arouse interest in his audience for the European problem?"). The establishent of an archive on questions of European pedagogics and the suggestion to introduce foreign language training in the Adult Education Centers in a sensible way into the European education efforts are serving the same fundamental purpose.

[1]) **Cf. A. Feickert:** *Europa-Arbeit in der Goehrde*, published in Heimvolkshochschule Jagdschloss Goehrde, 1946—1956.
[2]) **Issue No. 3 of** the *Arbeitsunterlagen fuer Volkshochschulen*, published by "Deutscher Volkshochschulverband e.V."
[3]) *Berliner Arbeitsblaetter fuer die deutsche Volkshochschule*, No. XI, 1960.

The Europaeische Aktionsgemeinschaft e.V.

This organization has its seat at Bad Godesberg. Its activities mainly extend to the planning, the organization, and the implementation of study seminars, study tours, and lectures as well as of *Europa-(Aktions-)Wochen* in towns and communities on behalf of, and jointly with other associations and educational institutions. A large part of the arranged events take place in the *Europa-Haeuser*; the local *Europa-Wochen* are carried through jointly with the *Europa-Union* and other local groups. Close cooperation is being cultivated, moreover, with the International Police Association and the German Salaried Employees' Union whose European occupation contest, with respect to the educational angle, takes place under the auspices of the *Aktionsgemeinschaft*. In addition, study tours for the Federal champions of the contest and study seminars for the *Land* champions are being organized. Moreover, European one-week meetings are being arranged by the institution for the teachers at Adult Education Centers and vocational schools.

These activities which have been going on since 1952 are exclusively aimed at the unification of Europe on a federative basis. They are supplemented by the publications of the *Aktionsgemeinschaft*[1]): *Taschenbuch fuer die Freunde Europas, ein Europa-Wegweiser (Manual for the friends of Europe, a guide to Europe)* by Hans Joachim Platz, whose revised edition is being prepared at the present time. Also a series of booklets on various countries have been published in which, in a tasteful and witty manner, an introduction to the ways of life of the neighboring European countries is given. These publications are connected with the new work program *Tourismus und Voelkerverstaendigung* (Tourism and understanding among nations) which the *Aktionsgemeinschaft* initiated with the help of a conference of scholars and experts on tourism. As future publications a European language manual, a pictorial volume *Family in Europe*, and a small manual of European integration efforts are planned. Also a few cleverly devised publicity pamphlets referring to the European question are worth mentioning.

[1] *"Was koennen wir fuer Europa tun? Aus der publizistischen Arbeit der Europaeischen Aktionsgemeinschaft"*, published in the *Bulletin des Presse- und Informationsamtes* of August 16, 1958, p. 1540.

The Europa-Bildungswerk e.V.

This institution was founded in Regensburg in 1947. Today it comprises a total of three associations in Duesseldorf, Regensburg, and Berlin which have the task of the dissemination of the idea of European unification by way of youth and adult education. This work is being carried through with the help of speaker services, especially on subjects of European impact, for lectures, informational conferences, and study seminars. The institution also makes expert lecturers available to a large number of organizations, among them the *Europa-Haeuser*, the subgroups of the *Europa-Union* on *Land* and *Kreis* level, the Adult Education Centers, the economic associations, youth groups, and individual occupational groups. In the past years the *Bildungswerk* used to supplement its work by a number of exhibitions on European subjects.

The Europaeischer Erzieherbund

The *Sektion Deutschland* e.V. (Darmstadt) which was founded in 1956 is the organization of teachers and educators — not aimed at the pursuit of group political interests — who cooperate in the *Europaeische Paedagogische Aktion* and work, within the framework of their professional activities, towards the unification of Europe on a federative basis[1]. The head office as well as the groups on *Land* level organize, on German and international level, European study and information conferences for their members at regular intervals. Ever since January 1960 the monthly *Europaeische Erziehung, Europa durch die Schule* (European education; Europe through the schools) has been published.

[1] Cf. *Europa-Arbeit in den Schulen. Die Ziele des Europaeischen Erzieherbundes* published in the *Bulletin des Presse- und Informationsamtes* of March 26, 1958, p. 555; *Die Tagung des Europaeischen Erzieherbundes* in Bozen of April 1 — 4, 1959 by B. Feige, published in *Die Berliner Schule*, Vol 6 (1959), No. 5.

The Volkshochschulen and Heimvolkshochschulen (Adult Education Centers and Residential Colleges for Adult Education)

The local Adult Education Centers and Residential Colleges for Adult Education, whose parent organization is the *Deutscher Volkshochschulverband* e.V. (Bonn), constitute the executive elements of European educational activities, some of them systematically pursued over the years, which are reaching all parts of the population.[1] Frequently, these activities are carried through in cooperation with the German Federation of Trade Unions in the joint working group *Arbeit und Leben*. In the *Europa-Seminar* of the *Heimvolkshochschule Goehrde*, which has already been mentioned, the Adult Education Centers have a cetral place of education at their disposal where specific attention is devoted to the European questions and where,

244

Young German Admirers Gather Around an American Serviceman

As Everywhere in the World Young People in West Germany, too, are Interested in Records

Photos: Bundesbildstelle Bonn

The Director of the Youth Department of the City of Nuremberg Hit Upon the Idea of Opening a House for Teenagers to Keep Them off the Streets. Here They are Given the Opportunity of Learning Various Trades and Pursuing Their Hobbies.

Photos: dpa

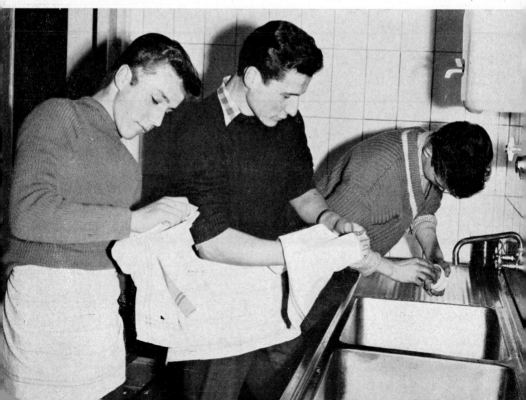

in particular, advanced studies for Adult Education Center teachers are being furthered. The two series of publications which the *Volkshochschulverband* issues, *Grundfragen zur Volkshochschularbeit (Basic Questions of Work at the Adult Education Centers)* and *Arbeitsunterlagen fuer Volkshochschulen[2]) (Working Documents for Adult Education Centers)* provide pedagogic instructions particularly for political education activities.

A survey, *Europa in der Volkshochschule (Europe in the Adult Education Centers)*, on which the *Paedagogische Arbeitsstelle* of the *Volkshochschulverband (Frankfurt)* is working at present, deals with the activities of the local Adult Education Centers as to their reference to European topics. As this survey shows, out of a total of 409 programs of the local Adult Education Centers in the time from April 1958 to March 1959, which were evaluated for this inquiry, as many as 206 programs, i.e., more than 50 %, had announced the discussion of European subjects. In detail, there were 165 courses, 44 series of lectures, 98 single lectures, and 165 study tours, 7 of which had Paris and Luxembourg as their destination. As an example of special European activities — which definitely is no isolated case — the Adult Education Center *Dinkelsbuehl-Gunzenhausen* should be mentioned which alone in the working year 1959-1960 organized a total of 83 series of lectures on European topics in 77 rural communities in which a total audience of approximately 2,800 persons participated.

The curricula of the 29 Residential Colleges for Adult Education, which are attached to the *Volkshochschulverband* as a rule, include the discussion of European subjects only within the framework of general political instruction. Some of these centers are also used by other organizations for their European events, sometimes in cooperation with the *Europa-Bildungswerk e.V.*

[1] Cf. *Die Volkshochschule in der Bundesrepublik und in Berlin*, published by Deutscher Volkshochschulverband.
[2] The No. 1 issue of *Politische Bildung*, edited by the Paedagogische Arbeitsstelle fuer Erwachsenenbildung, Inzigkofen, deserves special attention.

The Landeszentralen fuer Heimatdienst

It is not possible to outline here in detail the manifold and differently organized work of the *Landeszentralen fuer Heimatdienst* (Land Organizations for Civic Education) and of the respective central offices in some *Laender*, e.g., the working group *Der Buerger im Staat* (The Citizen in the State) in *Baden-Wuerttemberg;* the *Kuratorium fuer staatsbuergerliche Bildung* (Committee for Civic Education) in *Hamburg;* the *Institut fuer staatsbuergerliche Bildung* (Institute for civic education) in Rhineland-Palatinate. The activities of these institutions extend to the promotion of measures from which also the *Europa-Haeuser*, the *Europa-Bildungswerk*, and the *Land* groups of the *Europa-Union* benefit, as well as to the arranging of specific events of their own. These latter activities have been taking place, e.g., in Baden-Wuerttemberg, Bremen (where the *Landeszentrale* is identical with the Adult Education Center), and in Lower Saxony.

Individual institutions for political education

The following institutes concentrate their educational work on topics connected with the East-West conflict:

> Ostkolleg der Bundeszentrale fuer Heimatdienst (Cologne)
> Gesamteuropaeisches Studienwerk e.V. (Vlotho)

Ost-Seminar Koenigstein (Taunus)
Sozialakademie Friedewald
Heimvolkshochschule Hustedt
Ost-West-Institut Baden-Wuerttemberg (Freiburg i. Br.)

In these centers, European questions are regarded from the specific angle of the East-West problem. The far-flung work program of the *Akademie fuer politische Bildung* (Tutzing)[1] also includes seminars on European questions.

Haus Rissen, Institut fuer Wirtschafts- und Sozialpolitik (Rissen near Hamburg) also organizes at regular intervals, among other events, seminars on European affairs in the form of study tours to the organs of the European Communities, the Council of Europe, OEEC, and the NATO Secretariat General. In addition, *Europaeische Tage* and preparatory seminars for the developing countries are being held. A monthly circular, the *Rissener Rundbrief*, maintains contact with the former participants in the seminars and informs them with regard to political questions of present-day importance.

The task which the *Grenzakademie Sandelmark* has set itself is determined by its location in northern Schleswig. The close ties with the Scandinavian countries play a large part in this institution's dealing with European topics.

One of the oldest institutions for political education work is the *Friedrich Ebert-Stiftung zur Foerderung demokratischer Volkserziehung e.V.* (Bonn[2]) which was re-established in 1947. In the *Heimvolkshochschule Bergneustadt* this institution has set up for itself the necessary domicile for conferences and courses. European topics are being dealt with in a large number of courses and study tours.

Recently also the *Politische Akademie Eichholz* has concerned itself more pronouncedly with political education. Its programs include European questions in a number of contexts.

The *Deutsche Auslandsgesellschaft* in Luebeck with its working groups in Bochum, Flensburg, Hanover, Husum, Kiel, and Rendsburg can look back upon extensive activities throughout the last ten years[3]. The manifold program (lectures, exhibitions, movie shows, youth and students' exchanges, care for foreign juveniles and university students, as well as German language training courses for foreigners) is aimed at an improvement of the relations with foreign countries, and devotes its main attention to factual information. The relations with the Scandinavian countries, including Iceland and Finland, are being granted definite priority although the other European countries and America are not disregarded. Special interest is accorded to the subjects of a cultural policy nature. A large number of foreign lecturers could be enlisted for the discourses arranged by the institution. It publishes an information sheet *Ausblick* which is made up in the form of a news magazine[4].

Also the *Rheinisch-westfaelische Auslandsgesellschaft e.V.*, in Dortmund has a similarly wide range of activities which are meant to serve the purpose of a cultivation of human, cultural, and economic relations. A special field of work exists, moreover, in the training of and care for foreign trainees in Germany (in cooperation with

---

[1] Manfred Scheib: *Aufgabe und Wirken der Akademie fuer politische Bildung in Tutzing*, published in "Franz-Lieber-Hefte" No. 4, 1960, p. 55.

[2] G. Grunwald: *Die staatsbuergerlichen und internationalen Aufgaben der Friedrich-Ebert-Stiftung*, published in *Kulturarbeit*, vol. 11, No. 6.

[3] Cf. *"Deutsche Auslandsgesellschaft 1949—1959. Zehn Jahre Auslandsarbeit in zusammenfassenden Berichten und Ueberblicken.*

[4] Attention also has to be called to the publication *"Begegnung Deutschlands mit dem Norden"* (30 Oct.—1 Nov. 1959 in Luebeck). *Reden — Ansprachen — Vortraege, Zusammenfassung und Auswertung der Aussprachen.*

the *Carl-Duisberg-Gesellschaft*). A number of study circles (e.g., France, Italy, Great Britain, and the Commonwealth — *Die Bruecke*, Scandinavia, Ibero-America — — Spain) provides knowledge on the subject of foreign countries in the form of lectures, working groups, and language training courses. European information conferences are being organized, *inter alia*, together with the *Europa-Bildungswerk*, the *Europa-Union*, and the *Carl-Duisberg-Gesellschaft*.

The *Auslandsgesellschaft* also grants its support to the *Auslandsinstitut der Stadt Dortmund*[1]) which also, within the framework of its Adult Education program, deals with European affairs in series of lectures, seminars, and similar ways.

In Hamburg, the recently founded *Staatspolitische Gesellschaft e.V.*, and the *Neue Gesellschaft, Vereinigung fuer politische Bildung e.V.*, which was established in 1959, are engaged in activities of the same nature. Particularly the *Neue Gesellschaft* devotes detailed attention to European questions in its lectures and evening seminars Moreover, it organizes, at regular intervals, study tours to Paris, Brussels, Luxembourg, and Strasbourg.

The central event organized by the *Deutsch-Englische Gesellschaft* (Duesseldorf), which has been in existence since 1949 and called into life five subgroups on *Land* level and six Federal-level working groups, is the annual "German-English Conference" in Koenigswinter[2]). In addition, a large number of separate lectures, in most cases by English speakers, on questions of British policy and culture in the world political framework are being arranged. In this connection, also the association of the fourteen *Deutsch-Italienische Gesellschaften* (Hamburg) has to be mentioned as well as the large number of *Deutsch-Franzoesische Gesellschaften*.

The main emphasis of the work of the *Bund fuer internationalen Kulturaustausch e.V.* (Reutlingen), is placed on the international youth and adult exchange program as well as on the work on behalf of foreign occupational and university students' groups in the Federal Republic. Moreover, vacation and information tours to the neighboring European countries are being organized.

The *Deutsch-Franzoesische Institut Ludwigsburg* has been working in the same field since 1948[3]). Here, too, the exchange in all fields of public life in the effort to promote German-French understanding is considered to be of primary importance and is being cultivated and promoted in close cooperation with various French and German agencies, especially with the *Comité Français d'Echanges avec l'Allemagne Nouvelle*. Through these activities, the participation in vacation courses, study tours and work camps, the granting of school sponsorships, and the exchange of trainees and university students holding temporary jobs are arranged. In the domicile of the institute itself, French language training courses as well as conferences of teachers and trainees are being held. In addition, the cooperation in the *Deutsch-Franzoesische Juristenvereinigung* and in the *Internationale Buergermeister-Union* is being promoted. The subjects with which series of lectures and single discourses arranged by the institute have dealt are described in the *Ludwigsburger Beitraegen zum Problem der deutsch-franzoesischen Beziehungen (Ludwigsburg Contributions to the Problem of German-French Relations)* (Vol. I, 1954; Vol. II, 1957). Another publication of the Institute, the *Zwoelf-Jahres-Bibliographie Deutschland-Frankreich*, was planned for the summer of 1960.

The *Gesellschaft fuer uebernationale Zusammenarbeit e.V.*, maintains an institute

---

[1]) The Cultural Office of the town of Dortmund issues, at irregular intervals, the series *Dortmunder Vortraege* which frequently deal with European topics.

[2]) *10 Jahre Deutsch-Englische Gesellschaft — 10 Jahre Koenigswinter. Taetigkeitsbericht der Deutsch-Englischen Gesellschaft.*

[3]) Cf. *10 Jahre Deutsch-Französisches Institut Ludwigsburg, Taetigkeitsbericht.*

in Cologne which organizes international study tours as well as conferences and lectures concerned with international questions. It has arranged a private youth exchange program with France, and since 1945 has published the periodical *Dokumente*. The society is a member of the Council of the European Movement.

Another specific exchange organization is the *Europaeischer Austauschdienst e.V.* (Frankfurt/M.). The conferences in foreign countries and study tours abroad organized by it are arranged with respect to the occupational basis of the participants and include a large number of European countries. As a rule, the stays abroad are prepared with the help of short-term seminars in Germany.

Since February 1959 the *Haus Sonnenberg* (Oberharz) of the *Internationaler Arbeitskreis Sonnenberg e.V.*, has been the meeting place of adults and juveniles at international-level conferences which are being held in a spirit of national and group understanding. In the effort to promote this activity which also deals with European topics, the International Sonnenberg Association was founded in Copenhagen in 1958 to which Sonnenberg groups in Denmark, England, the Netherlands, Luxembourg, Norway, Austria, Sweden, and Switzerland have acceded. The *Sonnenberg-Briefe zur Voelkerverstaendigung (Sonnenberg Letters for Understanding Among the Nations)* appear at regular intervals; moreover, the series *Zwischen Gestern und Morgen (Between Yesterday and Tomorrow)* is being published.

Also the *Internationales Forum Burg Liebenzell (Schwarzwald)* is working in a similar way, foreigners and Germans discussing all sorts of present-day problems in working groups.

The Trade Unions

The German Federation of Trade Unions *(DGB)* and the German Salaried Employees' Union *(DAG)* also have taken up questions of European politics and European integration within their general educational programs, having done so, however, in a different sort of way. The work of the *DGB* is characterized by the fact that primarily it proceeds along the lines natural to an organization engaged in a socio-political struggle and, with few exceptions, is being carried through internally within the organization. It is supplemented, though, on a broad basis by the working group jointly established by the *DGB* and the Adult Education Centers *Arbeit und Leben* (Work and Life). Unlike the *DGB*, the *DAG* utilizes existing educational institutions for its European education activities.

The main part of the European education work of the *Deutscher Gewerkschaftsbund* is being done by the six Federal-level schools and by the instruction centers of individual trade unions. These latter institutions restrict themselves, however, to special events. The instruction programs include European topics within the courses *Die industrielle Gesellschaft und die Gewerkschaften, Sozialpolitik,* and *Volkswirtschaftspolitik.* As the composition of the programs shows, European questions have been granted somewhat greater attention this year, compared to 1959. Also the European education activities of the subgroups on *Land* level and of the *Kreis* and community committees is noteworthy; this work in many cases is carried through in cooperation with other organizations, chiefly the local centers of *Arbeit und Leben.*)*

The activities of *Arbeit und Leben, Arbeitskreis fuer die Bundesrepublik* (head office Duesseldorf) take place in the local field, in close cooperation with the Adult Education Centers. Due to the lack of documentary material in the head office it is not possible to say to what extent European subjects were included into the said educational activities. On Federal and *Land* level various evening courses extending over several days were held. Moreover, the European complex of questions also appears on the instruction programs of the more extensive courses in the Residential Colleges for Adult Education which *Arbeit und Leben* is supporting. From time to time, experts' conferences arranged by the head office take place as a means of assisting and facilitating the instruction work of the local colaborators. The head office also has drawn up a "Topic Proposal for a Local Basic Seminar on Questions of European Integration" in which the tasks, the topical and methodical procedure as well as references to working and information material, are described in detail.

The *Deutsche Angestellten-Gewerkschaft* has granted special emphasis to the subject of Europe in its political education work. The focal point has to be seen in the annual occupation contest which takes place under the auspices of the *Europa-Union* and which, starting from 1957, is carried through in a European framework. The actual European education work of the *DAG* is in the hands of the *Europaeische Aktionsgemeinschaft e.V.* In addition to international meetings for the champions on *Land* level in the *Europa-Haus Marienberg* and European study tours for the Federal champions of the occupation contest it regularly arranges European working weeks in the *Europa-Haeuser* at Otzenhausen, Marienberg, and Schliersee, as well as in the *DAG* instruction center *Haus Naumburg*.

* Cf. *Denkschrift Balser,* p. 23 seqq.

The Economic Associations

As a result of their institutional variety the European education activities of the economic associations can be surveyed only with difficulty. Partly this work is handled by the organizations united in the *Wuppertaler Kreis,* partly by the Chambers of Industry and Commerce, and partly by the agricultural cooperatives and associations. Exemplary institutions are the *Deutsches Institut zur Foerderung des industriellen Fuehrungsnachwuchses* (Cologne), which organizes the *Baden-Badener Unternehmergespraeche* and provides lecturers, the *Junge Unternehmer der Arbeitsgemeinschaft selbstaendiger Unternehmer,* the *Deutsche Volkswirtschaftliche Gesellschaft e.V.,* in Hamburg, the *Juniorenkreise der deutschen Unternehmerschaft,* and others. A special form of education activities on the part of industry are the 19 seminars which are arranged by some Chambers of Industry and Commerce and by several members of the *Wuppertaler Kreis.* The share of European topics in the programs of these institutions varies strongly. At any rate, economic policy points of view are being granted priority in every case.

Very lively educational activities have been introduced by the agricultural associations. In addition to a large number of *Laendliche Bildungsstaetten* and the *Bauernhochschule Fredeburg* especially the *Genossenschaftsschule Hohenheim* has to be mentioned with respect to the emphasis on European matters; this school is in charge of the task of dealing with the questions of agrarian politics connected with European integration. As an example for a number of similar institutions which, within the framework of professional instruction, also deal with questions of European economic policy the *Bundeslehranstalt Burg Warberg des deutschen Agrarhandels* should be noted. It publishes a monthly news-sheet, the *Warberger Merkur.*

Denominational Education Activities

The extremely diversified activities of church and denominational education facilities grant relatively little attention to European subjects. The examination of this sector has, however, not as yet been completed; as soon as the required information material is available, the respective report will be forwarded.

On the Evangelical side, some *Evangelische Akademien* organized European conferences. For the Evangelical Residential Colleges for Adult Education European matters only have a marginal nature. Mention has already been made in this report of the *Sozialakademie Friedewald*.

On the Catholic side, the interest for European questions appears to be more definite. As a central agency in this field the *Arbeitsgemeinschaft katholisch-sozialer Bildungswerke der Bundesrepublik* (Limburg) should be listed. Also the *Soziale Seminare* which are working in the dioceses in large numbers and the *Katholische Arbeiter-Bewegung* (Cologne) deserve special attention. Finally, the activities of several *Katholische Akademien* are noteworthy, too.

The Participants

The public character of the discourses and series of lectures renders it impossible to obtain general findings as to the composition and reaction of the public. At any rate, no research results to that effect are available. Thematically as well as pedagogically, the lectures are always adapted to that sort of audience which is about to be expected from the local population structure.

Things are different with regard to courses, weekend conferences, and evening seminars which can be prepared and carried through in a methodical manner. They are addressed to definite and surveyable groups of persons. Statistical investigations on the subject, however, have as yet only been published by the *Europaeische Aktionsgemeinschaft* and by the *Europa-Haus Marienberg* for the years 1956 and 1957*).

The overwhelming majority of the number of seminars, conferences, and study tours are carried through — in contrast to the practice of the Adult Education Centers — in cooperation with organizations, associations, schools, institutions of citizenship education and of the churches, and occupational groups. Some of the individual institutions are cultivating permanent partnerships. Through this method of procedure the invitation system is simplified and the certainty exists that qualified participants are being addressed.

*) In the case of the *Europaeische Aktionsgemeinschaft* this statistical evaluation refers to 14 one-week conferences with a total of 322 participants in the years 1957—58; 288 questionnaires were evaluated for this purpose. The *Europa-Haus* Marienberg examined the composition of its 1,489 visitors in the year 1957 (87.8 % of them foreigners). The percentage figures listed below are comparable only to a very limited degree and do not provide too clear a picture.

Composition by occupational groups in percent

	Europaeische Aktions-gemeinschaft	Marienberg
White-collar workers/civil servants	59.2	24.9
teachers	17.6	10.6
free professions/academicians/housewives, etc.	7.9	32.5
pupils/university students	10.1	10.4
laborers/craftsmen	5.2	21.6

Composition by sex groups in percent

male	86.2	65.1
female	13.8	34.9

Composition by age groups in percent

Europaeische Aktions-gemeinschaft:		Marienberg:	below 25:	59.5
below 18:	9.0		above 25:	40.5
21 — 30	61.1			
31 — 40	22.5			
41 — 50	23.2			
above 50:	24.2			

IV   The Mass Media

An American View of the West German Mass Media

The German press, radio and television have contributed to improving the moral atmosphere of Germany. By and large the more important of the newspaper are free of the bitter nationalist feeling that characterized them after 1918 and their tone is wholesome and objective. In the face of apathy and cynicism, a number have tackled the subjects of anti-Semitism, the Jewish tragedy, and the resurgence of Nazism. Generally, it must be stated that much of the German press has taken a strong and positive stand on the trials of German war criminals. Its coverage of these trials has also been impressive.

Among the newspapers to be commended are the *Frankfurter Rundschau* (the most fearless and vigorous exponent of democracy), *Die Welt* (Hamburg), the *Sueddeutsche Zeitung* (Munich), the *Frankfurter Neue Presse*, the *Mannheimer Morgen*, the *Frankfurter Allgemeine*, the *Stuttgarter Zeitung* and *Stuttgarter Nachrichten* (the latter two not as fervent in their determination as in earlier years); the Social Democratic newspapers like the *Westfaelische Rundschau* or *Telegraph* in Berlin can be compared with the *Frankfurter Rundschau*. Two weeklies, one the Catholic *Rheinische Merkur* of Cologne and the independent *Die Zeit* of Hamburg also deserve commendation. The latter periodical, in its issue of 10 April 1959, devoted a whole page to answering the question "Does a New Anti-Semitism Exist in Germany?" Mention must also be made of such magazines as the *Frankfurter Hefte* and *Deutsche Rundschau*, the latter published by the indomitable anti-Nazi Rudolf Pechel, who suffered with his wife for his enlightened opinions during the Hitler period.

Radio and television equal, and sometimes surpass, the press in the independence and coverage of themes relating to prejudice, tolerance and denazification. Especially during Brotherhood Week — for many years conducted under the auspices of former President Theodor Heuss — a wealth of material on the Jewish tragedy and problems of Christian-Jewish understanding has been carried on all nineteen West German radio stations.

---

*) From *The German Dilemma* — An Appraisal of Anti-Semitism, Ultra-Nationalism and Democracy in West-Germany p. 53; Published by Commission on International Affairs, American Jewish Congress, 1959.

Political Teaching and Mis-Teaching
by Anonymous Publicity Forces

By Dieter Geldschlaeger[1]

In addition to the political teaching provided by the home and the school, indeed, according to statements made by young persons, frequently exerting a stronger influence, is the political information and political teaching conveyed by the printed word. It goes without saying that this sphere of influence contains enormous potential force, whether it is an apparent elucidation of the past in the form of romantic stories from the last war, descriptions which are alleged to be "actual reports", the study of collections of documents from the past or polemic discussions concerning the past for the purpose of adopting an attitude with regard to important present-day political questions, as for instance in the East-West conflict. Moreover, a large number of radio and television programs doubtless exert considerable influence on the political education of young people.

A very predominantly, if not exclusively destructive influence on political education is exerted by the alleged reporting of facts in the combat pamphlets and "true stories" in the illustrated papers and several other products of the boulevard press — products which in their millions of dailies (boulevard press), weeklies (illustrated papers) or monthlies (war pamphlets) — regularly overwhelm young and older readers.

Since 1959 very diverse circles have repeatedly attempted to draw public attention to the combat accounts which appear in such serial pamphlets as *Der Landser*. This pamphlet series is published by the firm of Erich Pabel in Rastatt. In the course of three years over 200 numbers of the pamphlet series *Der Landser*, with a total edition of over 9 million copies, have been printed by this publishing firm alone. Observers of this phony literature are of the opinion that, together with comparable productions of similar firms, some 15 million copies of such "reports" are being printed yearly. In a court case which terminated recently, the publishing firm of Pabel, the largest of its kind, stated the motives by which it was allegedly actuated in the output of these pamphlets. The aim of the firm was to provide subject matter for teaching which described the abominable side of war, but which cleared the name of the German soldier before 1945; moreover these pamphlets helped to strengthen defense preparedness. After reading a considerable number of these pamphlets, a Hamburg journalist made the following pronouncement: "The whole thing is an untasty brew of watery pathos, misconceived heroism and mendacious longing for adventure, topped with pseudo-patriotic sauce, and saturated with embarassingly sweet nonsense about 'winning through'." In the Hansa cities of Hamburg and Bremen expert study teams have examined this type of "literature". In 1960 the Bremen study team delivered the following summary judgment: "In these writings war is detached from its historical and social background, from its disastrous consequences and its moral problems. It appears, not as a complicated social process, but merely as a sequence of soldierly acts. This description of war is one-sided and therefore untrue". Among the mendacious arguments of the publishing firms concerned is that these pamphlets are intended as reminiscence literature for

[1] From *Bericht ueber die Probleme und die Versuche ueber politische Bildung unter jungen Menschen in der Bundesrepublik* (Manuscript, autumn 1960).

the German soldiers of the Second World War. Is it really true that those are the readers? Here again we may quote a specialist: "The readers hardly come from the ranks of the 'front swine', to keep to the jargon. Those who read the *Landser*, the *Fliegergeschichten*, the *Soldatengeschichten aus aller Welt* and all the rest of it — are mainly juveniles. They are young people between 16 and 20, as was shown by an inquiry among the retailers of this superficial stuff. Young people who were toddlers as a war, which left nothing to be desired in the way of horror, came to an end, today read *General Ratsch-Bum* and *Die Rache des Hauptfeldwebels*, and they read that instead of 'killing' one can say '*vollrotzen*' and that 'dying' is called '*abschmieren*'. And when they lay the pamphlets aside they have been presented with sixty pages of war as a manly super-adventure for the price of 60 pfennigs . . . ." It is no wonder therefore that these combat pamphlets have been totally condemned as immoral. They have been described as "a sphere of commercialized danger to youth", the authors and publishers have been termed "bellicose sausage-makers" (Stefan Andres) or "evil post-war profiteers" (*Junge Stimme*), and their work has been designated "a dagger-stab against the law and the work of political education". The demand has frequently been made that all combat pamphlets should be prohibited, just as other writings which endanger youth, especially those of a pornographic character, have been prohibited in the past. The *Bundespruefstelle fuer jugendgefaehrdende Schriften* (Federal Organization for the Censorship of Writings which Endanger Youth) has not up to the present been able to decide upon a complete ban of combat pamphlets, and has only placed individual pamphlets on the index of writings which endanger youth, but is still considering the question.

The effect upon political education of many of the "actual fact" reports on the recent past and present-day problems in the illustrated papers and the boulevard press is scarcely any better. Under the cover of a historically accurate acount, they frequently conceal a remarkably one-sided description, and non-objectivity with regard to political events, which gives place to over-laden emotionalism. It is obvious that such reports encourage an unpolitical attitude towards political events and so work against political education. If it is recollected that between two thirds and three fourths of the readers of illustrated papers are, moreover, persons with only an elementary education, so that they probably do not possess very highly developed critical standards for judging such literary products, the danger of political mis-teaching contained in such forces becomes apparent.

The sort of reading matter described above, serial pamphlets such as the *Landser*, the illustrated papers and the boulevard press, are products which are particularly dependent upon their customers. The must exert a constantly renewed persuasion upon their readers. It is only natural that this persuasion should take the form of an appeal to the interest of the reader in sex and crime.

These literary products are only one example of the fact thar among a general public which is remarkably susceptible to commercial influences educational needs are frequently pushed to the wall by the "propaganda drive to encourage buying", even though this increased buying sometimes takes a highly unsuitable trend.

A very different contribution to political education is made by agencies of our public life which also exert an influence upon public opinion but which are not to the same degree dependent upon the spontaneous support of their customers. Highly commendable are the achievements of a number of publishing firms which supply young people with information and elucidation on political events in the form of paper-backs, as well as those of the radio and television programs.

"The age-groups between 18 and 25 buy more than one third of all the paper-backs. The next important groups are those between 25 and 30, and those between 30 and 40" (Hans Magnus Enzensberger). It is not only in the purchase of paper-backs that the younger age-groups play an important part. The fact has been established in various towns that half, and in some cases as many as two thirds, of the users of public libraries are juveniles. The largest German readers' circle has ascertained that 44 % of its members are under 30 years of age. It should be said that what characterizes this urge for books is not by any means only seeking for entertainment, but also for information, for professional knowledge, and the consultation of reference books. Thus it has been ascertained that every third book which is borrowed from a public library is purely non-fictional. Volumes on political subjects have now appeared in the cheap editions and have scored remarkable successes due probably in no small part to youthful purchasers and readers. The paper-back with the highest sales in Germany since 1945 is that illuminating work on contemporary history, *The Diary of Anne Frank*, of which more than 700,000 copies have been sold. Other volumes, such as the documentary work of Professor Hofer's, *Nationalsozialismus 1933—1945*, have not, of course, sold as many copies, but still are very frequently bought. Experts have often stated that the cognizance of documents alone does not signify adequate political activity on the part of young people, but again the study of these documents should not be underestimated, if it is considered that there are still a very large number of people among the older generation who are not even prepared to acquaint themselves with the facts.

A remarkably helpful part is played in this connection by the radio stations. Some very effectively functioning juvenile departments of the broadcasting companies have made a contribution to the political education of German youth, the repercussions of which cannot at present be adequately judged. In every form of political education which is carried on anywhere in North-West Germany, one is continually coming upon the tracks of what the juvenile program of North-West German Radio has done and is still doing under the guidance of Wolfgang Jaeger. The work of this juvenile radio department is also exemplary in the way in which political matter in the narrower and wider sense of the word, heavy and light fare are intermingled with each other, and the way in which a portion of political education is deftly introduced into the programs of the "Evenings for Young Listeners", while other programs on the other hand are entirely devoted to political education in the narrower sense. Some of these programs which deal with the coming into being of the Third Reich, with the history of the German Jews under the Third Reich and since 1945, or with the problems of divided Germany since 1945, have been in such demand among young people that the Munich publishing house of Juventa has decided to bring out these radio scripts as subject matter for study. Many a youth group leader would probably be glad to be able to borrow tape recordings of such programs, since the spoken word is often more forceful than the written word.

The wish for recordings of documents with commentaries has meanwhile been met by phonograph record companies, who have issued series of records of speeches from National Socialist times, with comments by expert historians. Abundant use has also been made of these study aids.

Critism of So-called *Landser-Hefte* Justified[1]

The County Court of Karlsruhe rules against the Pabel Publishing House of Rastatt

The Fifth Civil Chamber of the County Court of Karlsruhe, in the lawsuit concerning the critical radio broadcast "The War in the Ten-Penny Book", ruled against the Pabel Publishing House in Rastatt. The publishing house had issued 204 so-called "Infantryman" books, with a total edition of nine million copies in the past three years. The court had rejected its motion for provisional regulation against the author of the radio report.

The Court had, through its decision, confirmed that the sharp criticism of the Pabel Publishing House was not libel, injurious to business, insulting, or invitation to boycott as claimed by the publishing house, but rather the right to freedom of the press. In publishing house declarations, Pabel had, however, labeled the multiple criticism of his production as a Communist guided attack on the defensive readiness of the Federal Republic. Meanwhile, the lawyer of the publishing house had explained in court that Pabel's aspiration was to frighten his readers away from war and, simultaneously, to help restore the honor of the German soldier.

These descriptions of the war by the Pabel Publishing House, as they also presented themselves in the colorful "Infantryman" books, Neitzel had criticized as "mendacious turgidity" in his forty minute broadcast of 14 July. His sharpest argument was the assertion that he knew, through conversations with employees of the publishing house, that the complete truth about the horrors of war was not allowed to be reported in the Pabel production because it was not beneficial to business. Therefore, the readers, consisting chiefly of youths, would only be served half the truth about the war in well calculated doses.

---

[1]) From *Frankfurter Allgemeine Zeitung*, 15 September 1960.

The Swastika in German Novels [2]

By Lothar Kahn

Extracts from an article published in *The Jewish Spectator*, New York, April 1960

Writing on the Nazis in German fiction two years ago, I noted that an examination of German post-war novels did not substantiate the pessimism of Jewish critics fearful of a resurgence of Nazism in Germany. German fiction disclosed a completely changed attitude, including the most vehement reaction against Nazism and all its socio-political and racial tenets. It further revealed a rejection of all the elements which made Nazism possible. In general, the Jew received sympathetic treatment and was often accorded the place of an inspirational figure. Only one book, Wolfgang Koeppen's *Der Tod in Rom*, saw in the group of weak men who neither ardently supported Hitler nor dared reject him the chief clue to the German past and present.

---

[2]) From *Wiener Library Bulletin*, XIV, No. 2, p. 29.

Generally speaking, a more recent crop of novels would confirm this overall picture. At first glance it would seem that all is well in Adenauer's Germany and that the Nazi past is regarded as a crude and ugly joke that the Germans played on themselves and others. Some Germans started the joke and when most others knew that it was crude and ugly — and dangerous — it was too late to do anything about it. The Nazis are not taken seriously. They seem to stand in utter awe and amazement at their folly — not quite ready to admit that they had participated in Nazism, either by acts of commission or omission. As yet there are few convincing Nazis in German fiction, who are not merely disembodied men or political symbols. The fact that so many of the writers did not sympathize with the Nazis, and probably shunned those who might have served them as models, accounts for absence of convincing Nazis.

Willing to Face the Horror

If there has been a clearly discernible trend in the last few years, it is the greater willingness of German writers to face the horrors committed in the German name. Where once there was a marked tendency to shroud what happened in mystery, to imply that people thought and suspected — but did not know — has given way to a blank acknowledgment that these events transpired and that they were witnessed. Where in the late forties and early fifties some novelists suggested that it could happen elsewhere, that Germans were not alone in their guilt, that others were equally capable of committing crimes, more recent books ignore what happened across the trenches and are concerned with German guilt alone. Thus, the period which witnesses the first major outbursts of an anti-Semitic nature is also the one which first honestly faces German guilt and responsibility.

There is not necessarily a conflict between these two divergent German attitudes. It is clear that the acts of hooliganism were committed by young men of the same lower bourgeois class on whose shoulders Hitler was carried to power. The novels are written by men, often no older — some of the same socio-economic background — but having a different educational background and intellectual interests. Because it is the masses who make and break governments with the intelligentsia often standing idly by, some Jewish observers are inclined to attach little importance to the attitudes of the latter. In the case of Germany, this is not justified.

Intellectual anti-Semitism has been fasionable in both Germany and France where anti-Jewish writers, thinkers and teachers have often enjoyed considerable prestige, even in the universities. To be sure, in contemporary Germany they would, for fear of foreign reactions, get a minimum of governmental or popular support. But neither would a democratic government be able to suppress them. There certainly was considerable anti-Semitic activity by university professors and writers during the Weimar Republic, though without government support and sanction. As yet, despite isolated examples to the contrary, the post-war German intellectual scene has been devoid of anti-Jewish ideological agitation.

Also, the books which depict the Nazi horror in open and frank fashion have enjoyed consistent popularity throughout the past decade and a half. For the reading public of Germany at least — and it is widening there as elsewhere — the crimes of the Third Reich have been vividly dramatized. And the moral issues posed by them and the dilemma of guilt have been thoroughly — if not always intelligently — explored. Unlike in other periods of modern Germany history, contemporary literature has espoused the liberal, democratic cause and has in no way contributed to the resurgence of German nationalist militarism and to anti-Semitism.

Perhaps the most representative book in recent years as regards the Nazi past is *Am Grünen Strand der Spree* (the title of the English translation is *All Through the Night*) by Hans Scholz. Published in Germany in late 1956, it was a first novel by a man with a distinguished background in art criticism, painting, and motion picture advertising. Despite its frank treatment of German war crimes, it became a best seller in the Federal Republic. The initial episode related in Juergen Wilm's diary revolves almost entirely about the scenes he witnessed in occupied Poland in 1941. Wilm, the main character of the novel, describes a camp in which a Storm Troop's officer was in charge of a group of Jewish women, starving, barely able to stand on their feet, yet forced to work steadily or risk fierce beating. Wilms, a small factory owner before army service, was not interested in politics. What he sees, therefore, is considered entirely in human terms. "What right has anyone to humiliate a human being to this extent?", he asks. "Who has the right to do this?"

He tries to photograph the women at work but is stopped. Ponders Wilm: "If we think we are justified in taking measures against the Jew, we shouldn't have to hide it. Or don't we think we're justified?" Later he is present while a young Jewish girl is cruelly thrashed, but he stands helplessly by. Wilm is horrified by the mass execution of Jews. He recognises his responsibility and guilt.

The book describes scenes also of Polish anti-Semitism that is equally virulent and of Jewish cruelties to fellow-Jews. But the author is at no time trying to say, "You see, others are doing it, too. We weren't any worse than they." In assessing guilt and blame Scholz is solely concerned about German responsibility.

"They will say, we didn't want Hitler"

Heinrich Boell has established his reputation as West Germany's foremost young writer. In *Billiard um Halb Zehn,* a curious mixture of realism and symbolic allusions, he makes a family re-live its experiences during the time when people partook of "the sacrament of the buffalo". It is only in this fashion that Boell refers to the Nazis.

With the exception of one of its members, the distinguished Fahmel family had not "partaken" and had suffered mental and physical anguish in the process. Through the indirectness of his approach the very skillful, Boell succeeds in resurrecting all the psychological and moral dilemmas of "the cult of the buffalo". Though this is by no means a purely political book, any more than Scholz's novel is, Boell reminds his fellow Germans of the toll in lives, in suffering, in crushed personalities which "the sacrament of the buffalo" had cost them. One of his chief "sacrament of the buffalo" leaders, however, ends up in a very prominent position in post-war Germany.

Wolfgang Ott's novel of submarine warfare, *Sharks and Little Fish*, is reminiscent in its style and mood of Mailer's *The Naked and the Dead*. His main ire is directed against the German clergy which failed in its avowed tasks during the Nazi regime. Highly placed military men are next on his list. He presents some Germans as incredulous at hearing of Nazi misdeeds against Jews, but does not condone their ignorance. "They will say, 'We didn't persecute the Jews' — and that is a typical German argument: in Germany when the bakeries are on fire, the butchers stand looking on, and vice-versa. And the captains of industry will say, 'We didn't want the war' — no, they only financed it and made good money doing so. And the pastors will say, 'We didn't want Hitler.' ... Who did want him, anyway? Can you tell me what these people ever did to oppose him?" This able, youthful writer vigorously blames the Germans for lack of moral involvement in the destiny of their nation.

Another very popular novel, Manfred Gregor's *Die Bruecke*, depicts the horrors of the Nazi war and its utter ruthlessness. It is the story of seven sixteen-year-old students who, in the last stage of the war, are dragged from their classrooms and forced into uniform. They are instructed by a Nazi general to defend a bridge. While their non-commissioned officers know well enough to escape, the romantic-heroic notions with which the boys were indoctrinated keep them glued to their station. All but one are killed. As Gregor unfolds the tragic tale of their short lives, he is primarily concerned with the human element. Yet, as in the other books, he uses the treatment of the Jew as a measure for non-Jewish behavior. The only boy who comes from a Nazi home and whose father was an SS leader is instrumental, together with his mother, in saving the Jewish family next door. As this boy matures he learns to resist his authoritarian father and ultimately to silence his authority in the home. Yet the presence of the father destroys the son's equilibrium in all human relations.

On the whole, recent German novels develop on a human, rather than on a political plane. Still, they are becoming more honest with respect to the Nazi past and thus may be rendering a service to the German people and to humanity at large. The fact that most of these novels are lacking in depth and have strong journalistic overtones may be fortunate from a publicist viewpoint. For if hate literature is permitted to reach large numbers of people, the counter-message must be forthcoming at once. The contemporary German novel may serve this purpose. At least for the present, it belies the likelihood of a Nazi return. In fact, it looms as a bulwark against such a return.

It Began on the 30th January [1]

A radio script by Wolfgang Jaeger, Ludwig Schubert, Heinrich von Tiedemann and Dethardt Fissen.

After the discussion on "Our Jewish Fellow-Citizens", the Juventa Verlag has now printed the radio script of the second instalment in the Norddeutsche Rundfunk's series: "Problems Which Affect Young People"; a coming-to-terms with National Socialism.

Although the rebuff, which all the right wing radical groups and parties have suffered at the democratic elections in the Federal Republic since 1945, clearly shows that the danger of the revival of the National Socialist way of thinking is smaller than ever among us; we are still suffering under the unhappy heritage of the Hitler period: our Fatherland is still divided, and the longer this partition remains, the less probability of an early reunification.

Consequently, this broadcast in the Third Program on the 30th of January 1958, 25 years after the assumption of power by Hitler, captivated for three hours the interest of large numbers, particularly of young people, who had never before heard the voices of Hitler and his leading party confederates. The extracts from the original recordings of speeches and gatherings of the brown-shirt rulers gave the listeners to the broadcast a more vivid impression than it is possible to give the readers of this book. However this cold print by virtue of its contents is of itself evidence enough even without volume or tone control.

---

[1] From *Es begann am 30. Januar*, Juventa-Verlag, Munich, 1958.

Our Jewish Fellow-Citizens [1]

A radio manuscript by Wolfgang Jaeger, Charlotte Rothweiler,
Ludwig Schubert, Heinrich von Tiedemann and Dethard Fissen

Complaints have been heard now for many years from young people, 1) that the teaching of history in the schools usually finishes with the First World War, although exceptions do prove the rule and there are teachers whose teaching continues as far as 1930; 2) that modern history ignores the past decade, without which no teaching of the present can be given; and 3) that the teaching in good citizenship usually consists only of "Discussion of the Basic Law".

As the present 15—25 year olds have had conscious experience of only the latter years of the past quarter century and have had little opportunity to acquaint themselves with the recent past, the Youth Program of the Norddeutsche Rundfunk has commenced a series in the Third Program under the title "Problems Which Affect Young People"; broadcasts which will give young listeners the bases whereby they themselves can come to terms with the problems of contemporary history.

Our thanks are due to the Juventa-Verlag which has decided to print these scripts[2]) and now presents the first broadcast in this series "Our Jewish Fellow-Citizens".

The subjects dealt with here are: The persecution of our Jewish fellow-citizens during the Hitler period, the restitution with its problems, the relations between the Federal Republic and Israel, anti-Semitism and the attitude of young people of today to these questions about which many know less than about the Punic Wars or the Peace of Tilsit.

No one can say exactly today whether it was 4 or 6 million who fell victim to the Hitlerite racial insanity, who were murdered, gassed, burned, shot, beaten to death or who did not survive the inhuman treatment at the concentration camp. The immeasurable extent of the suffering is so impossible for the individual to imagine that many of the older generation have wiped these facts from their memories. The younger generation however simply cannot comprehend what happened then as they do not believe that their own parents could have sponsored such a regime or even only have tolerated it.

We have divided this investigation into our relationship with our Jewish fellow-citizens into four chapters: "The Federal Republic and Israel" — "Fate and Guilt" — "Homeland and Statelessness". But we have to begin with the chapter: "Persecution and Restitution".

---

[1]) From *Unsere juedischen Mitbuerger*, Juventa-Verlag, Munich, 1958.

The Whole of that Ghastly Era Revealed Inside Two Hours

"Juergen Wilm's Diary" televised[1]

By Walter Guenzel

Anyone who, in the fifteen post-war years, has managed to avoid settling his account with our recent past, had one of its darkest chapters served up to him in his own home on television last Tuesday evening. The bill of reckoning was presented on the screen before the eyes of the German viewer to whom it was addressed, in order to bring home to him what the world has chalked up against us, and what we ourselves must do in order to make sure that nothing like that can ever happen again.

Fritz Umgelter has filmed the novel Am grünen Strand der Spree, by Hans Scholz, for the Cologne Studio of the North-West German Broadcasting Association. The first of the five parts into which the whole is divided did not mince matters: it came as a shock to millions of people in Germany and neighboring Austria.

Polish children are playing at "shooting" Jews. Two of them must wear the Star of Juda on their breasts while the others fire at them, "Bang! Bang!", with wooden rifles. The children have taken the game and its rules from reality — a reality which the Germans brought to their country.

Or again, Polish children are seen standing close to a mobile canteen. There will be a helping of food left for them. But to them it is the most natural thing in the world that the little ragged Jewish boy in his ridiculously large and dilapidated shoes should stand aside and not make the slightest attempt to obtain even some left-overs. So natural, because the occupying army acts that way, and has taught them by example to do the same.

Who is that being shot dead in the ten-by-six meter pit by the Latvian "civilian volunteers" at a signal from an SS leader? That never-ending line of Jews, all those old people, men, women, children — or are those bullets in reality lashing our consciences, so long quieted and lulled to sleep?

Does that sight — hell let loose on a 43 centimeter screen — the sight of those people lining up to be shot — oppress the mind of the German viewer?

Curse of Yesterday

During that transmission the mark of Cain became visible, that mark which we Germans all bear in the eyes of the world, no matter whether we were involved or not. It also became clear that we can only get rid of that mark of Cain if we have full knowledge of the manner and substance of what went on in Poland, Russia, and elsewhere. For only if we know this, and meditate on it, can we understand the feelings of other nations towards us.

Seen in this light, this program was an eminently political act, just as, of course, Scholz's novel is a profoundly political work. Umgelter, as script-writer and producer, has presented us with a bill of reckoning from the past, with a frankness of statement rarely encountered.

---

[1] From Die Welt, 24 March 1960.

This bill, drawn up at home, is at long last an answer to the ceaseless hail of accusations from abroad which assert that we have not the courage to take stock of our curse-laden past. It is a more effective answer than the recent Polish and Czechoslovakian publications, which all too clearly reflect topical political intentions. Umgelter's types ring true, and so does his dialogue: there are no stereotyped monsters.

On Tuesday evening, millions of Germans were Lance-Corporal Juergen Wilms, incapable of doing anything to stem the tide of madness; who turned away screaming from that pit of massacre and pursued by a hail of bullets ran back to his unit, where at least there were still human beings; rough fellows, mercenaries, if you like, — but at least human beings. For two hours, within his own four walls, the viewer was a German lance-corporal, but Juergen Wilms lived through it all for four years. Two hours' confrontation with crimes committed on Hitler's orders, without verbiage, without inflammatory accusations — but for that very reason, perhaps, all the more telling in its effect.

14 x the "Third Reich"

Greatest documentary begins on TV

By Heinz Stuckmann

Today — Friday, 21 October — the television screens of Germany are showing the start of their greatest program. "The Seizure of Power" (8:25—9:15 p.m.) will be the first installment of a serial transmission lasting all in all 700 minutes, to be shown in fourteen parts. The last part will be on the screen on 15 May 1961.

The second installment has been shown to the press in Cologne. It is a documentary entitled Die Gleichschaltung ("Toeing the Line"), and shows everyone with the same Fuehrer, the same badge, the same shirt; they all give the same greeting, all have the same flag; they all eat the same "one-pot" meal on the same day; they were all to have the same car, the Volkswagen, and the same wireless, the people's set. This was Gleichschaltung. We are shown the organs of totalitarianism: the National Socialist Teachers' Federation, the National Socialist Students' Federation, the National Socialist Women's Organization, Hitler Youth and German Labor Front, National Socialist Social Welfare for the Poor and the Sick, National Socialist Motorists' Corps for drivers, the National Socialist Strength through Joy, movement for leisure — the list could be extended indefinitely. Everything, just everything is brought into the scheme. We are shown the leaders of this total control: Reich Youth Leader, Reich Press Chief, Reich Farmers' Leader, Reich Women's Leader, Reich Labor Leader, Reich Radio Chief, Reich Students' Leader, Reich Bishop, Reich War Victims' Leader — and we are shown, on a Nazi party poster, the only man who stood aside. A photomontage

---

[1]) From Die Zeit, 21 October, 1960.

shows the endless brown columns on the march and on the side of the road a single "shabby" civilian, if I may lapse into the jargon of the period. The caption reads: "How long are you going to be before you join?" The man is indeed a very shabby civilian, so shabby that he really can do nothing else but stand alone. Decent people joined the marching columns...

The rapid sequences of this film make it extraordinarily effective. When in the end millions of men and women are to be seen standing in neat blocks on the so-called *Reichsparteitag* grounds in Nuremberg, when it is no longer possible to recognize the individuals, but only the blocks, when out in front we see a single man with his arm raised — we can recognize the *Fuehrer* — we get some sense of what the Third Reich meant.

This program was planned eighteen months ago by the broadcasting organizations in Cologne and Stuttgart and was produced in the course of the last twelve months. Archives everywhere, especially those in Rome, Paris, Stockholm, Copenhagen, London, Warsaw, and the USA, were ransacked. Five hundred thousand meters of film were looked at.

After seeing the first part we will be awaiting the rest with keen interest. Young people, in particular, will be able to gain some idea of what the Third Reich was.

The editing of the series has been done by Heinz Huber, Artur Mueller and Gerd Ruge, assisted by Hannes Hoff and Eberhard Leube; documentary material was prepared by Dr. Kurt Zentner, and scientific advisor was Dr. Waldemar Besson.

Escapism of Consience [1]

Documents on Hitler's "Final Solution of the Jewish Problem" with commentary on and survey of the political situation

By Robert Neumann

I will begin by making an admission. I was in England as a political refugee during the war and I knew the Nazis as a specialist, so to speak. They had burned my books and had then already killed several of my relatives and I was engaged at that time of which I wish to speak, for reasons which do not belong here, with the desperate struggle of the Jews in the Warsaw Ghetto. An organisation with which I was connected was successful — do not ask me how — in actually bringing one single man out of the midst of this massacre, out of the Ghetto and to England. He was a man whose name we know and respect, one of the leaders of the Jewish Social Democrats in Poland, and he came to me and told me everything — and I refused to make use of the gruesome details of his information. I should thus compromise our cause, I thought, the poor devil's nerves have gone. He is just a wreck; things like that don't exist, it simply isn't true.

And here is another story, and this happened to me yesterday as I spoke with a man from Hamburg on this subject. He is a Jew but he had Aryan papers and actually survived as a political refugee in several concentration camps. In the winter of 1943/44 a corporal of the German army was put in beside them because of some

[1] Excerpts from *Ausfluechte unseres Gewissens*, Verlag fuer Literatur und Zeitgeschehen GmbH, Hanover.

civil offence. He related with glee and with all the gruesome details of the massacre of the Jews in which he personally had taken part. And my Jewish friend, understandably particularly interested in Jewish affairs, and the otherwise unusually alert political prisoners of that camp near Hamburg, took him for a braggart, a pathological liar. They simply didn't believe him.

We shall therefore take this source of error rightly into consideration when we now embark jointly upon a journey to that dark spot on the map of our conscience, to the continent of our repressions, our conative refusal to become aware of how much we knew, you and me, of the atrocities of the Nazi period, of the extent to which we looked the other way, out of cowardice, because it was dangerous to watch, or simply out of the apathy of our hearts, and how much we were still aware of, in spite of our looking away. We, I say, — not the leading group of the Nazi party, not the guards at the annihilation camps, not the SS and SD, but you and I, the German abroad, the German in the German concentration camp, the German in the German hinterland, the German who stood as a simple infantryman at the front, feeling that he was defending his Fatherland. How much did we know? For it is necessary that we become clear about this in our own minds, particularly in these days and taking into account the load on our conscience which the still, fortunately, insignificant events of recent times mean for us. The attitude of "I know nothing about it" and "It wasn't I" is insufficient. We must acknowledge once and for all to what extent it was our fault, otherwise we shall be unable to surmount it. We are, after all, men, let us look the matter squarely in the face. How did it begin? Recently, before the affair in Cologne took place, a prominent journalist recalled in a German weekly magazine that 18 years previously to the day on which he was writing, the Jewish star was introduced — you know, a six-cornered, yellow star, the size of the palm of your hand, an on it was inscribed in black letters *"Jude"* — Jew! And the journalist said: whatever we didn't know then of the fate of the Jews in Germany, whatever we only heard for the first time in 1945, we knew that, we did, after all, see these young girls, old men, school-children with the yellow Jewish star. And we can talk others and ourselves into believing that we could have done nothing about it — we could have done this: gone to one of these unfortunates and said to him, "My dear man — or dear lady — I am ashamed that you must wear that, I have not the courage to resist it but you should know that you are not alone and that you are not despised." And to this the journalist, Thilo Koch is his name, asks: "How many of us did at least that?" ...

The broadcast of these scripts in the *Norddeutscher Rundfunk* (NDR) in January and February 1960 resulted in an avalanche of listeners' letters — the greatest in the history of the Hamburg broadcasting station.

Franz Reinholz, the head of department *"Wort"* ("Word") in NDR undertook to reply individually and in detail to these letters, some of which were very important, some very shocking. Then he was unable to carry on and I took over from him. Then I, too, couldn't carry on — and decided on a last broadcast as a reply to the hundreds to whom we couldn't write. This is it ...

Your letters, dear listeners, in response to the series of broadcasts on Escapism of Conscience are too numerous to reply to individually. That is why we are making this broadcast. But that doesn't matter, for many of these letters concern you all and therefore many of my replies will also concern you all.

And all the more so, as your questions, protests, amplification, expressions of approval, of disgust, of shock are divided into clearly defined groups. One group is almost completely absent — that of the unconvincible. I have, until the moment of recording this tape — on a journey — actually only received two anti-Semitic letters.

I should like to be able to read you very many more from this group of excellent letters: the highly politically alert one of a business man in Düsseldorf, for example, on the chronic, cancerous evil of anti-Semitism in Germany — but I can't, there are too many. One letter, six typewritten pages long, comes from Göttingen. The man was a Nazi and at the end of his letter, says to me: "I could have been that boy who wrote the letter to 'Der Stürmer' then of which you speak, and I could have been that SS man who shot the little Jewish girl in the feet. That I was not, was just my luck — nothing more." And beforehand, he writes how his life has changed, but — no, I will read you these bitter lines, for we are here to hear bitter things: "And I come home from captivity as a POW and can vote, and vote for the party — he names it, I do not name it — which speaks of peace and Europe. Instead —" now, instead, he sees compromised men sitting in the government, they are named in every second letter from my listeners, and the man from Göttingen speaks of them with a vehemence, before which my own words, which, after all, are spoken before a radio transmitter, pale considerably. He continues: "And I see teachers sitting in office who have poisoned minds and who are now poisoning the minds of the children of their victims. And if they are not in office they are drawing their pensions. And I see judges sitting in office who have warped the law and if they are not sitting in office, they are drawing higher pensions than the relatives of their victims." Can I sell this man the idea that justice is being done, that in spite of everything, justice is being done in Germany, although he doesn't see justice? But that is just the point, my friends. I say to you: to find the man who shot the Jewish child in the feet — that would be the point. To that I say to you: the point is more to see that the man in Göttingen doesn't become lost to us again. As far as he was concerned, it was wrong what I said to you about the temporary harmlessness of these compromised ones. Because of their very existence they make cynics of good men and destroy their confidence. And this republic will only live if the man in Göttingen can have confidence in it.

My reply to him and to the very many others who wrote to the broadcasting station or to me personally, as he did, is that he lost heart too quickly. He thinks only of that which would have happened to him — if he had written his letter to Herr Goebbels' broadcasting station — if he had written it — perhaps he still believes to a small extent in this young, bungling, German democracy which was certainly not been freed by a long shot from these shadows of the past, when I say to him that I am recommending the NDR today to give just him a chance in one form or another to give us his opinion at the microphone. Our laws are all right. But a democracy is only as strong as the people who believe in it. A democracy is only built up from below. Vote! That is your democratic weapon. You have no idea how high the value of an elector's vote stands at the right moment.

And now, finally, comes the group which is almost of more consequence to me than that about which I have just spoken. These are the youths, those who are certainly blameless — they weren't there at the time. Their teachers prior to 1945 have not told them the truth. After 1945 they were nearly all the same teachers and of these, the overwhelming majority have now told them nothing more whatever about the Third Reich. And now we have to discuss with these youths the guilt of the older generation? "Loyalty" one lady writes to me, "on which most parents have decided, is better than teaching. This would only lead once more to discord whereas we all long for a life together in peace."

For this lady I have two letters in my correspondence. Here is one: "When your broadcast was announced I called my 14-year old son to me and asked him to listen. He squirmed on hearing your documentation and finally asked, "Was it like that?" I said to him, "That was how it was, my boy — and I knew all about it." We talked for a long time and my son found excuses for me — perhaps the pistol which I gave a Jewish fellow-student — but I had to admit to him — it was too little, I was afraid, it was not enough."

You see, listeners, that is a man. He is a doctor in Dönberg, near Elberfeld. Take off your hat to him. He has given his son something to carry with him through life and his son will never forget that of him. And now listen to this letter from Essen: "So that was my people! My father, an officer, and my older half-brother at the front, they too were there. It is as though the scales have fallen from my eyes and a peculiar hate is kindling within me, a rebellion against people whom I must regard with obedience and respect. But am I entitled to despise people just because they are cowards? A multitude of questions — but should I insist on discussions which I know will only bring me reproofs and reminders of the superiority of my father as the head of the family? Can I, with this overwhelming guilt, still hope at all for forgiveness?" Thus writes this young man. He is 18 years old. And then he writes further, "I am ashamed to belong to my nation".

And these two letters are not only evidence against the lady who found it so much nicer if one kept one's mouth shut. With these two letters alone, the whole work of collecting the documents for my four broadcasts and the entire agony of heart of that collection — more than one sleepless night — would have been richly rewarded. I hope this young person is listening to me. In spite of the small alterations that I have made to cloak his indentity, he will know that it is he to whom I am speaking. He and all the other young people have obtained a reply to most of their questions from that which has been said in the meantime. Also the 17-year old apprentice in Hanover. Also the engineer in Wetzlar who was worrying about his apathy of heart towards a child with the Jewish star — worries very honoring for him, but still senseless worries, for he himself was then still only a child. And also that girl, Hiltrud is her name, in Wuppertal, who didn't give me her address, but I hope very much that at least this broadcast word will penetrate into her room. She writes that she is ashamed. She should not be ashamed. None of you should be ashamed. There is no general guilt. There is only a general responsibility to know how and to be steadfastly resolved to do things better when it is your turn.

"The Diary of Anne Frank" As a Book, Play, and Motion Picture

To date, about 700,000 copies of The Diary of Anne Frank have been sold in the Federal Republic. Among the pocket books offered in the Federal Republic during the last few years, it has had by far the largest circulation.

The Diary of Anne Frank as a play has been shown to about 1.75 million persons in 2,150 performances in the Federal Republic and West Berlin from 1956 through 1959 — the figures for the 1959—1960 theater season are not yet available. In a Berlin theater 137 performances were given to a capacity audience.

It can be estimated that between 4 and 4½ million persons saw *The Diary of Anne Frank* as a motion picture.

Mention should also be made of the film *Israel, the State of Hopes* which was produced under a contract from the Federal Press Office and has been shown for six consecutive years in German cinemas and on the German TV screens. The Federal Press Office estimates that about 20 million people saw this film in the Federal Republic and West Berlin.

As of February 1959, there were 2,577 genuine modern-type pocket books, i.e. disregarding similar older-type series, such as, e.g., the *Reclam* books, *Inselbuecherei*, etc. Within the nine years being examined there was only one pocket book of which more than 500,000 copies were sold. Gratifyingly enough, this book was *The Diary of Anne Frank*. Of 1,212 pockets books, about which I received very precise information from the publishers concerned, only 151 volumes, i.e. 12.4 %, reached a sales total of more than 100,000 copies. On the other hand, between 1950 and 1958, there were 114 volumes of standard bound books which surpassed the success mark of more than 500,000 copies or 100 editions. During the period 1950—1958, there were 115 books that could be classified as bestsellers and among them only one pocket book.

From *Die Situation des deutschen wissenschaftlichen Sortimentsbuchhandels 1960*, by Hans Ferdinand Schulz, printed in Boersenblatt fuer den Deutschen Buchhandel, No. 60, 1960, reprinted in *Die Welt*, of 15 August, 1960.

A German Study of Youth and War [1]

By Thomas Quinn Curtiss

Who was it — in a burst of enthusiasm after a Schubert concert — that voiced the half-truth: "There are only two sorts of music: German music and bad music". In addition to their abilities for musical composition and the manufacture of beer, the Germans may well be proud of another unusual talent. They can dramatize the tragedies of youth better then anyone else. From Goethe's *Werther* to Thomas Mann's *Mario* and from Stefan Zweig's *Burning Secret* and Wedekind's *Spring's Awakening* to Frank Thiess's *Farewell to Paradise*, they have rendered the stories of children and adolescents first perceiving life's short-comings with such haunting magic, with such a lack of sentimentality and with such a fund of unerring artistry, that the stories have become more than mere stories, being elevated by genius into symbols of the eternal human aches and sorrows.

This gift — and one often wonders how they came by it — has been on occasion extended to the Teutonic film, as witnessed in *Maedchen in Uniform*, in Murnau's *Four Devils* — from the Hermann Bang novel about circus *kinder* —

[1] From *New York Herald Tribune*, 19 April, 1960, Int. Ed.

and now, once again, in the extraordinary motion picture at the Vendome and Studio Publicis: *Die Bruecke, (The Bridge)*.

The scenario — like most good ones — is simple. A group of high-school boys between the ages of 14 and 16 are called up for military service as the Nazi armies crumble and retreat before the invading American troops during the last month of the late war.

Though conscripted, it is decided to spare them by assigning them to the relatively harmless duty of standing guard over the bridge of their home town. But they are armed, and when the altruistic plan misfires, they are thrown with awful fury into the furnace of combat and, standing their ground, are brutally slaughtered.

The scenes of war at close hand serve as the picture's climax. No harrowing detail is spared the spectator, though the over-all feel of authenticity would not suffer if the sight of a disemboweled American soldier writhing in his death throes or the view of a civilian being eaten alive by flames were eliminated.

Though in its last quarter *Die Bruecke* is an impressive example of fearless realism, it is in its earlier sections — in which the characters of the boys are drawn — that one detects the remarkable expressiveness of Bernhard Wicki's direction.

The scenes of the oppressive life at home in war time, the dull days in classroom while the sunshine outside calls, and the problems of the various individuals growing up — one boy hates his cowardly father, another is experiencing the first pangs of love, another has a touch of the yellow streak, another is a born leader — are so imaginatively done and so perfectly performed that they capture one at once.

By some oversight, the cast is not credited on the screen — perhaps because, for the most part, it is made up of unknown youngsters. But each performance — and those of the adults as well — deserves the highest praise. *Die Bruecke* is certainly the most powerful film to have come out of Germany since the war, a gripping and unforgettable piece of cinema, terrifying, compassionate and deeply moving.

The Young Generation Sees Hitler in a Documentary Film [1]

By Nikolas Benckiser

The Bonn correspondent of a large English newspaper reported to his readers how Germans are reacting to the documentary film *Mein Kampf*. What, especially, do the younger people say, who did not consciously experience the Third Reich? Understandably enough, most of them left the cinema silently and without chattering in the usual manner, about what they had just seen. However, among the few bits of conversation the observer could pick up, he heard the remark, "what a ridiculous person this man Hitler was, and how difficult it is to understand how he could win such influence." Finally, one is inclined to shout, finally, we are right back at the beginning: — the funny man with the moustache and the brutally serious look on his face; the awkward gestures; the silly uniform

---

[1] From the *Frankfurter Allgemeine Zeitung*, 9 August, 1960.

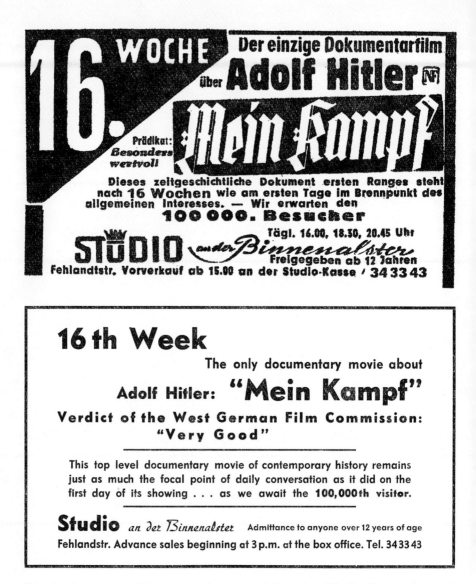

This advertisment appeared in *Die Welt*, Hamburg, on 1 November, 1960. The Film was shown until the end of the year. (Ed. note)

meant to cover up his physical clumsiness; the disgustingly hoarse way in which he shouted phrases, platitudes, or threats — this man is now seen as he actually was. In documentary pictures the younger generation, quite unprejudiced, sees him. They find what one cannot avoid finding, and what all of those who lived during that time could have found, when what are now only documents were the everyday hard facts of the years before 1933 and of the first years of the regime. And, necessarily, this question also comes up again, "how was it possible that this man could rise and control Germany?" "Weren't our fathers and mothers able to see correctly?", the younger people ask themselves in the cinema. The whole question of how Hitler gained control is one that continues to trouble the older people too. Every new document, refreshing the memory, brings up this question again and makes it still more impossible to give an answer. To the man who had a balanced mind, whose look was not clouded by misery, by nationalist delusion or by something else,—to him it must have been clear: he saw a ridiculous but repugnant figure. Sometimes, however, he began doubting his own eyes. When so many people seemed to see it differently, could it not be that he was seeing it wrongly, and that all the others were right? Well, if Hitler had been only a Tribune of the People, with all the seductive art that radiates from such persons, one could have unmasked him. However, just because he seemed so awkward, repugnant, and even ridiculous, and enchanted the people despite all that, must he not have had something which one did not notice? Did one just somehow miss the rhythm of the time? Or, as the Hugenbergs and the Papens thought, could one make use of this funny man anyway, since the people seemed to follow him? The documentary pictures, revealing the periods just before, and after 1933, now confirm how right those people were who did not allow themselves to doubt their first and incorrigible impression and judgment.

The question of how in fact everything was possible, remains in the end unanswered. However, it is significant that the young people see now what all should have noticed and realized at that time. The spirit of the demonic which drove Germany into the abyss did not lie in the funny man. There was nothing heroic about him; there is nothing to glorify now, and any desire to so glorify him will be lost by everyone who watches him in his last moments — (in the clips from the official motion pictures of those days). And that can be said too about the other parts of this documentary film, which is being shown under the title of the "Führer's" book, of which so many copies were sold and so few copies were actually read. The curse of ridicule which many a former opponent tried in vain to level upon Hitler, seems in spite of all belatedly to be finding its mark. Admittedly only after all of us, and particularly our fellow countrymen in the Soviet Zone, have had to carry upon our lives the curse of his truly inhuman seriousness.

"MEIN KAMPF" IN BERLIN[1]

By H. G. Sellenthin

The evening-filling documentary film Mein Kampf, by the German-Jewish emigrant Erwin Leiser from Sweden, which we praised as "very good" in our 5 August 1960 number, has now been shown in Berlin as well, and indeed in one of the largest motion picture theaters, the Titania-Palace in Steglitz.

A remarkable impression: both performances have been almost totally sold out every day, a result that not even Marlene Dietrich could achieve during her Berlin starring performance in the same theatre.

According to our observances, the visitors — among them strikingly many young people — received the film with deep emotion and left the theater in silence. There were only a few incidental remarks noticeable during the presentation. These appeared to direct themselves exclusively against the criminal position of the Nazi regime. In conversations before and after the presentation, we established that many pupils and also numerous students went to this film in order finally to become

---

[1]) From *Allgemeine Wochenzeitung der Juden in Deutschland*, 12 August 1960.

documentarily informed about the occurrences of the Hitler period, which they had not experienced themselves or had only experienced as small children.

Several young people voiced the opinion that they found it incomprehensible that such a clearly pied-piper-type of demagogue such as Hitler, was met by such a degree of trust.

A student said to me very thoughtfully after the film: "I do not believe that one can only speak of a 'seduction' of the people in Germany. For precisely this film has indeed shown that thousands, tens of thousands, and millions of people, many also best informed about the situation, continuously acclaimed the leaders of this empire and were willing to serve them right up until the time of the collapse. This shocking impression is awakened in this film. Hitler could only have had such a success because he quite evidently appealed to and awoke the expectations that the majority of the Germans had of life. With these serious facts, we must confront ourselves, in order to avoid a new evil!"

Many of the visitors, for the first time in their lives, saw Ghetto and concentration camp photographs of inhuman proportions. Although there were, over the past years, several similar films (such as *Night and Fog*), they had not yet seen them and were enticed by the theme, Hitler's Life — *Mein Kampf*. That is, therefore, how they also came to see these documents about the humiliation and annihilation of people.

A quite particular impression was called forth in Berlin by the scenes taken from the Peoples Court of Justice, where the quiet heroism of the victims of the screaming perversion of Freisler and his assassins were confronted in a historical portrayal. Again and again the film also wakened abhorrence, in as much as little Jewish children were at the complete mercy of, and subject to, complete neglect and destruction of their existence.

The film had a far-reaching effect in Berlin and was to be shown in all schools and universities. As the first official positive expression, the press service of the governnent of Berlin stated that the Film Critics Commission for Youth and School recommends the film, *Mein Kampf*, for fifteen years of age and on. The Voluntary Self-Control of the film industry even held it as recommendable for young people of twelve years of age and on.

It is to be hoped that this documentary film, though certainly a quite definite part of the population in Berlin will also again avoid it, will contribute to a far-reaching change of mind, as far as this has not yet been achieved.

Questions Answered[1]

The main box-office attraction in West Germany last week was a film that froze its packed audiences to stiff attention and sent them from the theater in silence with eyes averted. Compiled by a German-born Swedish intellectual named Erwin Leiser, it is a documentary that traces with graphic intensity the rise and collapse of the Third Reich. Its title: *Mein Kampf*.

At first, German audiences watch with embarrassed distaste, now snickering at the wild gesticulations of the early Hitler, now clearing throats in unison as Rudolf Hess shouts: "My *Fuehrer*, you are Germany. When you judge, the people judge." The shock comes with 1942, as the film moves on to footage shot by SS cameramen in the Warsaw ghetto and found by Leiser in mislabeled cans in East German archives (the Red government let him buy the ten reels for $8 a meter).

[1]) From *Time*, 5 September 1960, Atlantic Ed.

Originally intended by the Nazis for "instructional purposes" but shelved for fear they might provoke sympathy for the Jews, the SS shots show German soldiers looking on with pleasure as Jews with swollen knees and fleshless legs drop to the ground and die. Children lie dying on filthy cots. Then, as heads in the audience lower, the camera pans along a trundling line of corpse-filled push carts to the edge of a lime pit, where the bodies are sent sprawling down a chute.

A Jewish emigrant to Sweden, 37-year-old yournalist-TV Producer Leiser made the film to answer "the questions of German young people" from whom, in his opinion, much has been veiled by the "unsatisfactory, evasive, shamefaced answers of parents and teachers". In eight weeks, nearly half a million people have seen *Mein Kampf* in West Germany. (It is also set for distribution in East Germany.) Audiences, in the main, consist of people under 40, and the popularity of the film tends to contradict the notion that West Germans are unwilling to concern themselves with the facts of the Hitler era.

Exhibiton on the History and Persecution of the German Jews

Documents of a Horrible Past[1]

Outdoors the fountains murmur; happily chattering people — among them many Easter tourists from West Germany — enjoy the first summer warmth and admire the bold construction of the Congress Hall in Berlin's Tiergarten Park. Inside, however, all laughter and talking stops suddenly. Silence, shudders, and shame paralyze the visitors. *Die Vergangenheit mahnt* (The Past exhorts) is the motto written in big letters over an exhibition which the Berlin section of the International League for Human Rights shows in the Congress Hall. The past does not only exhort, it cries in silent lamentation from the super-sized photographs of hunted people, of piles of bones and starved skeletons, from businesslike official correspondence of the SS concerning mass extermination, or from the wise heads of Jewish poets, scientists, musicians who have made contributions to German culture for centuries.

In 1945, when the truth came over us, most of the Germans could say in a convincing manner: We did not know it, we had no idea about it. At present, the facts are known — or, at least ought to be known. This exhibition proves, however, that we still do know nothing, or much too little, since our imagination does not suffice to convert figures, newspaper articles or books into a lively picture of the horror. This show, however, breathes and lives, it gets under the skin. There is the big photograph of a cremation furnace, the doors opened like a greedy gullet. Those had been human beings who were pushed into this gullet; Germans, Poles, Russians, Frenchmen, Greeks, or Czechs; men, women, children who were first murdered in gas chambers or shot in the neck — only because they were Jews. Hundreds, tens of thousands, hundreds of thousands — almost six million people.

---

[1] From *Deutsche Zeitung*, 21 April 1960.

Slides are shown of the destruction of the ghetto in Warsaw. They were taken by the SS and still carry the original captions given these pictures by the butchers of men. "Bandits Defend Themselves with Arms" is one caption — whereas the picture shows women and children leaving a burning house with their hands raised. Dreadful horror is reflected in their eyes. The following excerpt is taken from an original teletype message sent by an SS headquarters on the destruction of the ghetto in Cracow: "180 Jews, bandits, and subhuman beings were destroyed. Total of the Jews registered and officially destroyed: 56,065". They talked about "subhuman beings" — while next to it there is a super-sized photograph with the caption: "The Master Race". This picture shows the faces — one could really only call them masks — of female concentration camp guards, brutal, mean, sadistic in every trait, but Nordic-blond. The drawing done by a child at the Theresienstadt Camp for Jews looks almost cheerful: barracks, toilets, the issuance of food — all in one picture. The camp was the only world of this unidentified child, a world which, very likely, he did not leave alive.

On one wall there is a big picture of Hitler. Not one of those showing the grimace of a hysterically screaming man, such as were not permitted to be shown during the Third Reich, but an absolutely normal picture of Hitler behind a lectern. Underneath the picture there are two telephone receivers, just as there are under a picture showing Hermann Goering in the defendant's bench in Nuremberg. The visitors to the exhibition wait patiently until a telephone receiver is free. They then listen to a few sentences spoken by the megalomaniac dictator, to part of a resounding speech by Goering, and a bit later to the statements of the same man before the Nuremberg Tribunal when he claimed not to have known anything nor to have given any orders. In between there are eye-witness' accounts of the "Crystal Night" when the synagogues in Germany were set afire, when Jewish retail stores were demolished, allegedly by the "boiling minds of the people". In fact, however, original documents show that the destruction was carried out under central orders given by the SA and SS headquarters.

This impressive exhibition does not only show the horrors of the Hitler regime but it also describes the history of Jewry from Moses to the Jewish settlements in Central Europe, from the persecution of Jews in former times — not costing lives — to the Emancipation in the 19th century which was eventually followed by the "factories of death" of the Hitler era, a movement "from error to crime".

A whole wall of the exhibition hall is filled with the portraits of 62 brilliant personalities, a wall honoring the "Jewish contributions to Culture in Germany and to the German Language". There are the portraits of Max Liebermann and Heinrich Heine, Einstein and Mendelssohn-Bartholdy, Karl Marx and Friedrich Gundolf, Franz Kafka, Hugo von Hofmannsthal, Jacques Offenbach... 62 names only from a list which can be prolonged at will. In the short, but instructive guide through the exhibition it is said: "For the intellectual development of man it does not matter whether its permanent values, as well as its non-permanent values, are created by people with a white or black skin, by the descendents of Jews, Christians, or Moslems. The experience of errors and crimes resulting from group and racial hatred ought to be a reminder for ever that the thesis of the equality of man regardless of race, religion, social background or political creed is not an abstract moral commandment, but a vital necessity for a humane world."

A Shocking Exhibition in the Congress Hall[1])

A truly shocking exhibition, "The Past Admonishes" — the history of the Jews and their persecution in the Third Reich — was opened in the Congress Hall yesterday. Photographic and written documents, unknown until now, which offer an unadorned insight into the German past, are for the first time to be publicly accessible.

The exhibition brings clarity and truth about our most recent past which must not be allowed to be covered up by passing over it in silence, but can only be purified and overcome by a laying bare and acknowledgement. Most highly effective is the make-up of the exbitition.

There are sixty-two portraits of famous Jews, men and women who, inextinguishable, belong to the German spirit, from Moses Mendelssohn to Leo Baeck. In sharpest contrast, thereto, is the extermination camp of Auschwitz in close-up.

The exhibition moves in this span: from the departure of the Jewish people out of Egypt, from their persecution in the Middle Ages until their terrible extermination in the Third Reich.

It is a shocking view, most shocking in the pictures of children. Tape-recordings, to be heard over telephones, report upon the history of National Socialism, about a visit to Auschwitz, and about a celebration hour at Bergen-Belsen.

Everyone is urged to visit the exhibition, naturally the youth in particular. To mobilize consciences and to move and disquiet hearts is its task, not in the service of any questionable propaganda whatsoever, but of the lucid truth.

---

[1]) From *Berliner Stimme*, 9 April 1960.

Youth Reflects[1]

For almost six weeks the exhibition "The Past Admonishes", which was arranged by the League of Human Rights, was to be seen in the Charlottenburg Town Hall. This exhibition, after having previously been shown for several weeks in the Congress Hall, must be booked as a great success. Next to adults, the pupils also stated their interest. In order to draw in the history lessons of the past — namely, the years 1933—1945 — in the upper classes, these students were, through the stimulation of the Senate for Public Education, led to the exhibition by their teachers. In thirty-eight days, it was visited by over three-hundred school classes! The District Office of Charlottenburg had "schooled" the schools, for us, the persecuted of the Nazi regime, a noteworthy fact. What must be especially emphasized, however, is the fact that the attempt succeeded in leading to a discussion with the pupils in order to learn their reactions in the question and answer period. It must be stated in advance that these conversations were led with the agreement of the teachers. They naturally only took place after the exhibition and a number of films had been viewed. There were high points and low points, not only among the pupils, but also among the teachers. One could immediately recognize if this

---

[1]) From *Die Mahnung*, the Central Organ of the Democratic Resistance Fighters and Persecuted Organizations of the Federal Republic of Germany, 17 July 1960.

theme had been touched upon in the classroom by the teacher or — as a red-hot iron — had not been touched. On behalf of the truth, it should not be passed over in silence that some teachers declined a discussion. There were those who allowed their students to go through the rooms alone, and others who thoroughly examined and discussed every picture. It was the pupils of the latter, among whom one could feel not only an interest but a frank understanding of the difficult theme. Perhaps it was somewhat too much that teachers took their twelve and thirteen-year-old pupils to the film presentation of *Night and Fog*. That may well have been an exorbitant demand. It was exactly the older pupils who were deeply impressed by this type of gruesome reality. They were the ones who, in the following discussion, showed the greatest interest and repeatedly asked questions. Which decisive impressions the students took home with them, however, should be evidenced by the entries which they wrote in the guest book. A few examples thereof:

I will always follow only my conscience. The exhibition was for me very instructive.

Thomas R., pupil

More of such exhibitions, which admonish us about the past, should be shown so that such a wrong will never occur again.

Karl St., pupil

I agree with the statement above.

Erika H., pupil

Many exhibitions of a similar nature are being shown at the present time, but this one is the best. As a youth, one stands shocked before these pictures of the past! Never again such a thing.

Christa M., pupil

May the terrible sorrows of the victims be a constant admonition. Out of love for the dead, render love to the living!

Hans Dieter K., pupil, Cologne

Must one first come to Berlin in order to see an exhibition of such kind!? Must first the events of the "Holy Night"*) have happened? We demand that the exhibition be shown in every city of the Federal Republic in order that the crime of the Nazi regime will finally be placed before everyone's eyes.

Helge Sch., pupil
Wermelskirchen/Rheinland

---

*) An allusion to the desecration of the Cologne synagogue on Christmas Eve, 1959.

V   Germany and the Germans

Cultural Reconstruction *

(1943)

By Kurt Lewin

Building a world of peace which will be worth at least the name "better than be-fore" includes many problems: political, economic, and cultural. Each of them is loaded with difficulties. Yet all of them have to be considered together and attack-ed together as interdependent aspects of one dynamic field if any successful step forward is to be achieved.

The implications of the cultural aspect seem to be particularly unclear. Has the culture of the German, the Japanese, the British, or Chinese anything to do with their likelihood or unlikelihood of going to war as an aggressor or fighting in a certain way when hard pressed? Are these cultural differences of any importance for intercultural co-operation?

The discussion of this question seems to have been retarded by philosophical and political sentiments. The difference between peoples has either been overemphasiz-ed and treated as innate racial characteristics, or underemphasized and treated as unessential, frequently by misinterpreting the democratic doctrine of equal rights of men. A realistic, scientific approach will have to consider differences between modern cultures as facts of the same nature as differences between "primitive" cultures. Such a scientific approach will refuse to consider cultural characteristics unalterable in principle. Instead, it will ask in an empirical fashion: How easily and with what methods can a certain degree of cultural change be accomplished and how permanent does such a change promise to be?

Definite answers to such questions can be supplied only by an "experimental cultural anthropology" which will study cultural changes systematically under spe-cially created conditions. Unfortunately, cultural anthropology is still in its "des-criptive" stage; it has its hands full with finding methods of observing and describ-ing modern cultures adequately and reliably. There have been but inklings of experiments about how cultures can actively be changed in a desired direction. Nevertheless, we will have to try to do the best we can.

A certain amount of cultural reconstruction will be necessary in most countries after the war; these countries will have to switch from a wartime to a peacetime "culture". Most nations will have to be able to do this without help from the out-side. This shift from wartime to peacetime culture should be less difficult than it might appear in view of the present hatred, particularly if peace should bring about a decent political world organization. After the last war sizable proportions of the population in most countries turned quickly to a radical pacifism. This ex-perience should warn us not to confuse the violence of a cultural sentiment with

---

*) From *Resolving Social Conflicts, Selected Papers on Group Dynamics.* New York: Harper & Brothers, 1948.

its depths and permanency. In this country, the let-down after the last war quickly turned into isolationism, thus setting the stage for this war. (The danger of a similar reaction after this war is again probably greater than that of a permanent imperialistic militarism in this country.) Even in Germany right after the last war the proportion of the population which turned to pacifism was probably larger than the group which started immediately to build for revenge and as a first step invented the *Dolchstosslegende*. (The home front was said to have stabbed the army in the back; in this way the prestige of the German army was maintained.)

The fact that superficial although violent cultural sentiments might change quickly in a nation does not, however, disprove those historians who claim that nothing can be changed so little as the deeper cultural characteristics of a people. It is these deeper cultural traits which we have to consider when thinking of the cultural aspects of permanent peace. In Germany, in spite of the pacifistic sentiment after the First World War and long before Hitler, every child was again playing war with toy soldiers. And soon, in line with long-standing tradition, militarists were again winning out. On the other hand, Mussolini has tried for more than a decade to build up in the Italians those soldierly characteristics which were obviously lacking in the First World War. In spite of a very thorough attempt which reached every age level down to early childhood he seems to have failed to alter these cultural characteristics. Similarly, certain peculiarities of the Russian or the British character seem to change very little. That these permanent characteristics are cultural rather than racial is shown by the fact that children taken from one country to the other will quickly and thoroughly adopt the characteristics of the people in the new country.

A democratic world order does not require or even favor cultural uniformity all over the world. The parallel to democratic freedom for the individual is cultural pluralism for groups. But any democratic society has to safeguard against misuse of individual freedom by the gangster or — politically speaking — the "intolerant." Without establishing to some degree the principle of tolerance, of equality of rights, in every culture the "intolerant" culture will always be endangering a democratic world organization. Intolerance against intolerant cultures is therefore a prerequisite to any organization of permanent peace.

To encourage change toward democracy a change of values in a vast realm would have to be accomplished. This change would include, for instance, increased emphasis on human values as against superhuman values, such as the state, politics, science. It would emphasize what the German "Iron Chancellor" Bismarck called far back in 1880 *Civilcourage* (morale courage of the civilians) and what he deplored as lacking in the German character (as against the courage and the blind obedience of the soldier). It would stress the value of manipulating difficulties rather than complaining about them. It would stress education for independence rather than for obedience.

In any attempt to influence cultural patterns it cannot be emphasized too much that the problem of changing single persons or small groups which are uprooted and transplanted into a new cultural background is rather different from the problem of changing the culture of a compact group remaining on native soil. The technique which seems to offer itself as the natural means to reach such a compact group for the purpose of changing the cultural backgrounds is "propaganda" in its various forms, such as radio, newspaper, etc.

Young Germans From Territories Beyond the Oder-Neisse-line Receiving Special Instruction to Enable Them to Attend West-German Schools Photo: dpa

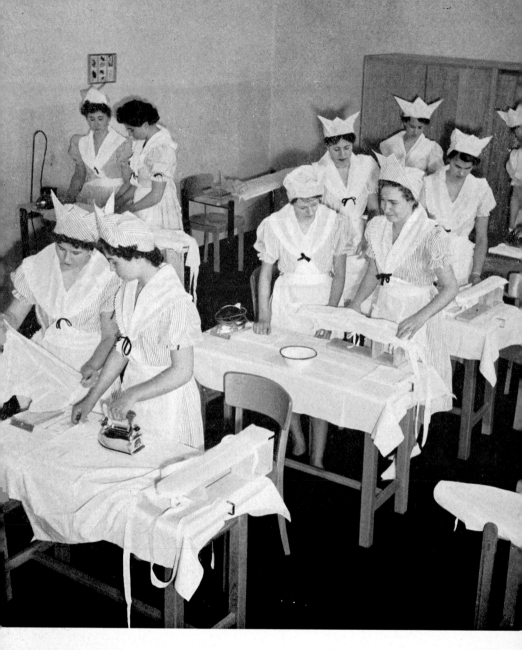

A Typical Scene at a Vocational School

Photo: dpa

However, even if such propaganda from outside or inside the country were success-ful it would not be likely to do much more than change the "verbal sentiments" of a people. When speaking about "democracy" the German is likely to mean in-dividualistic freedom. If an American defines democracy he too very frequently stresses individualistic freedom and forgets that leadership is fully as important in a democracy as in an autocracy. But the American happens to live in a country where the efficiency of the process of group decisions is relatively highly developed, at least in small groups, and where democratic leadership is thoroughly accepted as a cultural pattern and taught in practice to children in school. One cannot expect people living in a country without such traditions to understand a term like demo-cracy in any other way than in those conceptual dimensions in which they are accustomed to think. One cannot expect the member of a different culture to accept a never-experienced cultural pattern which even the people who have experienced that pattern are seldom able to describe adequately. It has been one of the trag-edies of the German Republic that the democratically minded people who were in power immediately after the war confused democracy with "being unpolitical" and under this slogan permitted the old reactionaries to keep their official positions as "experts". It was a tragedy that they did not know that "intolerance against the intolerant" is as essential for maintaining and particularly for establishing a demo-cracy as "tolerance for the tolerant"; above all, it was a tragedy that they did not know that strong leadership and an efficient positive use of the political power by the majority is an essential aspect of democracy. Instead, Germany congratulated herself on having "the freest Constitution in the world" because technically even a small minority gets its proportional representation in the parliament. Actually, this set-up led to dozens of political parties and to the permanent domination of the majority by a minority group in the center.

A second main obstacle against changing cultures is the fact that a pattern like democracy is not limited to political problems but is interwoven with every aspect of the culture. How the mother handles her child of one, two, or three years of age; how business is conducted; what group has status; how status differences are react-ed to — all of these habitudes are essential elements of the cultural pattern. Every major change, therefore, has to be carried through against such a highly interwoven background. It cannot be limited to a change in officially recognized values; it has to be a change in actual group life.

While it is correct that change of values will finally lead to a change of social conduct, it is equally correct that changes of action patterns and of actual group life will change cultural values. This indirect change of cultural values probably reaches deeper and is more permanent than direct changes of values by pro-paganda.

Excerpts from "The Special Case of Germany"[1] (1943)

Before discussing the problems of how a change might be accomplished, the ob-jective should be clear. This objective cannot for Germany be a copy of the English or the American way of living. Whatever occurs, the resulting culture will be some-thing specifically German. It will show the traces of its history and of the present

---

[1] Kurt Lewin, *Resolving Social Conflicts*, Selected Papers on Group Dynamics. New York: Harper & Brothers, 1948.

extreme experiences of war and Nazism. This would hold true even if the new German culture should become thoroughly democratic.

There is one more reason to strive for a "democratic German" culture rather than an American or English culture. The limitation of the democratic principle of tolerance toward others is defined by the maxim of "democratic intolerance toward intolerance". This right and duty to intolerance is very important if democracy is to live anywhere on this globe. This principle does not, however, demand conformity; it limits our rightful interest to certain minimum requirements which are probably not too different from the minimum requirements for international peace.

Cultural Changes of Individuals and Nations

Even formulated in this way, a change toward democratic German culture obviously includes very difficult problems.

There is no question but that the culture of individuals or small groups can be changed deeply in a relatively short time. A child transplanted from Germany or Japan to America will, as a rule, become thoroughly Americanized. Even grown-ups who are transplanted to a different culture may acquire the new culture to a high degree, and much can be done toward this end through proper education. Experiments with both children and adults prove that the social atmosphere of groups can be changed profoundly by introducing different forms of leadership. Experiments in leadership training have shown that it is even possible under certain circumstances to transform highly autocratic leaders of long standing within a short time into efficient democratic leaders.

All of these changes, however, are changes of individuals or small groups in a direction which is in line with some aspects of the general cultural setting in which these individuals or groups live. To change the culture of a whole nation is quite a different undertaking. The greater numbers involved present merely one of the difficulties. Even more important are certain dynamic relations between the various aspects of the culture of a nation — such as its education, mores, political behavior, religious outlook — which interact in a way that tends to bend any deviation from the established culture back to the same old stream.

There is no space here to discuss these dynamics in detail. I might merely remind the reader that the difference, for instance, between the American and the German culture is discernible more or less in every part of their respective cultural lives: in the way the mother treats a two- or three-year-old child, what the father talks about at the dinner table, how the worker talks to his foreman or the student to the professor, how the visitor behaves toward grown-ups and children, how the cookbooks are written, how opposing lawyers deal with each other after the court session, what type of photograph the candidate for political office uses for propaganda, and what religion means to a person in any denomination. A cultural change in regard to a specific item will have to be able to stand up against the weight of the thousand and one items of the rest of the culture which tend to turn the conduct back to its old pattern. As someone has put it, "Cultures are pretty watertight".

We may conclude: To be stable, a cultural change has to penetrate more or less into all aspects of a nation's life. The change must, in short, be a change in the "cultural atmosphere", not merely a change of single items.

The Heart of the German Problem

It seems to follow, then, that the basic requirement of a change in German culture toward democracy is a change in the role of the leaders and of the followers.

That German citizens have never known how to criticize their bosses has frequently been observed. In German culture "loyalty" is typically identified with "obedience". They do not see any other alternative to efficient group organization based on obedience but an atmosphere of *laissez faire* and inefficiency based on individualistic freedom. The Hitler regime has done everything to strengthen this view and to identify democracy with decadent inefficient lawlessness. After the last war the liberal German newspapers discussed the meaning of democratic leadership and democratic discipline in an attempt to educate the public away from the alternative of blind obedience or respectlessness and lack of responsibility. The English idea of "His Majesty's loyal opposition" was used to point out the positive functions and the responsibilities which the opposition parties have in a parliamentary system. To the German reader these articles sounded strangely unreal and unbelievable. They seemed as contrary to the German concept of human nature as the idea of fair play, a concept utterly strange to German culture.

Such articles, obviously, had little influence on the political action of the Germans; I doubt whether the results would have been better if they had been multiplied a hundredfold. To understand what is being talked about the individual has to have a basis in experience — as a child in a student council, in the hundred and one associations of everyday life; he has to have some taste of what democratic leadership and the democratic responsibility of the follower mean. No lecture can substitute for these first-hand experiences.

Only through practical experience can one learn that peculiar democratic combination of conduct which includes responsibility toward the group, ability to recognize differences of opinion without considering the other person a criminal, and readiness to accept criticism in a matter of fact way while offering criticism with sensitivity for the other person's feeling. The attempt to change one element alone will merely lead to a situation where the weight of the other elements will reestablish the previous total pattern.

Ways of Changing German Culture

Mere propaganda, and particularly propaganda from the outside, will not change German culture. If a sufficiently deep and permanent change is to be accomplished, the individual will have to be approached in his capacity as a member of groups. It is as a member of a group that the individual is most pliable. At the same time such a group approach can better influence relatively deeply large masses than either the individual approach or the mass approach through propaganda.

It is natural to think of the school system — from the nursery school to the university — as an organization through which the culture of a nation can be changed. Yet one should be clear about its limitations. The idea, for example, of using some 100,000 foreign teachers or former refugees seems to have been abandoned, because it would lead to nothing but a strong negative reaction. It has been suggested, again, that the Allies be content with securing certain minimum requirements concerning textbooks; that, of course, would not contribute much toward changing German culture.

I think one should neither under- nor over-rate the importance of the educational system. It is, of course, very important for long-range planning. Yet the atmosphere in education is but a mirror and an expression of the culture of the country; it changes with every change of its general social atmosphere — as the history of German education between 1918 and 1933 shows strikingly enough. Education of children, therefore, is in the beginning less important than a change in leadership.

Change in culture requires the change of leadership forms in every walk of life. At the start, particularly important is leadership in those social areas which are fundamental from the point of view of power. Ideology and power problems are closely linked. The shift of political power to other sections of the population and the change in leadership techniques in the fields of politics, law, law enforcement, and economics are, therefore, fundamental. Only as a part of such a political change can a cultural change toward democracy occur and survive.

To my mind, not too much can be expected from an exchange of potential leaders between countries, although such an undertaking is laudable. There is a definite limit to what a person can learn in the unrealistic setting of being a guest, outside of the particular atmosphere in which he will have to work. Much more promising would be a training "on the job". The reconstruction after the war should provide ample possibilities of collaboration for Germans and non-Germans, opportunities which could well be used for the training or retraining of youthful German leaders. This training does not need to bear the stigma of "education", because a job is to be done, a job of cooperation in the interest of Germany. It could be demonstrated there and experienced firsthand that "democracy works better". If strategically managed, such training on the job of leaders and trainers of leaders might well reach into every aspect of community leadership. It might help to set in motion a process of self-re-education.

The ideas discussed herein seem to point to a procedure which offers at least some realistic hope of success. Whether or not an attempt along this line can be made, and how successful it would be, depends on the world situation. Moses led Israel through the desert for forty years, until the generation that had lived as slaves might die, and the rest learned to live as free people. Perhaps there are still no faster or better methods for the permanent cultural re-education of a nation.

The Nature of Political Education [1]

by Arnold Bergstraesser

The present-day world situation and the course of history in our century force us to base our political thinking more scientifically than we have ever before. In this endeavor we could fall back upon older traditions which arose in Germany after the Middle Ages, and were especially prevalent in the eighteenth and the beginning of the nineteenth century. Germany has given the world, and above all America,

[1] From *Schicksalsfragen der Gegenwart*, Max Niemeyer Verlag, Tuebingen, 1957.

much stimulation toward a scientifically founded basis of political thinking. But on its part, Germany has neglected many of these same intellectual premises of political behavior which it should re-introduce. Political education is a necessity in our time, but in Germany it is only beginning to take effect.

Today we Germans are uncertain in a quarter where, in a decisive moment, we would need nothing more than certainty, since we find ourselves located on the border, as it were, of the Western world. One segment of our people lives under a system which is partly characterized by the fact that it is foreign controlled and also in part that a theory of society which contradicts our own prevails there.

German is an experimental station today where the tensions of the world are directly manifested. In such a situation we need clear views and a conscious line of behavior that is valid. Political instruction should be the task of education in these respects. Our view of what politics should be is often less determined by the political facts than by preconceived opinions. It has often been my experience that many in our State suffer from illusions and, as opposed to illusions, stumble over the facts and find themselves relatively quickly in some form of contrition, desparation or isolation and rather quickly afterwards pursue yet another illusion.

If we adopt a well-founded knowledge of political matters and of the social premises of political action and lead our larger numbers of our nation into a composed, masculine, and healthy way of political thinking, then this fluctuation from illusion to illusion would disappear and we would find it easier to make our political measures adequate for the political health of the individual, the masses, and their smaller and larger groups.

This achievement could result in the attainment of certainty, since democratic criticism and party politics, which have their justification under present conditions not in the German people only but in mankind, nevertheless turn toward a common goal — not toward an artificial unity, but toward a practical concern for the problem of existence and the nature of this very problem. I believe that our mutually binding principles with regard to the nature of politics can be so formulated that we all can consider the state to be an institution whose ultimate determination should be the concern for the healthy being and condition of human existence. This concern for the problem of existence is a common point of departure for the Christian teaching in both its Catholic and Protestant form in that it deals with worldly things. The concern for the fate of mankind is also the basis for the socialistic principle, where Karl Marx began with his analysis of the modern world and realized that modern man has fallen into a condition of self-alienation.

No sort of recognition can relieve us of this practical concern. No philosophy of history can free us from the responsibility which springs from our fundamental and universal respect for man as a creature. In this quarter we all have a common intellectual root. If we did not have this bond the mutual concern for the community entrusted to us would not be possible, since our conflict with one another would have no meaningful basis. The interest in healthy living conditions of the people — I know very well that it can be argued over what is to be understood by "healthy", and I consider such an argument worthwhile — depends on the view one has of the man for whom one can have respect as a fellow-creature, for whom one feels somewhat responsible, and from whom one can expect that he will likewise respect another equally as well.

In this respect we have certain common principles. In spite of commonality of principles, a diversity of opinion has arisen within political circles of the present-day. Intellectually speaking we find ourselves in an age of change. The world-picture of the nineteenth century has lost its importance, if it rightfully ever had any. That of science is in a state of continuous and remarkable development. Modern technology has awakened in us discomfort and opposition. It has brought some of us so far, that we are willing to resign ourselves to the influx of technical necessities on the organization of the modern world. I consider this to be a wrong idea. I am of the opinion that there has never been a period in the history of mankind in which man's life could be shaped with the help of technology as adequately and honorably in accordance with the idea of mankind as is the case in our own time today.

However, we must limit ourselves in order not to make one single idea or political ideology the basis of our thinking and action, but rather we must first accept the multitude of intellectual approaches which determine our political thinking and action, and thereby learn to live with others in a world in which these approaches conflict. The important question arises here of whether, in this multitude of fundamental concepts of the education of mankind in general and of political education in particular, a sufficiently well-founded commonality is to be found which would make it possible to determine an educational precedent. I have said that I believe in such fundamental commonalities. In Aristotle these commonalities, which are remote from contemporary antagonism, are most clearly to be seen. But there are many other authors in whose works such is to be recognized.

What can science do for political thinking and behavior? Political education cannot rest on knowledge and learning alone. It is also there to influence the mutual behavior of man in a supporting manner for the freedom and above all for the independence of judgment. This is the only practical way in which political education can influence — another way of influence is denied to it — the influence on behavior, the way of getting along with each other, and the influence on the knowledge, that is to say, on the objective premises of a conditional political judgment. Politics as a science and as a training also serves political theory and is intended for the future in general just as is education. It plans in advance, considers the things in question which have to be done. For the sake of these things which are to be done, it must have knowledge of the conditions which action or the planning of action must relate, because the facts of the present are the conditions under which we must think and educate for the future. But one can see from this formulation that for political education every tension in which we may at any time find ourselves as participants is in no way immaterial: the tension between the possibility of action on the one hand and that which has to be done on the other hand. In order to estimate the possibility of action, one has to have an insight into the conditions of society. I have had to be convinced of the fact that this insight is not easily found, but requires divers scientific investigation and also a special method. In recent years I have had the experience, when dealing with a whole series of questions, that empirical sociological studies have convinced me of other facts than those which I had been prepared to consider up to that time.

Recently in a discussion, for example, an empirical sociologist correctly tried to make me aware of the fact that, contrary to my beliefs at the time, the disavowal of the EDC on the part of the French was a shattering of the hope for the federal unification of Europe only for the intellectuals. The people themselves, however, were firmly convinced that the European peoples and nations would be lost individually, but united would be capable of resistence and recovery. For this reason, I should like to take the part of the empirical sociologist in this connection that such an assertion can be made.

We find ourselves in an age of social and political change amongst all the people of the world. Moreover we find ourselves in a unique, unprecedented period in which the world has never been. Such a situation is not so easy to understand. Perhaps it would be best to determine why the outbreak of the Korean Conflict some nine years ago was so important for Germany. The world has really become a unity, if only a tension-filled unity. Nothing of political importance that happens in South Asia or in South America fails to affect us. Even those European states which we as young men then considered to be the centers of power in economics, politics, and military matters are no longer the single possessers of such power, and are in turn also shaped by the development of a technical civilization of their own making which now encompasses the entire world.

In Germany, the center of continental Europe, in England and the United States, a modern society has been created on an industrialized economic fundation. This society has produced a technological organization of life which is today beginning to become the organization of the world and even extends to the former colonies, which are today known as the "underdeveloped" countries. The European way of producing goods, their distribution, and their administration are a specific characteristic of the Western world which is influencing the way of life in the whole world and which cannot be avoided in the long run. This technical organization of the modern working-world has its origin in Europe and has aready shown its inherent dangers to us Europeans. The overcoming of this danger decidedly depends on the meaning which we attach to living in general, and our social community in particular. For this reason the coming-to-grips with this modern way of life is essential and decisive for political education. Thereby the question which is directed to each one of us individually cannot be avoided: What are you by your example doing for the benefit of the community? And what are the intellectual foundations upon which you have built it? What characterizes your political point of view? Have you ever considered that there are others who have different political viewpoints based on other basic experiences and that it is precisely with these people that you must make yourself understood in order to achieve a common solution in a peaceful and orderly manner? The responsibility of a citizen means therefore not only that he understands the principles of democracy, but that he enforces these principles of self-education and self-determination upon himself and exercises them.

Political education firstly means the practise of what one believes. Such a principle was self-evident in the age of classical German literature and philosophy, in an epoch when Schelling held his speech on the Relationship between Art and Nature at Munich in 1807, on the occasion of the opening of the Academy of Arts. It was self-evident that which makes a man independent, self-sufficient, sound with others and for his contemporaries and citizens exercises a political effect and function. It is something essential for our education that beyond all party-political specialities there exists a fundamental necessity for our free and constitutional community order. But at the same time we need a concrete understanding of the matter. We have need of this especially because we are involved in a competition against and a conflict with the soviet form of totalitarian government. In the present-day world-situation there can no longer be politics between individual states, but rather between the countries of different social constitutions, between the totalitarian soviet concept of state and the free and constitutional. Within the free and con- stitutional concept of state there are different nuances, for example, in the concept of a healthy economical policy. This point is arguable. But before one can argue, one needs a high degree of expert knowledge of the consequences of one or the other measures which one takes. We are, however, of the same opinion that we do not want a totalitarian state, but free men, a free community, a self-determined way of life, and a state and policy which foster and protect these characteristics.

In the tension-filled community of the present-day politics of the world, modern man is now in the position to destroy himself. We know well-enough that one of the most important tasks of the present is to put in politically responsible negociation the control of the means of destruction which modern physics has made available without having been able in any way to foresee their consequences. Every political action today is connected with these modern technical possibilities. The preservation of peace has taken on priority of rank in the modern world. Man today must be defended against himself. Also we have to some degree landed in a situation in which it is not through our historical experience and intellectual deliberations alone, but through the situation of mankind with relation to its own technology that it becomes clear that politics is one of the arts that serve mankind and not a con- tinuous happening which runs according to its own rules and is superior to man. We must therefore convert this political thinking and concept of politics into a beneficial effort in order that one may be able to think of a happy future of man- kind and the entire world, and foremost for ourselves.
Political education is therefore meant to teach how one should serve the concept of community life and, moreover, in all its units, in the smallest group of a com- munity, in state politics, in the politics of the Federal Republic, and in all inter- national relationships between countries. As a pedagogical endeavor, it must be able to teach political behavior and to pass on knowledge. But why should a manner of behavior be taught? It should be taught because community behavior in the political realm is not self-evident. Even in the professions, it is required of us that we adapt ourselves to a meaningful order on the basis of our own under- standing and decision; and we are capable of this to a greater or lesser degree in relation to our own understanding and decision. In the family, school, neighbor- hood league, the community, in all levels of political life, we have the task of broadening our historical understanding of immediate problems and customs and the fruitful forms of modified action. Therefore, those educators are right who expect from the common endeavors in the school and the voluntary clubs outside of the school a definite support of the art of being able to work and live together. This is also valid for adult education and for the significant efforts of those in- stitutions of adult education which endeavor to communicate with others on and learn with them about the pressing problems of public life. But this task needs the support of the necessary understanding and the appropriate knowledge.

We all have the experience of how much more difficult it is today to give young people the proper preparation of the present-day world than was the case thirty or forty years ago, because our contemporary world and its situation is changing so quickly and in such a frequently inpenetrable manner. We therefore need research in the field of politics and teaching doctrine which can draw use from such research and employ them pedagogically. Such political thinking is dependent on different ways of thinking than those that we are used to, such as in the field of jurisprudence and historical studies. History tells how something happened. Politics tries to insinuate itself into the dynamics of being. It tries to explain the relationships and deals — as we have already pointed out — with problems of what has happened, not with reference to the "why", but to the future, querying what has to be done. History only seems to be logical since by necessity one historical event is linked to another and it is only afterwards that the chain appears to be an almost self-evident series of cause and effect. However, between these is the definite political work, the choice of politically responsible people between the various possibilities which are open to them. The individual is not spared such a choice, be it in private or in political life, and no one knows better than the politician how to prepare himself for this choice and how to sharpen and illuminate such a value-judgment in the light of this choice with regard to the subject at hand. This is the task which is presented to the teacher of political relationships.

In this endeavor at elucidation, the understanding of the structure of society is a fundamental principle. Politics as a science and politics as a doctrine is therefore not possible without an understanding of social structure. And in addition, the historical growth of this society and also not its present form alone, but rather the theoretical reality of human society has to be reasonable. We should learn to understand the relationship of labor and that of the spheres in which men live with one another, and should also learn to evaluate the relationship of the order of human relations as a sphere in which human beings mean something to each other. From that point on we would be in a position to understand the connection of order, of self-education, and self-determination as spheres in which men make common decisions and try to follow them through. Political science as a scientific discipline, therefore, tries to make the basic types of human behavior clear and to make out of them the basic bonds of the social order in which we live something lucid for the student, the grown-up, or the contemporary. The structure of work, of human relations, and that of self-education and self-determination, all three respectively constitute the whole of the nature of society. Man does not live in human conditions alone. He is not meant only to advance in self-education. That these spheres remain in proper relation to one another is the main concern of political thinking and also political action. Since whenever one or the other of these basic elements of the social order over-steps the limit which is accorded to it, then discontent appears, which is the harbinger of shock or even catastrophy.

As teachers of politics we have the task of building up a total concept of human society. At the same time, we have the task to explain the real problems of domestic politics, starting from the Basic Law and the state constitutions. We have, lastly, the task in Germany, be it the Federal Republic or the Soviet Zone of Occupation, to understand the relationship of world political tensions and circumstances and to make them understandable. All these things can so happen that they can be clear and understandable on various levels of simplification to anyone who attends or has attended a highschool. Perhaps there are too many people in our position who have too great a doubt concerning the degree of understanding of the so-called common man.

The teacher of politics as a scientific discipline has more to do than that. We must concern ourselves with the philosophy of politics. If we consider the thematic material which is expressed in intellectual and political circles, we see that there is not an astronomical number of political motifs which our political thinking has at its disposal. We have the possibility to make a relatively small number of classical works on political philosophy available to our students at the university as basic material. The standard classical authors of the political texts are Aristotle and Plato, Cicero and Augustine, Thomas Aquinas, Luther, Rousseau, Montesquieu — to name only a few in order to make it quite clear how greatly influenced the three-thousand-year-old history of politics in the Western world has been by a small number of excellent political thinkers — among these belongs also Karl Marx. Their effectibility becomes clear in the minutest remark, which is of and in itself a problem. This understanding of theory belongs to the indispensible knowledge which must be won in the field of political science. This knowledge should enable him, who should take a position — and he should do so — to take a position according to and based on principles. It should enable him to understand his partner or — let us say — his political opponent, that he knows why the other has a different opinion. For this a degree of humility is necessary — and I want to say quite openly — the humility to realize that we are all human, even in our understanding of one another with reference to our sureness of our own knowledge based on experience, even in the effort to be able to what is required of science by politics. The pupil, if we may call him such — since he is our fellow-citizen and would have much to tell us out of his own practical experience as we him out of our theoretical, historio-sociological studies — should have the opportunity to educate himself into a judicious contemporary. As a discriminating political observer he should evaluate on the basis of principles. He should have the ability to examine his own opinions critically and to understand his political opponents. The student should be able to limit a political argument which will always exist as such to factual precepts, to participate in a discussion for the sake of the matter which is at hand. Knowledgeably he should be able to defend his own position with the best arguments and a conscious understanding of why he represents this and not the other political conviction. We do not only want him to have his own convictions, we want to help him strengthen them consciously in that we give him the opportunity to defend his belief on the bases of understanding for himself and others. In the last analysis this education depends on the respect one has for other men. In this respect all political circles of the Western world have their very origin.

The Germans Cannot Afford Not to Change [1]

By Hendrik G. van Dam

This is a problem which is discussed from time to time, both in Germany and abroad. It is said that the Germans will never change, that it is their goal to cure the world of its ills through the spirit of Germany. To foreigners they are supposed to be either arrogant or servile, uncouth or over-courteous. They are put down as militarists and anti-Semites. Democracy has expelled them from its fold. The Germans, we are told, love to command and to obey. They have a bent for organization and are technically gifted. German women are either philistine or immoral. The Germans are systematic, but at the same time romantic. They are good-tempered when they don't happen to be otherwise. Finally, they are said to constitute a permanent danger to peace.

Though these generalizations are gross and clumsy, they do not fail to impress. There has been a great deal of such talk recently. Anti-Germanism is a deep-rooted collective sentiment based — like anti-Semitism — on quotations and experience. Statements of this kind can be neither refuted nor proven. They are founded on personal opinions, on sentiment, resentments, on understandable likes or dislikes. They are emotional and human as well as incompatible with the spirit of humanity. Though the subjects of such appraisal change, the basic attitude towards them remains the same. In trying to answer the question whether the Germans have changed, we must therefore rid ourselves of any tendency to generalize or moralize.

I believe the Germans change or fail to change just as much as any other nation. There are certain characteristics in mankind and in individuals, including the Germans as a nation and as individuals, which will assert themselves and develop under specific conditions. People influence each other; the form of society in which they live, its economic and social structure and its political system, all these have their effect. So do school and home life.

Like the citizens of other states, the Germans in Goethe's and Schiller's day acted differently from those living at the turn of last century. After 1871 the reinvigorated energy of imperial Germany exerted a strong and direct influence on all strata of society, and especially on the middle classes. In the Wilhelminian period we find tendencies reflecting the ambitious policies of the government. Compared with the British Empire, France, and Russia the German Reich was an upstart in power politics, which brought certain characteristics to the fore.

Military disaster brought the collapse of Imperial Germany, and the Weimar Republic was never able to overcome the inferiority complexes caused by that defeat. In addition, there was the silent and unwilled revolution accomplished by the inflation through the undermining of the bourgeois class. However, without the world economic crisis all these elements together would not have sufficed to bring about the victory of National Socialism.

[1] From *Magnum*, No. 29, April 1960, p. 53.

The Third Reich laid an absolute claim to the soul of its subjects; it commandeered teachers no less than soldiers. It succeeded in moulding its citizens to a certain type by absorbing them into para-military or semi-political organizations which linked the six-year-old Hitler-Youth with the SS *Fuehrer*. All these influences re-shaped the pattern of society. Just as the moustache of Wilhelm II had for years been typical of many German men, so in the Third Reich certain features were mass-bred, though much more consciously.

After the collapse of the Third Reich the Occupation Powers made Germany a present of democracy. Though there was no revolution, internal and external characteristics alike were recast. Excessive nationalism turned into lack of patriotism. Civic sense is poorly developed in the Federal Republic, and the political cabaret which flourishes there is hardly an adequate substitute. There is widespread distrust of all propaganda and this sometimes even extends to a dislike of straight information. The success of the Federal Republic's economic and monetary policy, known as "the economic miracle", has given great preponderance to economic interests. A process of Americanization has set in, and though the advance towards democratic maturity is still in its initial stage, the Germans of 1960 have different ideals and concepts of success than their forefathers.

The image of the individual German has changed, just as the picture of society in Germany has changed. The divided state of the country has played a part in this, but it is to be assumed that a reunited Germany would lean upon the Western — or the Eastern — example in a similar, if not in the same, way as the separate parts do today.

Finally, the Atomic Age, at the threshold of which we find the German-Jew Albert Einstein, and the growth of vast concentrations of power outside Europe, as well as the development of self-assured African and Asiatic nationalism, means that the struggle for the balance of power among the leading European nations now appears anachronous.

The Germans, like the French or the Italians, have been forced willy-nilly to change their concept of the world. A gradual social evolution is going on everywhere without any barricade fighting. Mankind faces different problems now than in 1914, 1932, 1939 or 1945. It is difficult to compare the Chinese of 1960 with those of 1903; the same holds good for the Germans of 1960.

It is difficult to tell whether they will be better than their predecessors. But if they wish to survive they certainly cannot afford not to alter. They have endeavored to change a great deal.

Research Requirements in the Field of Civic Education

By Walter Jacobsen

Special emphasis has been placed upon civic education in post-war Western Germany, for obvious reasons. The task has been made more difficult by problems of a particular nature.

These particular problems concern — which has in the course of the years become ever more apparent — 1) the object of education, i.e., the German citizen to be educated, differs in a complicated way from the German citizen of an earlier period, and, consequently, 2) also the methodology of education. On the other hand, the problems which are associated with the other components of the entire educational complex thus recede rather more into the background, i.e. the objective of education and the educational matter. Not that these factors have become un-problematical, rather the opposite. But 1) it is easier to achieve unity through them: one knows roughly what present civic education should be about and what the required fundamental reasonable views are, which go with it, — and 2) teachers philosophers, political scientists, historians, lawyers, and also theologists have not been sparing in the post-war years with helpful contributions; we are fairly well equipped now in these fields of research with sound knowledge and comparatively clear perceptions regarding the educational necessities and educational substance.

Where a deficiency does exist, on the other hand — apparently due to a lack of interest by the respective branches of research — it is in the knowledge about the individual in our State at this time. The result is a corresponding lack of suitable methods of approach to the individual as the object of civic education.

Why this is so, requires intensive individual study, — it would be, so to speak, the introductory problem which requires thorough elucidation; the causal-genetic backgrounds of the existing condition would alone provide valuable points for therapy and pedagogy.

For practical purposes today the important thing is, on the one hand, the reliable diagnosis of the present condition, namely the fundamental intellectual attitudes, the "mentality", the susceptibilities, etc., which prevail in the German people and, on the other hand, the methodical possibilities arising here and now out of these. At first glance a fundamental bisection of the object for diagnosis emerges: the "youth" and the "old". Not: here "youth" and there "the adult world", according to the usual classification of the educational establishments; but here those who did not yet experience in clear "awareness" the evolution of the Third Reich and there all the others who somehow — and be it through passiveness or resistance — have been jointly responsible and party to Germany's "chance for a destiny" in the nineteen-thirties. In these two groups are the greatest differentiations — from here also springs the great complexity of the relevant methodical problems of education — and also indeed the "don't meddle with me" attitude through which the relevant fields of research have been deterred from dealing this problem and have thus fallen back in their work.

The more urgent the call has now become for a careful "renovating" of past events and for a chastened, humane, and civic attitude of as many as possible of our fellow-citizens, the more inevitable has it become that all the spiritual and social difficulties, on which many a good effort to evolve a new type of fellow-citizen in Germany threatens to break down, be clarified, and put in its proper perspective. In education after all, these principles apply as in the treatment of the sick: therapy is only proper and can effect a cure if the diagnosis has been correctly made and the manner of action of the medicines prescribed are precisely known. Experimenting "on supposition" sometimes leads to success but very often makes the illness worse. In civic education today, unfortunately, experimenting "on supposition" is carried out to a very great extent and one already hears increasingly of certain doubts being expressed as to the success of the civic educational work carried out so far. It is probably time, therefore, that the appropriate branches of science decide to pay greater attention to the political-psychological fields of inquiry.

From abroad, principally from the USA, scientists, journalists, educators, and politicians often visit West Germany with the object of finding out what and how much has happened here in the field of education for democracy, and to "overcoming" the recent past; whether a fundamental change has occurred down into the deepest strata of personality attitudes. Much as the good will and the serious effort of those responsible thereby receive frequent recognition one senses again and again, in one point, the surprise of the critical visitor; he cannot understand why social psychology and sociology are called upon to such a small extent in Germany in order to assist in this large sphere of effort — which appears to them to be so exceedingly important — by providing reliable material concerning conclusions and methods. They are also surprised that the results of the educational endeavors are not systematically re-checked in order to confirm that the method adopted is the right one.

One often associates with the catch-phrase, "scientific underpinning of the work of political education", only the complex of problems of the historical, political and the constitutionally legal facts which support it and those of philosophical and pedagogical principles. In these fields there is in point of fact so much scientific material available that perhaps it appears unnecessary to increase production further. What has always been neglected is just the crux of the matter, the knowledge of the object of education; the individual in his environment here and now. One acts as though one knew exactly what he is made of, what his innermost thoughts regarding his attitude towards society, the state, politics, pressure of opinions, etc., are, in which social structure he lives, how he receives our efforts at education, what he does with them, which directions the tendencies of his intellectual development take, what we have to expect of him, what form the allurements and "susceptibilities" take to which he is exposed or subjected to, and so forth. In actual fact we rely only on suppositions and wishful thinking: "he should react in this or that way, and he will then of course do so". Pedagogic optimism is indeed indispensible but it must have a sound foundation.

In the process of educating our children and adolescents, the conclusions of the psychology of development have been observed very carefully for a considerable time and they are being applied systematically to the training of teachers and to methodology as well as to the choice of educational material. What actually justifies our assumption that the education of adults can be carried out without such scientific underpinning — most particularly in the delicate matter of political education?

I enumerate herewith some examples of concrete specific questions, the scientific treatment of which would be of considerable benefit to the efforts being made in civic education.

Suggestions of Subjects for Research in the Fields of Psychology and Sociology in Connection with Civic Education

1) The Problem of Susceptibility towards Communist Corruption.

To what extent are our fellow-citizens in the Federal Republic (with respect to their various ages, education, and social groups) endangered by communist propaganda and agitation efforts? Does the danger lie in the field of rational ideology, or in the field of self-deception and self-tranquilization, or in the field of fascination by the phenomenon of the manifestation of power, or in the field of credulity in respect to delusions in the personal sphere of life, or in the field of political disinterestedness, of indifference, of an egocentric "leave me in peace" attitude? How can such an attitude be explained characterologically and socio-psychologically? What type of action would be appropriate to effect a permanant change in this attitude? Or does the danger of corruption referred to hardly exist; is the West German citizen, apart from a few exceptions, immune to the corruption methods of the infiltrators and the manifestations of power of the East? If so, what is the explanation, what opposing forces assert themselves, how does he react emotionally to the news, comment and counter-propaganda on the subject of Communism and Eastern Block politics? How responsive is his emotion in the acute danger of a renewed loss of political freedom? Which motives, urges, impulses or "complexes" lie behind such emotion a) with young, b) with older persons? Is the readiness to resignation and "defeatism" detectable to some degree so that special attention must be paid to this? Which conceptions of a quasi-Marxist nature make any major contribution towards the political judgment of various sections of the community? How do intellectuals react who have had occasion to make a scientific analysis of dialectic or historical materialism? (Their attitude beforehand and some time afterwards).

2) The Problem of Indifference, of "Thinking in Conformity with Authority" and of the Susceptibility of the Sense of Joint Responsibility.

Does the "indifference" of the West German citizen referred to — and which must be analyzed in more detail — conceal other additional dangers than those of falling a victim to communist or camouflaged Eastern corruption? Does the economic security of the individual lull him into submission without criticism to the existing system? What reaction is to be expected if this feeling of security is sharply disturbed, perhaps as the result of a political or economic crisis? Can one then expect a readiness on the part of the individual towards a correspondingly more zealous joint responsibility or the contrary, with an intensified urge for tighter authoritarian leadership, renouncing democratic rights and responsibilities and with still greater readiness towards submission and loyalty without criticism? Which fundamental attitudes or characteristics — whether they be due to heredity, tradition or education — exist which either impede or encourage the success of education in the adult West German citizen of today towards active, conscious joint responsibility within the state? Do thinking, judgment and behavior cohere according to rigid preconceived ideas of order, *clichées* of imagination and stereotyped patterns of behavior in general with training and teaching methods employed in schools and in the home — which are the most important fundamental motives? Is there also a connection here with authoritarian behavior? Are the indifferent of today perhaps the docile fellow-travellers of yesterday? Which are the most important points of approach for education of character in the spirit of our present democratic educational ideals? What does the *Kretschmer* typology say to this?

3) The Problem of Collective Thinking, Conformism and Group Prejudice.

Man — a social being: to what extent do his group adherency, his social importance, his opportunities for prestige, his dependencies, his protective or aggressive tendencies, etc. affect his civic behavior? To what extent is he exposed to or in the grip of collective opinions? To what extent do language, manner of speech, reading material, habits of behavior of his environment, etc., sew stereotyped conceptions in his sub- and semi-consciousness? What importance for the civic attitude of the individual have his identifying or individualizing tendencies in regard to the collective community to which he belongs? To what extent are these development tendencies dependent on education and environment? Which educational and which sociological factors hinder the development of the courage of one's convictions? Which prejudices in respect to other nations are particularly deeply rooted in the German people? How dos the population in the Federal Republic behave towards foreigners staying in this country?

4) The Problem of National Consciousness.

Is the sense of responsibility towards the Fatherland (national consciousness) among our people underemphasized, overemphasized or "normal"? Does a disproportionate ethnocentrism (nationlism) still definitely exist among our people and if so, what urges, motives, repressions, overcompensations or similar factors are at the bottom of it? How many Germans and of which age and social groups "suffer" consciously or unconsciously under the loss of the erstwhile pipe-dream of "Germany's place in the sun"?

5) The Problem of the German National Character.

Which "national" characteristics do other peoples ascribe to the Germans and which do they ascribe to themselves? Which methodical possibilities are there of ascertaining such characteristics (behavior, essential traits, tendencies) by which the Germans objectively differ, comparatively uniformly, from other peoples, particularly those of the West? To what extent are the "characteristic" properties thus ascertained to be regarded as mainly damaging towards our standing in the world? Are there in addition patently unjustified characterizations of the Germans existing in other countries? What aims and possibilities are thus offered for self-education? Are the Germans particularly lacking in national self-criticism?

6) The Problem of the Political Type.

Does the prejudiced personality exist as a type? Which are his characteristic features? What psychological development conditions create these characteristics? Does the authoritarian personality exist as a type? What are his characteristic features? What psychological conditions create these characteristics? Does a kind of person exist as a type who tends towards political radicalism? What is the nature of his impulses? How is non-conformity "on principle" to be interpreted psychologically?

7) The Problem of Demagogy, of "Manipulation" of people, of Mass Contagion, of Autonomy of Judgment.

How much is true in the thesis of "manipulated people" (manipulated by means of influential attractions with an infiltrating effect)? What tricks does modern political demagogy employ? To what extent do fascination and suggestion affect the typical political manner of reaction? How does mass contagion in political reaction take place? Does modern school pedagogy encourage or hinder independent political thinking and judgment? What facilities can be provided to improve education towards independent thinking and judgment?

8) The Problem of Advertising Psychology in the Political Sphere.

In what way does advertising for consumer goods differ — from a psychological viewpoint — from advertising for ideas, particularly for civic demands? What is the nature of the reactions in various sections of personalities? To what extent can external attractive qualities be adapted to political advertising? What importance in forming an opinion can be attached to an apparent drop in a majority? What effect has modern "group pedagogy" on the manner of behavior and judgment, particularly in the spheres of working and professional life?

9) The Problem of Democratic "Consciousness" (of Rational Acknowledgement of the Democratic Principle).

To what extent and degree of conviction are the West German people prepared to acknowledge the parliamentary governmental system as better in comparison with others? What information, conceptions, feelings and valuations are essential for this decision? Which reservations are made? Which rationalizations also contribute towards acceptance of democracy?

10) The Problem of Tradition, of the National Symbol, of Consciousness of History.

What parts are played by certain traditional conceptions in the political consciousness of the Germans? What part is played by symbols — those accepted as well as those rejected? Which figures in German history are regarded today as exemplary or as national heroes?

11) The Problem of Materialistic Attitude to Life.

How much is true in the thesis of immoderate enjoyment of life by the present-day West German fellow-citizen — at the expense of his sense of moral responsibility? Which spheres of his world of values are particularly susceptible to appeals to his civic feelings? Repression — forgetfulness — psychic equipoise, . . . where is healthy reaction still to be found, where is there already ground for moral reminders of conscience? Is the possible verifiable prevalence of the materialistic way of life more the result of external conditions of the period or of education? Which influences intensify and which subdue it? Which psychological connection exists between materialistic interests in the way of life and a materialistic ideology?

12) The Problem of Checking the Success of Civic Educational Measures.

Which types of public work done by the Federal Office *(Bundeszentrale)* and other political education departments have proved to be fruitful and which less fruitful? (To be determined by a) systematic checking in the respective "consumer" groups in as far as these can be contacted, and b) scientific investigations by means of particular experiments.)

13) The Problem of "Renovation": the Conscience' Settlement of the Account with the Past.

What is the psychic nature of the inhibitions with which a sincere settlement of the account with the recent guilty past of Germany is confronted? In which psychic situation in relation to the collective accusation of guilt, are those born after 1920 and in which other situation are those born before 1910? *) Which impulses of fundamental attitude and conscience and which external psychic mechanisms contribute to the nature of the present attitude towards collective accusation? Which attitude can reasonably be expected of the Germans in the various age groups? In which forms and with which explanations does the collective (national) tendency towards self-justification (in regard to the recent past) attempt to assert itself? What is the importance in this respect of the level of education? With which types of mental conflict has the explanation of contemporary history principally to contend? How can it cope with them? What are the prerequisites of knowledge and the valuations regarding the past in the various age and social groups?

14) The Research Problem of Diagnostic Methodology in Attitude, Mentality, and Opinion.

What are the particular uncertainties of mentality diagnostics in the political field, particularly when at the same time representative statistics are required? What are the methodological opportunities offered today in social research for the solution of these probleme?

---

*) Those born after 1920 were, at the most, 13 years old in 1933 and thus lived through the "Weimar" period without any political awareness; those born before 1910 were then at least 23 years old and could thus, more or less with awareness, participate in political affairs then. We may for the present disregard the intervening group.

A Selected Bibliography of Studies and Monographs on Political Education and Political Science

By Wolfgang Gaebler

This bibliography is limited — apart from a few exceptions — to publications of the last five years. It makes no claim to completeness but serves to provide a picture of the intensity and thematic variety of the discussions of research as well as practice on the problem of political education in Germany. The commentary is only meant to give an idea of the respective contents. It deliberately refraines from advancing a critical appraisal of the various publications.

Arndt, Adolf: *"Staatskunst und politische Bildung"* (Politics and Political Education). *Die neue Gesellschaft*. Verlag Neue Gesellschaft, Bielefeld, Jg. 1957, Heft 3.

In this essay on statemanship and political education Arndt voices the theory that political education is not "what the political sciences can achieve in the form of research results and education successes". Also the *studium generale* and the academic education as such, he states, could not provide a political education, and it was a vain and arrogant prejudice to claim "that some professions more than others can make people qualified for political work and political responsibility". The political side of human and social existence could "only be experienced in direct application to oneself". Only the bearing of responsibility of one's own could provide the necessary practice for experiencing, as the essential core of political existence, the spiritual reality of creating confidence, "for which an intellectual accomplishment, be it ever so much acquired by way of academic studies, neither suffices nor authorizes anyone".

Badke, Rolf: *"Kann das politische Denken zur wahren Erkenntnis fuehren"*? (Can Political Thinking Lead to True Perception?) *Paedagogische Rundschau*. Aloys Henn Verlag, Vol. 12 (1957/58), pp. 1—10.

In this study of the question of whether political science can arrive at true perceptions, the author aims to contribute to the philosophical bases of political education.

Badke, Rolf: *"Vom Wesen des Staates"* (On the Nature of the State). *Paedagogische Rundschau*, Aloys Henn Verlag, Ratingen, Vol. 12 (1957/58) p. 433.

In this essay, Badke subjects to critical examination some conceptions (mainly the theses of Friedrich Oetinger) that have won wide influence in German political education. He does so because he considers it urgently necessary "to disperse the mists of illusions that threaten to prevent present-day political education from retaining a clear view of political reality".

Barthel, Konrad: *"Schule und nationalsozialistische Vergangenheit"* (School and National Socialist Past). *Gesellschaft — Staat — Erziehung*, 1959, Vol. 4, Nos. 6 and 7, Ernst Klett Verlag, Stuttgart.

After making a detailed analysis of "political education as it is to be correctly understood", with supporting excerpts from basic reading matter, the author arrives at practical conclusions for the teaching situation. In this situation, school, parental home and the teaching profession are each separately confronted with the unconquered phenomena of National Socialism. The difficulties are singular, if one considers that "political education today is not carried on, as almost all other education is carried on, within the traditional relationship between old and young, in which elders, as interpreters of an agreed field of experience, simply pass on to youth a stock of knowledge. Several factors contribute to the singularity of the situation. First, the attitude of today's older generation toward National Socialism was marked by error and failure, and for that reason the usual presumed superiority of the experienced teacher is lacking. Second, in many cases the older persons are not even capable of freeing themselves from their ingrained political conceptions and pre-suppositions even though these conceptions have been refuted by history. As a result, the political education of youth has to be conducted in part without, yes, even despite the 'old ones,' and to a degree that those who, as far as age is concerned, are qualified to teach must in fact first be taught themselves ..." In this whole process of "political self-education of the German people" (Litt), one should be concerned first of all with a scientifically oriented search for truth and a precise understanding of realities. As a "general guiding principle", it would follow that "the direct confrontation with the unveiled reality of National Socialism" is to be introduced with a combination of tact and purposefulness.

Beckel, Albrecht: "Demokratie in Deutschland als sozialpaedagogisches Problem" (Democracy in Germany as a Socio-Pedagogical Problem). Vierteljahresschrift für Wissenschaftliche Pädagogik. Vol. 35 (1959), No. 4.

The author deals with general problems of political teaching for democracy, as a prelude to discussing the special tasks and aspects of political education in Germany.

Bergstraesser, Arnold: "Wissenschaftliche Politik in unserer Zeit" (Political Science in our Times). Vierteljahrshefte fuer Zeitgeschichte, Deutsche Verlagsanstalt GmbH, Stuttgart, 6. Jg. (1958), 3. Heft.

In this essay Bergstraesser undertakes the attempt of defining "politics as a science" as an independent discipline with respect to its position in relation to the sciences as such. He finally arrives at the following definition: "Politics as a science is the attempt of utilizing the incorruptibility of scientific effort for the preparation of political judgment and political action. This attempt is made in the clear realization of the limitation of scientific work, of the creative nature of really statesmanlike action and, finally, of the unpredictable and ultimately indiscernible character of fate".

Bergstraesser, Arnold: "Das Wesen der politischen Bildung" (The Nature of Political Education). Freiheit und Verantwortung, Ernst Klett Verlag, Stuttgart, Vol. 1 (1956), pp. 4—12.

If for no other reason than the fact that Germany is located in the midpoint of the tension between West and East clear, political attitudes — and therefore the appropriate political education — are particularly necessary here. So observes the author, adding that, even given all differences in attitude within Germany, there is nevertheless a basic community of thought from which to build the foundation of a system of political education. Thus, all spheres of political thinking here, says the author, spring ultimately from respect for one's fellow-man. Nonetheless, he concedes manifold tasks confront a system of political teaching that both bases itself on and seeks to promote such respect. He sees the mission of political education as an effort to offer an over-all view of human society, to explain the tangible problems of both domestic and foreign policy, and, not least, to transmit the knowledge of the classic political philosophers. However, the author adds, political teaching cannot "be based on knowledge and learning alone". It must also, he says, "serve to shape us as members of the community ... with the community considered in all its elements: from the smallest grouping to the policy of the State or Land, the policy of the Federal Republic, and, finally, the world relationships among the nations".

Bergstraesser, Arnold: *"Warum ist politische Bildung nötig"*? (Why Is Political Education Necessary?) *Offene Welt. Zeitschrift für Wirtschaft, Politik und Gesellschaft,* 1957, Vol. 52, Westdeutscher Verlag, Cologne and Opladen.

Bergstraesser proceeds from the statement that the Germans "have not yet succeeded, at the level of foreign policy, in re-thinking the situation of the Federal Republic against a world horizon." Political education "with a view toward the present world horizon" is particularly necessary, he maintains, because "our teaching system is still oriented to the concept of a national culture". A goal of political education, writes Bergstraesser, is "to create within a growing number of contemporaries the capacity to form judgments in individual situations." But he adds that this goal can be reached only if efforts at political education become a major element of the curricula of schools and universities. He remarks: "For the *alpha* and *omega* of political learning consists in experiencing another human being, and in experiencing through him the realization of one's own limitations."

Besson, Waldemar: *"Politische Bildung im Zeitalter der Gruppengesellschaft"* (Political Education in the Era of Group Society), *Gesellschaft — Staat — Erziehung,* Ernst Klett Verlag, Stuttgart, 1958, No. 7.

Besson reasons from the premise that any discussion of the possibilities, tasks, and limitations of political teaching must presuppose an understanding of the structure of the political community for which human beings are prepared. An individual, dependent upon his own resources nowadays, would be condemned to more or less total political inefficacy, he notes; only a group has the attributes of political import. That circumstance gives rise to questions of the tasks and possibilities of political teaching within a group society, and Besson tries to provide an answer.

Bodensieck, Heinrich: *"Zur Aufgabe der Gegenwartskunde in unserer Zeit"* (On the Task of the Study of Current Events in Our Time), *Gesellschaft — Staat — Erziehung,* Ernst Klett Verlag, Stuttgart, 1958, No. 7.

Here the author considers pedagogic-sociological literature that has appeared from 1955 to the beginning of 1958, in the light of its usefulness for political education.

Bodensieck, Heinrich: *"Zeitgenössisches politisches Geschehen und Urteilsbildung im gegenwartkundlichen Unterricht* (Contemporary Political Events and the Forming of

Judgments in Instruction on Current Events). *Geschichte in Wissenschaft und Unterricht*, Ernst Klett Verlag, Stuttgart, Vol. 9 (1958), p. 218.

Borinski, Fritz: *Der Weg zum Mitbürger. Die politische Aufgabe der freien Erwachsenenbildung in Deutschland.* (The Road to Co-Citizenship. The Political Mission of Free Education of Adults in Germany.) Eugen Diederichs Verlag, Düsseldorf, 1954. Borinski espouses the view that a specifically political education can be conveyed to — and acquired by — only an adult individual. For him, the state is no independent entity, but rather an essential means of integrating the various aspects of life. He argues that only a democratic state, open to a continuous, living process of shaping and reshaping, is appropriate to our modern conditions of life. He observes that the citizen would best fulfill the tasks which come his way in a democracy, if he were to regard himself, not primarily as a citizen of his state, but rather as a "co-citizen" — applying that term to his behavior in every sphere of life, including the family, the school, his profession, and politics. Borinski sees the teaching profession as having the inevitable task of educating the human personality toward the formation of a political consciousness and a political attitude — and this by making clear the internal consistency and the logical necessity of a democratic form of life — that will help the individual to be a partner with his fellow-citizens.

Broszat, Martin: *Aufgaben und Probleme zeitgeschichtlichen Unterrichts.* (Tasks and Problems of Instruction in Contemporary Events.) *Geschichte in Wissenschaft und Unterricht,* Ernst Klett Verlag, Stuttgart, Vol. 8 (1957), p. 529.

The author cites examples of the treatment of the National Socialist era in history courses in order to illuminate some of the tasks and problems of instruction in current events.

Bungardt, Karl: *Die Macht der Ideen im Zeitalter der Technik. Zwei Beiträge zu den Problemen einer demokratischen Erziehung heute und morgen.* (The Power of Ideas in the Era of Technique. Two Contributions to the Problems of Teaching in Democracy Today and Tomorrow). Verlag Carl Winter, Darmstadt, 1956.

In the first of the two essays, Bungardt develops the view that teaching in today's Germany has dispensed with the idea of setting a goal for political instruction. On the contrary, he remarks, the only framework is that imposed by the laws and regulations of the various *Land* constitutions. In this freedom, he sees a danger that political education might be drawn too completely into the political currents of the day, unless an attempt is made to orientate the teaching not only toward the realities of democracy, but also toward the principles of democracy. In his second essay, Bungardt calls for the liberation of the teacher from too rigid supervision by the state. He reasons that only the teacher who is afforded a greater leeway can meaningly fulfill the challenge of political education.

Deutscher Ausschuss für das Erziehungs- und Bildungswesen: Zur Situation und Aufgabe der deutschen Erwachsenenbildung (The Condition and Task of Adult Education in Germany). Ernst Klett Verlag, Stuttgart 1960.

This *expertise* on the situation and the task of German adult education "develops and substantiates, after some remarks on the historical aspect (Section I), understanding for the development and, in particular, the tasks of adult education at the present time (Sections II and III); it applies these findings to several specially urgent fields of activity (Section IV; here the question of political education is primarily discussed), and then deals with the two basic forms of adult education in the narrower sense of the term, namely, the "independent" type (i. e., supra-partisan and supra-denominational adult education activities) and the "dependent" type (i. e., education activities sponsored by the political parties, the denominations, and the social organizations) (Section V); in Section VI it provides details on the structure and the tasks of the "dependent" adult education and finally, in Section VII, draws a number of practical conclusions.

Die Praxis der politischen Bildung in der Volksschule (The Practice of Political Education in Elementary Schools). *Schriftenreihe der Bundeszentrale fuer Heimatdienst,* Bonn, 1957.

This publication contains six lectures which were held at a conference of the *Bundeszentrale fuer Heimatdienst* on the question of political education within the elementary schools and the training of elementary school teachers. The lectures deal with the subjects: "Ways and possibilities of the instructional shaping of political education" (Otto Seitzer); "Political education in the practice of the elementary school" (Max Buchheim); "The fields of subjects of political education. Selection and main points" (Theodor Wilhelm); "The contribution of history instruction to political education" (Renate Riemeck); "The utilization of working materials for the visualization of political education" (Ferdinand Kopp); and "Working materials in political education instruction" (Franz Schoenberger). In addition, the publication contains a compilation of subjects which are recommended for political instructions in the elementary schools.

Die Praxis der politischen Bildung in der Berufsschule (The Practice of Political Education in Vocational Schools). *Schriftenreihe der Bundeszentrale fuer Heimatdienst,* Bonn, 1958.

This publication contains six lectures which were held at a conference of the *Bundeszentrale fuer Heimatdienst* in 1956 on the question of the practice of political education in the vocational schools. The lectures deal with the following subjects: "The instructional methods of political education in the vocational schools — ways and possibilities" (Jos. Protz); "Main points of topic selection for political education activities, seen from the angle of the educational task of the vocational schools" (Klages-Meinerzhagen; a supplementing lecture was held on this subject); "Working materials for the instructional shaping of political education" (M. Thiel); "Educational broadcasting and its instructional evaluation for political education in the vocational school" (R. Jaitner); and "Motion pictures and photographs in the citizenship education of the vocational school" (Paetsch). A summary of the conference results at the end of the publication contains recommendations referring to the question of political education in the vocational schools.

Dirks, Walter: *"Die Erziehung des Kindes zur gesellschaftlichen Mündigkeit".* (The Education of the Child to Social Maturity). *Hochland,* 1956/57, No. 49.

As Dirks sees it, the foundation of political education and maturity is social maturity — as expressed, for example, in the human co-relationship of marriage, family and school. "In a general sense, social maturity is the capacity to participate in the society of other human individuals, to take responsibility, to join in a conversation, to hold one's own . . . Maturity is education that has been implemented, and having been educated is equivalent to that state of the spirit and the heart that makes a human being come of age." Therefore the problems confronting the schools, says Dirks, call for "a propaedeutics of political education" — neither neglecting contemporary political realities, nor evading the responsibilities of fostering political understanding and political maturity. The schools, he declares, must make political instruction part of their training in social sciences. Yet the political material must be presented so objectively that no question arises of a *Politisierung* of the school.

Ellwein, Thomas: *Pflegt die deutsche Schule Staatsbürgerbewußtsein? Ein Bericht über die staatsbürgerliche Erziehung in den höheren Schulen der Bundesrepublik.* (Does the German School Cultivate Civic Awareness? A Report on Civic Education in the Secondary Schools of the Federal Republic.) Isar-Verlag, Munich, 1955.

In this report, the author seeks to present, as comprehensively as possible, a survey of civic education in the secondary schools of the Federal Republic. He bases his findings on personal inquiry and on talks with school authorities, teachers and pupils. Although the report does not take into account the development over the last five years, still it offers a detailed picture of the variety of endeavors to convey an education in political affairs to the pupils of the secondary schools of the Federal Republic.

Ellwein, Thomas: *"Zur politischen Bildung im Raum der Universität".* (On Political Education at the University Level.) *Gesellschaft — Staat — Erziehung,* 1960, No. 4, Verlag Moritz Diesterweg, Frankfurt-on-Main, Berlin, Bonn.

In this essay Ellwein seeks to assess the problem of political education from the standpoints "of the valid existing models". He finds that in German universities there is still a widespread overvaluation of scientific and theoretical qualification, while at the same time the student's preparation for subsequent community activity is largely neglected. The success of any activities in political education, however, will continue to be jeopardized, as Ellwein sees it, as long as it is considered sufficient to view the contributions of the universities in terms of theory or of an educational ideal. At the university level, he concludes. "there should be room for a model of political education that is not governed exclusively by theoretical educational values, but also by considerations stemming from the practice of democratic life and its requirements."

Ellwein, Thomas: *Was geschieht in der Volksschule?* (What Is Happening in Elementary School?) Franz Cornelsen Verlag, Berlin/Bielefeld, 1960.

A report on the elementary schools of the Federal Republic of Germany and West Berlin. It is based on the experiences of the author during an almost year-long tour during which he talked personally with parents, educators, pupils and officials of the school administrations. The topic of political education is dealt with in detail within the framework of this report.

Ellwein, Thomas and Fingerle, Anton: *Vernunft und Glaube. Ein Gespräch über die politische Erziehung in der Schule.* (Reason and Faith. A Discussion of Political Education in the School.) Cornelsen Verlag, Berlin, Bielefeld, Hannover, 1958.

The authors express the opinion that a strange taboo is dominant in the publications having to do with political education: That is to say, the relationship between politics and belief, the mutual confrontation of descriptive analysis and ethical evaluation, is rarely dealt with. The authors note that even the question of the attitude of the teacher is carefully avoided. The above-mentioned publication — the record of a discussion — is meant as a contribution toward stimulating the consideration of this question.

Elzer, Hans-Michael: *Der Mensch und die Politik — Fragen seiner politischen Bildung.* (The Individual and Politics — Questions of Political Education.) *Vierteljahresschrift für wissenschaftliche Pädagogik,* Vol. 35 (1959), No. 4.

Elzer builds on the premise that the usual formula for the teaching of European philosophy has its ultimate foundation in Aristole's conception of the human being as a "social animal". But in the present situation, the author suggests, the question arises whether this traditional concept of the human being is adequate to portray the individual in all the aspects of his existence. In this essay Elzer attempts to define some basic foundations of political anthropology — that is, to define the present situation of the individual in terms of politics, and to point out the consequences.

Erziehung und Politik. *Festschrift für Minna Specht.* (Education and Politics. Memorial to Minna Specht.) Verlag Öffentliches Leben, Frankfurt-on-Main, 1960.

This memorial to Minna Specht contains within the section *"Erziehung und Bildung in unserer Zeit"* (Teaching and Education in Our Time) the following contributions, among others: E. Ollenhauer, *"Erziehung und Bildung im demokratischen Sozialismus"* (Education in Democratic Socialism); O. Haase, *"Gedanken über den deutschen Charakter und seine nicht bewältigte Geschichte"* (Thoughts on the German Character and Its Unconquered History); W. Eichler, *"Erwachsenenbildung in unserer Zeit"* (Adult Education in Our Time); G. Weisser, *"Erziehung zur Freiheit in der Epoche der Anpassungszwänge"* (Education for Freedom in the Epoch of Compulsion to Adjust); H. Becker, *"Die freie Schule in der modernen Gesellschaft"* (The Free School in Modern Society).

Eschenburg, Theodor: *"Politik und Moral in unserer Zeit"* (Politics and Morals in our Time). *Politische Studien,* Isar-Verlag, München, 11. Jg. (1960), Heft 121.

In this essay in which he tries to describe the relationship between public institutions and political morals in their mutual influence upon each other, Eschenburg deals with various questions of political education. He is of the opinion that the first repercussions of political education activities can already be noted, although these only set in a short time ago. With regard to political questions, he states, youth of today is less passionate and credulous than his own generation "but maybe more critical and more observant because they know more about politics and the political institutions than we used to know". Eschenburg states that the juveniles respect the institutions to an extraordinary extent, pay great attention to justice in their dealings, and in general show suprisingly great interest in the position of the legal sector within the political sphere. In the section of the book dealing with the discussion of National Socialism in school instruction Eschenburg points to the necessity of outlining also its antecedents; for the fact remains "that the National Socialists did not simply conquer the republic but the republicans also surrendered it".

Fackinger, Kurt: *"Wie sehen Schüler Fragen der Zeitgeschichte"*. (How Pupils See Questions of Contemporary History.) *Gesellschaft — Staat — Erziehung*, Ernst Klett Verlag, Stuttgart, 1959, No. 4.

In this essay Fackinger analyzes the results of an inquiry made among 250 pupils of various secondary schools in Frankfurt-on-Main as to the problems of contemporary history.

Fischer, Wolfgang: *"Jugendliche Entwicklungsphasen und politische Bildung"*. (Political Education and the Development Phases of Youth). *Gesellschaft — Staat — Erziehung*, 1956, No. 2.

The author undertakes an attempt here "to view the matter of political education of youth with reference to the specific mental-psychological attitudes of the young at various phases of the maturing process". This approach leads him to reject "the indifference of a so-called traditional pedagogy, which keeps only the subject matter in view" and which fails, according to Fischer, sufficiently to take into account the pupil's maturity level.

Fischer, K. G.: *"Die Misere des politischen Unterrichts"* (The Lacks of Political Training). *Neue politische Literatur*, Ring-Verlag, Stuttgart und Düsseldorf, 4. Jg. (1959) Heft 6.

The author deals with the question of political education, using as an example a representative selection of currently used German textbooks. He states with regard to the textbook situation: "The problematic nature of the instruction material seduces one into prolixities and encroachments on many other disciplines; in this way, the political aspects are dealt with in a dilatory manner." What political instruction requires, Fischer states, is "a clearly defined goal which places the political aspects into the center and starts from the basis of our political situation; only definite realization can be objectives of instruction; and whoever thinks everything else to be too problematical should at least accept the fact that they are faced by the definite alternative: democracy or dictatorship." With respect to instruction material Fischer asks for "prepared material, in order to make possible the 'passage through the matter' towards full insight, without devaluating it pedagogically by way of a popularization through a methodical dissection of the big lumps into small tidbits, without an effort toward the visualization of the concept — authentic background material and reading material which will exemplify, from the material afforded by history and the present times, what is meant by the questions — an encyclopedia of high quality, understandable to the normal citizen and at the same time comprehensive."

Flitner, Andreas: *Die politische Erziehung in Deutschland. Geschichte und Probleme* (1750—1880.) (Political Education in Germany. Its History and Problems.) Max Niemeyer Verlag, Tübingen 1957.

This study is based on the idea that our education system constitutes a historic structure and that it has to be recognized and understood in its historic connections if its meaning is to be ascertained and if its substance is meant to be maintained or modified. Flitner deals in details, on the basis of extensive background material, with the questions of state and education in the 2nd half of the 18th century, Rousseau and the French Revolution, Germany under the thrill of the Revolution, the reform days and the national liberation, pedagogics as a science, political theory from Adam Mueller to Karl Marx, school politics in the days prior to March 1848, the pedagogic movement of the year 1848, politics and education theory up to 1870, and, in conclusion, the educational associations in the 19th century.

Flitner, Wilhelm: *"Pädagogische Probleme der Erziehung in den Demokratien".* (Pedagogic Problems of Education in Democracies.) *Hessische Hochschulwochen für staatswissenschaftliche Fortbildung,* Vol. 9, Verlag Dr. Max Gehlen, Hamburg and Berlin, 1956.

Flitner suggests in this lecture that the demand on educators in the democratic areas of the world that they produce some concept with which to oppose the Marxist-Leninist ideology is not without its dangers. He reasons: "If we wish to set up some opposite concept on the same level, then the opponent has already wrested away from us a significant concept that it would behoove us to protect. We could set up as a counterweight only the negative attitude of freedom and the political attitude of responsibility . . ." Such a move, and all other attempts to create a uniform way of looking at the world and a uniform ideology and philosophy of life, the author argues, could only succeed in depriving the human being of what makes him a human being: responsibility and self-evaluation. He grants that, like all teaching, political education has the task of seeking, within a certain ethical framework, a common denominator of communication with other individuals, including those who have other attitudes and other outlooks on the world. But political education, he continues, cannot be effective in a vacuum; it must be linked with rational experiences. In Germany, says Flitner, if the experiences of the totalitarian dictatorship can be successfully absorbed and digested, "then we shall have gained what has been lacking up to now: a common basic field of experience, accessible to the whole community — a mutually shared foundation on which the State can be established anew."

Geissler, Rolf: *"Zur Problematik des Bildungszieles und der Methodik des Geschichtsunterricht".* (On the Determination of the Goal of Education and a Methodology of Instruction in History.) *Geschichte in Wissenschaft und Unterricht,* Ernst Klett Verlag, Stuttgart, Vol. 9 (1958), p. 129.

In dealing with history, says the author, one's major point of reference should be the present. This circumstance, he continues, contains possibilities as well as dangers. Civic education, in his view, must not take its goals and values from external traditions or sources. Instead, the study of history, says Geissler, should look within its own current environment and recent past for guides to the creating of goals and landmarks of signifiance. Basing his reasoning on this conception, Geissler poses question as to the methodology and the educational goals of instruction in history.

Giese, Gerhart: *"Erziehung und Bildung in der mündigen Welt"* (Education and Culture in a Mature World). Verlag Vandenboeck & Ruprecht, Göttingen, 1957.

This book endeavors to demonstrate from the basis of the Christian faith the possibilities of education and upbringing in our world. With reference to the subject of "Education and Philosophy of Life" Giese states "that all education ought to give to the developing individual, as part of his 'upbringing', also a 'philosophy of life' in the sense of a definite world concept as an aid for his world orientation"; in this respect the difference would have to be considered carefully "whether the philosophy of life is foundation or goal, whether education activities take place from the basis of a philosophical attitude or toward one, whether the philosophy of life becomes part of education unnoticeably and undeliberately like an atmospheric propensity or whether the entire instruction activities are tendentiously aligned according to one special philosophy of life." In the chapter "Tolerance as a Theological and Pedagogic Problem" special remarks refer to political education which is termed to be essentially an "education towards cooperation, towards a social behavior" and "thus, a *conditio sine qua non* for political education in the spirit of genuine democracy which is not conceivable without 'fair play', without chivalry and, consequently, without tolerance."

"Grundlagen staatsbürgerlicher Erziehung". (Foundations of Civic Education.) *Vierteljahresschrift für wissenschaftliche Pädagogik,* Vol. 32 (1956), No. 4.

The title is that of a lecture by Josef Esterhues, published as an introductory contribution to the above-named issue of the *Vierteljahresschrift für wissenschaftliche Pädagogik,* which is devoted exclusively to the sphere of political education. Besides this lecture, the issue contains detailed contributions on the church as a medium for teaching civic affairs (Adolf Heuser), the family seen in the same connection (Kurt Haase), the contribution of the elementary school to civic education (Hugo Reiring) and political parties viewed as playing a similar role (Peter Nellen.)

Grundlegung der politischen Wissenschaft. (Fundamentals of Political Science), published by Ossip Flechtheim. Verlag Anton Hain KG, Meisenheim, 1958.
A new adaption for the German reader of the book "Fundamentals of Political Science," which was published in the United States in 1952.

Gutachten des Deutschen Ausschusses für das Erziehungs- und Bildungswesen zur politischen Bildung und Erziehung. (Findings of the German Committee on Training and Education in Regard to Political Education and Teaching.) Bonn, 22 January 1955 (published in *Geschichte in Wissenschaft und Unterricht,* 1955, pp. 79—90). A report by the German Committee, in which a clarificaton is attempted of the foundation of political education. Guiding principles are set forth, in the form of recommendations on both goals and methods of political education.

Habermas, Jürgen: *"Zum Einfluß von Schul- und Hochschulbildung auf das politische Bewußtsein von Studenten".* (On the Influence of School and University Education on the Political Awareness of Students.) *Gesellschaft — Staat — Erziehung,* Vol. 4 (1959), No. 8, Ernst Klett Verlag, Stuttgart.

A sociological study in connection with the thesis formulated by Georg Picht: "The unpolitical attitude of the secondary schools is so deeply rooted in their concept of education that it can only be conquered if we decide to re-examine our whole attitude toward education." From that thesis, Habermas derives the following observations: 1. "The pedagogical attitude toward the social sciences" consists of a determination "to transmit facts and figures about the mechanics of politics and the other social sciences" and of "an experiment in playing pseudo-parliamentary games." 2. Still in evidence are motivations "based on an attenuated humanistic tradition," which keep the teaching of the social sciences from having a "deeper-reaching influence." 3. The result is not "inevitably indifference," but rather a climate in which "political authoritarian tendencies frequently appear." 4. Where educational humanism cannot attain anything, there will not occur "a reflective, awakened and watchful awareness, but rather a kind of pragmatism with politically ambivalent consequences." In such a situation, education becomes the prey of ideology, where-as what is needed is a "critical education and one capable of synopsis" — an education that could cope with scientifically based facts.

Hahne, Heinrich: *"Philosophische und politische Bildung"*. (Philosophic and Political Education.) *Die Pädagogische Provinz*, Hirschgraben-Verlag, Frankfurt-on-Main, Vol. 13 (1959), No. 4.

An evalution of the thought-processes of Wilhelm von Humboldt in the light of the problems of the present-day political situation.

Heckel, Hans: *"Rechtserziehung als politische Erziehung"* (Legal Education as Politi-cal Education). *Gesellschaft — Staat — Erziehung*, Verlag Moritz Diesterweg, Frank-furt/Berlin/Bonn, Jg. 1957, Heft 7.

As Heckel states, agreement could generally be found to exist regarding the idea that political education is "the preparation of the population, particulary its youth, for an active cooperation in the shaping of the entirety of democratic life". Political education "means education towards political ethics, towards a realization of the ideas of morals and justice in the sphere of political action". In this "accentuation towards morality", Heckel states, political education is similar to the legal education which, too, is "not a training toward the profession of a jurist but towards a right-eously thinking and lawfully acting human being". With regard to the discussion of the question what legal education means to political education, Heckel attempts to develop the basic principles of law in his essay.

Hennis, Wilhelm: *"Das Modell des Buergers"* (Model for the Citizen). *Gesellschaft — Staat — Erziehung*, Moritz Diesterweg, Frankfurt/Berlin/Bonn, Jg. 1957, Heft 7.

Hennis starts from the basis of the idea that the clear realization of the essential nature of politics and of education which is required as a prerequisite of political education has largely been lost in our times. Since the days of Rousseau the peda-gogic spirit of the respective era has been reluctant to accept the fact that education essentially amounts to the heteronomous shaping of man in his natural form toward the form of lawful man. In the test being passed by political instruction the limits of the pedagogics of modern times, which are based on the idea of an autonomous development of the natural dispositions, are being disclosed, and the insufficiency of our modern concept of politics is revealed. At present, e. g. the fact is being denied "that politics essentially deals with authority, that type of good, just authority which has been forced into accepting responsibility". In view of the lack of a proper orientation in political education activities it would be necessary "to draw up a model of the citizen ... which might serve as a pattern for political education". Hennis sees the decisive task of political education in the "education towards a proper adequate experiencing and moral reacting to the reality of the political facts" with the objective of "showing the way to greater human fullness and per-ception to stunted imperfect man of our time".

Hennis, Wilhelm: *"Bemerkungen zur wissenschaftsgeschichtlichen Situation der politischen Wissenschaft"* (Observations on the Historical Development of Political Science). *Gesellschaft — Staat — Erziehung,* Ernst Klett Verlag, Stuttgart, Jg. 1960, Heft 5.

The essay voices the basic thoughts of a detailed study of the author which is going to be published in the near future. Hennis starts from the basis of the idea that political sciences are searching for their proper subject. "They try to determine once more what politics mean. That they have to do so is the result of a historical development", which Hennis briefly outlines in this publication (the essay is a contribution to a memorandum on the situation of political sciences which the Federal Ministry of Interior had commissioned to be written).

Hillgruber, Andreas: *"Zeitgeschichte als Aufgabe des Geschichtsunterrichts am Gymnasium".* (Contemporary History as the Task of History Instruction at the *Gymnasium* Level). *Gesellschaft — Staat — Erziehung,* 1956, No. 1.

In this essay the author rejects the usual arguments that are brought forward against the treatment of contemporary history in history classes. He argues that the young generation has the right to learn the full truth about Germany's most recent past. Particularly in the *Gymnasium,* he declares, it is the task of instruction in history to sharpen the critical faculties occupying them with contemporary problems, and in this way also to protect young people against a new attempt to misuse their idealism.

Hilligen, Wolfgang: *Plan und Wirklichkeit im sozialkundlichen Unterricht. Untersuchungen, Erfahrungen und Vorschlaege.* (Plan and Reality of Sociological Training.) Bollwerk-Verlagsgesellschaft, Frankfurt, 1955.

With respect to the purpose of his study the author states in his introductory remarks: "In it, the forms, subjects, and results of (political) education as well as the experiences, objections, and proposals of the teachers are intended to be compiled, examined, and compared to the curricula and to the demands voiced in the relevant literature. On the basis of this attempt, proposals for a new teaching program are to be the outcome." The most important instructional aids for the proposed new teaching program are listed by the author in a bibliographic annex.

Hornung, Klaus: *"Über das Verhältnis von Geschichtsunterricht und politischer Bildung".* (On the Relationship of History Instruction and Political Education). *Freiheit und Verantwortung,* Ernst Klett Verlag, Stuttgart, 1957, pp. 4—10.

History instruction is set forth as the central element in political education ... but together with development of a political outlook, as a decisive principle of the success of education in history. From this premise, the author goes on to examine the close interrelation between political education and instruction in history. He delves particularly into the question of whether the most recent past should be included in courses of history instruction. His conclusion: The treatment of problems of current history is essential to the whole teaching process.

Junge, Walter: *"Zur Frage des jugendlichen Interesses an den Inhalten der politischen Bildung".* (On the Question of Youthful Interest in the Contents of Political

Education). *Pädagogische Rundschau*, Alois Henn Verlag, Ratingen, Vol. 13 (1958/59), p. 686.

As political education would be of little effect without an interest on the part of young people the question is posed: Is today's young person receptive to political problems? In his essay, Junge presents results of an inquiry that he conducted among pupils. He also makes some suggestions regarding didactic possibilities of stimulating students' political interest.

Kindler, Karl Friedrich: *"Not und Aufgabe der politischen Erziehung"* (Predicament and Purpose of Political Training), *Gesellschaft — Staat — Erziehung*, Jg. 1960, Heft 2, Ernst Klett Verlag, Stuttgart.

In this essay, Kindler observes: "As cheering as are the efforts by our schools and institutions of higher learning, press and radio, Federal and *Laender* Centers for Democratic Education, colleges of political and pedagogical sciences, the church academies, the national associations, the parties and the legislative bodies, towards political training of our younger generation and our entire people ... all of these efforts still constitute only the initial, quite unsteady trial steps on the soil of unregimented, representative democracy with government under law." He first sketches what he considers to be the most important causes of this unsteadiness and then attempts to answer the question as to what must be done in order to overcome the unsatisfactory state of political training prevailing even today in Germany. The essay contains references to the significant literature relating to the problem of political education and provides a survey of the progress and present status of discussion.

Kittel, Helmuth: *"Politische Erziehung durch Behörden"* (Political Training by Admistrative Authorities), *Die Sammlung*, Vol. XIII (1958), p. 481. Göttingen: Verlag Vanderhoeck & Ruprecht.

Kittel writes that if it is true that politics, the actions of the politicians, exert a substantial influence on the political training of the people, then this obtains similarly for the administrative authorities representing the public powers. He adds that as a matter of fact, the average citizen most frequently comes in contact with the administrative authorities. In this essay, Kittel investigates the influences that can be exerted by administrative agencies in regard to political training.

Kopp, Bernhard: *"Staat und Erziehung"* (State and Pedagody), *Die Pädagogische Provinz*, Jg. 1956, Heft 7, Hirschgraben-Verlag, Frankfurt.

The author investigates in this essay the correlative connection between State and pedagogy with respect to the field of poliical education.

Krockow, Christian, Graf von, *"Grenzen der Gemeinschaft"* (Boundaries of the Community), *Gesellschaft — Staat — Erziehung*, Jg. 1957, Heft 7, Verlag Moritz Diesterweg, Frankfurt.

In this essay, the author tries "to depict the boundaries delimiting the character of the community in our political and social system," and at the same time "to warn against the dangers that may arise out of making 'training for the community' the paramount objective of social-studies instruction."

Landshut, Siegfried: *"Zum Begriff und Gegenstand der politischen Soziologie".* (The Concept and Scope of Political Sociology) *Koehnes Zeitschrift fuer Soziologie und Sozialpsychologie.* Westdeutscher Verlag, Köln-Opladen, 1956, p. 410.

"What is involved", asks Landshut in his introduction, "in the present day transformation of the term 'political' into an adjective qualifying another branch of science, sociology — a branch, moreover, which by comparison with the venerable study of politics is of very recent origin?" Landshut attempts to answer this question by demonstrating how, with the eighteenth century's conception of Natural Law, the spheres of State and society became separated in the general conception of political community, i. e. how a sphere of society distinct from that of the State first became recognized and then developed into the subject matter of a new science, sociology; and how, with the gradual emergence of the modern type of parliamentary democracy, the problems of the antagonism between State and society acquired increasing prominence and the State and its organs eventually became "wholly and exclusively a product of social forces"; "politics thereby indeed becoming transformed into sociology". However, as soon as "the concept of 'political existence' is at issue the conditions under which political sociology is at all possible themselves appear worth invesitigating". Thus political sociology is not an appropriate starting point for reflection upon the essential nature of politics.

Landshut, Siegfried: *"Die Schwierigkeiten der politischen Erziehung in der egalitaeren Massengesellschaft"* (The Difficulties of Political Education in Modern Mass Society). *Gesellschaft — Staat — Erziehung,* Verlag Moritz Diesterweg, Frankfurt, Jg. 1957, Heft 7.

The problem of political education, Landshut states, actually only came up when after World War I that gigantic process of social upheaval had been moved into the sphere of general awareness which had set in already one century ago and which dissolved and leveled, with ever-increasing rapidity, traditional society. In a disintegrated egalitarian mass society which is only kept together by a network of administrations and organizations political education now was meant to replace ... and this fact is regarded by Landshut as the principal calamity of political education activities . . . the previously existing and today no longer feasible matter-of-course entry of youth into the political community, with the help of stimulating instruction and of the effort of thought. Landshut sees another difficulty in the fact "that the factual circumstances and conditions of political every-day life definitely are not identical with the principles and prerequisites corresponding to the norms and articles of the constitution". This situation should not be hushed up, so that the juveniles whenever they notice these contradictions shall not become suspicious and perhaps seek salvation in a disastrous idealogy of world improvement. The best way would be "to take the juveniles in the top grades of the schools into our confidence and to tell them that we all are living in this world and that this is the world which is imposed upon us".

Lemberg, Eugen, *"Ideologie und Utopie in unserer politischen Bildung"* (Ideology and Utopia in our Political Education), *Gesellschaft — Staat — Erziehung,* Jg. 1958, Heft 2, Ernst Klett Verlag, Stuttgart.

The author believes that German political education in the post-war period has been oriented too one-sidedly to the negation of the Nazi past and that there is

Photo: Ivan Koeves

Above: View of the Building

A Forum on Educational Problems at Adult Education Center "insel" in the Town of Marl, Westphalia

Photo: Werner Luecke

Youth Leaders at Jugendhof Barsbuettel Discussing their Problems

Photo: dpa

the "danger of an ideological vacuum". He writes that any political education is in the long run doomed to failure, "if it does not, in addition to criticism of past errors that might still be repeated and to training for a specific spirit of partnership, impart an image of the cosmos and of history, a basis for self-interpretation and a vision of the future". He adds: "Willingly or unwillingly, the scheme of any political education on a long-range basis must also come to grips with these matters, that is, with mythos, ideology and utopia." The author intends his essay as a contribution to a discussion of this kind.

Litt, Theodor: *Die politische Selbsterziehung des deutschen Volkes* (Political Self-education of the German people), *Schriftenreihe der Bundeszentrale fuer Heimatdienst*, 1957, Bonn.

In this publication, Litt gives expression to the view that the present generation of educators must first of all educate themselves before they can go about educating the younger generation; for as he writes, we come "out of a political past that during protacted periods was less democratic than anything else and was consequently not able to bring forth a theory of the State from which democratic consciousness might draw nourishment." He adds that the conception widespread particulary among German educators to the effect that the State is merely a means to an end must be revised. He states that the result of this conception is that the individual leads a double life as an "individual" and as a "citizen", which is detrimental both to "political" and to "individual" life. According to Litt, the State is not first and foremost a means of preventing infractions of order or guaranteeing the material welfare of the citizen. He points out that a pure police and welfare state becomes an arbitrary state only too easily. Litt writes that on the contrary, the State is the highest court of decision for all disputes that constantly arise efforts for a community life in freedom and dignity. He adds that by imparting the direction to our lives, the State cannot be isolated from these lives at all. He infers that everyone is called upon to participate in shaping the State, that is, to take part in the struggle for the power necessary for the maintenance of order and in the regulation of this struggle for power. Litt deduces that since leadership and decision are at stake in politics, it is mistaken to favor transferring forms of social life such as partnership and cooperation (see Oetinger, *Partnerschaft*) — which he says are in fact only possible under the protection of political power — to the field of politics.

Messerschmid, Felix: *"Politische Bildung heute"* (Political Education Today), *Freiheit und Verantwortung*, Jg. 1956, Heft 1, Ernst Klett Verlag, Stuttgart.

Messerschmid considers the central task of political education to be the attempt "to counteract the truly terrifying inclination of modern man to reject active responsibility for universal and political matters, to conceal himself in the mass and to sacrifice his liberty to this concealment". He adds, "If this attempt does not succeed, totalitarianism is the inevitable result; and it is not very significant whether this totalitarianism bears a Bolshevistic or democratic stamp." In regard to the kind and method of political training, Messerschmid refers among other things to the fact that pedagogical authority is not "supreme authority" and that political education must not restrict the sphere of personal decision.

Messerschmid, Felix: *"Die Ausbildung der Lehrer für den Unterricht in Politik"* (Preparation of Teachers for Instructing in Political Subjects), *Gesellschaft — Staat — Erziehung*, Jg. 1958, Heft 3, Ernst Klett Verlag, Stuttgart.

This paper on the objectives, ways and means of training teachers for political pedagogy in Germany was presented by the author at the First Conference of German and French University Presidents in Berlin (19—22 February 1958). The theme of the Conference was: "The University and the Political Sciences: Approaches to Educating Students as Citizens."

Moebus, Gerhard: *Das Fehlen einer politischen Bildung* (The Lack of a Political Education), *Probleme einer Schulreform* (Problems of a School Reform). Stuttgart: A. Kröner, 1959.

Anyone who is expected to impart political education must in the author's opinion have an adequate specialized training for this purpose. He adds that without science of the political field at the college and university level, there can be no satisfactory instruction in political subjects in the schools. He points out that the communication of knowledge is, however, only one phase of political education. The author states that knowledge must be complemented by dispositions and attitudes manifested in performance and if necessary in self-denial and sacrifices as well. Moebus contends that the historical development of Europe has led human beings to "an incomparable plateau of existence" with respect to their outward and inward freedom of action. He states that this elevation is readily conducive to a feeling of giddiness and insecurity. He adds that it is therefore all the more necessary to seek a firm footing in a well-founded education of the individual in political knowledge and dispositions.

Moltmann, Guenter: *"Zeitgeschichtlicher Unterricht"* (Instruction in Contemporary History), *Geschichte in Wissenschaft und Unterricht,* Jg. 1956, S. 158, Ernst Klett Verlag, Stuttgart.

In this essay, the author presents a detailed treatment of the question of the educational value and methodological problem of instruction in contemporary history.

Monsheimer, Otto: *"Politische Bildung als Forderung, als didaktisches Problem und als akademisches Studienfach"* (Political Education as a Requirement, as an Educational Problem and Academic Subject). In *Erziehung und Bildung im Zeitalter der Technik. Festgabe fuer Paul Luchtenberg,* Verlag Ph. C. W. Schmidt, Neustadt/Aisch 1960.

The demand for a political basic orientation, in Monsheimer's opinion, results from the political immaturity and uncertainty of the German people which is documented in the fact that within one single generation the Germans tried out all existing modern forms of government. Also today we are still far away from real political majority, Monsheimer claims. In addition to these points of view, he deals with the didactic problem of political education and refers to the training of the teachers in the field of political education, trying to demonstrate the possibilities of this type of training by pointing to the example of the academy practice in Hesse. The publication also contains the memorandum issued by the Examining Board of the University of Frankfurt in 1959 which deals with the "reorganization of the state examination in social sciences (the science of politics)" and provides an impression of the knowledge demanded from the future teachers by the university.

Monsheimer, Otto: *Drei Generationen Berufsschularbeit* (Three Generations of Trade-School Endeavors). Weinheim: Verlag Julius Beltz, 1955.

In this book, Monsheimer takes up the question of political education in detail in the course of a historical exposition of trade-school endeavors. Following a discussion of theoretical questions of principle, he tries to point out approaches for an effective political training, referring to a number of examples taken from trade-school teaching practice.

Mueller, Lorenz: *"Politische Bildung und Erziehung im Studienseminar"* (Political Education and Training at the Study Seminar), *Gesellschaft — Staat — Erziehung*, Jg. 1959, Heft 6, Ernst Klett Verlag, Stuttgart.

In the author's view, political education is still receiving far too little attention in the education of teachers. On the basis of a report concerning the efforts of the Study Seminar in Frankfurt, the author discusses the requirements and possibilities of teacher training for pedagogy on political subjects.

Oetinger, Friedrich: *Partnerschaft: Die Aufgabe der politischen Erziehung* (Partnership: the Objective of Political Training). Stuttgart: Metzeler'sche Verlagsbuchhandlung, 1956.

Oetinger starts wih a critical exposition of traditional forms and conceptions of political training. In this regard, he presents a particularly detailed treatment of so-called "citizenship training" and "national political schooling." He adds that at the present time, it is no longer possible to establish a connection with either of these two pedagogical concepts, which have been predominant in Germany in the past. He contends that both of them are based on the characteristic German view of the State, which led to isolating political life from private life. Oetinger regards efforts in favor of a disposition to partnership — a disposition upon which our commonwealth's transformation into a democracy is predicated — as a means of political training and education suitable to our contemporary situation. He states further that providing it is once recognized that in the last analysis survival is at stake, it is not unduly difficult to infuse a disposition to partnership and cooperation, to fairness in settling antagonisms, and to compromise.

Philosophie und politische Bildung an den Hoeheren Schulen. (Philosophy and Political Education at the Secondary Schools). Edited by Heinrich Holzapfel. Paedagogischer Verlag Schwann, Duesseldorf 1960.

The book contains lectures which were held at a conference in the year 1959 at which recommendations for the shaping of philosophical and political instruction in the high schools were drawn up. The lectures deal with the following subjects: "Possibility of and dangers to freedom in the democracy" (Karl-Heinz Volkmann-Schluck); "The Aristotelian-Thomist state idea" (Bernhard Lakebrink); "The state in the present-day Evangelical-theological way of thinking" (Grete Schneider); "Philosophy and political education with reference to W. von Humboldt" (Heinrich Hahne); "The Soviet ideology in philosophical instruction" (Heinrich Sauerwald); "The State science of dialectic materialism and its discussion in school instruction" (Kurt Klein). In a summary of the conference results at the end of the book the main principle is defined as amounting to the fact that "political education is essentially philosophical education" since political education has to inquire into the essence of things, and this amounts to a philosophical question".

Pohl, Bruno: *"Die Erziehung zum Menschen in der technischen Welt"* (Training for Human Living in the Technological World), *Gesellschaft — Staat — Erziehung*, Jg. 1958, Heft 7, Ernst Klett Verlag, Stuttgart.

The author advances three considerations in regard to training for political thinking:

1. The social-studies consideration. "It must be asked in all seriousness whether political education in our era should not also include psychological comprehension of man, embracing in particular a psychological inquiry into the culture of the pedagogical groups . . . The problems involved in existence, soul and spirit must have a part in determining political judgment."

2. The cultural and anthropological consideration. The author states that this is a matter of personality training. "The more profound consciousness of freedom, human dignity and social justice is not gained through social studies. Especially in view of the relentless dehumanizing tendencies of the technological world, pedagogy must consistently endeavor to lend effect to the spiritual values . . . . The values of the personality are the foundation of all human freedom."

3. The religious consideration. "A merely secular training is in the long run not adequate in a society increasingly permeated with spiritual insecurity, where the conscious mind is increasingly focused upon the estrangement of man." The author adds that only a religion surpassing morals and laws provides the foundation for genuine patterns of community, meaning that "even democracy in the technological world cannot be stabilized without religion's weight as a source of solidarity."

Politische Bildung und Erziehung im Bereich der Berufsschule (Political Education and Training in the Scope of the Trade School), *Schriftenreihe der Bundeszentrale für Heimatdienst*, Bonn 1956.

This issue contains lectures by K. Abraham, W. Krefting, T. Litt, G. Möbius, O. Monsheimer, W. Roessler and E. Wingerath delivered in 1955 at a conference on the topic "Political Education and Training in the Scope of the Vocational School."

Politische Bildung und Erziehung im Rahmen der Volksschule (Political Education and Training in the Scope of the Grammar School), *Die neue Volksschule in Stadt und Land* (The New Grammar School in City and Country). Bonn, *Bundeszentrale für Heimatdienst*, special issue 1956.

This special issue contains the following papers presented at the Tutzing Conference on Political Education and Training (1955):

A. Huth, "Psychology and Political Education."

A. Klein, "Political Education as a Component of the Training of Grammar-School Teachers at the Academies, Colleges and University Schools of Education.

W. Schultze, "Approaches to Political Education and Training in Countries Outside the German Area."

O. Seitzer, "Political Education in the Practice of the Grammar School."

E. Weniger, "Pedagogy's Demands of Political Education."

H. Wenke, "Political Education's Responsibilities in View of the Composition and Situation of the Younger Generation."

T. Wilhelm, "The State Oriented to Democracy, Social Justice, and Political Education."

Ritter, Gerhard: *Wissenschaftliche Historie, Zeitgeschichte und "Politische Wissenschaft"* (Scientific History, Contemporary History and "Political Science"). Heidelberg: Carl Winter, 1959.

In this essay, Ritter opposes the widespread conception that the science of history is purposeful only if it is immediately applicable to practical political life. He adds: "It has probably been believed that a combination of the kind attempted by the modern science of politics between the historical and sociological approaches would also be able to penetrate the darkness of the future sufficiently to establish the goals of political action.... Yet the future is always shrouded in mists, and action is in this regard always a venture extending beyond scientific insight."

He remarks further that no one will contest the view that science should bend earnest efforts to expand "the realm of certainty" and restrict that of venture by illuminating reality. He then asks: "But in what measure is it at all possible to intuse and mould political life by rational means?" Ritter refers to the sometimes incredible misinterpretations and false prophecies of distinguished savants, which provide striking proof "that learned knowledge by no means prevents blind failure to recognize reality," especially not in our times, in which the "overview of historical processes" is "also rendered quite difficult by the endless expanse of the stage of world history." the author adds that critical personal reflection concerning the tasks of political history is the necessary prerequisite for its success in exerting influence in the future.

Rodenstein, Heinrich, *Die pädagogische Bewältigung der Vergangenheit* (The Pedagogic Problem of Coming to Grips with the Past). *Die Neue Gesellschaft*, Verlag Neue Gesellschaft GmbH, Bielefeld, Jg. 1960, Heft 3.

Since National Socialism had not been defeated from within, i. e., not by German democratic resistance elements, but had been crushed by the power of the allied armies, the existence of "living National Socialist rudiments" still had to be reckoned with. The mastering of the past certainly amounted to a pedagogic problem. "It is a mistake, however, to think in this respect only of the conscious educators, particularly the family and the schools; in this very wide field more secret educators are at work today than the conscious pedagogic elements want to admit". Rodenstein thinks that for this reason the entirety of all consciously or unconsciously active educational elements should be examined critically if we want to solve the political-pedagogic problem of mastering the past.

Schallenberger, Horst: *"Politische Bildung in der Volksschulwirklichkeit* (Political Education in Practical Grammar-school Application), *Pädagogische Rundschau*, Jg. 1958—59, S. 71, Aloys Henn Verlag, Ratingen.

The author tries in this essay to illuminate the necessity and objectives of political education and the possibility of implementing it within the grammar school.

Schilling, Konrad: *"Beitrag zur Behandlung von Judentum und Antisemitismus im Oberstufenunterricht"* (Observations concerning the treatment of Jewry and anti-Semitism in the last two years of secondary-school instruction), *Geschichte in Wissenschaft und Unterricht,* Jg. 1960, S. 132, Ernst Klett Verlag, Stuttgart.

In this essay, the author tries to show in what manner questions pertaining to Jewry and anti-Semitism may be treated appropriately in the upper grades of the secondary schools.

Schörken, Rolf: *"Welches Bild haben Obertertianer vom Nationalsozialismus?"* (What Image do Second-Semester Sophomores have of National Socialism?), *Gesellschaft — Staat — Erziehung,* Jg. 1959, Heft 5, Ernst Klett Verlag, Stuttgart.

In this publication, the author reports on the answers given by 15 and 16-year-old secondary-school pupils (95 in all) to the question: "What do I know about Hitler and what do I think about him?"

Schuette, Ernst: *Demokratie und politische Bildung* (Democracy and Political Education). *Die Neue Gesellschaft,* Verlag Neue Gesellschaft GmbH, Bielefeld, Jg. 1960, Heft 2.

"Democracy and political education depend upon each other", Schuette states in this essay. Whereas a dictatorship can manage with an ideologically restricted instruction system aimed at certain objectives, democracy needs the "citizen who is eager to acquire factual knowledge and who is open to problems as well as critical". Therefore we ought to "take political education seriously, if we take our democracy seriously".

Smend, Rudolf: *Politisches Erlebnis und Staatsdenken* (Political Experience and Thought). *Gesellschaft — Staat — Erziehung,* Verlag Moritz Diesterweg, Frankfurt, Jg. 1957, Heft 7.

"An educational objective always becomes the subject of special pedagogic interest when it has become problematical. At the present time, this is specially true for the task of political education, namely, the task of showing people the way towards finding their political place", Smend states in his introductory paragraph. The State, he declares, has become problematical in the sphere of political experience, probably as a result of the fact that during the last 150 years the attitude towards the State in Germany had fluctuated between a passionate demand for political experience and a complete lack of political interest. Smend then tries to find an answer to the question "for the road and the education possibility towards a more appropriate attitude."

Sozialkunde im mathematischen und naturwissenschaftlichen Unterricht (Social Studies in Mathematics and Science Instruction), by E. Löffler (editor), W. Dreetz, W. Flörke, T. Litt, E. Sellien, and W. Siedentrop. Heidelberg: Verlag Quelle & Meyer, 1956.

This book is based on the idea that academic studies and natural sciences must collaborate in political training. It tries to illustrate possibilities for supplementing the pupils' political education in the course of instruction in mathematics and natural sciences.

314

Spranger, Eduard: *Gedanken zur staatsbürgerlichen Erziehung* (Thoughts on Citizenship Training), *Schriftenreihe der Bundeszentrale für Heimatdienst* 1957, Bonn.

Without a political power to maintain order, a comity of human beings is not possible for any State, according to the author. On the other hand, he adds, no State is possible without the foundation of a morality rooted in the population and without the responsible commitment of the individual. On the basis of this observation, Spranger takes up the methodological problems of citizenship training. He remarks that political training can only be successful if it is able to build upon the pupil's own experiences. The author's view is that it is necessary in this respect to establish a connection with specific "primeval experiences" the pupil gains in his human environment, especially in the family (for instance, the phenomena of power, dependence, liberty, justice, etc), and in this manner to try gradually to bring about comprehension of the interrelationships of political life.

Stammer, Otto: *Politische Soziologie und Demokratieforschung* (Political Sociology and Research on Democracy), *Kölner Zeitschrift für Soziologie und Sozialpsychologie*, Westdeutscher Verlag, Köln-Opladen, Vol. 8 (1956) p. 380.

In this essay on the implications and tasks of political sociology Stammer takes as his starting point the following proposition: "Political sociology can hardly claim to be able to cover the whole broad field of political action and political power on its own; on the other hand, the disciplines which have traditionally played a special part in the evolution of political science — social philosophy and the sciences of history and government — cannot dispense with sociology as an ally in the treatment of both general and specific aspects of political phenomena." In Germany, where "the establishment of a social democracy appears to be an important objective of communal policy", political sociology is faced with two essential tasks: "first, analysis of the structural and functional relationships between social, political and ideological forces in their concrete context; and second, ... analysis of the conditions requisite for and the consequence of establishing a social democracy, including the demands which such a task imposes on all ... the forces concerned".

Sternberger, Dolf: *Bemerkungen ueber den Gegenstand der Politik* (Observations upon the Content of Politics), *Kölner Zeitschrift für Soziologie und Sozialpsychologie*, Westdeutscher Verlag, Köln-Opladen, 1956, p. 396.

In this essay Sternberger raises the issue of "the true object of political science", of the "unifying bond" which joins the numerous disparate elements covered by the study of political science into a meaningful whole. He draws attention to Thomas Aquinas' assertion that the soundness and well-being of a political community consist in the preservation of unity and peace, and sets this assertion beside the various power theories. Both peace and power are involved in politics, he maintains. "Power, since at all times and on all sides it obviously plays a part — but only a part; peace, since in the last resort tension exercises pressure in the direction of a solution, conflict in the direction of reconciliation, of decision, in fact, of a kind which is accepted and becomes legally sanctioned by the actual society. To comprehend such a field of forces, such a system of rules, together with all the possibilities of infringement and disturbance pertaining to it — to grasp this as a whole seems to me to be the true task of political science: the study of the social organism in its actual living state ..."

Tietgens, *"Skeptische Generation und Politische Bildung"* (Sceptical Generation and Political Education), *Gesellschaft — Staat — Erziehung,* Jg. 1958, Heft 5, Ernst Klett Verlag, Stuttgart.

The remarks in this essay relate primarily to the political education of adolescents outside the school. In the author's view, a large proportion of these experiences and perspectives are also true of political education in the schools. The expression "Sceptical Generation" relates to a study by H. Schelsky *(Skeptische Generation: Eine Soziologie der deutschen Jugend,* Düsseldorf, 1957), to which the author makes reference in this publication.

Tietgens, Hans: *Nationalsozialismus und politische Bildung* (National Socialism and Political Education). *Die Neue Gesellschaft,* Verlag Neue Gesellschaft, Bielefeld, Jg. 1960, Heft 5.

In this essay on National Socialism and political education, Tietgens arrives at the following conclusions, *inter alia:* Political education "must not be limited to the imparting of formal knowledge in the spirit of traditional citizenship education. It must offer help for the process of becoming part of society, a fact which today, without any ritual support, is no longer a matter of course ... Whatever remains undigested in the form of failures is charged to the debit of politics. This situation can only be counteracted by a watchful and sharpened consciousness". The central question is "in what way political education can provide support to the sober, hardly attractive concept of democracy among people whose emotions are more effectively aroused by authoritarian or totalitarian systems and who allow themselves to be impressed by them".

Topitsch, Ernst: *"Ideologie und Utopie in der Erziehung"* (Ideology and Utopia in Education). *Deutsche Universitaetszeitung,* Verlag Deutsche Universitaetszeitung, Göttingen, Jg. 1958, p. 712.

An education towards scientific perception, that is, with conscious reference to the science theory of the Era of Enlightenment is today, in the opinion of the author, one of the main demands "that are addressed to us by life within modern society". This education is even more urgently required in view of the fact that particularly in Germany pre-scientific anti-Enlightenment tendencies had soon attained predominance over the "modern" movements and had brought about that "breach between ideology and social reality" which largely determines our situation also today. This breach looms in the background of the problem of the relationship — which is willingly discussed by German cultural philosophy, sociology, and pedagogics — between "culture" and "civilization", "community" and "society", and "organic-entire" and "mechanical-atomistic" methods or world concepts. Frequently these antithetic pairs of terms can "not be rendered at all in western languages". It is true that the "ideological and utopian elements in the way of thinking of Enlightenment" no longer have relevance in the general awareness of today, but what has remained and should be cultivated is the "critical achievement, the impulse toward the systematic examination of the ideologies and the no longer cancelable realization that scientific perception ... constitutes one of the foundations of the modern way of shaping our lives".

Weinstock, Heinrich: *Die politische Verantwortung der Erziehung in der demokratischen Massengesellschaften des technischen Zeitalters* (The Political Responsibility of Pedagogy in a Democratic Collective Society of the Technological Era), *Schriften-reihe der Bundeszentrale für Heimatdienst* 1959, Bonn.

According to Weinstock, pedagogy is faced with the task of political education because man is by nature a *"zoon politikon"*, if for no other reason. He states that in Plato's view politics, philosophy and pedagogy were still an inseparable unity, but in Aristotle's mind the path towards de-politicizing pedagogy had already been taken. In order to re-politicize pedagogy, Weinstock writes, it is consequently necessary to come to grips with the entire post-Aristotelian pedagogical tradition. Weinstock tries to render a contribution to such a discussion by subjecting funda-mental pedagogic and political conceptions to a critical investigation. In keeping with the thesis he advances in closing to the effect that the individual decision dictated by conscience has priority over the demands of the collective group, Weinstocks finds that the task of present-day political training is the endeavor to counteract the tendency towards "de-personalization" in industrial, democratic collective society by promoting a consciousness of responsibilities and the sense of justice.

Weinstock, Heinrich: *"Der Nationalsozialismus im Schulunterricht"* (National Social-ism in School Instruction), *Gesellschaft — Staat — Erziehung*, Jg. 1959, Heft 8, Ernst Klett Verlag, Stuttgart.

In the author's opinion, it would only be detrimental to ourselves if we were to expel the guilt-laden history of National Socialism from consciousness. In this essay, Weinstock tries to demonstrate that discussion of National Socialism involves plentiful opportunities for education in ethics and politics. The author states that a discussion of this kind is the only means of strengthening ourselves against the danger of a new catastrophe. He infers that teaching the lessons taught by the history of National Socialism is therefore the moral obligation of every educator.

Weniger, Erich: *Politische Bildung und staatsbürgerliche Erziehung* (Political Educ-ation and Citizenship Training). Würzburg: Werkbund-Verlag, 1954.

"Our deliberations on political education and citizenship training", writes Weniger in this essay, "must proceed on the basis of as precise an investigation as possible ... of those changes in the conformation of our intellectual, social, and political existence that might be of permanence and force us to seek new approaches to education." He adds that political education should, on the foundation of a general education of the individual — a training in humanity — guide him to direct, active participation in poltical developments and in political responsibility. The author remarks that this also includes thorough preparation of adolescents for the functions they will someday be expected to perform in youth organizations, in connection with co-determination in industry, in professional societies and in political organi-sations. He is moreover of the opinion that the attempt must be made to illuminate the complicated interrelationships and problems of our political life. He writes that pure "drill in facts concerning the constitution, administrative bodies, political pro-cedures, types of government, and the like" is "quite pointless". He states that it is on the contrary a question of imparting experiences, "mental experiences leading to realization and insight".

Wilhelm, Theodor: *Paedagogik der Gegenwart* (Contemporary Pedagogy). Stutt-gart: Kröner Verlag, 1960.

In the course of a general presentation of the problems of present-day German pedagogy, the author provides a summary of the theses concerning the objective of political training advanced in his volume *Partnerschaft*, which was published under the pseudonym "Friedrich Oetinger" (q. v.).

Wittram, Reinhard: *Das Interesse an der Geschichte: Zwoelf Vorlesungen ueber Fragen des zeitgenoessischen Geschichtsverstaendnisses* (Interest in History: Twelve Lectures on Questions Concerning Contemporary Comprehension of History). Goettingen: Verlag Vandenhoeck & Ruprecht, 1958.

The fundamental view of this work may be illustrated by the following quotation:

> "An interest in history that orients itself only to what happens to be of note at the moment will become short-winded and devoid of vision. Comprehension must have a vast range and a great deal in mind. There is nothing in history that is not interesting — if it is understood. Anyone who calls the outlived and extinct matters of the past "rummage" does not know what he is talking about. The interesting thing is that it has to do with me — not in the sense that everything can be brought into verifiable relationship with my era, but in the spirit that it involves the human race. The whole is present in every part."

The bearing of the present upon historical perception is not denied by any means. Yet history's relation to the present presumes a certain "advance comprehension" of the historical aspects, according to Wittram. It is "felt ... to be the at once, consternating and liberating, painful and challenging discontinuation of history".

Germany in American Eyes [1]

By Norbert Muhlen

Sometimes wind and sometimes rain,
Then the sun comes back again;
Sometimes rain and sometimes snow,
Goodness, how we'd like to know
Why the weather alters so.
Ford Madox Ford, *Children's Songs*

In a recent book in which he attempted to acquaint Americans with *The Unquiet Germans* of our time, Charles W. Thayer, an American diplomat, army officer and author, observed: "The thankless task of analyzing nations' souls becomes hopeless when, as Goethe said of his compatriots, they have two souls in every breast." Does it matter that Goethe never said such a thing about his German "compatriots?" When his Docor Faust confessed,

Zwei Seelen wohnen, ach, in meiner Brust,

he merely proclaimed that there dwelled two souls — one divine, the other, mundane — in his own breast. And if one must generalize, this dichotomous nature is human rather than German.

But what made Mr. Thayer's slip so significant was its rather Freudian revelation of the uneasy image which he — and many other Americans with him — held of postwar Germany.

The Germans "have two faces ... The enigma of Germany is permanent ...", V. S. Pritchett in 1959 likewise asserted in *Holiday Magazine*. As it seems to Americans, these "two souls", two characters, two sets of traits of Germany stand in sharp and eternal conflict with each other — one being good, the second, wicked. While they are locked in a fight that neither wins, the Germans remain "unquiet" — or so the stereotype has it.

This image of the double-souled, double-faced, enigmatic, and therefore "unpredictable" Germans, as it prevailed at the outset of the 1960's in American eyes, reflected not so much the German realities of our time as it did the sum of varying stereotypes of Germany (based on yesterday's realities, it is true,) which Americans had accepted over the past two centuries. In quick alteration, Germany had appeared as Europe's model country and then again as the world's worst nation, now populated by peaceful people, and at the next moment, by addicts of war and violence, yesterday to be feared, today to be trusted, and tomorrow — who knows? The question-mark was a symbol looming large over the American image of Germany in our time and the answer consisted mainly in a vague "it remains to be seen".

First and foremost, these swiftly and thoroughly changing past images of Germany in American eyes were formed, of course, by the changes in the realities, the structure and spirit of Germany which underwent equally abrupt and deep changes.

---

[1] From *Meet Germany*, published by Atlantik-Bruecke, Hamburg, 1960.

The more similarities to the values and institutions of the United States Americans thought to see in new German realities, the friendlier was their image of "the Germans". Americans gauged and evaluted the foreign country according to the degree by which it developed "in their own image", and this yardstick might well be called "typically American", for it has been produced by the very philosophy if not theology on which the American republic was founded.

Public opinion of other peoples rarely results, though, from the use of one single yardstick, and if there are actual political relationships with a foreign nation — as there came to be between America and Germany since the turn of this century, — the image tends to reflect their course. More precisely, while genuine conflicts of interest divide the two countries, the picture generally held of the other country and its people takes on darker colors and many unpleasant traits, — and *vice versa*. As it would seem from a study of American public opinion of, and policies toward, Germany, public opinion has followed rather than caused the ups and downs in actual relationships.

But the interrelation of domestic ideals and interests of America with those of Germany (or other countries,) are often counterbalanced, or at least slowed up by a third factor which also helps to form American public opinion. It is the longevity of stereotypes and clichés; they survive for a long time after the realities that created them have come to vanish. This power of survival innate to international images has been established by social psychologists in their study of prejudice — which, after all, is often merely a petrified image surviving realities, and resisting rational observation. Hence, in the case of present-day Germany, the image of the "two souls"; it is an amalgam of yesterday's image transformed into prejudice and of today's emerging new image. Yet in turn, yesterday's image as well as today's also contain the remnants of images from considerably more ancient times.

For almost one century after the inception of the United States, Americans accepted a highly positive picture of Germany and the Germans. While in that period actual political relationships between the two nations — and with them, actual tensions and conflicts — hardly existed, American opinion of Germany could originate almost exclusively from the comparison of Germans with the image in which Americans saw themselves.

Throughout the first half of the 19th century, the voices of American public opinion — editorialists, authors, preachers, politicians — described the Germans most frequently as "calm", "moderate", "hardy", "staid", "economical and hard-working", "kindly", "domestic", "quiet"; these were the traits which the early republicans, the pioineers, the burghers of the Jacksonian era liked to attribute to themselves, too. In contrast with the British — seen at the time as the "hereditary enemy" and consequently as evil, due to the conflicts of mutual political relationships, — and in contrast with the French — to which then none of these qualities were applied, — the Germans, who were observed with a detachment based on distance, seemed more similar to Americans than any other people; therefore they appeared as "the good Germans", and "the quiet Germans".

Only in their political order prevailed a deep dissimilarity, as Americans found. But when in 1848 Germany attempted its democratic revolution, it seemed to remove the last facet that set it apart from America, and America was carried away by a wave of Germanophile emotions unparalleled ever before or since. Germans, it seemed, took to a democracy in the American pattern, based on human, civil and States' rights, successfully steering a middle course "between royalty and radicalism" which were equally unpopular in America. In fact, it was the way in which the

Germans went about their revolution as much as that revolution itself that impressed Americans with the similarity between the German character and their own; rather than in the "tumultuous" and "blood-thirsty" ways of the French, the Germans were reputed to overthrow their rulers in a "calm" and "moderate" way, in brief, on the middle of the road which Americans glorified a long time before Dwight D. Eisenhower made it his slogan.

Once this revolution was defeated, however, Americans reverted to their previous image; Germans, as in 1866 *The Nation* magazine summed it up, were "the most learned, patient, industrious, civilized people on the face of the globe, which has attained the highest distinction in arts, in science, in arms, in literature, in everything, in short, but in politics". For politics, as Americans then believed, was the branch of civilization in which their own people had attained the highest distinction on the globe; seeing the happy results of their great social experiment, other nations would eventually come to copy it by their own will, as Americans confidently hoped. In the meantime, they remained politically underdeveloped nations who deserved America's moral support on their way to freedom. For the time being, the *New York Herald* in 1852 noted, the Germans were "incapable of republican institutions until they had been better prepared by a long democratic education". It was merely a matter of time and education, Americans thought, until the United States of Germany would be the first foreign equivalent of their own United States; Germany seemed well ahead on this road.

Apart from politics, Germany was already seen as closely resembling the American self-image. It was "the land of Luther" at a time when America was identified with Protestantism; it was also the land of free and general elementary education which Americans considered one of the main pillars of their own egalitarian and progress-minded order. (The systems of German schools and universities were widely copied in America.) Like America, Germany — or, all the kingdoms and other sovereign states called Germany — seemed averse to conquests and victories by arms; rather and also like America, they appeared bound on building a new, powerful domestic industry able to compete with the economically superior British. "Germany is, I find, very nearly related to our country", William James wrote after attending a German university.

When in 1870 war broke out between France and Prussia, American sympathies were with Germany which, as the *New York Times* expounded, "embodied, to our minds, the freer ideas of the age, freedom of thought and constitutional progress". While Germany was still politically underdeveloped, France — in addition to being characterized as Catholic or atheistic, at any rate "frivolous", "unstable", "impatient", "sexually depraved" and "vainglorious", a true catalogue of traits hated by Americans — had its two opportunities of being a democracy, but both times had refuted the saving grace, and therefore deserved contempt for being stubbornly wayward, rather than charity for merely being backward.

But while Prussia won the war, it lost American sympathies. The new German empire — founded on power rather than freedom, apparently left the road toward a democratic republic. In turn the French once again reverted to it, in addition to their transformation into the European underdog — and by tradition American sympathies go to the underdog. Over the next fifty years these American feelings were continuously strengthened while a new image of Germany emerged — the image of "the bad Germans", militaristic, lusting for power, authoritarian despoilers of domestic freedom and international peace, in brief, the opposite of the American self-image. Germany was now personified by Emperor William II, as repulsive, ridiculous and fearsome a figure in American eyes as had been before that of Emperor Louis Bonaparte who personified France. With the new naval and colonial ambitions of imperial Germany, actual political relationships evolved between that country and the United States, but more often than not they were in the nature of hostile encounters spanning from Venezuela to Samoa and China. The new negative picture of Germany superimposed the old positive picture.

The First World War carried this hostile image of Germany to new heights. With the exception of many members of the academic, Jewish-American, and German-American communities, each having special ties with and sympathies of its own for Germany, the majority of Americans accepted the new stereotype of Germans as "the Huns". At war's end, as the historian John Gerow Gazley reported, Americans had passed through a period when it was popularly believed that... every German was instinctively and unalterably a babykiller. If this somewhat overstated the case, no doubt the prevailing American temper was different only in degree, not in substance. The image of the "bad Germans" now rooted as firmly in the American imagination as before that of the "good Germans"; however, the first image was deepened by the emotions of conflict and war, and therefore probably more intense.

In the years of the Weimar Republic this picture underwent new alterations while Germany made a second try at democracy, worked hard and peacefully, excelled in technology, science, the arts, — in short, took on again the contours and colors of its first, "good" image. Furthermore, it was now Germany which was the international underdog. In brief, the reversal of 1871 was again being reversed. Once again, the Germans appeared primarily as "industrious" and "scientifically-minded," as in 1931 Princeton University students — in the first test in which social psychologists used the word-list assocation method — asserted. Over the years, the two images of the Good Germans and the Bad Germans merged in an uneasy balance; on the whole, the new attitude of Americans toward Germany from 1923 to 1933 was far from its war-time freezing point, yet far removed also from its original warmth; it was rather lukewarm, and slowly, though steadily improving.

In the eyes of many Americans, the Third Reich at first seemed merely a German regression to the realities of the Kaiser to which the old stereotypes could easily be refitted. (People everywhere have an almost compulsive tendency of seeing new realities through old cliché-colored glasses.) The persecutions of the Jews added the new trait of anti-Semitism to the old image; and the Communists who took the lead in the propaganda battle against Nazi Germany, tried hard and quite successfully to superimpose their Marxist stereotype; their image of Nazism as the "dictatorship of monopoly capitalism" out to destroy the workers' rights at home and the Soviet Union abroad added a new left-wing coloration to the old hostile picture of Germany. (Before, liberal and radical left-of-center opinion had been traditionally "pro-German".

However, Americans at large were uncertain whether or not to agree with those who now saw and presented the Germans as a people basically corrupted, if not "mentally pathological", (as an early analyst of Nazism, the historian Frederick Schuman, put it, thus initiating a series of new "German traits" in which psychiatry was misused as irresponsibly as the Nazis misused biology.) The majority of Americans were reluctant to identify traits of Nazism (whose totalitarian character was still widely unknown,) with the character of the German people.

Due to its own pre-assumptions, the American mind tends perennially to waver between two contradictory reactions to a dictatorship abroad. On the one hand

America's democratic axiom holds that a people has the leaders and also the form of government which it deserves, which it wants, and which it has brought about itself, either by commission or omission of democratic activity and civic responsibility. Therefore, the people are blamed as much as their leaders for what Americans dislike in their country, until in the end the disliked dictatorial form of government appears as the very outcome of the national character of the foreign people. But on the other hand, the democratic axiom accepted by Americans also takes it for granted that all peoples have an innate desire for democracy (which in American usage stands for institutionalized forms of civic decency), although "gangsters" may control the government for a while by sheer force. In this case, the "oppressed" people deserve sympathy and suport in their struggle for liberation. And so with Nazi Germany. While both images militated against each other, Hitler's claim that all Germans stood behind him helped to identify Germans with Nazism, to taint the image of the people with the sinister colors of the system, and to make them responsible for the deeds of their leaders.

But even in the first years of the Second World War, the majority of Americans remained unwilling to accept the claims of either Hitler or of American cryptoracist German-haters. True, by 1942 the adjectives used to describe Germans most frequently were now "war-like" and "cruel", while the older favorable qualities such as "hard-working" and "intelligent" also still remained in the foreground; but other old traits of the "good Germans" such as "religious", "quiet", "dull" were rarely attributed to them any more. Nevertheless, as late as 1943 the overwhelming majority of Americans still affirmed that they "did not hate the Germans". In addition, they affirmed their conviction that the Germans, once they were given an opportunity and the required education, would join the ranks of peaceful and free nations, as they did not really want the Nazi rule.

What was more, Americans were willing to back up these convictions by their own sacrifices. In the midst of the war, with tragic casualties abroad and rationing at home, the majority, for instance, supported the suggestion that after the war food be sent to Germany, and that the reconstruction of German industry be encouraged rather than interdicted. American advocates of a vindictive peace remained a small minority.

Only toward the end of the war, and increasingly so for several months after V-E Day, did the American majority tend to accept the identification of Germans with Nazis, and to support proponents of a "tough" postwar treatment of Germany. There is not sufficient evidence to show whether this new mood stemmed from the revelations of Nazi atrocities in concentration camps and occupied countries, or from the progressive impact of war-time propaganda which slowly made the older images vanish. Yet by the end of 1945, this brief interval of emotional hostility toward the German people in which the German character was seen accordingly, and which lasted less than a year, ceased winning new adherents; it slowly receded, and gradually the dark image paled.

The first inroads toward a new image were made in 1948 when the people of Berlin, supported by the American armed forces and the American people, resisted the Soviet blockade. As Americans saw it, it proved that Germans were not Nazis; or perhaps, Americans thought, Germans had learned their lesson, and the value of freedom. Over the subsequent decade, the policies and posture of the new German government, and its approval as shown in the national elections, seemed to confirm this ney image. Rather than Hitler, it was now Chancellor Adenauer — and to some degree, Ernst Reuter and Willy Brandt, the two mayors of Berlin — who personified this Germany of the new image, as its symbol appeared in American eyes the Volkswagen — small, sturdy and successful, — which took the previously symbolic place of Big Bertha guns and Tiger tanks.

Yet the stereotypes of Nazi Germany were slow to disappear. No image, as we learned, tends to disappear overnight. But in the case of the Nazi-German image, the impact had been so uniquely deep, often traumatic, and its causes beyond comprehension, that in many American minds it remained associated with Germany. Furthermore, some writers and analysts purposely kept playing up this image, — sometimes from their own traumatic experience. In other instances they misrepresented the new Germany in the interest of Soviet policies out to destroy mutual trust between the new alliance of free nations to which the United States as well as the new Germany belonged, and also out to distract attention from Communism's terroristic dictatorship.

Over the years of the 1950's, the Nazi image submersed increasingly in many American minds, but on slight provocation it was brought to the surface again. Often a single minor news item from Germany reporting some isolated incident of a Nazi nature was viewed as an alarm signal of Nazi revival; and with it, the old hostile stereotypes of Nazi times in American opinion came to life again.

By the beginning of the 1960's, American opinion had arrived at a point rather distinctive from previous attitudes; while before it had frequently held that the German people were "good," while their leaders and their political order were "bad," now the opposite was often accepted. Most observers were impressed by the democratic goodwill of leaders such as Adenauer and Brandt, — two names widely known and respected in America, — while they were less certain about the thoroughness of democratic beliefs among the people at large.

But the response of American opinion — through its press, the voluntary religious, political, other organizations, its political spokesmen — to the outbreak of anti-Semitic incidents after Christmas Eve of 1959 in Germany significantly differed from the response to similar incidents of previous years; and this new response of 1960 clearly demonstrated that the new, friendlier image was coming to the fore, and beginning to be widely accepted. As Americans now found, the social values, the "way of life", the devotion to work, industry and science, also the emphasis on output and consumption of goods, the peaceful ambitions and the thoroughly "quiet" character of present-time Germans again closely resembled the characteristics of their own. Yet for the first time, Germany also closely resembled the United States in its political structure and institutions, its respect for civil liberties, its democratic system. In addition, actual political relationships united rather than divided the two countries; in a consent of interests as well as ideals, they stood side by side in the defense of their common values and their national existence. What once William James had observed, was now again discovered by many G.I.s on NATO duty in Germany: "Germany is, I find, very nearly related to our country". In American eyes, this near relation was bound to be seen in a new — or again in the old — light of respect and understanding.

Although some of the old misgivings, prejudices and fears were still alive, they paled under the impact of the new reality. As long as this new reality would keep prevailing, the new American image of Germany would keep improving. In the view of most Americans "the Germans" have developed a character by force of which they became trusted partners in the new alliance for freedom and peace. This is today's dominant American image of Germany.

Questions and Answers on West Germany [1]

By Sebastian Haffner

What is the mood of West Germany? For a long time we have been told it is comfortable, materialistic, selfish, pacifist, against all adventures, lacking in confidence, not even very interested in the reunion of Germany. Is this still true or is the mood slowly changing?

It is still surprisingly true. Among the politically minded, of course, the mood is no longer as placid as it used to be — rather a little uneasy, even a little glum. They know that they are at the moment being subject to a drumfire of world-wide denunciation, for which every resource of Communist and Communist-influenced propaganda is employed. They sense that this propaganda is having its effect, and that British, and perhaps also American — feelings for West Germany are no longer what they were a few years ago. They are worried, but remain passive. They keep their fingers crossed and hope for the best. No real sign of a nationalist revival yet.

As far as the big non-political majority is concerned, almost nothing of all this has yet sunk in, and people just continue to enjoy their regained prosperity and respectibility, their supposed holiday from history, their chromium-plated idyll, and hope that it may last for ever.

In so far as there is a visible reaction against this still predominantly happy philistine complacency, it comes from the intellectual and literary Left and not from the Right. A left-wing radical "non-conformism", neither Communist nor Social Democratic, but anti-Governmental, contemptuous of the "economic miracle", nationally self-critical to the point of sometimes being anti-German, calling for a belated repentance of Nazi sins and sometimes for a belated prosecution of former Nazis — this has become a growing force in West German public opinion over the last three years or so. It forms the mainstream of the reviving German literature, has strong points in the universities, in the Protestant Church, in the press, and has established a complete hold on German television. Whether it will in its turn bring about a right-wing reaction (of which the swastika daubings around the New Year may have been an inarticulate premonition) is too early to say.

A word about reunion. No German will ever admit that he does not passionately care about it, and a substantial minority, especially in Protestant Northern Germany, really does passionately care. But pessimism about reunion in the foreseeable future has been growing, and sometimes this pessimism is hard to distinguish from resignation. Still, this is a subject about which only a fool would dogmatize. Nine out of ten Germans, in cold blood, reject the idea of a war for reunion with genuine horror. But how they would react if one day there were a Hungary in East Germany I would not dare to say.

---

[1] Sebastian Haffner, Berlin correspondent of the *London Observer*, has answered questions put by the London staff of his paper. The article was published on 24 April 1960.

European Union

> Do West Germans still believe in a united Western Europe or not?

Yes and no. As a popular political movement, European federalism in Germany is far weaker than it was ten years ago. At the same time, the new friendship with France and the new intimacy with Western Europe in general are taken for granted; anti-French resentments are not only dead but are regarded as positively quaint, like Victorian interior decoration, and masses of Germans now habitually take their holidays in France and Italy without a conscious feeling of going "abroad". The idea that Germany could ever be at war again with her Western European neighbors has dropped right out of existence. Perhaps it would be truest to say that West Germans today — mistakenly — regard and treat West European unity as if it were an accomplished fact, something to be enjoyed rather than something still to be achieved.

The Forces

> How strong is their Army and how efficient? Is it popular? are the people proud of it? And the Air Force? Navy?

In round figures, the German Forces today total 250,000 men, of which the Army has around 150,000, the Air Force 80,000, the Navy 20,000. The planned ultimate peacetime establishment, to be reached in about two years time, may be 350,000 in all. The efficiency rating, on the basis of the last manoeuvres, is fair to good; but it is still a force in the making, which will need several more years to reach maturity.

Public attitudes towards the new forces vary from mild popularity via tolerant acceptance to grudging indifference. The active (*ohne mich*) anti-militarism of the early fifties has died down, but there is none of the old popular enthusiasm for the Army.

There are two other new features. First, the forces are entirely under civilian control, and the high brass has no say in politics. Secondly, internal discipline follows the American rather than the Prussian model: the soldier is regarded as a "citizen in uniform" and treated as the social equal of his military superiors. There is even a military *"Ombudsman"*, through whom every soldier who feels wronged can, over the heads of the whole military hierarchy, appeal direct to Parliament.

Nationalism

> Are there then any strongly nationalist groups or parties waiting in the wings for Adenauer to die? If so, are these led by old Nazis, or are they new men?

The answer is in the negative. Nazi revivals have been attempted by little groups or parties ever since 1949, with constantly declining success. At the moment, neo-Nazism in West Germany is a lunatic fringe, not more. As for old Nazis (real ones), a few of them live discreet professional lives, under assumed names, in Germany (and provide the occasional scandal when dug out); rather more form little *émigré* circles in Cairo and Buenos Aires. None of them has any political influence or following in Germany.

Whether a Nazi revival is possible if West Germany were ever cast out from the West, and/or subject to an economic depression, is a matter for speculation. My own opinion is that it is improbable even then, and that a new German nationalism would take different forms. Today, at any rate, Nazism in West Germany is a figment of Communist propaganda.

Ex-Nazis

> Was Adenauer's policy of deliberately soft-pedalling de-nazification and letting time heal the wounds wise or not? How many real (as opposed to formal) Nazis are there really in power and office?

In my opinion, the policy was very wise indeed. The real and effective de-Nazification of Germany took place during the last stage of the war and was largely the work of Hitler himself. In May 1945, Nazism, as a political creed, was dead in Germany, and personal persecution of the numerous former adherents of this discredited creed could only have revived it by creating a massive vested interest in Nazi apologetics.

The number of real present Nazis in positions of power and influence in West Germany is, to the best of my knowledge, zero. The number of real ex-Nazis is probably still quite substantial though in a natural way diminishing year by year. The difference, which the question does not formulate, seems to me decisive — more decisive than the difference between real and formal ex-Nazis, which is very fluctuating.

Genuine Recoil from Past

Not even Communist propaganda can deny that present West German justice is a model of mildness, humanity, and civilized sophistication. This is so although, or possibly because, many of the older judges once had, willingly or unwillingly, to dispense Nazi justice; it represents, in them, a genuine recoil from, and compensation for, their own past.

One can generalize from this example and say that, in a sense, the whole present West Germany represents Germany's genuine recoil from, and compensation for, its Nazi past, and this is naturally embodied in hundreds and thousands of cases of individual persons who had a Nazi period in their lives and have turned their backs on it. It seems to me a far more respectable and confidence-inspiring phenomenon than the forcible imposition, under anti-Nazi auspices, of another intolerant and persecuting political creed, which is what we witness in East Germany.

Education

> What is education like, particularly in the universities? What do German historians and philosophers teach young people? And what do the young people say to their professors? Do the young men and women really know what the Nazi regime was like, and do they care? Are they secretly a bit proud of Hitler?

Education in West Germany, including the universities, is very much what it was in all Germany before Hitler, or even before 1918 — at which point history-teaching in the schools often stops. It imparts much solid factual knowledge, and, in the case of the universities, sound methods of research. With few exceptions, it does not impart either a coherent philosophy of life or an established set of manners. It never did.

There is no recognized German school of history or philosophy at the moment. There are individual scholars, teaching differing, often eclectic, doctrines. As everywhere in the West, science dominates the universities at the expense of the humanities, and probably attracts the best talents.

German academic historians have, on the whole, despite one or two brave freelance attempts, so far failed to review and rewrite German history in the light of twentieth-century experience. The great nineteenth-century historians still retain their authority, and modern events are often judged in the incongruant terms of the Bismarckians and their Liberal critics. An authoritative scholarly German history of Hitler does not exist, and textbooks and school books have to make do with scrappy facts and conventionaly adverse snap judgments.

The young — with individual exceptions — know and care little about Hitler, but then they know and care little about history altogether. (They do know and care about cars, rockets, and space travel). I have never personally come across signs of secret pride in Hitler's exploits among the young, and I don't think it is at all widespread among the general run of them. But there are odd little youth circles here and there in which, usually under the guidance of middle-aged misfits, a brew of *Germanic mystique*, military glory, and *Wandervoegel* romanticism continues to be distilled.

Altogether it is probably true that education is the weakest spot in the present West Germany. Partly this is a weakness Germany shares wih the agnostic West as a whole. Partly education is the field in which the secret insecurity and sick conscience of the German elder generation — the Hitler generation — has its most damaging and most lasting effect. But the result of weak education among the young seems to be shapelessness and disorientation, rather than any positive evil.

Rule of Law

How deeply rooted is democracy and Parliamentary government?

What is deeply rooted and really valued in post-Hitler Germany is the rule of law, personal liberty, humane decency, and orderly constitutional process of government — "normality". Democracy and Parliament are certainly less deeply rooted, but they are now soberly accepted by almost everybody as the necessary political basis of the aforementioned values. There is, in any case, no alternative. Monarchy and aristocratic rule are past reviving; dictatorship and totalitarianism are completely discredited, and there is no serious opposition to democracy and Parliamentary government, in striking contrast to the days of the Weimar Republic.

Power in the present West Germany is distributed between (in rough order of importance) the Chancellor, the Parliamentary majority party, the Cabinet, Parliament as a whole, the States, and the big lobbies. The Christian Democratic party machine is hardly a power factor at all. The German Christian Democrats, like the British Conservatives, are the sort of party that outside Parliament and between elections leads an obscure, almost unnoticeable existence. They are not a machine party.

Opposition

What has happened to the Social Democrats, and what do they want? Who will succeed Adenauer anyway?

The Social Democrats have taken a grip on themselves and — to judge by the latest State and municipal elections results — are on the upgrade again. The two great — connected — events of their recent party history are the meteoric rise of Willy Brandt, and the adoption of a new party programme which repudiates Marx and remodels the party on Scandinavian lines.

Willy Brandt, the Social Democrat Mayor of Berlin, is now the only serious rival of Adenauer in popular esteem in Germany, and appears as the predestined successor. The question is whether even he can carry his party — the natural minority party in West Germany — into government.

After Adenauer, this might not be wholly impossible in a straight electoral fight; in the meantime, the possibility of a coalition — towards which Herr Brandt is edging his party via a bipartisan foreign policy — is for the first time a matter of serious talk in political Germany. German post-war politics were never as interesting as they are beginning to be just now; and the question of the Brandt succession to Adenauer is the key to everything.

It is, incidentally, a mistake to think of the German Social Democrats merely as a frustrated permanent opposition party. They have been for ten years in opposition in Bonn, but they lead five of the eleven State Governments and dominate most of the big municipalities. They have also, on a bipartisan basis, cooperated in some of the most important legislation in Bonn, such as the new military constitution and the new model law on old age pensions, with which Germany leads the world in this field. They definitely belong to the West German establishment.

Lost Lands

> What about the Oder-Neisse line? Do most Germans accept it as final? Do they feel wronged? Do they think that one day, somehow, they will get back Silesia, Sudetenland, etc.?

There was a time — and not so long ago — either when practically every serious German politician would privately say that, of course, in return for reunification, Germany would have to accept the Oder-Neisse line, or something very like it. In the last year or so, this has changed, partly through increased counter-propaganda of the Association of Expellees — which, with more than two million members, is a powerful lobby — but mainly, and paradoxically, through the fading of reunification hopes. As long as even the claim to reunification has to remain theoretical, what inducement have the Germans to give up the further theoretical claim to the lost Eastern provinces? (A claim to Sudetenland is not officially made.) One advantage of getting nothing is that one can dream of everything.

Popular feelings about the whole question vary, of course, greatly between the expellees and the indigenous West Germans. Obviously there is a sense of grievance — which might still be overcome if this were the price of a genuine reunification. Perhaps it would also be overcome if there could ever be a real deal with Poland; but for this it seems at present too early or too late. So the claim will linger on for the time being. How many people really think it can ever be realized, I don't know.

Fear of East

> Do the West Germans ever talk or think of doing a deal with Russia? Do they feel strong enough to play that kind of game?

Some outsiders, yes. (Among them remarkably, the little German Reich Party, often considered neo-Nazi). Any responsible politicians, no. Among the general public, deep fear and horror of Communism stand in the way.

And yet I could imagine a situation in which many Germans would begin to think and talk of a deal with Russia, not from a sense of strength, but from a sense of weakness. If the West, on which West Germany relies, were proved too weak to hold Berlin, or too unfriendly to stand by the West German alliance, or too disloyal to hold out against recognition of East Germany, there might be panic and a clamor to come to terms with Russia while reasonable terms could still be had. If Russia then made a generous reunion offer, anything might happen.

Industry

> What part does big industry play? We said we must split up German heavy industry, and this was not done — probably rightly. But does it matter or not?

If education is the weakest point of the present West Germany, industry is the strongest. The professional achievement of West German industry since 1948 — not only in sheer production, but also in technological planning, marketing, and social relations — is beyond praise. It seems as if the German capacity for excellence, shifting from field to field, has now, after a succession of music, scholarship, and soldiering, settled on industry.

Of course it matters greatly that German industry was not split up after the war. Had it been, this would have imposed artificial misery on Germany and would have made Germany safe for Communism. As it is, the "economic miracle" has given the new German democracy and Western orientation a solid basis of prosperity.

The "economic miracle" is only very partly the work of the old industrial families. A vast stream of managerial talent from the middle and lower middle classes has flowed into German industry since the war, and many of the biggest industrial names of today are entirely new men. (For instance, the present director-general of Krupps, and virtual re-creator of this gigantic combine, is the expellee-son of a washerwoman from now Polish Stettin).

The industrial climate, too, is new. Despite over-full employment, there is an almost complete absence of strikes, due to remarkable relations between industrial management and trade unions. In fact, there is something like a secret coalition between them against bankers and hard money politicians.

Industry is, of course, a powerful lobby in economic affairs, but — in contrast to Weimar days — it is rather kept out of real influence on major foreign policy. Mr. Khrushchev's toast to Herr Krupp at the Leipzig Fair of 1959, and the fraternization scenes between Herr Ulbricht and some representatives of big Ruhr industries at this year's Leipzig Fair, are curious reminders of the difference between myth and reality. It is a myth that German capitalism is the most reliably pro-Western force in Germany. It is pro-business, wherever business can be done. It is, however, also a myth that the big capitalists make German foreign policy. This is made by Dr. Adenauer today, and perhaps by Herr Brandt tomorrow.

Churches

> What part is played by the Churches — Roman Catholic and Protestant?

Since we were on the subject of myths: the idea that Adenauer's policy is inspired by the Cardinals is as mythical as that is it inspired by the big industrialists. The Chancellor is a good Roman Catholic and an adherent of free enterprise, but his politics are strictly his own.

The role of the Churches in present West Germany is easily overrated. The religious revival, which was often expected after the catastrophe of 1945, has not taken place. The direct political influence of the Churches is very limited — because they are two and not one, partly because their chief sphere of political interest, education, is a State, not Federal, affair, and many State Governments are led by Social Democrats.

Nevertheless, the fact that the ruling party is explicitly "Christian" helps the Churches; and so does the general West German climate of restored, deliberate respectability. People no longer leave their church, as was the fashion under Weimar and also under Hitler; rather they tend to drift back to the fold for decency's sake, even if they remain semi-agnostics at heart. The Christian festivals are again kept with some strictness; so are the individual church rites of baptism, marriage consecration, and Christian burial.

This somewhat formal restoration of the outward decencies of Christianity favors the Roman Catholic Church more than the Protestant one; so does its stricter discipline over its flock. In the result one is often tempted to think of West Germany as a predominantly Roman Catholic country, although the number of Roman Catholics and Protestants is almost exactly equal, and the Christian Democratic Party insists almost pedantically on strict denominational parity in its patronage.

It is true that the Protestant Church, which has its centre of strength in the poorer northeastern parts of West Germany — and beyond, of course, in East Germany — which sticks to an all-German church organization and has a strong nonconformist left-wing, easily appears in a somewhat opposition-like role. But these are subtilties, of which not too much should be made. On the whole the interdenominational peace, and the spirit of mutual toleration between the two churches, as well as between Church and State, belong to the many achievements through which the present West Germany scores over every other modern German State, — not excluding Bismarck's famous German Reich of ninety years ago.

Impressions of Germany

By Oscar Cohen

During the spring and summer of 1960 I visited the Federal Republic of Germany twice in connection with my responsibilities as Director of Program and Education of the Anti-Defamation League of B'nai B'rith. I approached my first trip to Germany with deep emotional involvement. My reaction to setting foot on the soil of Germany for the first time — a revulsion amounting almost to physical illness — is I suppose a common one. However, I think if one is determined to be objective, it is difficult too to come to sweeping conclusions.

While my trips to Germany were brief and were limited to visits to Frankfurt, Wiesbaden, Bonn, Cologne, and Berlin, I tried to make the most of my time by interviewing those who would be in a position to provide me with information I was seeking. I had met with knowledgeable people in the United States and in other European countries both before and after my visit to Germany. Moreover, I made it a point to seek out those who were the political opponents of the party in power in Germany and those in other countries who were ideologically opposed to the present Christian Democratic regime. I was in a position therefore to compare the reactions of opponents of the Christian Democratic party with the statements of representatives of the present administration.

My primary concern was the status of education and research concerning democracy in Germany. I centered my questioning and investigations around two questions:

1. How deeply rooted is democracy in Germany at the present time?
2. Is an adquate program being undertaken to build democracy in Germany and root out any residue of Nazism and anti-Semitism?

I found what to me was an amazing degree of unanimity in answers to these questions. There was general agreement that democracy was well established in Germany. There may have been a difference of opinion upon the degree to which democracy exists in Germany, but no one felt there was any immediate danger to the democratic framework at this time. If there was any doubt about the future of Germany, it was always expressed to me in the words "at the present time". There were varying degrees of confidence about the future, but there was absolutely no fear about the present.

It was pointed out that democracy had been imposed upon Germany twice. The first imposition was a failure for a variety of reasons, most of them quite evident. This time, however, the situation is very different from that existing during the days of the Weimar Republic. This time Germans know they were defeated. At the end of the first World War no foreign soldiers were on German soil. It was easy to impress upon the German people that they were in some way cheated or betrayed. However, the results of defeat under Hitler are all around. The German people have paid a price for their defeat. Secondly, Germany has experienced two dictatorships, the Nazis and, in the Eastern Zone, the Communists. Both have been painful. The rewards of the Nazi dictatorship are readily evident in the deaths, the mangling of individuals, and the destruction of cities. The Communist dictatorship has left its mark on people wherever they have had physical contact with it. Where they have not, there are a large number of refugees and a constant flow of escapees from East Germany which remind people about Communism. West Germany has absorbed 12,000,000 refugees since the end of the war. Before the war the area now known as West Germany had a population of 36,000,000. Its population is now 55,000,000. Finally, a compelling reason for at least the apparent solidity of democracy in Germany is the fact that it works. Germany is extremely properous. One-quarter of the workers in Germany now own their own homes. From 1950 to 1960 real income for workers has increased from 50 to 60 %. From 1948 to 1960 the real income of German workers rose from ⅓ that of United States workers to ½. One out of every five cars sold is being purchased by workers. Democracy is the philosophy of success.

There is general agreement that Communism in West Germany is dead. Also there was complete agreement on everyone's part that the extreme right wing is dead also. It was pointed out with apparent logic by most of those to whom I spoke that people who had Nazi leanings would vote for right-wing parties. The *Deutsche Reichspartei*, the only party which might possibly be considered as the successor to the Nazis, received 1 % of the vote. It would seem that this extreme right-wing movement is of little political consequence. (The pro-fascist parties in Italy received an estimated 14 % of the vote in the last election.)

There was agreement also that anti-Semitism is no threat, at least at the present time. It was pointed out that Hitler had solved the Jewish problem. There simply were not enough Jews left in Germany to form any basis for an anti-Semitic movement. Whatever people may feel in their hearts, there is no open anti-Semitism, and in fact in many ways Jews are favored both by official Germany and by many segments of society.

It is evident to me that not nearly enough is known about how German people feel about Nazism and the degree to which the residue of Nazism has disappeared. Research might be able to throw some light upon what the public reaction might be under less favorable conditions than those which exist in Germany at the present time. What would happen under crisis situations nobody knows. This is the big question. Yet there is a high degree of confidence in Germany. Even the Social Democrats point out that a severe economic depression is unlikely. They indicate that nations have learned how to deal with severe economic crises at last. While there is a difference of opinion as to the degree to which nostalgia for Nazism remains imbedded in the consciousness of the German people, there is agreement that the German people would never again embrace Nazism. If the German people turn toward the right, it was stated, it would be toward an authoritarian form of government, perhaps more like the administration in Portugal. Moreover, no one seemed to think that the German people would turn to open and violent anti-Semitism again.

Some seemed to think that the problem was more one of indifference and insensitivity than a residue of Nazism. All agreed that the desecration epidemic, although representing a sympathy toward Nazism and/or anti-Semitism on the part of the desecrators, had done a great deal of good. No one felt that the desecrations constituted any representative attitude on the part of the German people. If it did, they pointed out, there would have been much more of a right-wing or crackpot vote. However, the desecrations have pointed up the fact that there remained a residue of Nazism and as a result a number of good things have happened, particularly in terms of sensitizing people to the possible menace of Nazi sympathy. The program of education for democracy has been stepped up greatly as a result.

An example of this lack of sensitivity was told to me by the Minister of Education of the state of Hesse, who said he was using this incident in his speeches around the country with great effect. A high school teacher had come upon a Nazi textbook in mathematics which had been used in some schools in Germany during the Nazi regime. The problem in the Nazi text book went something like this: "There were a number of people on a boat which was sinking. There was one lifeboat and room in it for 30 people. On the sinking ship there were 15 Christians and a larger number of Jews. The problem involved lining up the people in a circle so that every ninth person would be a Jew and would therefore be excluded from the lifebot." This is not exactly the problem, but the general idea. The teacher decided to try this on his class in high school, and to his amazement the students accepted the problem and tried to figure it out. Nobody made any comment on the Jewish aspect of the problem. Somewhat startled, the high school teacher then took the problem to a group of his colleagues who were meeting at lunch. Here again the mathematically inclined took out their pencils and tried to figure out how it was done without any comment on the Jewish aspect of the problem. Once the fiendish character of this problem was pointed out to people, they were shocked. But the point is that there seemed to be a low degree of sensitivity to the problem.

Favorable Developments

These are situations which appear to be supporting the development of a firmly rooted democratic society in Germany:

1. An extensive program is being undertaken by many institutions in Germany to educate for democracy. This includes the national administration, state administration, school systems, radio, press, TV, and various publications. It should not be assumed that the educators in Germany are unaware of or insensitive to the potentialities of education in countering pro-Nazi sentiment or in building democratic attitudes. They are doing a great deal. In terms of what is happening in the mass communication field, they have just about reached the saturation point. To find substantiation of this claim, one has but to read the account of how the press treated the desecration phenomena in Germany as described in a special bulletin by the Wiener Library in London. There was a tremendous outpouring of anti-Nazi sentiment in Germany. An important Social Democratic member of Parliament said to me, "In terms of education, we are doing a good job. No effort is being spared and we are constantly seeking new ideas. If you have any ideas which we think are good, they would probably be carried out regardless of expense."

2. The labor movement constitutes a massive bulwark against many right wing tendencies. Moreover, the labor movement is conducting an extensive adult education program among its members to build knowledge of and favorable attitudes toward democracy. In its education program the full horror of Nazism is emphasized. The labor movement is constantly seeking out important former Nazis who have secured positions of power and tries to remove them from these positions. For example, the Civil Service Union was investigating every important civil service official in Germany. Importantly, the Civil Service Union includes the police in Germany, and a number of police chiefs who were former Nazis have been removed as a result of the Union action. While not according any great importance to the extreme right-wing movement, the labor movement is vigilant. They cover most right-wing meetings and engage in heckling, and although this is not democratic, they sometimes break them up. I was told by labor people that they would fight if an attempt were made to impose an authoritarian government on the nation. Coming from people who spent several years in concentration camps or in exile fighting Nazism, this statement must be taken seriously.

3. There is a vigorous movement in both major political parties to root out important former Nazis from positions of power. All those who wish to join the Social Democratic Party are screened.

4. The youth of Germany who were not exposed to the total social, economic, and educational impact of Nazism present a hope for the future, according to nearly everyone. They appear to be more enthusiastic for democracy than their elders. They appear to like the American way of life and to pattern their own behavior after Americans. A great deal of imitative behavior on the part of young people is based on American customs. The young people are more questioning than they used to be before World War II, I am told. More importantly perhaps, there is a strong spirit of anti-militarism among young people. There is great difficulty in recruiting among the young for the armed forces.

5. I was assured by many that there is a high degree of democracy in the armed forces and that the army constitutes a democratic influence. When the armed forces were established in Germany, a civilian committee screened the first officers so as to eliminate any leading Nazis. All officers must go to school where they are given courses on democracy and Nazism. Printed material provided to soldiers includes publications on democracy and the Jews. Moreover, I am told that the traditional German relationship between officers and men no longer exists.

A well known writer told me of a number of his experiences. For example, he was visiting a class of young soldiers who were being admonished for smoking in the tank park. At the end of the lecture, a young soldier stood up and said, "We saw the Colonel smoking in the tank park. What are you going to do about it?" On another occasion, the writer was talking to a Major on the parade grounds when a soldier approached and said he would like to speak to the writer. The writer agreed this was all right, but the soldier said that he would like to speak to the writer alone. The Major simply walked away. It would be surprising to hear of these incidents (which are said to be typical in Germany) in any army without consequences to the soldiers concerned, let alone the German army.

6. The lessons of history are abundantly clear in Germany. The ruin which was the result of Nazism in Germany, the bloodshed, the disgrace, the horrors of war are all very evident. The consciousness of the terrible things that happened to Germany is a deterrent for a return of the Nazi way of life.

Unfavorable Development

These are the forces and situations in Germany which seem to me to bear danger to some degree toward the development of a democratic culture in Germany:

1. The educational system has certain grave deficiences which, from the point of view of education for democracy, might be summarized as follows:

a) Up to 85 % of the young people of Germany leave school, outside of technical training, at the age of 14. Support is growing for a compulsory school age of 15. (Apart from the financial aspects involved, there is a grave shortage of teachers.)

b) There is a severe scarcity of teachers with adequate training and experience which would enable them to handle teaching about Nazism in the classroom.

c) Education is under state jurisdiction and each of the states does not have equal emphasis or uniform regulations concerning teaching about Nazism.

d) Considerable difficulties are being experienced about the introduction of discussions of Nazism into the classroom. Here one finds conflict between the school and the parents. For how does the teacher indicate that the movement in which so many students' parents participated was evil, or, for that matter, how would teachers get around the fact that many of them participated in the Nazi movement? Students have sometimes reacted unfavorably to forceful presentations. I was told of the case of one high school student who indignantly jumped to his feet and said, "My father was a Captain in the SS and was killed fighting for his country. How dare you tell me that my father was an evil man." The student then left the room. The class was sympathetic to this young man. Presentations of horror films of the Hitler period sometimes evoke a defensive response from students. They will react with statements like "All Germans could not have been that bad. Their defensiveness will be indicated in other statements like "After all, Hitler solved the unemployment problem", and, on a more elementary level, "He built the autobahn". These are examples of the kind of difficulties which teachers are encountering. There appears to be no agreement as to how best to meet this problem. While there have been a number of conferences on this matter, extensive scientific research is not taking place.

2. Much reference is made to the nebulous thing called the German character or German culture. The noted anthropologist Margaret Mead has defined the culture of a people as everything that people are accustomed to doing, from the way a

Prime Minister signs an edict, to the manner in which a mother shushes a baby. Over a period of time Germans have become identified with certain cultural characteristics — a tendency toward authoritarianism, for example. One notices these characteristics in personal relationships — the fine manners and courtesy between individuals on a peer level, and the undemocratic treatment of subordinates. No one would claim that Germany has a democratic tradition. The problem in building a democracy in Germany involves a change of national customs and habitual ways of life built up over a long period. As an example of characteristics which retard the development of democratic practices, there is a lack of activity at the grass roots level in political matters. People vote in large numbers, but there is little individual involvement in civic or political movements. Political party leaders complain that members consider that once their vote is cast, their responsibility is ended.

Organizations and pressure groups do not operate in the same way they do in the United States. Many of these groups are subsidized with government funds. American organizations would reject this paternalism and dependence. It is true that in Germany the percentage of people who vote is larger than it is in the United States, but the involvement of a large proportion of Americans in local, regional, national movements, political, service and cultural organizations, is an indication of the strength of democratic life in this country. The lack of organizational and political activity makes for complacency and indifference in Germany.

3. The denazification program in Germany has been only partly successful. There is strong feeling on the part of many that former Nazis of any consequence should not be given positions of influence — above all, not in the national administration. The denazification process, however, may have reached a point of no return, where further denazification in any except glaring cases might result in an unfavorable reaction. There seemed to be strong feeling that after fifteen years of denazification, it was time to forget except for former Nazis who were guilty of the most serious crimes.

4. One of the most serious drawbacks to the development of democratic practices and education in Germany, in my estimation, is the lack of research about problems of democracy in Germany. This became quite apparent at a two-day conference of American, German, and other European social scientists who met at the University of Frankfurt to consider this subject.

Not only has research been fragmentary and unrelated on the problem of democracy, but whatever knowledge to be gained from these studies is not being transmitted. There is inadequate exchange of information.

The most serious shortcoming is the lack of systematic research on problems which would have practical results. There is a tendency for studies in Germany to be concerned with "pure" rather than action research. A group of younger social scientists, some of them with American training, are eager to engage in practical research. They were frustrated by the dedication of the institutions with which they are associated to academic rather than practical problems. A more serious problem is the lack of adequate funds for a systematized and coordinated effort to probe the grave problems facing the German nation. It seems unlikely that without government funds and encouragement that needed research will be undertaken.

In building a democratic way of life, certain basic knowledge is required. What do the German people at various age levels actually believe and know about their past and present? What methods should be used in the training of teachers? What are the effective techniques for teaching about Nazism in the classroom? What is the effect of programs to promote democratic attitudes in the mass communication media, in organizations, in the armed forces? These are only a few of the questions to which answers are badly needed. No one knows the answers and yet responsible officials must take action. Some of these actions, in the education field for example, may be doing more harm than good.

There are social scientists in Germany capable of undertaking the needed research but funds and some coordination are required. In the development of these studies, social scientists and practitioners in the intergroup relations field in the United States have much to offer. Research and experience in the building of democratic attitudes are comparatively well advanced in this country. Unfortunately, however, even the American literature on this subject is not well known in Germany.

I believe that inadequate exchange of information and lack of systematic and large scale research are major roadblocks to the securing of insights into the problems of democracy in Germany. An adequate program of applied research could result in major advancements in the development of democratic attitudes.

An Appraisal of the Anti-Semitic Outbreaks [1]

By Sidney Gruson

The majority of the 100 or so persons arrested during the outbreak of anti-Semitism were youngsters who had either no exposure or the lightest of exposures to the Nazis' credo of race hatred. This is the aspect of the whole affair that is causing the greatest anguish.

It has shown that there is at least a fairly large hard core ready to pick up the Nazis' anti-Semitic slogans, though there are only 30,000 Jews among West Germany's 54,000,000 people, and none of the 30,000 is in the public eye.

Now that the outbreak has receded some thought is being given to its meaning for Germany's future. It is easier however, to estimate what it does not add up to than what it may represent.

It does not signal to most observers here the resurgence of dangerous German nationalism panting to lead the world into new disasters. Nor does it signify to these observers that the Germans as a people have retained the Nazis' racialist teachings.

At least to this reporter, the group in a Darmstadt bar who threatened to rough up a man shouting anti-Semitic slogans was more representative of the German people's feelings and attitudes than the muted voices of approval for the swastika painters and slogan smearers.

Of course some of the tears being shed included crocodile tears by groups and individuals who thought that the timing rather than the deeds themselves were wrong. This seemed to be the general reaction of members of the German Reichs Party, which is the major extreme right-wing political organization in the field today.

---

[1] From the *New York Times*, Int. Ed., 25 Jan., 1960 (Excerpts). Original subtitle: Demands Rise for Action by Bonn After Anti-Semitic Outbreak.

Small Party

The party, which most people consider the ideological successor to the Nazi party, is an insignificant speck on the German political body with its 16,000 members and its 307,331 votes, 1.2 per cent of the total, in the country's last general election.

It is easy — perhaps too easy — to draw an analogy to the early days of Nazism, when Hitler and his followers also represented no more than a speck. But the West Germany of 1960 is far different, in moods and conditions, than the Germany in which Hitler clawed his way to power.

The country is fat and prosperous. It is deeply woven into the fabric of Western political, economic and military organizations. What remains of military pride has been satisfied by West Germany's place in the Atlantic alliance, and there is a thorough understanding of the shift of military power in the world.

All this is not to say that in another harsh depression, with hunger and unemployment rife in the land, the democratic spirit fostered since the war would easily survive.

There are issues enough for a dangerous nationalist appeal if things went bad. The country's division could easily be made into a banner for a crusade. So could the loss to Poland of the eastern territories — still the "homeland" to millions now living in West Germany.

But the dangers do not exist now nor do they loom on any visible horizon. Nothing has happened in the last month in Germany to warrant changing this.

Germans Eye Prosecution of Nazis [1]

By Gaston Coblentz

The atmosphere surrounding the prosecution of war criminals in West Germany is gradually undergoing a remarkable change after years of hesitation and reluctance.

With at least 1,200 former Nazis currently under investigation, and many of them scheduled to stand trial during the coming months and years, there appears to be less open public resentment of the proceedings than at any time since the war.

Until recently, it appeared that public opposition to the trials would increase rather than decrease as time went by. The argument was constantly heard that the Nazi era had become a thing of the past and that bygones should be bygones.

However, contrary to expectations, there has in fact been an increase in willingness to deal with this grim chapter of German history. Tonight, by way of example, two of West Germany's main radio networks broadcast to their Sunday evening audiences long, detailed accounts of the career of Nazi Josef Eichmann, now held by Israel and charged with the murder of 6,000,000 Jews.

The turning point in the public's attitude seems to have occurred, with some delay, after the assumption of responsibility for war crimes prosecution by the West

---

[1] From New York Herald Tribune, Int. Ed. 28 June 1960.

German authorities. This took place after the Western Allies ended their occupation and declared West Germany a sovereign nation five years ago.

It required another three years before Chancellor Konrad Adenauer's government and the local governments of the individual West German states decided to establish a central bureau near Stuttgart to accumulate and coordinate legally valid evidence for the purpose of purging West Germany of the worst unpunished war criminals still at large in the country.

With German thoroughness, the Stuttgart bureau assembled evidence pointing to the guilt of some 950 SS (Elite Guard) personnel and other persons who served at the large Auschwitz concentration camp in Poland, and implicating more than another 100 Nazis who were active at the Treblinka, Chelmo, and Belzec camps, all also in Poland. Another 200 persons are under suspicion of murdering Jews and other victims in Estonia and Lithuania.

New arrests are taking place almost every week. The statute of limitations for manslaughter will expire soon, but murder charges can still be lodged. The Justice Ministry says that the time limit in the cases named above was automatically extended by deliberately launching the inquiries before the 15-year limit ran out.

The ministry has also stated that it will use every legal device to prevent important still uncovered criminals from being spared by the technical expiration provision.

German Verdict More Impressive

It has been the transfer of the prosecution from Allied to German hands that has given the proceedings a greater meaning to the public than was the case while war crimes were being dealt with by the Allies under military occupation law. The average German appears to be more prepared to respect the verdict of German than of Allied courts in dealing with Nazi defendants.

Bitter grumbling about the trials continues in nationalist and neo-Nazi quarters. Part of the general public also regards the trials as an obeisance by the Adenauer government to "world Jewry". However, the continuing arrests have the support of both of the largest political parties, the Christian Democrats and the Social Democrats, as well as of the nation's most influential newspapers, radio stations and publicists.

Tonight Klauss Harprecht, a prominent radio commentator, began a broadcast on Eichmann and the Third Reich's "liquidation bureaucracy" by stating that the German people would have to leave the prosecution of Eichmann to Israel, but that, nevertheless, "we must know who this man was and what he did".

There is, however, one crippling limitation to the current court proceedings.
Under post-World War II West German law, the maximum sentence which can be awarded is life imprisonment. The death penalty is forbidden.

Postwar Germany

Germany divided: The Legacy of the Nazi Era. By Terence Prittie.
Illustrated. 380 pages. Atlantic-Little, Brown. $6,00.

By Maurice Dolbier

In 1953 and 1954, before he crossed over into the Eastern Zone (patriot, traitor, idealist, kidnap victim?), Otto John, then head of West German's security services, made frequent use of a statement that might well be taken as a motto for Mr. Prittie's book: "Whatever things look like, nothing has really been settled."

Terence Prittie has been a correspondent in Germany since 1946 — for much of that time head of the *Manchester Guardian's* German Bureau. Despite the fact that, as a prisoner of war, he was a witness to bestial and sadistic behavior on the part of German officers and men, despite the fact that, as a journalist in postwar Germany, he has seen ex-Nazis returned to positions of political power, has heard the West blamed for both Hitler and the war, has reported on resurgences of anti-Semitism — his attitude toward the German people is neither unfriendly nor pessimistic.

He dedicates his book to "the Youth of Germany — the future of their country is their trust, and their responsibility. A clear knowledge of the German past will enable them to discharge their task." They have not been encouraged by their elders. As late as 1959, in Baden-Wuerttemberg, a textbook devoted "five sentences to the Jewish problem in Germany", in North Rhine-Westphalia "children were once again being taught the fable of 'hostile powers' organizing the 'encirclement' of a peaceful Germany", and a standard textbook for 17-year-olds, while mentioning (in 13 lines) the Nazi persecution and annihilation of European Jewry, gave no figures. ("One German schoolmaster told me, in all good faith, that this was because the figures were so horrific that nobody would ever believe them — not even children").

Mr. Prittie has found, however, that against all the odds, "a new generation of Germans is growing up who are open-minded, alert, and intent on getting to know the outside world and divorcing themselves from the stale atmosphere of mock-heroics, party-cracker slogans and false gods." For them and for a Western world which, for its own survival, must be more open-minded and alert to the problems and promises of today's Germany, Mr. Prittie provides an intimate, detailed, and troubled report, covering such matters as the refugee situation, the industrialists, politicians and statesmen of the new Germany (with a special study of Dr. Adenauer), the dangers that come from the Communist East and from the unhappy characteristics of too many Germans of forgetting the past and of blaming others for their own failures.

---

[1] From the *New York Herald Tribune*, Int. Ed., 21 Nov. 1960.

Close-up of the Throngs of Youth during the Annual Ceremonies at the Site of the Former Concentration Camp at Bergen-Belsen where Anne Frank is Buried alongside Other Thousands of Victims. Photos: Erich Andres

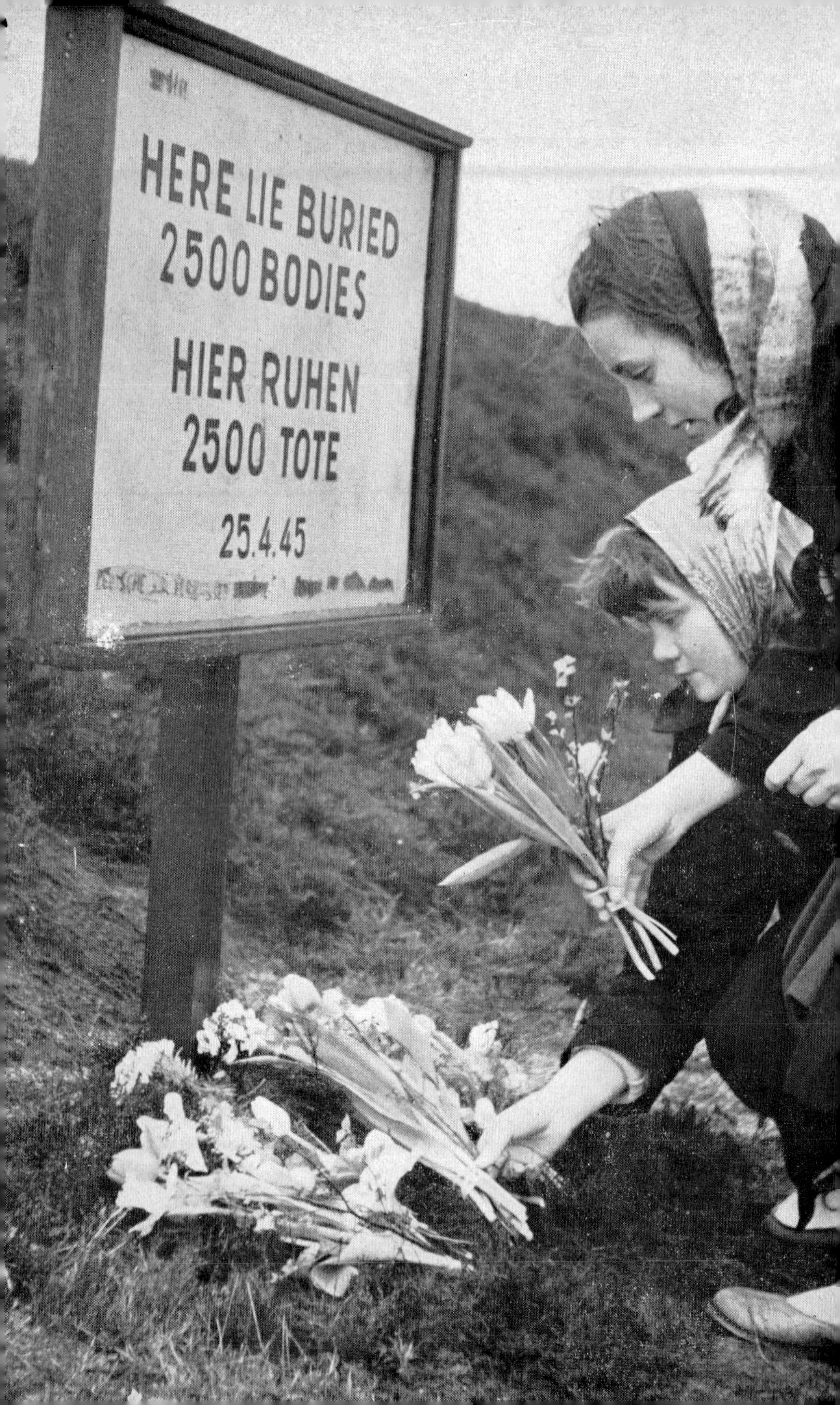
HERE LIE BURIED
2500 BODIES
HIER RUHEN
2500 TOTE
25.4.45

Memorandum on "The Militaristic and Chauvinistic-Education of the West Germans" [1]

Recommendation to UNESCO: Put a stop to militarist education of West German youth

The opposite course of West Germany[2])

As a peace-loving democratic state which faithfully fulfilled the obligations of the Potsdam Agreement and the contracts of the anti-Hitler coalition, the Government of the GDR is entitled as well as obliged to call the attention of the member countries of UNESCO to the completely opposite development in the German Federal Republic.

Although West Germany is a member of UNESCO and thus assumed the obligation to do everything to protect the coming generation against the scourge of a new war and to make an active contribution to the preservation of peace and to understanding among the nations, the West German Government, in complete disregard of the aims and principles laid down in the UN Charter and in the UNESCO Constitution, is preparing a revanchist war with the objective of reversing the outcome of World War II and of turning into reality the old conquest plans of German militarism. It is the only government in Europe to advance territorial claims against other states.

The entire education and instruction system of West Germany is subordinated to these aggressive aims. It serves the purpose of creating the ideological prerequisites for new war adventures and of poisoning youth with the pernicious way of thinking of revanchism, chauvinism, and hatred between the nations. It is, thus, a direct part of the preparation for new aggressive adventures.

Military poisoning of youth

The West German Government already spent more funds for the rearmament of West Germany than what had been the total direct expenditures of the Hitler State for the preparation of World War II; at the same time, it restricts the expenditures for education and cultural purposes to a minimum.

Although the West German UNESCO delegation approved of the already mentioned resolution of Taormina and accepted certain obligations, there exists in West Germany, in ruthless disregard of these obligations, a comprehensive system for the militarist and revanchist poisoning of the juveniles which is steadily being intensified.

"Teaching principle Eastern Affairs Instruction"

The scant beginnings of democratic reforms in the school system which could be found in West Germany after 1945 were abolished step by step simultaneously with the revival of German militarism. Former active Nazis and war criminals who rule over the Bonn State also exercise decisive influence in the key positions of the education system and of the formation of public opinion.

---

[1] From the Communist daily, *Neues Deutschland* of 1 December 1960.
[2] This heading refers to the first part of the Memorandum (left out here) in which the "democratic education" in the GDR is described and praised.

The evil spirit of agitation against other nations and of a revanche policy is permeating instruction activities more and more strongly. In order to incite feelings of hatred already in the children, the so-called "Eastern Affairs Instruction" was introduced into the West German schools. The emotional and imaginative world of the students is meant to be ripened for another "crusade toward the East" with the help of the "Teaching principle Eastern Affairs Instruction" in all subjects.

65 "Eastern Research" Institutes

The pseudo-scientific basis for the so-called Eastern Affairs Instruction is supplied by the same "Eastern researchers" who under Hitler helped prepare the attacks against Eastern Europe in an ideological way.

Today, a total of approximately 65 specific "Eastern research" institutes, Eastern academies, chairs for Eastern questions, and societies for "Eastern research" exist in West Germany. All of them are fostering grounds of the revanchist indoctrination of youth as well as of the entire population.

In the schools and education centers of the Federal Republic the Hitler dictatorship is embellished and its cruel terror against the peace-loving anti-Fascist elements in Europe is ignored or minimized. For the purposes of school instruction, that type of background material is recommended which is contained, e. g., in the periodical *Unsere Volksschule* in serial form since May 1960 under the headline "National Socialism", or which is published by the Ariola corporation, in the form of tapes and records, with reference to subjects such as "Germany in World War II" and "The Third Reich in Documents" within the section "Hitler Loved Us so Ardently".

Falsifiers of history

The acts of aggression for the unleashing of World War II are interpreted as having been "necessary defense measures". In the textbooks, the Fascist attacks against the European nations are not described as carefully prepared aggressions but as "fateful events". The treacherous attack against the Soviet Union even is claimed to have been a "crusade for the Occident".

The description of the heroic anti-Fascist resistance struggle of the best elements of the German nation and of the nations attacked and subjugated by Hitler Germany more and more disappears from the textbooks every year, and Fascist military elements are asserted to have been the alleged resistance fighters.

The spirit of race hatred and neo-colonialism permeates the West German school system. Studying youth is talked into believing that the suppression of the peoples of Africa is a cogent necessity. There is an open return to the Fascist race ideology which declares people of a different color to be inferior and unable of independent creative achievements.

Neo-Fascist youth organizations

Besides the militarist and revanchist poisoning of the West German juveniles by the official school system these are greatly threatened by the large number of the militarist, revanchist, and neo-Fascist youth organizations which exist in West Germany and which were founded upon direct instructions from the West German Government or with its approval.

The said organizations are granted spiritual, material, and financial assistance by the Government and, in particular, by the West German War Ministry. The leaders of these organizations are, in their majority, former youth or SS leaders of Hitler.

They have not abandoned their Nazi attitude nor their objectives. They opinionate the imaginative world of the children and juveniles by way of abusing the homeland concept, of distorting legal aspects, and of glorifying the Nazi system. The revanchist and militarist influence exercised upon West German youth is effected with direct assistance from the West German Government. With the help of governmental and semi-governmental institutions the Office for Psychological Warfare is taking care that, at school as well as in their spare time, the juveniles are being educated towards war-preparedness, and are influenced in a revanchist sense. For this project sums amounting to millions are being spent every year. To a special extent, the Bonn War Ministry has been introducing the militarist ideology into the schools.

A flood of war and filth literature

An important instrument for the ideological poisoning of West German youth exists in the mass produced or mass-imported war, crime, and trash motion pictures. These pictures against whose showing the West German authorities undertake nothing serve the purpose of brutalizing the juveniles. They are meant to exonerate the Nazi criminals, to justify the Hitler war, and to create new war enthusiasm among the youth. Moreover, the West German youth is exposed to a veritable flood of war, filth, and trash literature. Nothing is being done against this by the West German Government. At the present time, as many as twelve series of publications with militarist and war literature are being sold in West Germany with a circulation total of 20 million copies per year. With regard to their outward appearance and their contents these publications are entirely identical with the respective war literature of the Nazi days. In half of the cases they were written by the same authors.

Appeal to lowest instincts

This "literature" glorifies Fascist war and is meant to create renewed war enthusiasm among the West German youth. The descriptions of brutalities and cruelties, race hatred and agitation among the nations are typical components of these publications. The same can be said about the novels and so-called eye-witness accounts referring to the time of the Fascist war which appear in many West German illustrated periodicals.

More than one hundred West German publishing houses publish Fascist and militarist literature. Up to the year 1955, already 700 militarist and Fascist publications with a total circulation of three million copies had appeared in West Germany, including books by war criminals such as Rosenberg, Doenitz, Raeder, and Hess.

The so-called *Bundeszentrale fuer Heimatdienst* (Federal Organization for Civics) last year issued a total of 75,000 books and 120,000 booklets as well as 2,000 motion picture copies with militarist and revanchist contents.

A large portion of the Fascist and militarist literature is being supplied to the readers by way of a special mail order book-selling system; in this respect it is a characteristic fact that the West German War Ministry figures as a wholesale buyer for troop libraries and thus contributes quite deliberately to the contagion with Fascist and militarist literature of the West German youth serving in the West German armed forces.

While the responsible organs of West Germany in this way open all doors to the ideological poisoning of youth, while Fascists and militarist can exercise their tainting influence upon youth without restriction, West German parents and pedagogues who want to safeguard peace for their children and pupils, as well as scientists and artists who claim the right to free expression of their opinion also with regard to the rejection of atomic armament, people from all population levels and walks of life who support a peaceful policy as well as the education of youth in a humanist and anti-militarist spirit are today declared to be enemies of the state in West Germany and are reprimanded. Attention only has to be called in this respect to well-known personages such as Professor Renate Riemeck[1]), Professor Walter Hagemann, and headmistress Philomena Lehnert.

These facts are incompatible with the basic principles of the constitution of UNESCO.

Recommendations of the Government of the GDR

In view of this development, the Government of the German Democratic Republic recommends to institute a commission for the examination of this situation in the German Federal Republic which is endangering peace, and to introduce appropriate measures so that in West Germany the education of youth will take place in a spirit of peace and of understanding among the nations, as demanded in the theses of Article 26, Paragraph 2 of the General Declaration of Human Rights and in the theses of Principle No. 10 of the Declaration on the Rights of the Children.

The Government of the German Democratic Republic requests the member countries and the Secretariat of UNESCO to examine carefully the evidence, submitted in the memorandum and in the attached documentation, of the education of West German youth in a spirit of militarism and revanchism, as well as to deliberate on measures which can put a stop to this development. The Government of the German Democratic Republic declares its readiness to submit additional documents on the poisoning of West German youth with the way of thinking of revanchism, militarism, and Fascism and, if desired, to set forth its views before the 11th General Conference of UNESCO.

The Government of the German Democratic Republic declares that it will continue to do everything in its power to make the principles of UNESCO, the principles of humanism, and of friendship among the nations the basis of youth education in all of Germany. The Government of the German Democratic Republic welcomes sincerely support granted to the realization of this noble effort.

---

[1]) Frau Riemeck is President of the "Internationale der Kriegsdienstgegner" and a leading member of the "Staendiger Kongress gegen die atomare Ausruestung der Bundesrepublik" (neutralist); Dr. Hagemann is a member of the board of "Bund der Deutschen", a neutralist splinter-group. Ed. note.

A Word on the Impotence of German Literature [1]

By Johannes Gaitanides

Blushing with shame, I'll come right out with it! I lack discontent. With such a statement I toss away every chance for a place among the literary *avant garde* who manipulate disgust with the Federal Republic as if such were a criteria of good style. Some of the members of this elite are therefore emigrants in spirit, some are even actual emigrants. As for me, on the other hand, a political journalist with a partially foreign background, I live in the Federal Republic of my own free choice. And what makes it still worse, I enjoy it here on the whole.

I like living in the Federal Republic because the government at least does not hinder me from enjoying life — I am allowed to go my own way; because I can do and say what I please and what I consider right; because there are no insurmountable limits set for my potentialities (including the baser ones). Yes, this country even finances my profession adequately; that is, to be honest and to be myself. Twelve years of Hitler and the Communist neighborhood suffice me to consider this situation acceptable. I dare to endorse it, because I share it with all my writer colleagues, including the most vehement critics of Bonn. No matter what they say and put on the market, it is printed and sells. The more furiously they cut away at the ground under their feet, the better it sells.

Admittedly this is a private and subjective judgment (although it also objectively invalidates some of the criticisms of the Federal Republic). My view cannot and would not deprive wrath of its right to be heard — the wrath with which for years our left-wing intellectuals have been campaigning passionately, if in vain, against the "cankers" in our land of the economic miracle. After the catastrophy, the great catharsis or purification did not come about. With presumptuous arrogance, we minimize our portion of guilt and complacently skip over the smoldering past. The intellect has no power in our public life and not to the extent that domestic politics quite ignore ideological aims in their planning and the great tasks of our time are left dangling in mid-air. Our economic proficiency is coupled with brutality and indifference. Free initiative subjugates itself to the dictates of security. Indolence and "keeping up with the Joneses" dominate private life and all moral obligations are ignored and so on and so forth. Doubtlessly, others will describe more colorfully, with more details and nuances, the opulent manifold list of the vices of the Federal Republic, so I may save myself the trouble of further enumeration.

This criticism hits the bulls eye. Why, then, does it miss the mark at the same time? Why doesn't it "land" instead of getting lost in ineffectiveness? I wish to concentrate on this question.

First answer: it does not "land" because our left-wing intelligentsia, which is largely identical with our literature, presents this critique in the form of a wholesale damnation "across the board", and because such scathing criticism tends "to throw out the child with the bathwater". I flatly assert that painting things black and white doesn't catch on with the Germans anymore. Hiler dulled the dagger of polemics (on which he largely built his career) for some decades to come. Only those persons who tend toward radical solutions (this being a question of personality and circumstances) are susceptible to polemics. But if the Germans learned anything from the experience of National Socialism, it was this: to renounce radicalism, thus auto-

[1] From *Der Monat*, June 1960.

matically closing their minds to polemics — or to put it in positive terms, to demand of criticism and opposition soberness, fairness, matter-of-factness, objectivity, and the careful weighing of pros and cons. Right or wrong, they feel they do have something to lose — armed with this awareness, they are impervious to every criticism of the polemic kind. So polemics is dead ... as a style, method, and species (here we have hit upon something which could be entered as an asset on the balance sheet of the citizen of the Federal Republic) — it can win no more battles for the soul. After 1945 the Communists and the right-wing radicals learned this lesson, as did — I ask their absolution for mentioning them in the same breath ... the intellectuals of the "homeless Left". People might applaud the brilliant escapades of Erich Kuby one day, yet elect Adenauer the next. Instead of winning his potential sympathizers to his side, Kuby's wild exaggerations push them from a state of indecision over into the other camp. Polemics today convinces no one but the already convinced. As for the doubters and seekers, the group that counts, it acts in the capacity of a barker for the opponent.

I must ask my colleagues a second time for their forgiveness — I welcome this novel immunity to polemics on the part of the Germans. Yes, I even consider it a symptom of growth towards democratic maturity.

What happened during the Weimar Republic? At that time the criticism of Kurt Tucholsky and others like him, justified as it was with respect to content, its polemic form wounded democracy — and not the enemies of democracy — and so it even removed some of the obstacles in the way of the major foe, the National Socialists. We are not eager to have this happen again.

The material to be worked is the deciding factor in the choice of the tool. The material is our public. The left-wing intellectuals, however, do not respect the fact that this psychologically and sociologically transformed material can no longer be impressed with the old worn-out instrument of polemics. This sin of craftmanship is in no small measure responsible for the ineffectiveness of their criticism.

Second answer: the present-day criticism is futile because it is based on a falacious argument. All insight into the weaknesses, mistakes and vices of the Federal Republic notwithstanding, it is nonetheless impossible — as the left-wing criticism attempts — to dismiss the country's impressive achievements in one fell swoop, not even by appealing to the Christian doctrine according to which the gain of earthly goods does not make up for the loss of the soul. This alleged loss of the soul — this is the point around which the critique of the literary intelligentsia culminates.

If I am permitted to say so, this charge seems a bit haughty, even insolent. How much louder would this critique thunder against the Federal Republic if it had not produced an "economic miracle", if we didn't have full employment, if there had been no rise in the social status of the worker, no assimilation of those expelled from the East and of the refugees from Communist Germany, no further development of social securities, no reduction in working hours, no voting power for the workers in the Montan-Union industries, no restitution for the victims of Nazism! The reconciliation with the "hereditary foe" France, West Germany's gradual integration into Europe, free communication with the intellectual and artistic trends in the West (which at no time in recent history has been so intensive as today), the sterilizing of nationalistic feelings, and the broadening of the geographical horizon — anyone who does not take these new values into account in his critique robs his argument of persuasive power. Nor can these new values be swept aside by dubbing them with the derogatory common-denominator "material" goods, not to speak of the fact that the alleviation of physical need transcends far beyond the material realm. In the light of this state of affairs, to go so far as to doubt and damn the Federal Republic as a whole is to lay oneself open for a judgment of political incompetence. This applies also to those who think they can brand the German post-war development with the formulation "restoration". Such persons overlook the fact that the growing separation of business leadership from business ownership, the increasing influence of pressure groups, the expansion of government authority in the economy, the rise of the worker into the middle classes and the impersonalizing of work in the automatic factory have created a new, revolutionary state which makes it impossible to draw a sociological parallel between post-war and pre-war Germany (or to use the label "restoration"). The credibility of our intellectual critics is impaired primarily because they more or less fail to recognize these fundamental changes.

Could our intellectuals, who put the blame for the dashing of their hopes on the "economic miracle", be only victims of a misunderstanding? It is true that the fantastic dynamics of the economy in West Germany is confronted with a general stagnation in all other areas of life. Great is the temptation to interpret this optical juxtaposition as a causal relationship and to make the economic dynamics responsible for the intellectual and spiritual stagnation — a manoeuvre eagerly and monotonously pursued by our critics.

But it is not the businessmen who are responsible for the intellect. Responsible are the intellectuals themselves! They are the intellectual life, it is their job to stimulate the life of the intellect and spirit. They cannot claim that the forces of the economy hinder them in their productivity. Publishers and the theater, radio and television compete with each other to grab up the fruits of their labor. They can hardly save themselves from the avalanche of literary prizes. The reviewers even up the number of editions, if the book has the good fortune to receive a review which tears it to pieces. And the dear public buys their books with the same patient composure with which they "buy" the ordinances of Konrad Adenauer.

The practice of avoiding the encounter with the *mea culpa* and saddling all one's own guilt on a scapegoat is of course not confined to the literary world. The writer may plead that the tone which reputedly makes the music is not only a question of the musician but also of resonance. This argument, however, is as senseless as the problem of which came first, the chicken or the egg.

Basically the complaint of today's writers is that we have no dream anymore, no hope for a better, more beautiful tomorrow. Since it is the dream which sets the goals and standards, one may well ask whether a culture without a dream can still be considered a "culture". Be that as it may, the function of literature is to be the megaphone for our dreams. But our literature forbears dreams (and turns their fabrication over to the film industry). It still owes us the dreams — whether this lack of dreams is due to honesty or incompetence is a topic which we won't go into now.

Thus deep down the complaint of our intellectuals against the Federal Republic is a dissatisfaction with themselves — the suffering of the insolvent debtor, whose resentment against the creditor increases in proportion to the amount of the debt. Third answer: the ineffectiveness of our literature is due to a constitutional flaw. Every literature which deserves the name stands in opposition to its society. It measures what is by what should be. Since this difference cannot be abrogated, since reality never attains to its dream, literature is necessarily exiled to the negative. Nowhere, however, is the gulf between literature and society wider than in Germany. Never was it as deep as it is today.

The reason for this might be sought in certain typical national tendencies which are attributed, not unjustly, to the German: his tendencies towards "abstraction", towards "all or nothing", towards perfection. These tendencies may have a hand in the current row between literature and the people. However, from what I hear these tendencies are supposed to have gone out of style even here in this country, so they cannot account for the whole explanation. They only come into sharp focus in combination with another factor.

Historical developments drove the European intelligentsia into the ranks of the Left after the First War — a quite legitimate development at that time, provoked by the war and by economic and social conditions. Since then quite a few things have changed. The expansion of Bolshevism, the arbitrary opportunities to become thoroughly aquainted with it, the realization of certain principles of the welfare state even under conservative governments, the constantly increasing aggregation of "bourgeois" and the movement of the worker into this middle-class aggregation thus shedding the label of proletarian — as a result of all these phenomena, the leftist impetus of West European intellectuals has been greatly reduced and robbed of radicalism, if not actually smothered. The intelligentsia of Western Europe have shifted their position from anti-bourgeois to un-bourgeois.

Not so in Germany. Time is not to be cheated and the nature of the intellect requires a continuous process of development. Therefore, our generation, from whom Hitler stole more than a decade, has a long way to go to catch up. In other words, we lag behind our Western European counterparts by a considerable number of years.

Under the compulsion to make up for lost time, our painters and sculptors race into abstraction, our musicians into twelve-tone music, and our writers into the anti-bourgeois effect. If these writers engage in political argumentation they find themselves in a quixotic position. The development of capitalism in Germany was not interrupted by Hitler, as was the intellectual life, but kept pace with the sociological changes in Western Europe. Consequently there is a time-gap between our intellectual and sociological stage of development. The left-wing intellectuals don't seem to find any better way to bridge this gap than by calling forth the phantom of "restoration" to help them date back our social reality to their intellectual stage of development. Thus they need "restoration" like they do their daily bread — to give it up would be almost suicide. The use of this unrealistic make-shift construction dooms their critical efforts to futility, but the price of relinquishing it would be higher.

All this would still not be so bad if only that peculiarly German brand of "conscientiousness" tending toward extreme expression, which I sketched above, did not get mixed up in this time-lag problem. The combination of the two leads our intellectuals to condemn middle-class existence, as an "abstraction". They do not refer to a particular middle-class citizen in a particular time and place, but to the citizen, retaining the connotation of the former usage of "the bourgeois". The German writer doesn't say, as do his Western European and American counterparts: You are a bad citizen; instead he says very fundamentally: the citizen is no good, and with this flat statement he is guilty of a gross injustice. As for "the" people, the mass, Mr. Everyman and Miss Jane Doe — their optimal possibility for self-realization within any social system (including the Communist system) is and will remain in their position as the much-abused "citizen". Thus the inhabitant of the Federal Republic today acts in self-defense when he closes his mind to a literature which denies him his right to live. He can only defend himself by turning a deaf ear to the boundless, impossible demands placed on him. Taking a lesson from this, a basic principle emerges: the social effectiveness of literary social-critique must start with the recognition of the citizen's right to exist. (Up until the First World War, German literature was whole-heartedly committed to this principle.)

Now, let us consider that same perfectionist mania usually oriented toward the model or the laboratory, toward the desk or toward paradise, which takes it upon itself to condemn in total the Federal Republic. The extravagance of this claim blinds its author to the fact that there is no such thing as a perfect democracy, that democracy can never be more than the smallest evil and the least harmful form of resignation to human imperfection. I am inclined to understand this mania for earthly perfection (which springs from love and manifests itself in uncharitableness) as a perversion of mankind's primeval longing for transcendence. We and our literature no longer seem able to offer a response to this longing. The Western European intelligentsia, longer practiced in the art of life without transcendence, seems to have found its way out again from this dead-end street of evasions.

As to the question of who is responsible for the gulf between literature and society, our intelligentsia automatically and with naive self-righteousness nails the public to the cross. It apparently doesn't occur to them to knock at their own door with this question.

Fourth answer: the impotence of our literature is the result of a failure to perform its social function.

The friends of literature accord it the role of a social conscience. In this capacity, literature functions by ordering and disturbing (solidifying the fluid and making the solids fluid). According to the particular disposition of the society, literature will concentrate on one or the other of these two functions. When society becomes rigid and numb, literature is provoked to disturb things. In times of upheaval, unrest and uncertainty, literature is challenged to bring things into order and to clarify — to act as a guide. This is an ideal construction — I prefer to think of it as a thermometer which may be used to determine to what extent literature in a specific period and among a particular people fulfills its social function. What is our situation in this respect?

We have a thoroughly unbalanced, disordered and uncertain society. Yet we are confronted with a literature which exhausts itself along the lines of a "disturbing" therapy. It is a reflex when it should be an action. It liquifies the fluid. It empties the empty and doesn't fill. Our writers give expression instead of answering. They throw stones at the society which is asking for bread from their hands.

Intellectual unrest is a softening agent, a means of breaking a rigid object apart, a defrosting process. As such it is required as a therapy for crystalline souls and for those social *milieux* in which the hearts and minds are dulled, satiated, frozen. Literature of harrassment flourishes and finds resonance only in such an atmosphere, and may become an "event". Because only in these conditions and against these conditions is such literature "necessary" and then its effects are felt.

Just for this reason, one may interpose that disturbance is the need of the hour for German literature, for the symptoms mentioned do characterize our present society. Yet this objection is not valid for two reasons. Firstly, because symptoms are never unambiguous, but may be caused by a variety of diseases. There is a callousness resulting from exaggerated complacency, conceit and self-confidence. There is another callousness which serves as an armor against weakness. The defense is put up to hide an excess of anxiety, a sense of insecurity and an awareness of the dubious quality of all existence. One withdraws into oneself like the snail, conscious of its defenselessness, draws back into its protective shell when attacked. It is this type of callousness we are dealing with here in Germany today. It is the result of an over-consumption of disturbing experiences. We are dealing with the boisterous whistle of the frightened boy walking through the woods in the black and ominous night pretending courage, with dancing on the rim of a volcano, with the attitude "after us the deluge", with petrifaction as a reaction to fear — not to well-being.

The second misunderstanding is based on negligence in the matter of dosage. Medicine dispensed in an overdose changes its character from that of a curative agent to that of a poison. In such a case the patient either succumbs or he develops immunizing defenses. This is happening in Western Germany. The citizen of the Federal Republic "thrown" into complete uncertainty, flees for the sake of his self-assertion into egocentric isolation and bolsters himself with the protective insulation of psychic indolence. Moreover, any pain is dulled by repetition and continued exposure produces insensitivity. As for literature intended to disturb, it is like the surf: at first it irritates and stimulates, later it rocks one to sleep.

The real ailment of our writers is to see the function of the intellect in terms of harrassment alone. Our literature has been successful, however, as a useful mirror bringing into approximate view things as they are, if in caricature form. But our literature doesn't offer any food to the hunger for examples and standards. It defines the hunger but does not feed it. Moreover, our literature says no, a comprehensive no, which in our confused and disintegrated world is not (as our intellectuals believe) a sign of courage (because they take no risk). It is an indication of indolence which takes the path of least resistance. It is the path of least resistance because the literature intended to disquiet has the opposite effect and helps to ease the minds of the contemporary Philistines who like to think that all the guilt for the bad state of things belongs with the neighbor, the boss, the government, current events, NATO, the atom bomb, the Devil or even with a malevolent God, but is certainly not to be found in himself, His Majesty, the reader.

The place of literature is in the opposition. But in which opposition? How can anxiety be remedied by harassment, or chaos by creating chaos! What we need is opposition to intellectual and moral anarchy. And one can only speak of such an opposition when the progression has been made from describing to answering, from diagnosis to therapy. The disquieting — let us say expectorate literature might well keep its place as a mirror of our time used to aid the society in becoming self-conscious. But it is only an "engaged" literature which can become an "event". A committed literature (with horizons stretching far beyond the dogmatism of our religious and political doctrines of salvation) which would offer the present generation something to look to in their task of bringing order and meaning into life. As long as our literature does not accept the risk of saying "yes" the society feels rejected by it. And rightly so.

The main flow of our literature is oriented towards the left. Our society, however, (that of all Western Europe) has a tendency to conservatism. In the eyes of our intelligentsia this is a sin against the intellect, a mistake for which they blame the belly and mammon. This interpretation is another gross misunderstanding on the part of the intellectuals which further widens the gap between literature and readers. Two categories of natural laws are active in history. Human existence remains the same in its essential aspects throughout all time: in the laws of death and birth, hunger and might, in the finiteness of the human will, in its desire for law and justice, for liberty and equality, happiness and recognition, salvation and fulfillment. And at the same time life changes in each second in an irresistible process of transformation. History thus unfolds as a network being woven by the constant interplay of the laws of constancy and timelessness with the laws of change. Life has a solid basis and richness whenever both laws check and modify each other, penetrate each other, and keep each other in balance. Our time, however, suffers under the rapidly expanding cancer of change which overgrows and devours all timelessness. From one day to the next the map is altered, new inventions tumble over one another, our horizons run away from us towards an ever receding infinity. The stream of knowledge has turned into wild rapids and therefore we fear to lose our footing. We sit in a car with a high-powered motor and the brakes are out-of-order. This unleashing is the accomplishment of our natural sciences and of technology. The lawyer is the progressive Left which attempts to derive new rules for human society out of this flood of changes.

It is this process, the race of events, which drives men into the arms of the conservative parties whenever they are able to have a voice in their destiny by means of the ballot. They turn to conservatism following their instinct that a racing motor must be combined with a safeguarding system of brakes; not in order to stop the vehicle (or even to put it into reverse as claimed by leftist critics) but rather to control its course and to prevent it from plunging headlong into the abyss. Barrels of ridicule and wrath are poured over this "middle-class security complex" which is as easy to do as it is foolish. This desire for security is not only a reflection of satiety, it not only is concerned with a high living standard, property ownership and uninterrupted pleasure. It is also a defense mechanism of timelessness against time — more exactly: the subordination of change under the law of timelessness. Seen in this context, the desire for security is in tune with the function of the conservative: not to return to the past, but to retain timelessness in time, and, if necessary, to defend the former against he latter. The more and faster a period changes, the more it tends to entrust itself to conservative leadership as an act of self-correction. This is especially true for our period because the disciples of change in the shape of the Soviets have attained such threatening power. This is the real reason why the free societies of Europe decided in favor of the conservatives and against the progressive Left: the subconscious knowledge of the necessity of reducing the galloping pace of our time to a less dangerous speed and to direct it into more navigable roads.

The gap between literature and society probably cannot be closed — it could be bridged by an emergency foot-bridge if our left-wing intellectuals would strive towards a proper understanding of the actual state of our society. This would and should not mean that they give up the role of "the pike in a fishpond".

Glossary

Abitur	Final high School examination entitling the successful candidate without further tests to enter any German university
Bundesrat	Federal Parliament (Upper House)
Bundestag	Federal Parliament (Lower House)
Bundeswehr	Federal Forces (Army, Navy, Air Force) of West-Germany
Land, pl. *Laender*	a state of the German Federal Republic, which is composed of ten such *Laender*
Landser	the German equivalent to GI
GDR	German Democratic Republic (Communist-controlled part of Germany)
German Committe on Training and Education	advisory council of experts
Gymnasium	a nine-grade high school
Mittelschule	a lower secondary school, Graduation from it does not entitle the student to matriculate at a university
Permanent Conference of Ministers of Culture and Education	Coordinating council of *Land* ministers. West-Germany has no Federal minister of culture and education
Rector	head of a German university. Annually elected from among the professors
Volksschule	primary (elementary) school
Volkshochschule (VHS)	adult education center
Volkshochschulverband	adult education association

List of Authors

Dr. Theodor W. Adorno Professor of Philosophy, Director, *Institut fuer Sozialforschung,* University of Frankfurt/Main

Hellmut Becker Lawyer, President, *Deutscher Volkshochschulverband,* Kressbronn

Nikolas Benckiser Asst. Editor, *Frankfurter Allgemeine Zeitung,* Frankfurt/Main

Dr. Arnold Bergstraesser Professor of Political Science, University of Freiburg

Eberhard Bitzen Bonn Correspondent, *Frankfurter Allgemeine Zeitung*

Gaston Coblentz Bonn Bureau Chief, *New York Herald Tribune*

Oscar Cohen National Director of Program and Education, Anti-Defamation League of B'nai B'rith, New York

Thomas Quinn Curtiss Film Critic, *New York Herald Tribune,* Europ. Ed., Paris

Hendrik G. van Dam Secretary General, *Zentralrat der Juden in Deutschland* (Central Council of the Jews in Germany), Duesseldorf

Maurice Dolbier Book Reviewer, *New York Herald Tribune,* Europ. Ed., Paris

Dr. Georg Eckert Professor of the History of Pedagogics, Director, *Internationales Schulbuchinstitut* (International Institute for Textbooks), Braunschweig

Dr. Kurt Fackiner *Studienrat* (High School Teacher), Bad Homburg v. d. H.

Dr. Juergen Fijalkowski Social Scientist, *Institut fuer Soziologie,* Free University, Berlin

Dr. Juergen Fischer Executive Director, *Westdeutsche Rektorenkonferenz,* Bonn

Wolfgang Gaebler Political Scientist, University Hamburg

Johannes Gaitanides Writer and Publicist, Unterschondorf/Ammersee

Dieter Geldschlaeger Student of Theology, *Evangelische Akademie,* Schleswig

Dr. Marianne Grewe *Paedagogische Arbeitsstelle des Deutschen Volkshochschul-Verbandes,* Bonn

Sidney Gruson Bonn Bureau Chief, *New York Times*

Walter Guenzel Assistant Editor, *Die Welt,* Hamburg

Juergen Habermas Social Scientist, *Institut fuer Sozialforschung,* University Frankfurt/Main

Sebastian Haffner Berlin Correspondent, *London Observer*

Dr. Andreas Hillgruber *Oberstudienrat, Studienseminar* (Teachers' College), Darmstadt

Dr. Walter Jacobsen	Psychologist, Bonn, formerly at *Bundeszentrale fuer Heimatdienst*
Dr. Walter Jaide	Professor of Psychology, *Paedagogische Hochschule* (Pedagogic Academy), Hannover
Dr. Lothar Kahn	Teachers' College, Connecticut
Dr. Ekkehart Krippendorf	Student of Political Science, Tuebingen
Dr. Hans W. Kuhn	Political Scientist, *Seminar fuer Politische Wissenschaften,* University Freiburg
Wilhelm Langenbeck	*Oberstudienrat* (High School Teacher), Wiesbaden
Helmuth Leichtfuß	*Studienrat* (High School Teacher), Wiesbaden
Kurt Lewin	Late Director, Research Center for Group Dynamics, Massachusetts Institute of Technology
Ernst Matthewes	*Landesschulrat* (Superintendent of the Hamburg School System), Hamburg
Dr. Felix Messerschmidt	Director, *Akademie fuer Politische Bildung* (Academy for Political Education), Tutzing/Oberbayern
Dr. Norbert Muhlen	Writer and Columnist, New York
Robert Neumann	Writer and Publicist, Locarno-Monti, Switzerland
Terence Prittie	Bonn Correspondent of the *Manchester Guardian*
Gerhard Reyl	*Studienrat* (High School Teacher), Limburg/Lahn
Dr. Jost Riedel	Political Scientist, Otto-Suhr-Institut, Berlin
Rolf Schoerken	*Studienassessor* (High School Teacher), Duesseldorf
Dr. Walter Stahl	Executive Director, *Atlantik-Bruecke e.V.,* Hamburg
Werner Veldmann	Assistant Editor, *Die Welt,* Hamburg
Adelbert Weinstein	Journalist, *Frankfurter Allgemeine Zeitung,* Frankfurt/M.
Dietrich Wetzel	Chairman, *Verband Deutscher Studentenschaften* (German Students' Association), Bonn
Frans Woerdemann	Documentary Programs, Inc., Washington

Members of the Atlantik-Bruecke

Chairman:

Prof. Dr. Arnold Bergstraesser University of Freiburg

Vice Chairman:

Dr. Gotthard   Personally Responsible Partner in the Banking
Frhr. v. Falkenhausen   House of Burkhardt & Co., Essen

Treasurer:

Erik Blumenfeld   President, Norddeutsche Kohlen- und Cokeswerke
                        A.G., Hamburg

Prof. Dr. Paul Baumann President, Chemische Werke Hüls AG., Marl

Dr. Hans C. Boden   President, Allgemeine Electricitäts-Gesellschaft
                        (AEG), Frankfurt/Main

Dr. Wilhelm Borner   Member of the Managing Board, Schering AG.,
                        Berlin

Dr. Hans Karl v. Borries Montagnola (Tessin)

Dr. h.c. Mac Brauer   Bürgermeister a. D., Hamburg

Dr. Rudolf Brinckmann   Personally Responsible Partner in the Banking
                        House of Brinckmann, Wirtz & Co., Hamburg

Prof. Dr. Arthur Burkhardt President Württembergische Metallwarenfabrik,
                        Geislingen-Steige

Prof. Dr. Constantin   University of Freiburg, President of the General
von Dietze   Synod of the Evangelical Protestant Church of
                        Germany

Dr. Marion Gräfin Dönhoff Journalist, Hamburg

Ernst Friedlaender   Writer, Siena, Italy

Otto A. Friedrich   President, Phoenix Gummiwerke AG.,
                        Hamburg-Harburg

Gerhard Geyer   President, Esso AG., Hamburg

Prof. Dr. Ulrich Haberland President, Farbenfabriken Bayer AG., Leverkusen

Karl Haus   Personally Responsible Partner in the Banking
                        House of Sal. Oppenheim jr. & Cie., Cologne

Dr. Konrad Henkel   Personally Responsible Partner in the Firm
                        Henkel & Cie. G.m.b.H., Düsseldorf

Dr. Günter Henle   President, Klöckner & Co., Duisburg

Prof. Dr. Max Horkheimer University of Frankfurt

Dr. Hermann Jannsen   Member of the Managing Board, Frankfurter Bank,
                        Frankfurt/Main

Dr. Fritz Könecke	President, (ret.), Daimler-Benz AG., Stuttgart
Dr. Heinrich Kost	Chairman of the Board, Rheinpreussen AG., Homberg
Prof. Dr. Helmut Kuhn	University of Munich
Dr. W. Alexander Menne	Member of the Managing Board, Farbwerke Hoechst AG., Frankfurt/Main
Dr. h.c. Friedrich Carl Frhr. v. Oppenheim	Personally Responsible Partner in the Banking House of Sal. Oppenheim jr. & Cie., Cologne
Dr. Wolfgang Pohle	*Generalbevollmächtigter*, Friedrich Flick KG., Düsseldorf
Dr. Hans Reuter	President, DEMAG AG., Duisburg
August Rohdewald	Member of the Managing Board, Norddeutsche Kreditbank AG., Bremen
Dr. Hans Günther Sohl	President, August-Thyssen-Hütte AG., Duisburg
Klaus H. Scheufelen	Personally Responsible Partner in the Scheufelen Papierfabriken, Oberlenningen/Wttbg.
Prof. Dr. Karl Schiller	University of Hamburg
Fabian von Schlabrendorff	Lawyer, Wiesbaden
Dr. Ernst Schneider	President, Industrie- und Handelskammer, Düsseldorf
Curt E. Schwab	Publisher, Stuttgart
Dr. Kurt Sieveking	Bürgermeister a. D., Hamburg
Dr. Gerd Tacke	Member of the Managing Board, Siemens & Halske AG. and Siemens-Schuckert-Werke AG., Munich
Werner Traber	Member of the Managing Board, Hamburg-Amerika Linie (Hapag), Hamburg
Dr. Hans Christoph Frhr. v. Tucher	Member of the Managing Board, Bayerische Vereinsbank, Munich
Franz Heinrich Ulrich	Member of the Managing Board, Deutsche Bank AG., Düsseldorf
Dr. Ernst Hellmut Vits	President, Vereinigte Glanzstoff-Fabriken AG., Wuppertal
Prof. Dr. Carl Friedrich Frhr. v. Weizsäcker	University of Hamburg
Dr. Hermann Winkhaus	President, Mannesmann AG., Düsseldorf
Casimir Prinz Wittgenstein	Member of the Managing Board, Metallgesellschaft AG., Frankfurt/Main
Otto Wolff v. Amerongen	Personally Responsible Partner in the Firm Otto Wolff, Cologne